THE VANDEMONIAN WAR

THE VANDEMONIAN WAR

The secret history of Britain's Tasmanian invasion

NICK BRODIE

Published in 2017 by Hardie Grant Books
Hardie Grant Books (Australia)
Ground Floor, Building 1
658 Church Street
Richmond, Victoria 3121
www.hardiegrant.com.au

Hardie Grant Books (UK)
5th & 6th Floor
52–54 Southwark Street
London SE1 1UN
www.hardiegrant.co.uk

All rights reserved. No part of this publication may be reproduced, stored in a retrieval system or transmitted in any form by any means, electronic, mechanical, photocopying, recording or otherwise, without the prior written permission of the publishers and copyright holders.

The moral rights of the author have been asserted.

Copyright text © Nicholas Dean Brodie 2017

A Cataloguing-in-Publication entry is available from the catalogue of the National Library of Australia at www.nla.gov.au

The Vandemonian War
ISBN 978 1 74379 311 4

Cover and text design by Nada Backovic
Typeset in 10.5/15 pt Sabon by Kirby Jones
Cover image of Major-General Sir George Arthur, Government of Ontario Art Collection, 693137
Printed by McPherson's Printing Group, Maryborough, Victoria

The paper this book is printed on is certified against the Forest Stewardship Council® Standards. FSC promotes environmentally responsible, socially beneficial and economically viable management of the world's forests.

Dedication

*For Mumma Duck,
who taught me to pick my battles.
And for Kristyn,
who has accompanied me through a few.*

CONTENTS

Preface   1

Chapter One   Conquest and Division   5
Chapter Two   Scouring the Country   22
Chapter Three   Clearing the Settled Districts   37
Chapter Four   Mercenaries and Aboriginal Guides   53
Chapter Five   The Oatlands Roving Parties   71
Chapter Six   Offensive Defence in Reality and Record   87
Chapter Seven   The Methods and Landscape of Settlement   104
Chapter Eight   Aboriginal Auxiliaries   120
Chapter Nine   Pushing Further while Debating Peace   138
Chapter Ten   Roving Still   156
Chapter Eleven   Beyond the Limits of Law
                       and Documentation   176
Chapter Twelve   Keeping up the Pretence and the Pressure   193
Chapter Thirteen   Captivity, Qualms and Escalation   208
Chapter Fourteen   Agitation and Armament   223
Chapter Fifteen   Propaganda and the Preliminary
                       Manoeuvres   245
Chapter Sixteen   Necessity Has No Law   262
Chapter Seventeen   Harass Them if They Cannot Be Taken   280
Chapter Eighteen   From Open War to Black Operations   301
Chapter Nineteen   The War after the War   322
Chapter Twenty   Allies, Enemies and Ambiguities   338
Chapter Twenty-one   Ending the Vandemonian War   361
Afterword   377

Endnotes   383
Acknowledgements   408
Index   411

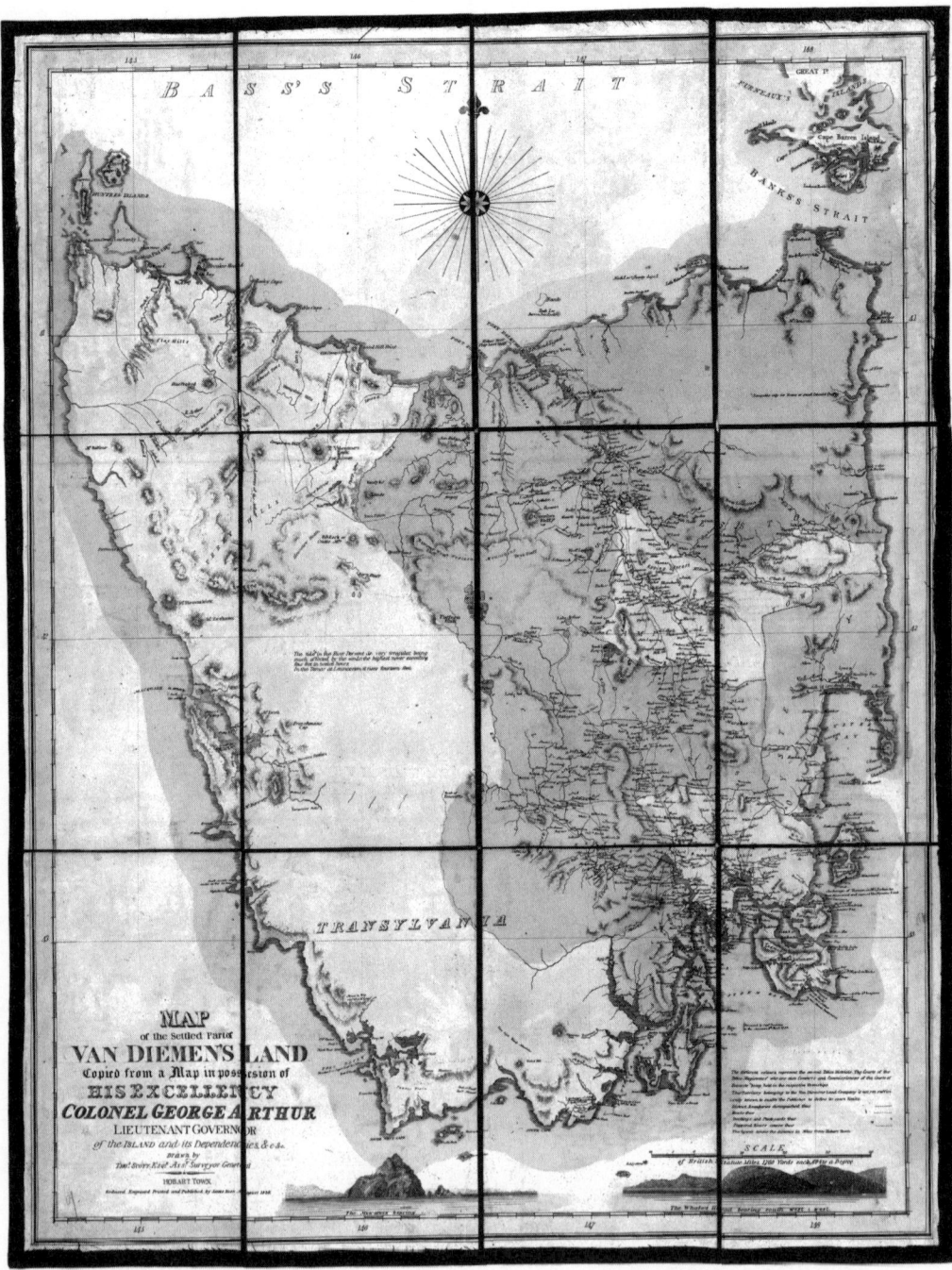

Assistant Surveyor Thomas Scott's map of Van Diemen's Land, 1830. *Allport Library and Museum of Fine Arts, Tasmanian Archive and Heritage Office: Thomas Scott, Map of the settled part of Van Diemen's Land, 1830.*

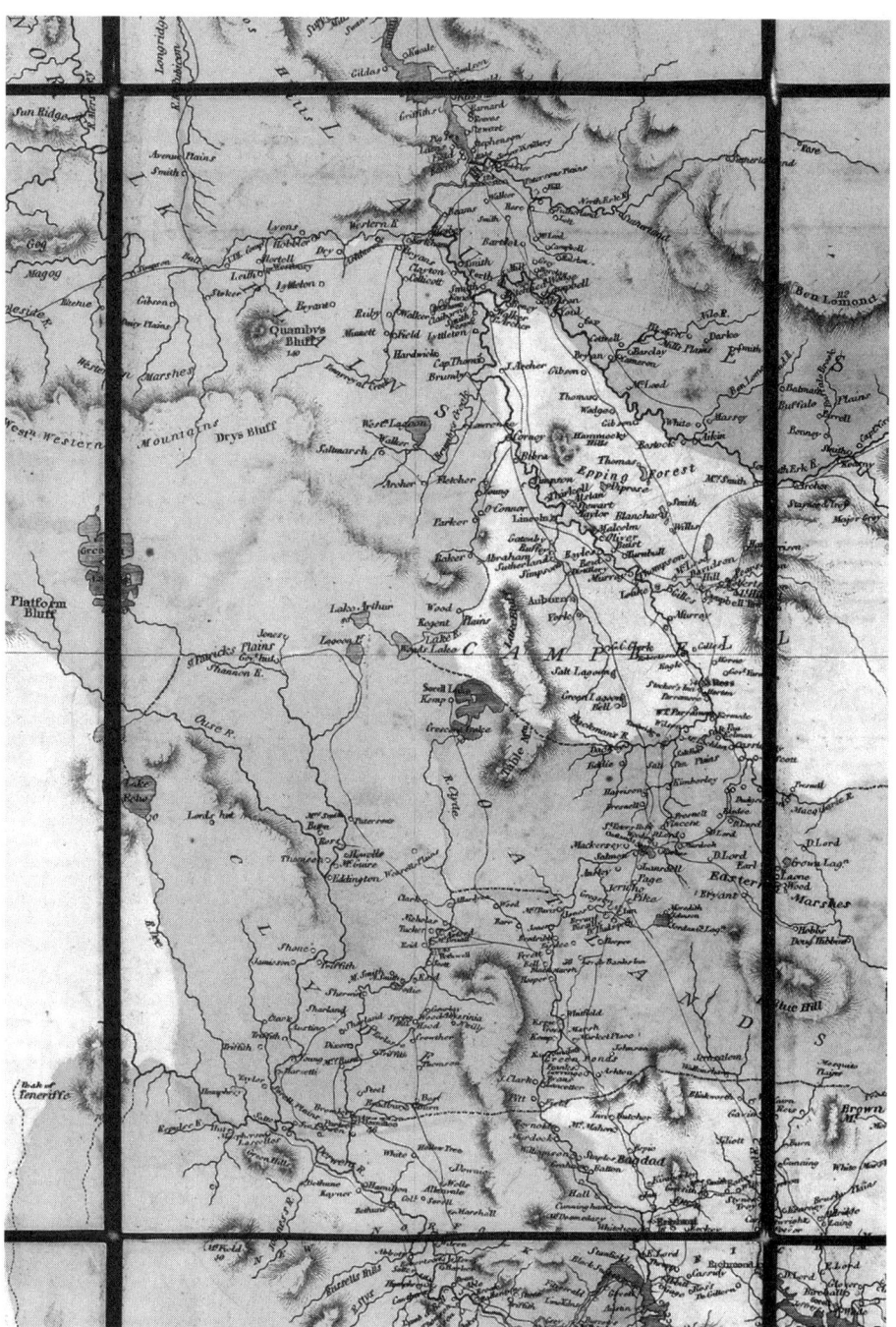

Detail of Scott's map, 1830, showing the western midlands. *Allport Library and Museum of Fine Arts, Tasmanian Archive and Heritage Office: Thomas Scott, Map of the settled part of Van Diemen's Land, 1830.*

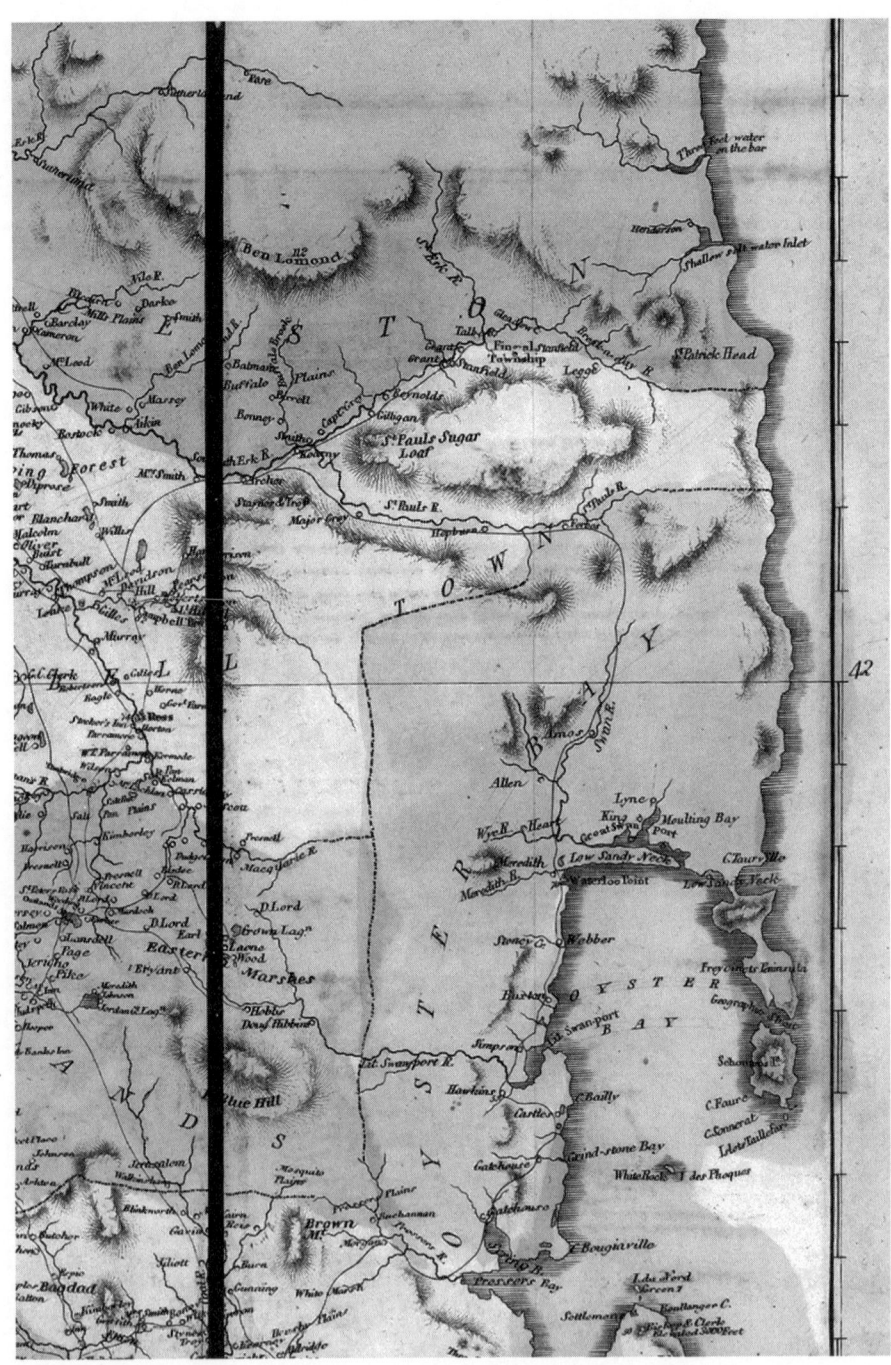

Detail of Scott's map, 1830, showing the east coast. *Allport Library and Museum of Fine Arts, Tasmanian Archive and Heritage Office: Thomas Scott, Map of the settled part of Van Diemen's Land, 1830.*

Preface

The Vandemonian War was the British Empire's best-kept secret. Invasion was called settlement. Ethnic cleansing was called conciliation. Genocide was naturalised as extinction. Even Van Diemen's Land was renamed Tasmania.

Conflict racked the eastern half of the island of Van Diemen's Land during the 1820s and 1830s. But this violence went much further than the vague and unofficial frontier fighting between settler folk and Aboriginal people of popular misremembering. The Vandemonian War was far more conventionally warlike than is generally acknowledged, the colony more militaristic than posterity was led to believe, and the colonial government more culpable than it would publicly admit.

There was no room for the old Aboriginal tribes in modern British Van Diemen's Land – they could be British subjects or nothing. It is no exaggeration to say that the Aboriginal tribes and most of the Aboriginal people were extirpated from the island. Whole societies were deliberately obliterated. And genocide, I have come to realise, can be a starched white-collar crime.

The Vandemonian War was planned and executed through extensive chains of command, leaving a rich documentary archive. The following pages offer unambiguous evidence that the colonial government condoned atrocities, and that it deliberately covered the truth through propaganda and obfuscation.

Under Lieutenant Governor Colonel George Arthur – a man that historical tradition characterises as a sort of humanitarian hero – the British prosecuted a series of military campaigns with great fervour against the Aboriginal people of Van Diemen's Land. British regulars, paramilitary police forces, convicts and mercenaries were deployed to harass Aboriginal people into surrender or degrade them into annihilation.

By any serious estimate the collective Aboriginal population of Van Diemen's Land was reduced from unknown thousands to a few dozen survivors within only three decades. This is uncontested. This dreadful outcome of colonisation became one of the darkest stains on the British Empire.[1] But while the conflict in Van Diemen's Land has never been forgotten, it has not been accurately remembered either. A colonial lie has been perpetuated in popular memory for nearly two centuries.

Here for the first time is the story of the Vandemonian War as fought by the British Empire and its representatives. Compiled from long-lost handwritten instructions and reports, government orders, correspondence and annotations, this is the real story of Australia's most infamous colonial war. It is confronting reading. Folklorists attached to the repetitive mantras of Australian mythology will be challenged. Everyone will be shocked.

Excised of the accretions of the ages, this is a story of command chains and subordinates, soldiers and militiamen, enemies and allies. This is more than European-born farmers and Aboriginal people skirmishing over land, sheep and kangaroo on vague frontiers made hazy by the distances of space and time. This was no unofficial frontier conflict. It was an orchestrated invasion prosecuted by an empire.

My discovery of the truth about the Vandemonian War started with a certain manuscript volume in the Tasmanian Archives and Heritage Office in Hobart. It is labelled 'No. 7/ Records relating to the Aboriginals', and has the archival designation CSO1/1/320 (7878). It comes from the records of the Colonial Secretary's Office, and contains hundreds of pages of inbound correspondence, only a tiny fraction of which has ever been previously examined, analysed or cited by historians.[2] These letters detail military and paramilitary operations against Aboriginal people in the interior of Van Diemen's Land in the 1820s and 1830s.

Previous historians of the 'Black War' rarely used these files, seemingly encouraging subsequent historians to neglect them too –

PREFACE

even when they knew of them. This under-appreciated volume helped guide me to find more volumes and discover the real Vandemonian War with its strategies, campaigns and missions.

The Colonial Secretary was the colony's senior civil bureaucrat, whose office orchestrated the administration of Van Diemen's Land under the direction of the Lieutenant Governor. The letters collected by his office detail the crucial connections between London and Hobart and various districts and front lines. These documents reveal a tremendous amount of information about the war.

Piecing together the conflict through these documents is, however, no simple task. There are hundreds of letters in the volume – generally archived by correspondent rather than date – and yet it is frustratingly incomplete. Some letters are obviously missing, meaning certain geographical areas or key weeks are un- or under-represented. This is what happens when letters are bound together at a later date for archiving – things get lost. But there was more, and even I was unprepared for what I found.

Covering a huge expanse of territory from Hobart in the south to Launceston in the north and encompassing the grassy midlands and the scrubby valleys from the central highlands in the west to the rugged east coast ranges, these letters gave a more detailed picture of the whole conflict than any I had ever seen.

It would be easy to get lost in the immensely detailed accounts of military and paramilitary operations against Aboriginal people in the interior of Van Diemen's Land, but many little annotations upon them intrigued me too. These revealed layers of government reading them, commenting upon them and issuing instructions. As with the letters themselves, these small details revealed a bigger picture, this time not only of what a government knew, but of how a Lieutenant Governor and his subordinate officers acted and reacted. Here was the command and control structure of the war, written in ink by the officers and combatants themselves.

I also examined the records of the Lieutenant Governor's Office and of police magistracies, and investigated the accounts of the Commissariat. What I found were underlying scribal and command patterns that told a story quite different from official narratives and historical traditions. From these I began to reconstitute the government's Vandemonian War from the archival darkness in which it had been deliberately hidden.

Among all of this disparate and neglected evidence, one file particularly stood out. Upon receipt of letters, the Colonial Secretary's Office gave them a numeric identifier to help manage so much correspondence. The code 7578 was part of this system. A letter would be numbered something like 7578/2, the second letter or subject in the 7578 file, making it easier for the Colonial Secretary to locate. This system allows inbound and outbound correspondence to be matched.

As I read through CSO1/1/320 (7578) I kept wondering whether the matching outbound 7578 letters had survived somewhere, the ones the government sent to its officers. They had. In the seemingly innocuous copybook of correspondence CSO41/1/1 (sent from the Colonial Secretary to the police magistrates of Van Diemen's Land) were the outgoing 7578 letters – and more besides. Here, in astounding detail, were the plans and operations directed by the government during the Vandemonian War. Lieutenant Governor Arthur's intentions were clear. As a letter dated 5 September 1828 from the Colonial Secretary to the Police Magistrate of Campbell Town reads:

> With regard to the hostile appearance which you represent these people to be assuming, the Lieutenant Governor has no hesitation in stating that He thinks you should expressly intimate to the Military Force which is placed at your disposal, that they should adopt decided measures, in driving the Natives from the settled Districts.

Through thousands of such letters, annotations, replies and orders I saw the conflict as no other historian before me. The Vandemonian War is the story of an empire conquering an island and calling it settlement.

CHAPTER ONE

Conquest and Division

1803–28
Van Diemen's Land

Landings and Land Grabs

The British Empire invaded Van Diemen's Land with a pincer movement. They landed in the southeast in 1803 and then the north in 1804. They dug in, planting flags and crops. With that, the large island south of mainland Australia was claimed for Britain.

For the first few years, the occupation was relatively precarious. Contact was limited and sporadic. The two outposts could mostly defend themselves against Aboriginal groups and runaway convicts-turned-bushrangers, but they struggled to project control beyond that.

But there was conflict from the start. In 1804 some soldiers fired on a group of Aboriginal people spotted approaching Risdon Cove, the original southern beach-head. It was remembered and recorded because they had used a small cannon, killed a few people, and captured a boy. Other encounters certainly went unrecorded.

Within a generation, the pincers closed. Colonisation advanced, helped by shiploads of sailors, surveyors, settlers, convicts and soldiers. The southern outpost became the busy port of Hobart Town, growing along the Derwent River. The main administrative focus of northern occupation shifted eastwards, becoming Launceston. Settlers took land in the fertile valleys cut by the island's rivers, moved into the grassy midlands between Hobart and Launceston, and pushed right up into the edge of the central highlands. Small port settlements and interior river-crossing towns were founded and fortified, and served to support the invasion. Many Aboriginal people were even absorbed into the colonial advance – taken into the occupiers' homes and raised as their own or trained as servants. Soldiers were strategically stationed to contain convicts, chase bushrangers and deter insurrection, but also to protect what came to be known as the settled districts. Aboriginal people were left to roam the thick forests, scrubby hills and rugged highlands. For now.

The ways, cultures and societal structures of Aboriginal Van Diemen's Land were poorly understood by the newcomers. Even today, colonial-era Aboriginal Van Diemen's Land remains obscured by thin evidence and the accretions of myth and history. Early maritime visitors had made some contact and recorded a few details about appearances and tools, but they also fostered a misguided impression that the ways of these people at that first contact were the ways they had always been.[1] Certainly the societies the colonists encountered in the nineteenth century were not unchanged relics of humankind's nativity.

The colonists gradually learned that there were several distinct Aboriginal entities throughout the island, which they generally called 'tribes'. Each seemed to have their own geographical ranges, so the colonists named them by key locations: the Oyster Bay tribe, the Big River tribe, and so on. This was part of a wider process of mutual learning, where colonists and Aboriginal people interacted with each other, learned from each other, and changed each other in different ways across the island. Tribes that were close to the colonial bases, especially in the southeast, learned more than their more isolated counterparts, and were better understood in turn. Sailors in the southeast, using Bruny Island as a replenishing station for journeys further afield, sometimes exchanged gifts with Aboriginal people – just as Captain Cook had done. Other seamen landed to showers of stones and spears.[2] But the great irony for colonial-era Aboriginal societies is that they were recorded and documented through the same processes that vanquished them. And so the uncovering of the real Vandemonian War also reveals much about the Aboriginal Vandemonians.

Towards the Autumn of 1828

By the mid-1820s colonial Van Diemen's Land was expanding its effective reach. A new convict penal settlement placed a strong British presence at Macquarie Harbour in the island's southwest. The Van Diemen's Land Company was established, and commenced occupying the northwest. Although one was a convict outpost and the other a resident corporation, they formed a new pincer movement taking the western half of the island. Both had military support. On paper the conquest seemed nearly complete.

Van Diemen's Land also became a colony in its own right in 1825, when it was declared independent from New South Wales. Wielding considerable executive power, Lieutenant Governor George Arthur oversaw the development of several familiar attributes of civil society, from local legislative councils and law courts to roads and bridges, and the continued growth of a flourishing local press.

And so the mid-1820s has come to be seen as a key period in the history of European settlement in Tasmania. Even the actions of some Aboriginal people seemed to point to a new epoch of colonial amity. As the *Hobart Town Gazette* reported in November 1824:

> [W]e announce with the most cordial satisfaction, that, from some cause yet unknown, no fewer than sixty-four Aborigines came into town on Wednesday, of their own accord, and in a pacific manner well calculated to conciliate even those who had been most prejudiced against them.[3]

The Lieutenant Governor ordered them fed, and they were accommodated in the market house building. Bonfires were lit for them, and a police guard was ordered to watch over them, ostensibly 'to guard their repose from interruption'. It was the very picture of colonial paternalism. The Lieutenant Governor reportedly had a 'lively interest in these poor creatures' and it was his 'desire to at once conciliate their feelings and promote their welfare'.[4] Moreover, a 'plan for civilizing and evangelizing them' was apparently being developed by Arthur, with the aid of several interested gentlemen and clerics.

Attempts at diplomacy had been undertaken as early as 1814, when Lieutenant Governor Thomas Davey had pointedly visited some Aboriginal people near the mouth of the Derwent River, gave them clothing as gifts, and then encouraged some of them to Hobart, where the Reverend Robert Knopwood welcomed them into his home.[5] Over the years, many Aboriginal children were also adopted into settler families, baptised and effectively resided within colonial society in various parts of the island.[6] One boy even travelled to England, was educated in English ways, and then returned to Van Diemen's Land in the hope of becoming an example to others.[7]

Such attempts to mould Aboriginal people into labourers, agriculturalists and Christians did not spring suddenly from the mind of any particular gentleman or governor. Rather, they were part of the organic processes of the age, common to the paternalistic logic of empire, and had other colonial precedents, especially in New South Wales.

By the late 1820s, a generation of Aboriginal people had grown up either in, familiar with, or aware of the colony's various outposts. In the north, many had encountered sealers working among the islands of Bass Strait since the colony's beginning. In the interior, Aboriginal groups increasingly met surveyors, shepherds, stockmen and 'settlers', as well as runaway convicts and bushrangers. In the southeast, Aboriginal people had regularly encountered maritime outsiders since the days of Captain Cook.

In early May 1828 the *Hobart Town Courier* printed a short vocabulary, acquired from some Aboriginal men visiting Hobart.[8] A survey party that had been charting parts of the coast for potential harbours brought these men to town from nearby Bruny Island. In one sense the event reflected the relative amity that could exist in parts of Van Diemen's Land, but it also hinted at the increasing colonial expansion that surveying generally portended.

When Lieutenant Governor Arthur learned of the men's arrival, he instructed the Colonial Secretary to supply them with 'biscuit from the Commissariat. And let them be persuaded to return to Bruné Island where an establishment will be formed for them, as I am fearful they will get spirits or be otherwise corrupted in the Town.'[9]

A few days later Arthur again communicated with the Colonial Secretary. 'I consider it especially important to conciliate their tribe,' he noted, giving orders to:

> send a quantity of biscuit and Potatoes to be under the charge of a Soldier of the Veteran Company, who will issue them regularly to the Natives. By this means, they may be persuaded to settle and cultivate Potatoes for their future support.[10]

Arthur also insisted that 'a discreet man should be selected for this service'. There were many applicants for the job to run the Bruny Island Establishment, each stressing their bush skills, familiarity with Aboriginal people, or general resilience for an onerous task. A bricklayer named George Augustus Robinson was finally selected for the job, seemingly because of his enthusiasm for the Lieutenant Governor's general plans, and the patronage of the Reverend William Bedford. Through strategic and effective patronage, Robinson would transform himself into the 'Conciliator' of popular memory, the man who peacefully brought in the Aboriginal tribes. But in early 1828 all that lay in the future.

From these discreet beginnings, a false narrative bloomed. Arthur's pacific approach to the Aboriginal visitors from Bruny Island belongs to a highly specific set of circumstances, but his broader policy reflected an aggressive colonial plan. Just a few weeks earlier, in April 1828, Arthur had responded to reports of increased violence in the interior by issuing a proclamation that the settled districts be cleansed of Aboriginal people.[11] The closing pincers became an armed frontier – the Lieutenant Governor was preparing to divide and conquer.

War and Partition

Sporadic violence had been endemic in Van Diemen's Land for two decades, but in early 1828 it escalated to war. Though Arthur did not issue a document or instruction to Aboriginal tribes informing them that the British Empire considered itself at war with them, the April 1828 Partition Proclamation serves as a useful marker of several operational threads coalescing, and can be regarded as the official acknowledgement of major hostilities.

The Proclamation opened by carefully reciting some prior proclamations and orders, thereby establishing the colonisers' patient and beneficent intentions. Frontier violence was acknowledged but attributed to the misbehaviour of 'Shepherds and Stockkeepers' and 'Sealers', thereby implying these to have been the illegal acts of individuals, and therefore classified as criminality. The Proclamation further absolved the government by brushing over the invasiveness of colonisation itself, instead pointing to the intransigence of Aboriginal people who exhibited 'a state of living, alike hostile to the safety of the Settlers, and to the amelioration of their own habits, character and condition'. There was a state of mutual animosity so intense, the Proclamation avowed, as to require the segregation of the country. The Aboriginal people were to 'be induced by peaceful means to depart, or should otherwise be expelled by force from all the settled Districts'. Any pretence of peaceful settlement was officially over.

As a legal instrument the Proclamation applied a logistical structure for fighting the war. It proposed that 'a line of Military Posts will be forthwith stationed and established along the confines of the settled districts' through which Aboriginal people could not pass without the personal approval of the Lieutenant Governor. Magistrates were ordered to effect the 'expulsion of the Aborigines from the settled Districts', although they were to be treated well if captured, like other prisoners of war. Furthermore, the application of force by convicts and civilians could be authorised by 'a Magistrate, Military Officer, or other person of respectability named and deputed to this service by a Magistrate', providing a legal mechanism for allowing militia operations. All Vandemonian subjects were enjoined 'to obey the directions of the Civil, and to aid and assist the Military Power (to whom special orders adapted to situations and circumstances will be given)'.

The British Empire had been preparing for war in Van Diemen's Land for several years. The initial invasion was part of a global strategy of empire-building, and resistance was to be expected. Led by military officers, effected by soldiers and supported by convict labour, the establishment of a penal colony was intended to prevent rival claims in the region, tap into existing trading routes and develop new ones, and facilitate broader settlement. It worked, just as it did around Australia – from Port Jackson in the east to King George's Sound in the west.

Much like the new colonial outpost of Singapore, which supported a British push into southeast Asia through the Malayan Peninsula, the broad processes of Australasian British settlement were guided for wider imperial objectives, orchestrated under the careful supervision of the British Secretary of State for War and the Colonies. By the late 1820s, the continent was ringed with frontier bases, projecting British influence into their subregions, controlling key sea routes and approaches, and supporting continued advances into the interior. Hobart and Launceston were parts of this big picture.

But by 1828 the British were overstretched. Wherever the British landed, indigenous inhabitants generally fought back, resisting encroachments into their territories. Although often treated more as a tactical nuisance than a strategic problem – a side effect of settlement particular to each situation – there are clear trends in the encounters between colonisers and Aboriginal peoples. Curiosity, conflict, cohabitation, collaboration, avoidance and adaptation all highlight the multifaceted but singularly recognisable nature of colonial invasion. The ringing of Van Diemen's Land with coastal settlements by the late 1820s, coupled with continued moves to settle and pacify the interior, revealed that Aboriginal people could be dispossessed only so far. Eventually they would have nowhere to go.

Arthur's Armaments

Arthur had been aware of Aboriginal resistance from the beginning of his term in Van Diemen's Land. He was also cognisant of the colony's larger strategic role in the British Empire. In May 1824, his predecessor Lieutenant Governor William Sorell had appraised Arthur of the conditions in the island,[12] detailing the regimes for the management of convicts and the assistance given to free settlers.

Sorell's briefing also articulated strategic apprehensions. One point concerned the means of communication between settlements, highlighting the importance of ensuring the smooth flow of information and supplies. More particularly, with fewer than 230 soldiers on the island, Sorell believed that the occupying force required 'augmentation'. He had requested 'Guns and Horses, Sufficient for Batteries to cover the Harbour' as well as 'a Supply of arms and accoutrements Suitable to a small local force, and of arms and equipment for a Small corps of yeomanry'. Sorell desired, in effect, to be able to raise a local militia.

In part this was because the professional soldiery was mainly occupied with guard duties at the major settlements. George Town, Launceston, Hobart and Macquarie Harbour all occupied a significant proportion of the total force available. But as Sorell informed Arthur, there were also soldiers in the interior:

> there are three Interim Stations, one at New Norfolk, one at Ross and one at Jericho. There has been a party temporarily on the Clyde, where the Natives had been very troublesome, and where I projected a Hut Barrack for a permanent Station and a small Prison.[13]

It was not just convict guard duties that determined military manoeuvres across Van Diemen's Land. Two and a half weeks after Sorell's briefing, Arthur wrote to Earl Bathurst, the Secretary of State for War and the Colonies, about Van Diemen's Land's 'very defenceless state'. He amended Sorell's earlier requisition, and sent it with the despatch to Bathurst in London.[14] He wanted:

24 x 24 Pounders, with iron Garrison Carriages, Side Arms and other Stores Complete.

50 x Barrels of Gunpowder.

6 x 6 Pounders Field Pieces, cars complete, to act with or without Horses, with Sides, Round Shot, in fixed bottoms, Harness and Drag Ropes complete.

1000 x Muskets, with Bayonets, Belts, Pouches, etca., etc., complete.

200 x Swords and Belts for Yeomanry.

200 x Brace of Pistols.

Between the field cannon, a thousand bayonet-bearing muskets, and hundreds of swords and pistols, Arthur was clearly making preparations for a land war.

Arthur continued agitating for arms and soldiers in his first year in office.[15] He informed Bathurst in August 1824 that he thought 'Five hundred men' would not be 'too large a Force to protect an Island so extensive, if the exigencies of other Colonies will admit of it'. He acknowledged that 'as the Natives have been also troublesome in New South Wales, I do not believe any considerable reinforcement can be well spared from that Colony'. But he pointed to his own colony's trouble with 'the late unusual hostile proceedings of the Natives' in the interior as being a key concern, as well as runaway convicts and 'Bushrangers'. He suggested the formation and armament of local district corps to address the growing insurgencies.

Bathurst agreed. Replying almost a year later – seaborne communication with London was a very slow affair in those days – Bathurst told Arthur that further reinforcements 'for placing at the disposal of the respective Governors' were underway.[16] Van Diemen's Land was not, after all, the only colony with 'troublesome' Aboriginal people.

Troops came from a variety of sources. Some were initially bound for New South Wales, while 'three Companies consisting of 50 Men each [were] formed from the "Veteran Battalions"', which would be sent to the island for the purposes of overseeing convicts. Bathurst also informed Arthur that London was considering the idea of a local yeoman militia, and was generally amenable to the notion, but that no firm decision had yet been made. In the interim, Arthur was given approval 'to organize a Police Establishment, until the Military Assistance ... shall become available'.[17]

Police Magistrates and Field Police

By early 1828 Arthur presided over something closely resembling a military-run police state where the operational reality of Van Diemen's Land saw a close alliance of the civil and military powers.

Much of the island was divided into police districts centred on the major towns, where magistrates and field police were responsible for policing the 'settled districts'. In the central midlands between Hobart and Launceston, gentleman settlers occupied the positions of police magistrates – Thomas Anstey at Oatlands and James Simpson at Campbell Town. The remainder of the interior police magistrates were military men, strategically covering the midland's flanks. In Richmond, near to Hobart and the head of the Coal River Valley, was the ex-soldier Thomas Lascelles. In the region of Norfolk Plains, in the north-west of the midlands, was another ex-soldier, Malcolm Laing Smith. At New Norfolk, in the upper reaches of the Derwent River, was the ex-naval administrator William Hamilton. Soldiers occupied the crucial perimeter posts. At Great Swan Port on the east coast was Captain George Hibbert of the 40th Regiment. At Bothwell, by the edge of the central highlands, was Lieutenant Joseph Curtin, also of the 40th Regiment. And at George Town on the north coast was Captain John D'Arcy of the New South Wales Royal Veteran Company.

Arthur had established a field police in 1825, with an initial complement of 30 men. Intended to be flexible, responsive and familiar with the territories to which they were posted, the field police's role went beyond simply capturing runaway convicts and bushrangers. They also served as guides and worked as a sort of official 'civil law' presence on settler-led and military expeditions.

By 1827 Arthur had further combined the civil and military powers, appointing Major Tobias Kirkwood of the 40th Regiment as 'Commandant of the Field Police'.[18] In July 1827, Arthur reportedly spent some time personally 'directing the movements of the Field Police and Military'.[19] Their actions often went unrecorded, but they were an active presence in the colony. In one incident in November 1827, when three field police were capturing a runaway convict, they reportedly encountered 'about 150 natives who attacked them with stones'.[20] The *Hobart Town Courier* reported that one of the field police was hit in the head. In response, these field policemen:

> expended seventeen rounds of ball cartridge and killed two of the dogs, but are not certain whether any of the natives were hurt, on fixing their bayonets and charging, the natives retreated. The plan of the Field Police cannot be too highly appreciated, they are a most useful and active set of men.

Arthur clearly thought so too. With instructive timing, and revealing his wider strategic thinking, Arthur reviewed the administration of field police rewards in early March 1828. He had found the force 'highly beneficial' and 'an Augmentation of the Band' was being implemented.[21] Because field police duties were potentially onerous, and could make them decidedly unpopular with the broader convict population, these convicts were offered reduced sentences in return for this special service. The new incentives would, the Colonial Secretary informed the police magistrates, come into force in April 1828 – just in time for the Proclamation.

Military and Paramilitary Dispositions

This 'augmentation' of the field police highlights the escalation of operations against Aboriginal people in early 1828. Even the early dispositions of the growing force points to the 'augmentation' of a wider strategic situation, not merely the supporting of existing duties policing convicts and settlers.[22] The military-run police districts of the perimeter, with their sizeable military stations, only attracted a total of 10 field police appointments. Army bases had little need of field policemen. The other interior stations, however, could certainly do with paramilitary support. New Norfolk, Oatlands, Norfolk Plains, Campbell Town and Richmond gained 15, 18, 18, 21, and 12 field police respectively. Having tested the system over a few years, Arthur was growing his small mobile force into something resembling a militia, answerable to a network of officers mostly composed of soldiers or ex-soldiers, and strategically stationed to respond to incursions through the partition line.

As well as arming and expanding a mobile police force, during March 1828 Arthur focused on the situation and orientation of military posts in the island. When he travelled to Launceston late in the month, ostensibly to be at a church consecration, the Colonial Secretary noted in internal government records that the purpose of the journey was also for 'inspecting the Military stations and Road parties in the interior'.[23]

Earlier in the month Arthur had even created a new garrison situation. 'It is necessary', he informed the Colonial Secretary, 'that a Military station should be permanently established in the vicinity of the Western River'.[24] The detailed instructions Arthur gave were for a sizeable post: an officer, 25 soldiers and four horses. He also noted that it was an 'urgent' priority and he wanted it to be 'durable' and ready 'before the winter sets in'.

Arthur's plans for the military station of Westbury, and his touring of military posts, were evidence of a broader plan, and not just reactions to the specific circumstances of each locality or moment. Strategically placed on annual Aboriginal migration routes from highlands to coastlands, the Westbury station helped form a protective ring around the main settled districts of the interior, worked as a military link between the major areas of colonial expansion in the eastern and western parts of the island, and provided imperial troops to protect the interests of the Van Diemen's Land Company. Not for the first time in the empire's history, British soldiers were defending the investments of British stockholders.

Ever since assuming command of Van Diemen's Land, Arthur had strategically deployed the military to help effect colonial expansion.

In November 1826, he authorised civilians to respond to attacks (or simply the threat of attack) by combining with military forces and driving Aboriginal people away, 'treating them as open enemies'.[25] These sorts of general island-wide orders and regulations were supported by specific deployments, like that at Westbury in the north. In another instance, Captain Hibbert was sent 'with a detachment of Military' to occupy a part of Oyster Bay on the east coast at Great Swan Port in mid-1827.[26] They were initially stationed at the property of a prominent local colonist – himself an ex-soldier – for his 'protection'.[27]

It was not the first time the military had been stationed there, but this time it was a greater and more permanent military presence. A newspaper correspondent enthused that this could be 'the forerunner of a populous settlement', pointing out that the added protection would encourage more colonists to the area. But when the settler asked to be reimbursed the cost of hosting the army, Arthur was incensed. He replied through the Colonial Secretary 'that any other settler would have given twice the accommodation to have obtained the like security.'[28] Whoever's expense it was, garrisons of redcoats stationed in the barns of colonists cast protective shadows and enforced a peaceful settlement. This is how the Australian colonies were established.

On the Legality of Conquest

The deployment of the military was not merely passive. In 1827, Arthur issued a government notice for 'the protection of the settlers', clarifying 'that the black Natives may be driven from the settled districts'. He called it 'a measure of indispensable necessity',[29] and promised 'Sufficient troops ... will be at the disposal of the civil power'. On the same day he sent a garrison order instructing 'two subalterns, two sergeants, and 30 rank and file, of the 40th Regiment' to march from Hobart into the interior.[30] Some of this force was sent to 'Ross Bridge to strengthen the detachment at present stationed there', while the rest continued on to Westbury. He sent Major Turton of the Engineers Department on a tour of 'all the out-stations' to determine what further military aid was required 'for the protection of the different districts' and also requested that Turton liaise with the police magistrates for their opinions.

While the main body of redcoats marched northwards from Hobart, Captain Hibbert was ordered to send one 'sergeant and 10 privates' from the Oyster Bay station on the east coast westwards into St Paul's Plains in the Oatlands' district. He would receive replacement troops directly from Hobart, while this advancing party commenced operations to 'protect the country' in the central midlands 'from the attacks of the Natives.' When Arthur took his tour of the stations in early 1828, he was not just checking their camping conditions – he was personally inspecting a broad strategic deployment directed towards a specific purpose. The colony was effectively in a state of war, and had been for some time.

While framed as a new strategy, Arthur's Partition Proclamation represented a culmination of measures already being implemented. While formally using a future tense – instructing the Vandemonian public that 'a line of military posts will be forthwith stationed and established along the confines of the settled districts' – such measures were already clearly in place or underway. When the Brigade Major's Office forwarded the Proclamation to the key army officers on the island, it meant sending copies to 11 significant military stations. And while orders and Proclamation alike expressed the desire to avoid unnecessary bloodshed and hoped that diplomatic overtures could have some impact, the underlying concept was that the military was tasked with effecting the removal of Aboriginal people. The Proclamation spoke of peace, but articulated war.

Arthur's Proclamation established a neat chain of command that bypassed the niceties of civil society. Hostilities could therefore be directed by the police magistrates, sanctioned by their subordinate officers, and conducted by the army. Operations were coordinated at the direction of a man holding the dual role of Lieutenant Governor and Colonel Commanding. All this was perfectly legal, because delegated authority to represent the empire emanated from the King and passed through a sequence of duly appointed officers right down to field policemen and army officers. Each bore a little bit of the power and authority of the Sovereign.

Such practices were not entirely new, and all operated under a prism of theoretical legal civility. Conflict with Aboriginal people in the interior was hardly a secret, or even unique to Van Diemen's Land. In New South Wales, conflict in the Hawkesbury district had led Governor Lachlan Macquarie to send redcoats out in punitive raids in the 1810s, ordering the soldiers to hang the corpses of slaughtered Aboriginal people from the trees.[31] Such measures were, Macquarie asserted, to 'Strike them with Terror against Committing Similar Acts of Violence in future'.[32] Some of the violence of New South Wales translated to the transportation of Aboriginal men to Norfolk Island and Van Diemen's Land, in part rendering the realities of Australian colonial warfare as mere criminality, all while using British law as a weapon.[33]

Over several decades a number of Aboriginal men were absorbed into the convict system. One such man was Musquito, a warrior from New South Wales who later served as a guide on expeditions against Vandemonian bushrangers, before becoming something of a bushranger himself.[34] After killing a Tahitian on the east coast he was tracked down with the aid of Aboriginal guides, and was eventually hanged in Hobart after a public trial.

Several Aboriginal Vandemonian men were also hanged or sentenced to transportation from Van Diemen's Land, but these were rare exceptions to the general rule that conflict was dealt with extra-judiciously in Van Diemen's Land. Men who were well known to newspaper-reading colonists were generally seen as part of colonial society and could be dealt with as such. For the unnamed people of the interior, however, the situation was a bit different. While they could be known to some colonists individually, as a body they were still largely outside of the structures of colonial society, economy and culture. It was this separateness that encouraged the process of 'effecting the retirement or expulsion of the Aborigines' from April 1828.

Here several threads overlap. Arthur was undoubtedly genuinely interested in the possibilities for a negotiated settlement. Promoting the use of Bruny Island for acclimatising the less 'troublesome' Aboriginal groups south of Hobart into colonial society, Arthur was also investigating the possibilities for direct negotiation with the more hostile tribes of the interior.

Arthur seized an opportunity that appeared in late 1827, when a young Aboriginal man was captured. He had been raised by a settler family but had returned to the bush for a time before being captured. Arthur wanted to put him to work as a go-between. Named Kickerterpoller, he was known widely throughout the colony as 'Black Tom'. As a one-time accomplice of Musquito, he was also considered a bushranger and murderer. Brought to Hobart Gaol, Kickerterpoller was quizzed on whether he might 'be employed to mediate and explain to the Natives the impropriety of their conduct', to which he apparently agreed.[35] A few months later Kickerterpoller was 'examined' in Arthur's Executive Council on the 'endeavour to negotiate with the Chiefs of the Tribes and dissuade them from their present system of hostility'.[36] While the exact details of the conversations and plans are a bit unclear, one roughly contemporary report of the conversation suggests that Arthur and Kickerterpoller discussed the causes of conflict, the feasibility of the partition plan, and options for protective exile for Aboriginal people on islands off Van Diemen's Land.[37]

Another factor connected with the Proclamation concerned pressure from settlers, as it seemed to answer calls for action. Some settlers even explicitly asked Arthur for protection or assistance. Newly arrived colonist John Allen wrote of his recent acquisition of land in the Great Swan Port district on the east coast, where he had built a hut and planted crops – and lost both to an Aboriginal raid.[38] Arthur read Allen's petition in mid-March 1828, and recorded in a memorandum for the Colonial Secretary that he was 'sorry to find that the natives have evinced a very wanton disposition for outrage, in destroying the Stacks and premises of this individual'.[39] Arthur ordered Captain Hibbert to provide Allen with help for rebuilding and provisions from the government store for three months. Arthur then addressed the Colonial Secretary directly:

> Be so good as to prepare a memorandum exhibiting some of the more daring and sanguinary outrages recently committed by the

Natives, for the purpose of being laid before the Council, in order that some counteracting measures may be adopted on the part of the Government.

While he was potentially looking for some strategic insight into the operations of Aboriginal hostilities, he was also clearly gathering evidence to establish the political case for an offensive. The Partition Proclamation was issued just a few weeks later.

Public opinion was also at play. But here again this was more complex than the newspapers would have us believe. While Arthur's autocratic inclinations often led to conflict with the press, he was not above using it to suit his own needs. Close examination of the manuscript archive of the Colonial Secretary's Office and the content of colonial newspapers reveals an adept manipulation of the press for propaganda purposes. In this case it is at least suspicious that in the weeks leading up to the Proclamation, the *Hobart Town Courier* focused attention on the question of 'the distressing subject of the blacks'.[40] In late March the editor advocated that Aboriginal people be 'removed to one of the islands in Bass's Strait'. In early April he referred to 'the hostile tribes that infest the settled districts', and advocated a Proclamation or implementation of Martial Law as had been done at Bathurst in New South Wales.[41] Later in the month he presented the new Proclamation on the front page of the paper 'with no small pleasure'.[42]

While newspapers only captured a fragment of the whole story, their frequent reporting of 'outrages' and discussion of negotiation, exile, infestation, segregation and assimilation all combined to mould public perception. Although it seemed that Arthur had succumbed to public pressure to confront the insurgency, the arrival of more than 100 troops before he issued the Proclamation is unlikely mere coincidence.[43]

The government was preparing to dig in. Over the winter of 1828 it consolidated its positions and geared up for a series of spring offensives.

CHAPTER TWO

Scouring the Country

1828, Autumn and Spring
The Midlands

Pursuits and Captives

Operational military records from colonial Australia are frustratingly rare, and so there is little documentary evidence of the soldiery holding the line against Aboriginal people or expelling them from the 'settled districts'. But the military was not inactive. Even the public reports of self-interested gentlemen, glorifying their actions in the colonial press, reveal snippets of coordinated missions of deputised civilians and red-coated soldiers.

In early April 1828 the *Hobart Town Courier* reported that a local settler, two of his servants, two soldiers and three field policemen were in pursuit of an Aboriginal group.[1] Traversing the northeastern midlands near Ben Lomond mountain, they spotted smoke trails, which guided them to the Aboriginal position. The settler 'hastened, creeping on his hands and feet within 20 yards of the place', but was spotted making his approach. It was later reported that 'one of them was in the act of throwing a spear at him, when he fired at him in his own defence'. Like most settlers' narratives, it was Aboriginal violence that prompted a stern colonial response. Violence begat violence in a righteous circle of blood and gunpowder.

With the blast of the musket the spearman 'fell, but got up again and ran off'. The pursuit continued, and they eventually 'overtook a boy about 16 years of age, whom [they] took prisoner'. The party then returned to the deserted camp, and 'found 20 blankets, 24 knives, 2 muskets loaded, about 4 pounds of buckshot, a canister of gunpowder, a bayonet' as well as spears and waddies (clubs). The discovery was the colonists' worst fear: the arming of Aboriginal people and the disarming of the settlers. It was just one of numerous reports from the period of Aboriginal assailants taking guns from huts or stockmen.

One of the guns was recognisable. It had been taken a few days prior from a farm, where Aboriginal people also killed a servant. The young prisoner confirmed the story, giving details of the attack. The story matched what the settler knew of this incident, apparently confirming he was on the trail of the right people. The next day they made the prisoner guide the party in further pursuit, but during the night 'the boy made his escape, by groping his way up the chimney of a room in which he was confined.'

The settler was John Batman, who later helped establish the settlement of Melbourne. Though his attempt at retribution had been thwarted, it highlights that the war was being fought by mixed paramilitary parties even before the Proclamation. Significantly, Batman commended 'the soldiers and field police constables' for their good service. Over subsequent days Batman met up with other nearby settlers, no doubt with the aid of other militiamen and soldiers, and attempted to regain the Aboriginal tracks. But they 'did not find any traces of them whatever'. Someone wrote an account of the proceedings, and sent it to Hobart. It was published in the *Hobart Town Courier* a week before Arthur's Proclamation.

In the months that followed, the *Hobart Town Courier* hinted at other actions being undertaken in Van Diemen's Land. In May, 'a native girl 16 or 17 years of age was taken, who spoke English, but who escaped in the night up the chimney'.[2] The similarity of the escape suggests multiple interpretative possibilities, from standardised practices to misinformed rumour. But the reports of conflict that made it into print were just a proportion of a greater whole. For the most part, the press was generally ill-informed about military operations to maintain the partition. So instead of describing wartime actions, there was much editorialising on the cause of the conflict. There were even expressions of sympathy for the general position of Aboriginal people, despite the widespread angst about Aboriginal hostility and the economic cost of the war. The colonists knew that settlement caused the conditions for conflict, but continued to settle anyway. For many, the profits exceeded the risks.

Command Structures and Designation 7578

Preparing for spring incursions into the 'settled districts', Colonial Secretary John Burnett acted to support the war by making it easier to document. In August 1828 he created a correspondence code for addressing issues connected with Aboriginal people, designating it 7578. This administrative decision marks the moment from which the Vandemonian War became extraordinarily well documented, and by which such documentation was preserved.

The first outbound 7578 letter from the Colonial Secretary's Office was in response to a query from James Simpson, the police magistrate of Campbell Town in the northern midlands. Simpson was concerned with the 'course to be adopted against an aboriginal Native who attacked Mr Reynold's Hut'.[3] The Colonial Secretary responded that the offender 'should be proceeded against in the same manner, that any other person would be, who was taken under similar circumstances'.

About a week later he wrote to Simpson again, pointing out the Lieutenant Governor's advice to get the military to 'adopt decided measures' against Aboriginal people who were making a 'hostile appearance' in that district.[4] Through the Colonial Secretary's Office Arthur kept close tabs on operations throughout the island and provided more and more instructions to the police magistrates over the following months. In early September the Colonial Secretary again communicated to Simpson in reply to information about an attack on a hut, pointing out that the Lieutenant Governor 'recommends that you should concert with the Officers commanding the Military Parties some decided measures for restraining the Aborigines from entering the settled Districts.'[5]

Later in September the relationship between the civil and military authorities in the midlands was further clarified. The Brigade Major wrote to Captain Walpole of the 39th Regiment, commander of the military station at Ross, just south of Campbell Town.[6] Walpole was informed that 'the object of stationing the party under your command at Ross is to protect that neighbourhood from the attacks and aggressions of the aboriginal Natives', and told to 'pay the most ready attention to the application of James Simpson, Esq., police magistrate at Campbell Town'. The Brigade Major also conveyed the wishes of 'the Colonel Commanding' that it was important to attach policemen to the military operations 'who will represent the civil power'. This ensured the legality of the military operations when it would 'be found necessary to remove the Aborigines from the settled districts by force'. Weekly reports 'for his Excellency's information' also ensured Arthur was kept up to date with all military manoeuvres.

A Day of Infamy

In October the colony's attention was drawn to the southern midlands where the police magistrate of Oatlands, Thomas Anstey, was facing a crisis. Aboriginal attacks on stockmen and settlers' huts were hardly unusual by the spring of 1828, but on one day in early October a series of events shocked the readers of the *Hobart Town Courier*.[7]

A woman named Anne Geary 'had seen the natives coming', advancing towards the hut she occupied. She fled to her neighbours, the Goughs. Upon hearing the news, Mr Gough and two other men formed a party, and raced to the hut from which Anne Geary had just fled. They were concerned to retrieve a gun and ammunition stored there, which they wanted to prevent the Aboriginal people from acquiring. Unfortunately, the three only had one gun themselves, so the others carried dark sticks, hoping to fool any Aboriginal people they may have encountered. But, reaching the hut, they were too late. The door had been broken open, and the gun and ammunition were gone.

While Gough was out, an Aboriginal group attacked his home and family. Attempting to fend off the assault Mrs Gough pleaded with her assailants for mercy, 'begging them to spare the lives of her *Picanninies*'. But it was to no avail. Even her 13-month-old infant 'received several contusions' during the assault. She was told, 'in good English, that they should be all killed', and she was beaten herself.

Returning home, Gough 'was met by his eldest daughter Mary, covered with blood, calling upon her father to hasten home as the natives had killed her mother and sisters'. He saw his wife 'sitting on the ground, resting her back against the fence, with her infant child in her lap'.

'My dear Gough', his wife managed to say. '[I]t is all over with me, I am killed by the natives'. Then she passed out. Gough bandaged her head as best he could, tearing strips from his own clothing. He then ran to the hut, where he found 'his infant daughter Alicia lying breathless in front of the door with her arms extended'. Remarkably, she was still alive. Inside was Anne Geary, prone on the floor, with wounds to her head and torso. He helped her to a sofa, where she commenced vomiting blood. Within hours both Anne and the infant Alicia died of their injuries. Mrs Gough and her other infant daughter recovered over the following weeks.

The *Hobart Town Courier*'s report of the attack appears to have been derived directly from the coronial inquest, because the printed story drew directly – often verbatim – from Gough's own testimony.[8] Tenses and perspectives were tidied, and the original comment of the Aboriginal man to Mrs Gough's pleas – 'no you white Bitch we'll kill you all' – was toned down for readers.

But while the story was not exaggerated, its publication demonstrates how the press helped prepare the political ground for government action. Gough's story seemed to provide confirmation 'that the natives have formed a systematic organized plan for carrying on a war of extermination against the white inhabitants of the colony'. The attacking war party was thought to be a 'horde' consisting 'of about 20 men, no women or children', rather than simply a migrating tribal group. Only in passing was it mentioned that after the attack, a 'party of constables and soldiers' pursued the assailants for three days, creeping up on their campfires, even while other raids occurred around the district.

Midlands Recruits, the Case of John Danvers

Newspaper reports of attacks, especially those upon women and children, stimulated individuals within the district to mobilise against Aboriginal people. One such person was 'an athletic young man, of a most courageous disposition' named John Danvers, who 'offered his Services to conduct a party of Soldiers or Constables to those parts where the natives resort'.[9] Danvers was a convict who had a long association with the district. He had been transported for life for 'Housebreaking', arriving in Van Diemen's Land in 1824 on the *Asia*.[10] He had also previously been tried for horse stealing, but had been acquitted. When Danvers offered his services as a guide, he was serving as a 'Watchman at the Commissariat Stores at Lemon Springs'.

Danvers possibly wanted the rewards associated with good service to the government. His convict conduct record shows that Anstey had twice before sentenced Danvers to punishment for ill behaviour. In 1825 Danvers received '25 lashes' for 'Neglect of Duty & insolence to his Master' and in 1827 he lost his ticket of leave for 'being frequently drunk', disorderly and under suspicion for involvement in multiple felonies.

Tickets of leave were a reward for good behaviour, and allowed convicts to gain their own employment rather than serve their sentences as assigned servants or on public works chain gangs. The loss of a ticket was a significant punishment; its prospective reissue was a powerful incentive. Danvers' offer to chase Aboriginal people was probably a hope for personal freedom and a more amenable way to serve his sentence, as well as a genuine desire to aid king and country. But the dangers were real, and Anstey was convinced that Danvers 'seems anxious to distinguish himself in all that may be required of him'. Such men made excellent paramilitaries.

With Danvers expecting he could 'fall in with them in two or three days', Anstey informed the Colonial Secretary of the convict's offer. But while he was focusing on pursuing the group connected with 'outrages recently committed', Anstey also alerted the government of another 'two or three tribes' that were 'hovering about the hills'. He had 'constables stationed in some huts in the Eastern marshes and Blue hills to have a watchful eye over their movements'.

Later in the month Anstey sent a circular to his subordinates, providing them with general operational instructions. Referring to the 'late outrages', he stated that it was 'indispensably necessary that some prompt and efficient measures should be adopted'.[11] He reminded the men of the Proclamation, summarised 'the most prominent clauses' and informed them that they were 'empowered in cases of urgent necessity, to call upon all His Majesty's civil subjects for assistance'. Moreover, Anstey instructed his men 'not to wait till the Aborigines shall have shewn some actual demonstration of hostile intentions', but to send word to 'headquarters' as soon as they were sighted. That way the district operations could be developed into a 'combined plan'.

Anstey already knew he would soon have even more troops at his disposal. On 24 October, a detachment of the 40th Regiment was ordered from Hobart into the interior because 'the Colonel Commanding deems it necessary to augment the military detachments for the purpose of strengthening the out-stations'. It comprised '5 sergeants, 5 corporals, and 58 privates'. As they marched out on 27 October, Anstey issued his circular. Three days later Arthur proclaimed martial law.

November 1828, Martial Law

Citing attacks on 'unoffending and defenceless women and children' and the 'insufficient' powers 'afforded by the common law' to his magistrates, Arthur formally declared on 1 November 1828 that 'martial law is and shall continue to be in force against the black or aboriginal Natives, within the settled districts of this island'.[12] He wanted 'all soldiers' to be ready to 'obey and assist' when called on 'for the purpose of carrying on military operations against the Natives'. It contained an unambiguous command that the military were to take orders from the police magistrates. But soldiers were already in the field, and operations were already underway.

The declaration of martial law was as much a call to action as a legal instrument. In communicating it to his police magistrates, Arthur also provided some general instructions,[13] which were similarly reiterated to 'Officers in command at the out-stations'.[14] Arthur clarified that he was not 'seeking the destruction of the Aborigines' but was rather concerned with 'punishing the leaders in the atrocities'.

Arthur also hoped for the opportunity 'to take by the hand, and give a certain predominance to, some one particular tribe, which may have been less guilty than others'. He was still hoping for a negotiated settlement, but knew this was only likely to occur with some tribes. The colonists were well aware of intertribal conflicts, and Arthur hoped to use this to his advantage by forming alliances with certain tribes – which was gradually happening with the Aboriginal people south of Hobart – and bringing them into the colonial fold. Both civil and military authorities were ordered to send weekly reports for Arthur's information.

Over the following weeks the police magistrates sent reports of their operations to the Colonial Secretary for Arthur's attention. In the westernmost of the main settled districts, the focus tended towards deploying forces, managing information and ensuring communication and cooperation between different parties. In New Norfolk one 'military party is stationed at the Lower Clyde', while other military forces were deployed at settlers' farms, ready to respond when 'the Natives may shew themselves'.[15] In the Bothwell district, where Lieutenant Williams had taken over the police magistracy from Lieutenant Curtin earlier in the year, he instructed his constables to respond to Aboriginal groups by collecting 'as many armed Persons as he can, divide them into small parties, placing an authorised person with Each, and to follow the Natives up for several days' whenever they appeared.[16]

To help avoid 'Bloodshed', Arthur ordered 'that the Chief and one or two men appearing to have most authority in the Tribe should be taken'. Regarding these plans, the Colonial Secretary responded to Williams that 'His Excellency altogether approves thereof', especially the additional use of 'the Services of the Post Office Messenger'. Being so close to the highlands, Aboriginal people could relatively easily slip by colonial posts, so tactical and terrain intelligence was of central concern.

At Norfolk Plains in the northwestern midlands, the ex-soldier and police magistrate Malcolm Laing Smith was being given more explicit direction by Arthur.[17] Laing was convinced 'that conciliatory measures are not likely to succeed', and focused on deploying the military in a chain of posts up 'to Westbury Barracks' and establishing 'a cordon along the remote Stock Huts'.[18]

Arthur supported this scheme and authorised Smith to determine where best to station 'Military Parties' in his district. But because Smith was troubled by the small number of field police at his disposal, he asked for six more men so he could attach a field policeman to 'each Military Party'. It is a pointed indicator of the number of military parties deployed in his district that Smith already had 12 field policemen at his disposal and wanted a further six, suggesting perhaps 18 military parties were operating throughout Norfolk Plains at the time.

But Arthur had other ideas. 'I am further directed to acquaint you', the Colonial Secretary informed Smith, 'that it is hoped by swearing in a few steady Soldiers as Constables, any Augmentation of the Field Police will be unnecessary.' Having already placed regimental officers in charge of key districts, Arthur had just advocated further militarisation of the police magistracy by giving soldiers civil powers.

The Roving Parties

The Oatlands district had experienced many 'atrocities' and so Anstey developed a plan for the 'Capture of Aborigines'. His plan had Arthur's full support because, as the Colonial Secretary put it, 'very little differs from what His Excellency had already contemplated':[19]

> If sufficient force could be found, it appears to His Excellency desirable to occupy the Country by Posts, placed at considerable intervals from Campbell Town to St Paul's Plains and from thence to the Tier above Oyster Bay; and another line of Posts from Oatlands towards Prosser's Plains, and extending to little

Swan Port. The first named Division it appeared might commence by surrounding the Tract which is called the 'Native Hut Valley', at the source of the Elizabeth River; and subsequently if unsuccessful in that attempt, they could act in separate Bodies by watching for the Native Fires at night, and endeavouring to trace out their haunts by day.

Arthur was advocating deploying two lines stretching from the midlands strongholds to the coast, one veering north and the other south. These posts could serve to support mobile forces, striking into territory occupied by Aboriginal people, starting with the 'Native Hut Valley' along the hills directly east of Campbell Town. Arthur directed Anstey to 'try the effect of sending out two Parties ... with Danvers and Hopkins as Guides'.

James Hopkins was another convict, who had been punished in Worcester Gaol for an assault, before being transported on the *Arab* in 1822 for 'Highway robbery'.[20] Like Danvers, it seems his prior conduct qualified him for arduous duties. But they would not be alone. As Arthur told Anstey, 'an additional Military force will be immediately sent to you for the purpose; and you will be pleased to concert matters with Mr Lockyer, so as to insure that the Parties are well directed.'

Mr Lockyer was an ensign with the 57th Regiment, and had arrived in Van Diemen's Land just a few months earlier on the *Phoenix*. It was an appropriate name for the ship, which brought a detachment to Hobart before embarking some of the 40th Regiment for India.[21]

It was a year of change in the composition of the redcoats in Van Diemen's Land, with the long-serving 40th Regiment moving on and other regiments coming in. In November 1828, for instance, 30 privates of the 63rd arrived in Hobart in time to help enforce martial law.[22] Even some of the police magistracies changed hands between regiments as part of the shifting deployments of 1828. But while regiments came and went, the British Army remained, and Ensign Lockyer was soon enough at the front.

Oatlands was increasingly the major operational centre for military action in the colony. It was close enough to Hobart for relatively effective communication with the Lieutenant Governor. On 8 December, Anstey reported to Arthur that 'the Military Parties of this District have not yet fallen in with the Natives'.[23] As he explained:

> There has been no want of zeal exhibited by either the Soldiers or Constables employed in this service, but in consequence of the small number of Troops stationed at Oatlands, Ensign Lockyer was not able to detach more than one Party until Monday last the 1st instant when, by the arrival of Lieut Vicary with a Party of the 63rd Regt our means were increased.

'We have now five Parties in the Bush in the Eastern Division of this District', Anstey added, promising to forward the Lieutenant Governor 'a report of the proceedings of each party' as soon as feasible. Soon thereafter, the documentary trail of the Vandemonian War was greatly enriched.

Danvers' Mission to Tooms Lake

Danvers' party departed Oatlands on 26 November and spent that day travelling between various settlers' huts.[24] At one of these they were 'joined by Constable Longworth, and three Soldiers'. The next day was similarly spent in transit, and the party acquired the services of 'two others of the Military'. That night, in the hills of the southeastern midlands, they entered enemy territory and were 'on the look out the whole of that night for their fires'.

After continuing eastwards the following morning, they 'came to seven Native Huts'. From the remains of a butchered kangaroo, they surmised that the camp had been occupied within the last couple of days. They climbed a nearby hill for the night so they could again try to spot campfires. Crossing the 'Eastern Tier' on their fourth day out, the party failed to find any clear tracks, so they divided 'into two parties each taking a Hill' to increase their chances of spotting the telltale glows of fire. Again there were no sightings, so in the morning the parties separated again, this time to pass around Tooms Lake. Each group encountered abandoned Aboriginal huts near the shorelines. One party found eight, the other 10, pointing to a reasonable Aboriginal population in the area. That night they watched the lakeside, but still saw nothing but darkness.

Over the next four days they variously backtracked and traversed different hills. One settler reported that Aboriginal people had been seen in the area, but the party did not find them. On the ninth day they rested. Explaining this delay Danvers reported that 'some of the party being Foot Sore could not travel any further'. They had marched an incredible distance over difficult terrain.

On 5 December, after dividing again and taking different hills for the night, 'we saw a fire appearing about three miles distant'. Danvers tried to regroup with the rest of his force on the nearby hills. He could not find them in the dark, so he led his party toward the fires, climbing another hill to keep a watch. Unknown to Danvers, the other party had already moved off and soon regrouped with Anstey.

Early the next morning Danvers spotted another fire, situated about two miles from the first one. Following their general orders, the party 'advanced towards them', probably choosing the closer of the two fires. But the Aboriginal people were on alert and, perceiving the approach of the armed force, 'got to the Top of a high hill'.

Controlling the high ground gave several advantages as it made observation, defence and escape easier. Recognising the situation, Danvers attempted a ploy. 'Two of us went part of the way up without our fire arms thinking to decoy them down'. Meanwhile, 'the others of our party were laying in ambush'. But these Aboriginal people were not deceived and did not come down. Instead they escaped in a different direction. Danvers' party tracked them some '13 miles' back towards Tooms Lake, and then 'got as near as possible to them that night'. His party prepared to attack at the following dawn.

'At Daybreak we formed ourselves to surround them', Danvers later reported, but his party was spotted by a man getting up to tend the campfires. He 'gave the alarm to the rest, and the whole of them jumpt up immediately and attempted to take up their spears in defence'. The small military party was only six men strong, and thus outnumbered by more than 20 people. But the colonial force still had the relative advantages of surprise and training. They 'immediately fired and repeated it', pouring volleys of shot into the frantic camp.

In the aftermath of the attack, the party cleared the site. 'We destroyed 11 Dogs', Danvers noted, 'and brought one alive'. Keeping dogs for hunting, and their services as canine alarm systems and additional protection, was one of the major Aboriginal adaptations to British colonisation. But there were other signs of adaptation in the camp. As well as 52 spears and 29 waddies, there were 14 blankets, 28 knives, 6 partial sheep shears, 2 razor blades, '1 Fowling piece', some gunpowder, and 'A quantity of ball and shot'.

Of the Aboriginal people, Danvers reported that 'two only were, unfortunately, taken alive'. These were conveyed back to Oatlands under guard, where the party arrived the following day. There were other casualties – 'several of whom were killed', Danvers simply but matter-of-factly reported to Anstey. He did not report what the soldiers did with the bodies, but he did note that the blankets were 'destroyed by Fire'. They also 'burned all the Native Huts'.

Upon successful completion of this operation Danvers signed a mission report, titled 'Statement of Proceedings of an armed party of 9 Soldiers, two Constables, and John Danvers guide, sent out in Pursuit of the Aborigines by the Police Magistrate of Oatlands'. William Holmes, one of the field police constables attached to the expedition, also signed the report on 9 December 1828. This was forwarded to the Colonial Secretary's Office for Arthur's information.

On the same day, someone in Oatlands wrote to the *Hobart Town Courier* with a glowing commendation of 'their indefatigable exertions on this most harassing service'.[25] While offering a terse description of the mission, the writer clearly had exact information, listing the same numbers of trophies taken in the raid. But the letter also gave extra specifics not detailed in Danvers' account. 'Ten of the Natives were killed on the spot,' the writer asserted, 'and the rest fled.' Of the two 'prisoners' that the party brought back to Oatlands, they were apparently 'a black woman and her boy'.

Other Soldiers, More Scouring

Danvers' mission was just one part of Anstey's plan to scour his district with roving parties of armed men. On the same day that Danvers first spotted the Aboriginal fires, another mission departed Oatlands 'under the Command of Ensign Lockyer and led by James Hopkins Special Constable and Guide'.[26] They followed a similar path to Danvers, and spotted fires on their second evening out. The next morning, while Danvers' party was attacking the camp, Lockyer's party headed 'towards the fires', and soon 'saw about Thirty natives marching in Indian File about 150 yards' away. 'They were well armed, and well loaded with Plunder'.

'Lockyer thought it best to watch them till night', Hopkins reported, so as 'to surprise them by their fires.' The party 'lay in the scrub' and was not spotted. They watched the Aboriginal group head into some nearby hills, where they 'threw their firesticks on every side of them and thus the Bush began to burn for miles'. The soldiers lost the trail in the smoky conflagration. They tried for a few more days, but returned to Oatlands, seeking fresh shoes and supplies. Anstey thought the thing was 'very badly managed', annotating Hopkin's report with the suggestion that the party 'should have marched towards the Fires under cover of the night' as soon as they first spotted them. That way they could have approached the camp 'at day break' and 'seized and bound the Natives between sleeping and waking'.

While Lockyer's party was laying in the scrub on 7 December, yet another 'party of military' from Oatlands was 'scouring the Country in every direction during the day and night'.[27] This was a detachment of the 63rd Regiment under the command of a sergeant, attended by one of Anstey's field police constables, and guided by an assigned convict servant. The next day this party got word from Lockyer that he had intercepted an Aboriginal group, and he instructed them to proceed to a particular marsh to try to 'fall in with them'. That evening the sergeant saw fires, and identified one in particular attended by 'two natives'. In the morning they advanced on this camp, but were spotted. 'One shot was fired' at the fleeing figures as 'they attempted to make their escape'. The field policemen thought it 'took effect', but noted that 'we could not wait to look for the body' because they went in pursuit. After three more days they too returned to Oatlands 'for want of provisions'. As he did with most reports, Anstey annotated it before forwarding the detailed account of the mission to the Colonial Secretary. They 'will do better with the next Party', he noted.

On 8 December a fourth party from Oatlands spotted where Aboriginal people had 'set the bush a fire'. The next day they 'saw another fire' raging in the bush, which seemed to have been ignited by 'the Tribe which had been attacked by John Danvers' party'. This was a combined party of seven soldiers from the 63rd and 40th Regiments, similarly under the command of a sergeant in company with a field police constable. Temporarily occupying a stockman's hut, a soldier was left behind to guard it while the stockman guided the remainder of the party towards this Aboriginal group. They first headed towards Tooms Lake, but veered off along a road into the hills. The guide proved a bit unfamiliar with the landscape, and so they missed the lake completely, but did get to see the Schoutens – now known as the Freycinet Peninsula – 'on the Sea Coast' to the east.

By then, however, the party was 'totally exhausted' and short of provisions. They headed back towards the farms and stockmen's huts, and stumbled across a 'brush hut' occupied by 'some white person' who had fled upon their approach. It was probably built by 'bushrangers or sheep stealers', they surmised, 'as a great number of mutton bones were strewed about'.

Even once back at occupied settlers' huts, they tried to draw rations so they could stay in the field, but due to a shortage of flour they decided to return to Oatlands. The party's 17 December report suggested that future parties should be issued 'with biscuit' because it lasted longer and could be consumed without the aid of a campfire. Stealth and a secure food supply were going to be crucial in the weeks and months ahead.

CHAPTER THREE

Clearing the Settled Districts

1828–29, Summer
East, South, North, West

Roving Towards the Coast

Hoping that each mission could improve on the last, Anstey continued to send out roving parties. Other districts most likely followed suit, though no other left such a rich documentary trail. The valleys, hills and forests of Van Diemen's Land were being swept clear in an effort to make tribal habitation of the 'settled districts' unviable. In explaining his decision to enact martial law to his London superiors, Arthur implied that the ends would justify the means: 'Terror may have the effect which no preferred measures of conciliation have been capable of inducing.'[1] Arthur's superiors sanctioned his measures, and so terror became British policy in Van Diemen's Land.[2]

Only a few days after returning to Oatlands, Danvers and Holmes and six others were again sent out 'in pursuit of the Natives'.[3] They tracked south and east 'to the source of Prosser's River'. It seems that Danvers had learned from the encounter at Tooms Lake, which sat at the upper tributaries of the Macquarie River, that the upper waterways were likely places to find Aboriginal people. They found nothing of interest on this occasion, so they moved on in the morning.

Continuing eastwards, they found 'a very high hill, the name of which is unknown to us'. Despite declaring this territory part of the 'settled districts', the eastern tiers that separated the midlands plains from the coast was poorly known. Failing to spot any campfires or smoke trails, the party continued east 'as far as where Prosser's river empties itself into the Sea'. They had no luck securing 'intelligence' or provisions from settlers and stockmen they visited, so some of the party crossed over to Maria Island to get provisions from the military station there. The remainder 'scoured the bush in every direction', but found no Aboriginal traces in the area. Once the parties had reunited, they all headed to a settler's farm, 'and stayed there the remainder of the day to take bread, and repairing our knapsacks, shoes, and clothes'. The expedition took a heavy toll on the soldiers' equipment, as well as their bodies.

With repairs done, the party headed towards Little Swan Port, hoping again for information. But despite having 'been in great strength thereabouts' a few weeks ago, these Aboriginal people had since moved on. The party continued up the 'little Swan port River at the distance of eight or nine miles', and on 'towards Oyster Bay' the next morning. Here they finally found something:

> We came to several places where the natives had lately been, and where we saw several Native huts. In these places they seem to have made warlike preparations, which we judged from the fresh scrapings of spears which we saw there.

Now on the alert, the party headed to a nearby creek, thinking the Aboriginal people 'might have made for that place'. Instead, they 'found two Soldiers and a constable stationed there in a government hut', waiting and hoping to ambush Aboriginal hut-raiders. These would-be ambushers said that they had 'been two or three days before in Mr Meredith's hut' (the settler who had housed the east coast military station in his barn and asked to be reimbursed). It was another small example of the mutual assistance between the colonial forces and the settlers. Van Diemen's Land was a military colony in a multiplicity of ways.

The party then headed to Waterloo Point. The small coastal settlement was named for the battle where Napoleon was finally defeated, and reminds us that many of the soldiers and ex-soldiers of the Vandemonian War had other recent experiences of war. The party reached Waterloo Point on 23 December, and 'saw Captain Dalrymple in the Evening'. Dalrymple belonged to the 40th Regiment, and had replaced Captain Hibbert as police magistrate of the Great Swan Port district. On Christmas Eve, Danvers and Holmes' party 'remained this day at Waterloo point to refresh ourselves, by order of Capt Dalrymple'.

Dalrymple spent part of Christmas Day 1828 making plans and preparations with Danvers and Holmes. He 'added four Soldiers' to the party, and then 'ordered this party to be divided into two parties'. Dalrymple thought the Aboriginal people may have gone either to the Schoutens or to St Patricks Head further north along the coast. Danvers was to guide one party, Holmes the other, but they all set off together continuing their northwards journey up the east coast. They learned little from the stockmen and settlers they encountered, but they did hear 'that the Natives had speared two of Mr Meredith's horses'. Following Dalrymple's orders, the party then split up in their continued searching.

A Casualty, and the Veneer of Civility

On 27 December, Anstey and Lockyer had to deal with an annoyed Lieutenant Governor. The day before, the Colonial Secretary had written to Anstey to express Arthur's 'extreme regret' about certain events concerning another military party 'sent in pursuit of the Natives by Ensign Lockyer'.[4] This itself was possibly a bit of administrative sleight of hand. The original mission report had recorded that the mission was sent out by Anstey, as such missions nominally were, but Anstey had crossed out this line and written in Lockyer as the directing authority for this particular mission.[5] In all probability Lockyer had authorised the mission, but Anstey was obviously keen to distance himself from its outcome.

This small party commenced their expedition on 10 December – the same day that Danvers and Holmes had set off – although they left from one of the marshes in the district rather than Oatlands itself. The group comprised four men of the 57th Regiment, guided by Constable Thomas Benison of the field police. By coincidence, they headed in a similar direction to Danvers towards the coast. Benison's party, however, saw smoke and found 'fires by which the Natives had been roasting Opossums'. Soon Benison's party was in sight of the coast, 'and crossed some of the Native hunting grounds, where the blood of kangaroos indicated that the natives had been there recently'. Then, again shadowing Danvers' group, they entered Prosser's Plains. After that things went awry.

The party stopped 'on the banks of a considerable river'. Benison ordered privates Wood, Price and Splint to prepare a camp for the night and stay put while he and Private Monaghan climbed a nearby rise 'to make what observation we could'. On the hill, Benison and Monaghan 'saw no fires nor any thing else which could guide us in the dark', so they descended back down the hill towards their companions. On the way, Monaghan went a little ahead, declaring that he 'would shoot a kangaroo' to supplement their diminished provisions. As Benison neared the camp he heard a shot in the darkness.

Reading the account later, Anstey expressed his frustration and noted for the Colonial Secretary's benefit that he 'told every Party that a shot must never be fired, nor a word spoken, except in whispers'. Anstey did not want the Aboriginal people on alert for the roving parties. But in the darkness of that night Benison had more immediate concerns. 'I was apprehensive', he later recalled, and 'went down in the direction where the shot had been fired, but could see nothing on account of the darkness'. His apprehensions increased when he and Monaghan returned to camp to discover that Private Price was missing.

In the morning the party 'went in search of the missing man, and found poor Price lying weltering in his blood dead, a ball having passed through his head'. His musket was nearby and still loaded, so it was not suicide. It seemed Monaghan may have mistaken him for a kangaroo.

By now the party was very short of provisions and the soldiers' shoes had worn out so completely that they travelled barefoot. They took Price's 'firelock' but left 'the body behind' and continued with their mission, heading towards fires they had spotted, although without success. They visited a few huts, and then made for home, returning to Oatlands on the evening of 17 December. Benison gave his report the next day, and Anstey forwarded it to Hobart.

A week later the Colonial Secretary wrote to Anstey:

> I am directed to express to you His Excellency's extreme regret that a cart was not immediately despatched for the Body that an Inquest might with as little delay as possible have been held upon it, and as the Lieutenant Governor considers it very important that the most minute investigation of this mysterious affair should still take place, His Excellency is desirous that a Jury should be summoned and an Inquest held as soon as it is possible reporting to me fully thereon for His information.

By contrast, Arthur showed no concern for the people killed near Tooms Lake. The peculiar application of martial law during the Vandemonian War made inquests about Aboriginal deaths unnecessary, while the charade that it was a civil operation meant 'friendly fire' casualties were given coronial rather than military investigation.

The Northern Line

Danvers' and Holmes' parties also had little luck in late December. While Holmes headed east then south down the peninsula, Danvers struck further north towards St Patricks Head. He started by following what he called the 'Big River' (probably what is now the Apsley), which fed into a large lagoon at the north of Oyster Bay. After following the water for 'about six miles' the party 'ascended the Tiers' and then continued towards the coast. Here they found a midden of shellfish and abandoned camp fires, but nothing else. On 30 December, 'within one or two miles of St Patrick's head', Danvers turned his party back:

having been given to understand that Martial Law did not
extend beyond these boundaries, and being likely to be short of
provisions, and seeing no signs of natives, we retraced our steps,
at the same time pursuing a different route going homewards.

Holmes' party also decided to turn back on 30 December. They had traversed the difficult terrain of the peninsula – eventually being reduced to clambering 'from rock to rock' – but had found no 'traces of the natives'.

In the new year Danvers' and Holmes' parties reunited at Waterloo Point. Captain Dalrymple's extra soldiers detached and stayed at Oyster Bay while the rest returned to Oatlands, 'examining the country very minutely' as they travelled via Tooms Lake. Upon their return Danvers and Holmes told Anstey that they 'entertain no doubt that most of the Native Tribes have crossed the Country, and proceeded to the Westward'.

The Western Line

Anstey had instructed several roving parties to scour the southern midlands towards the west. On 12 December, two days after Danvers' and Benison's parties had departed, Anstey sent another 'armed party' south from Oatlands.[6] They tracked towards the small town of Jerusalem (now Colebrook), crossed the Coal River in its valley northeast of Hobart, and to their surprise discovered 'a whole line of trees marked'. These were, they realised, the secret markings for a cattle-rustling highway through the bush. This was the party's only useful discovery, and they returned to Oatlands on Christmas Eve without making contact with any Aboriginal people.

Another party operating to the east of Oatlands from 15 December did spot Aboriginal fires, but lost sight of them 'when it began to rain excessively and the Fire disappeared'.[7] Later they found old campfires, where Aboriginal people 'had been making Spears', but little else of note. They 'heard a shot' one day in the distance, 'crossed a range of Hills or Mountains of which they did not know the name', and returned to Oatlands via 'Toom's Lagoon'.

The mid-December rain also impacted another 'party of military' roving to the west and northwest of Oatlands, guided by field police constable John Tattersall.[8] They had departed on 15 December, and quickly 'found a small uninhabited hut on fire' in a marsh west of the town. They could see 'one or two more fires' a little further on. These fires were probably evidence of deliberate Aboriginal targeting of isolated stockmen and farms and the destruction of buildings and haystacks. On 15 December a correspondent at Bothwell wrote to Hobart, describing the incursion:

> A horde of Aborigines entered this district yesterday, after killing James Jones, a freeman, servant to Michael and Henry Jones the lime burners at the Black marsh. The body of the unfortunate man was found this morning covered with spear wounds in a water hole in the Jordan, near his master's house. Intelligence has reached this township that a soldier of the 40th stationed on the Shannon was this morning wounded severely in the shoulder by a spear. The man was unconscious of a foe lurking so near him until he received the wound.[9]

Tattersall's party, however, failed to meet with any of these assailants. 'The whole of this day', he reported on 20 December, 'the rain came pouring down incessantly'. While the party pushed on towards the hills, 'the rain and wet rendered all further exertion impracticable'. They tried twice more, but were thwarted by 'heavy fog and wet'. At the end of the month they were sent northwest towards Lake Sorell.[10]

While operations west of Oatlands met with little initial success, the incursions reported at Bothwell were being addressed. The same correspondent who reported the death of James Jones praised '[t]he incessant activity and vigilance displayed by Lieutenant Williams of the 40th for the protection of this district.'[11]

Like Anstey, Williams sent regular missives 'for the information of the Lieut Governor', giving the key points of his operations 'to effect the expulsion of the Aboriginal Natives'.[12] Although Williams' surviving correspondence is not as detailed or voluminous as Anstey's, it is clear that the deployment of military parties dominated his strategy. His brief summaries include reports of civilians and constables accompanying military parties on excursions as well as limited information on the movements and pursuits throughout his district. Williams also conveyed his various attempts to warn settlers and to 'collect a party of settlers & their servants to proceed against the Natives' – effectively calling upon settlers to form militia in areas not adequately covered by the military.

But not all settlers and servants shared Williams' notions of public service. There were clearly some recruitment difficulties in Bothwell in the summer of 1828–29. Arthur responded to one report of a man who 'refused to assist the Parties employed against the Aborigines' by regretting that 'nothing can be done against this man in a legal way', but suggesting 'the only means therefore to punish him will be to deprive him of any indulgence which he may be receiving from the Government'.[13] Arthur was happy to informally punish such shirkers. He also approved Williams' dismissal of ineffective guides.[14]

Although Williams' report states that roving parties in the Bothwell district were unsuccessful 'in capturing any of the Natives' in December 1828, they were not without success. One of the missions sent out from the Shannon River on 15 December 'fell in with the Natives' two days later 'and took about 200 spears, some sheep shears &c'.[15] Apparently 'the Natives Escaped', but they had clearly been disarmed and dispersed.

When some Aboriginal people were spotted again about a fortnight later, one of Williams' constables 'formed a party and cooperated with the Military Parties' in that area.[16] When 'a Tribe of Natives made their appearance at the hut of Mr Clarke on the River Ouse late in the afternoon, twelve Rounds were fired at them ineffectually.' They 'retired without doing any mischief'. Two parties were formed to go after them.

Division Constable Young led one of the parties, and 'fell in with the Natives early on Wednesday morning'. Unfortunately, 'he was unable to get within shot of them but succeeded in Capturing between 2 & 300 Spears'. Combined with the shooting at the hut, Williams' report implies that military in the Bothwell district tended to shoot first and attempt captures later, if at all. This probably reflects longstanding military practice in the area, and probably the wider colony too – shooing Aboriginal people away by shooting at them.

In fact, later the same day, a roving party was 'proceeding down the Eastern Bank of the Derwent, and saw the Natives on the opposite side making spears'. It was likely the same group attempting to re-arm. '[B]eing unable to cross the River, [they] fired at the Natives to disturb them.'

In Williams' report to the Colonial Secretary, he also mentioned that Aboriginal people approaching a hut were met with 'twelve Rounds'. Arthur wrote 'Very Cunning' in the letter's margin, and signed it 'GA'. But Williams felt their efforts were in vain:

> I fear that the exertions of the Civil and Military Power will be attended with little success in capturing the Natives, except if guides can be procured capable of tracking them. By keeping the Soldiers & Constables actively employed, the District may be protected, but I do not think the Natives can be captured.

Arthur's Excursion and Strategic Oversight

A few days after Williams posted his letter, the Lieutenant Governor left Hobart for the north of the island. Arthur planned to travel towards Launceston then head west towards Westbury 'to examine the Lands in the occupation of the Van Diemen's Land Company'.[17] He ordered the Surveyor General to explore some of the nearby hills, and conscript a few soldiers to help build temporary huts by convenient riverbanks to facilitate his travels. He also requested an additional four packhorses to carry his baggage, and 'that the Horses are in good condition' because he intended 'to return across the Country from the Mersey to the Great Lakes', traversing what was still relatively unknown territory to the colonists. It meant that he was likely going to return to Hobart by either the western midlands or Bothwell.

While the main operational details of the Vandemonian War were recorded through the colonial secretariat, the records of the Lieutenant

Governor's Office also preserve much often-overlooked information, like the evidence for this planned excursion as well as Arthur's concerns that Williams 'has occasion for the services of a Clerk to keep the Commissariat accounts' at Bothwell.[18] In a more telling memorandum from December, Arthur approved a horse being purchased 'for the use of Lieut Williams in his Police Duties at the Clyde'.[19] Arthur was making an exception, because he usually wanted 'to see every horse myself before the purchase is complete'.

Other government department records also detail elements of the Vandemonian War, further highlighting Arthur's general oversight. We know that there was a small mounted military police force operating in the interior in December 1828 because Arthur again provided consent for the Brigade Major to get 'the usual dress for the soldier, and purchase a horse for his use'.[20] While the role of the mounted police remains unclear, the records indicate they could be 'permanently attached' to various stations throughout the colony.[21] They were likely used to provide mobile support to parties in the field.

Police magistrates also kept their own accounts and records, but these have hardly survived, and do relatively little to illuminate the war. Even centralised Commissariat and Ordinance accounts, detailing macro-governmental expenditure, only survive in small exemplars from the period. One such volume, however, itemises and enumerates the issuing of goods for government service from July 1827 into early 1828.[22] Through this, it is possible to reconstruct the main components of a mounted policeman's gear, which included bits, bridles and saddles for the horses, as well as spurs, coats, pistols and swords for the riders.[23] The same volume also notes that 'Alexander an Aborigine' received a blanket and a coverlet on 1 November 1827, but this was a rare example of official government philanthropy.[24]

All these records suggest the government was more inclined to militarisation than humanitarianism. Over the course of roughly half a year the Commissariat issued 89 bayonets and 2366 cartridge rounds.[25] The colonial police received 57 muskets with ramrods and 84 gun flints, although even this was dwarfed by the 908 gun flints given to the military in the same period.[26] Twelve of the flints went to police forces stationed on the Lower Clyde in the Bothwell district, and were probably among those used to 'disturb' the group manufacturing spears on the far bank of the Derwent River. With hundreds of weapons and thousands of rounds of ammunition distributed, as well as the demonstrably deliberate disarmament of Aboriginal people, the Vandemonian War was far more industrial than has previously been recognised.

Aboriginal Auxiliaries, the Deployment of 'Boomer'

Intelligence was a critical resource in the war, although it was recorded with less clarity than bayonet numbers. In early 1829, likely in response to Williams' requests for better guides, an Aboriginal man known as 'Boomer' or 'Bruné island Jack' was 'sent up to Bothwell by the government'.[27] This indicates that an establishment for feeding, housing and training Aboriginal people was being actively administered by the government in ways that also supported combat operations.

Details about the Bruny Island Establishment are relatively scant. But during the previous winter Arthur explored the possibility of getting 'any inferior or half-worn blankets at the Prisoners' Barracks' to send to Bruny Island 'for the purpose of being distributed among the Natives'.[28] By November 1828 there were apparently 'about fourteen' Aboriginal people living there.[29]

Although Arthur was mostly concerned with operations in the interior and other matters concerning the administration of the colony, he did give some attention to the Bruny Island Establishment and the project of pacifying the tribes south of Hobart. He wanted 'three steady well conducted convicts who are expecting indulgence in 12 months' to be sent there to oversee the distribution of 'blankets and rations', and to busy themselves 'cultivating a few acres of Potatoes', most likely for the instruction of the Aboriginal residents. It seems likely that Boomer was recruited from this scene of government paternalism to assist the campaigns against the tribes of the interior.

Although there are few records from the campaigns in the Bothwell district, Boomer's operations are broadly discernible through a range of reports published in the press. When he arrived in Bothwell it was in company with a woman, variously described as his 'Jin' or 'wife'. They were both attached to 'a party of 5 soldiers and a constable', along with another man named Nelson. The party joined a broader campaign including '14 parties out in all directions' drawn from 'about 80 rank and file' stationed in the district, who were scouring the district for Aboriginal people.[30] They were all on alert because of a series of hut raids where the assailants had taken muskets.

After a few days out, Boomer was reportedly sick of the 'pork and biscuit' rations on which the party subsisted, and 'was permitted to go with Nelson' to hunt game in the bush. In the evening Nelson returned to the party, but Boomer remained away until morning. The soldiers reported that he had been exhibiting a 'sullen' disposition. Whether from being on foreign country, traversing the territory of traditional enemies, or simply disagreeing with the premise of the whole exercise, his thoughts and attitudes are unclear and rendered only in fleeting characterisations based on the perceptions of witnesses. But his actions do reflect a general concern with the mission. After seeing a 'soldier's hut' later that morning, Boomer and his companion 'both ran away'.

The military party separated to search for them, and Private Malony soon found Boomer apparently hiding 'in the hollow of a tree'. Responding to his rediscovery, Boomer reportedly 'shook hands with Malony saying that soldiers were very good & would not hurt him', before trying to deflect the conversation by explaining that 'he had lost the woman'. Then, while going 'looking for her, Boomer suddenly put his leg behind the soldier, and pushed him down, biting him severely in the arm'. As they scuffled, Boomer and Malony rolled down the hill. When they thumped to a halt, Boomer kicked Malony down, grabbed his gun, pointed it at Malony, and fired.

But there was no spark from the flint. To save the powder from the damp, Malony had a handkerchief tied over the mechanism, keeping it dry. Seeing his chance, Malony grabbed the gun, and the two again started rolling down the slope, until falling over a precipice. Striking the ground, Malony's arm was injured and he was unable to maintain a grip on Boomer, who 'eventually ran away'.

In the evening Boomer was spotted by another military party. The corporal in charge, 'not knowing he was tame', called out to Boomer 'to induce him to come quietly'. Boomer 'steadily refused', and tried to flee the situation. The soldiers went after him. Boomer 'made for the Clyde and dived many times', it was reported, 'but each time he put his head up the soldier fired, and at last killed him'.

Word of this incident was forwarded to Hobart. In its 'Chit Chat' section, the *Colonial Times* rather snidely reported that Boomer 'endeavoured to escape, and received the merited reward of his treachery and presumption, by being shot dead'.[31] The *Launceston Advertiser* ran the same story.[32] In the meantime, Arthur returned to Hobart without exploring the lakes, and Boomer's wife was recaptured. The soldiers continued to go out into the bush. Reports came in from the interior, some of which were reproduced in the newspapers. The history of the war was being written just as it was being fought.

Press, Propaganda and History-making

The press's coverage of the Vandemonian War both reflected and informed public opinion, but it also made for an unusual evidentiary mix. While there was broad consensus that something had to be done to resolve aggressions by Aboriginal people, public sympathies ranged from dovish to hawkish. While the *Hobart Town Courier* sarcastically awaited 'the result of the coroner's inquiry' following Boomer's death, and advocated that colonial forces 'beware then of wantonly firing upon them',[33] the *Colonial Times* proclaimed that,

> A profound peace now ranges throughout the country. The bush-rangers are thoroughly extirpated, and if the operations against the Aborigines are as vigorously carried on as they have been for some time back, these marauders will shortly share the same fate.[34]

These editorials were often printed next to reports of settlers or servants who had been attacked – and the reprisals that followed – or discourses about the social and economic opportunity for the landholding settlers in a future peace. While the *Hobart Town Courier* hoped 'that a subsidiary colony of these Aborigines, will shortly be formed in some convenient place or island', the *Colonial Times* rather bluntly looked forward to the successful 'extirpation' of the Aboriginal population of the interior. But despite their differences in language, they both amounted to the same thing: a landscape cleared of the tribes.

The key conceptual differences expressed in editorial commentary lay mainly in the method by which this could be achieved, and the effects upon the displaced people. The doves hoped that Aboriginal people's 'offspring at least may acquire civilized habits ... and at last become useful and industrious members of the community', fostering the view that Aboriginal people could be gradually if forcibly integrated into colonial society. The hawks tended to focus more on the needs of the moneyed classes, asserting that Van Diemen's Land 'requires only an honest and industrious Peasantry to render it one of the most desirable countries in the universe', carrying the implicit principle that Aboriginal ways of living on the land would not be permitted.

And so the British Army and the Vandemonian field police continued their pursuit of Aboriginal people across the hills of the interior. In December 1828 Garrison Orders were issued to the military stations in Van Diemen's Land:

> the Colonel Commanding is desirous of impressing upon the minds of officers on duty in the interior of the importance and necessity of exerting *every energy* to repel from or capture the aboriginal Natives in their respective districts during the summer months. All the small parties from the detachments should be instructed to be constantly on search, and by forming themselves into parties of eight or ten each, with provisions for 14 or 16 days each at a time, with properly organized plans and arrangements, little doubt can exist of the beneficial results which would arise from such a combined system of operations.[35]

It was all part of the general principle of projecting 'Terror' upon Aboriginal people. One correspondent from Great Swan Port commented in January that the 'parties are continually out in quest', adding that he personally 'saw but one black during the whole of our journey, and he escaped among the scrub'.[36] He also mentioned that one settler 'shot a black man' recently, before offering a brief list of reported encounters in the wider area: 'Nine were killed and three taken, near St. Paul's River, ten days back, and about the same time ten were shot and two taken near the Eastern Marshes.'

Whether read as confused rumours or reasonably reliable reports – the 'ten' and 'two' could refer to Danvers' mission near Tooms Lake, for instance – such messages spoke to a wider colonial agenda and revealed a determined campaign of ethnic cleansing. This plan was conducted by British regulars and authorised paramilitary forces at the Lieutenant Governor's behest. A few months later, Arthur echoed sentiments he had expressed to other magistrates when he ordered Lieutenant Lane of the 63rd Regiment (another new police magistrate for Great Swan Port) to 'take the most active and decisive measures to drive the Natives out of the settled parts of your district'.[37] The tribes had to make way for settlers.

By this time, the military and paramilitary operations were increasingly aided by Aboriginal guides, although they rarely attracted the press's attention. This disjuncture between reality and reportage spoke less to events and more to emphasis, highlighting how the press version of the conflict was often skewed for the reading public of the day – subtly misleading historians and posterity alike. For instance, when a group of '5 Soldiers' traversed the territory between Oatlands and the east coast during late December 1828 and early January 1829, the party found no Aboriginal people but did encounter an abandoned settler's hut with a human skull inside.[38] Ensign Lockyer, who personally commanded this mission, 'took the skull with him'. This part of the story proved newsworthy, especially as it seemed to offer a lonely and pathos-riven proof of the isolated hardship of frontier lives.[39] That the party also had 'a black Native Boy' with them did not merit public attention. That fact remained quite separate from a developing public narrative of the conflict, which principally structured the war in terms of distant frontier murders and inveterate racial animosity. Literally, the war was fought far away from urbane Hobart and preening Launceston – close enough to titillate and worry, but sufficiently distant to be discretely obscure.

CHAPTER FOUR

Mercenaries and Aboriginal Guides

1829, Summer–Autumn
Eastern Front

Kickerterpoller and Gilbert Robertson Capture Eumarrah

In early 1829 the Lieutenant Governor arranged 'a Salary at the rate of £150 per annum' for a settler named Gilbert Robertson 'to take charge of a Roving Party of 10 or 12 men to be employed against the Aborigines'.[1] Robertson was already involved in the war, holding the post of chief district constable of Richmond, although he effectively took leave of that position to be employed as a sort of colonial mercenary. Capturing Aboriginal people was a far more lucrative occupation. But, while placed outside the parameters and restrictions of policing duties, he was not entirely autonomous of all the colonial chains of command. Robertson was 'placed under the Orders of the Brigade Major, and supplied in the same manner as the Military Parties'.

Robertson was contracted by the government in part because he had some prior success capturing Aboriginal people. During November 1828, just a few weeks after the proclamation of martial law, a party led by Robertson and guided by Kickerterpoller crept up on an Aboriginal camp and captured five people, although at least five others escaped the raid. Robertson conveyed his 'satisfaction' to the Colonial Secretary that he had 'succeeded in Capturing two chiefs "Yumârra and Jemmie", one young warrior, a Lance Man and Chiefs wife (five persons in all) of the Stoney Creek Tribe'.² He reported that,

> 'Black Tom' [Kickerterpoller] (of whom I cannot speak with too much praise) told me of their habits for he states that they seldom take up their <u>abode</u> near the coast in any case and that after having committed a Murder or other outrage they invariably retreat to some remote situation in the interior.³

Kickerterpoller also advised Robertson of a regular spear-making place, which illustrates how Aboriginal allies helped the colonists take the war into tribal geographies. This knowledge, however, had its limits; when Robertson's party travelled through an area where 'Tom was a stranger' they soon got lost. Nonetheless, they were eventually able to track and intercept their target, and seize a good proportion of them.

The captives were taken to Richmond and then to Hobart, where they were placed in the gaol. Unsurprisingly, considering the war had been brought into town so visibly, Robertson's exploit attracted the interest of the press. As the *Hobart Town Courier* reported:

> On Tuesday Mr. Gilbert Robertson arrived in town with 5 native blacks, whom he apprehended near the Eastern marshes. The whole tribe consisted of 10, but five made their escape in some thick scrub, which bordered their encampment. Among the captives is their King, named Eumarrah, whose indignation at being deprived of his liberty is very great.⁴

This success seemed an early proof of concept for Arthur's hopes to use intermediaries like Kickerterpoller to help capture Aboriginal people, so Arthur and his Executive Council met with the newly captured members 'of the Stoney Creek Mob of Natives'.⁵ Kickerterpoller acted as translator, although at least some of the captives 'understood sufficient of the English language' to be quizzed by the Lieutenant Governor on 'the cause of their grievances and aggressions'.⁶ Their replies were minuted by the council's secretary:

> The five Natives denied having speared the White People or that any of their Tribe had been concerned in any of the Murders; but they admitted that the White People had been murdered by the Port Dalrymple Tribe, because they had been driven from their Kangaroo Hunting Ground.⁷

This was all that was officially recorded of the 'considerable communication with the five Natives'.

Captivity and Conscription

While the Bruny Island Establishment had developed organically as a site for feeding and clothing Aboriginal people, the government had not yet provided any formal or centralised mechanism for dealing with captives. When the woman and child captured by Danvers were conveyed to Oatlands, Anstey advised the Colonial Secretary that they were going to be 'forwarded to Hobarton in a day or two'.⁸ Government injunctions simply advised captors to treat their prisoners well.

Many Aboriginal captives were absorbed into colonial gaols, though their legal status remained ambiguous. In April 1829, for instance, the police magistrate of George Town on the north coast, Captain D'Arcy, wrote to the town adjutant regarding a captive 'Black Native Girl'.⁹ Despite contacting the military officer, he placed her 'in the Factory' – the nearby female convict establishment. The Lieutenant Governor approved this arrangement 'for the present', but reprimanded D'Arcy for corresponding about her through military channels. He was advised that 'the subject would have been more properly communicated to the Civil Department'.

In the south of the island, where more captures were being recorded, Richmond Gaol served as a major place of Aboriginal confinement, at least following Robertson's first success. After examining the Stony Creek captives in his Executive Council in November 1828, Arthur ordered them removed to Richmond Gaol and kept secure 'so as entirely to prevent their return to the settled Districts of the Island'. As the police magistrate of Richmond, Thomas Lascelles, was informed:

> His Excellency has therefore directed these Natives to be removed to the Gaol in your district, there to be confined, with the exception of the younger lad, who may be rationed by the Crown and permitted to reside with the Chief District Constable, in the expectation that his services may be made useful in furtherance of measures for the apprehension and future disposal of the Aborigines; until further instructions shall be given you.[10]

Arthur's broader plans were beginning to take shape. On the same day the Colonial Secretary wrote to Lascelles, detailed plans for dividing the midlands with military posts were approved, as well as coordinated operations with Lockyer and Danvers from the Oatlands district. Arthur also approved two experimental missions in the relatively under-documented northern midlands district of Campbell Town.[11] In the first, a man named 'Low' was proposing to 'endeavour to conciliate some Tribe', although there was some confusion about whether he planned to go out alone or with a party. The second proposal was an 'experiment of taking some of the women', which suggests that captures had probably been taking place in that district in tandem with military operations. Through the centralised information systems of the colonial secretariat, district practices cross-fertilised under a centralised command structure. Arthur was overseeing both military and paramilitary movements as well as the confinement of captives and the deployment of Aboriginal guides.

While making plans for the use of Richmond Gaol, Arthur also approved of the provision of victuals at the gaol to 'Black Tom, and the two prisoners named Arthur and Lee' while possible arrangements with Robertson were worked out. Thomas Arthur and Robert Lee, like Kickerterpoller, had served on Robertson's previous expedition, and it was expected they would support his next one.[12] Like Danvers, they were convicts who likely hoped for reduced sentences. In January 1829, reminding the government of his good service, Danvers applied to have his ticket of leave reinstated.[13] Instead, he was offered the opportunity to gain the rewards of further good service by being appointed to the field police in the Oatlands district in a more formal capacity. Without many options, he accepted the position.

Other convicts who had already performed good service similarly found rewards were not immediate. Lee had been transported for life in the 1810s, and in late 1828 the Colonial Secretary annotated his conduct sheet with the comment that 'A worse character cannot well be conceived'.[14] Since arriving in Van Diemen's Land, Lee had been punished many times. He officially earned a total of 275 lashes for a range of offences from drunkenness to various absences, as well as periods of confinement in barracks or gaols, extra labour and time in penal stations. While getting a ticket of leave, he lost it after being found 'on board the Ship Kent whaler without a pass with intent to escape from the Colony'. Moreover, several of his offences exhibited violence, including 'striking a superior officer'.[15] In 1822 he was flogged for 'Assaulting & beating' a constable, and the following year he earned three years at Macquarie Harbour penal station for 'Cutting & maiming Mary Lee his wife'. After reading it, Arthur annotated the back, stating that 'This man must positively be sent back to Maria Island'. But he was soon enough again in Robertson's service.

Guiding Robertson into Tribal Country

While the midlands were swept by soldiers and field police during the summer campaigns of late 1828 and early 1829, the captive segment of the Stony Creek tribe presumably remained confined at Richmond Gaol, and Robertson remained relatively inactive. Only on 2 January 1829 was Robertson allowed 'to select 10 or 12 Convicts who are likely to be useful'.[16]

Details of Robertson's missions can be reconstructed from a variety of sources, but most importantly from his own writings. He produced two journals for 1829, seemingly drawing on a mix of personal reminiscence, various papers and perhaps mission reports and diaries.[17]

While less clear than some of the midlands evidence, they nonetheless record his movements and actions with relative reliability.

Things moved slowly at first. Robertson started the year in Hobart, and visited the Hobart town adjutant arranging military rations before leaving for Richmond. He spent several days at Richmond waiting for 'some of the party' to arrive as well as 'the Arms and Accoutrements', and occupied himself with various preparations such as negotiating for rations and 'making ammunition pouches and other articles'.

During this time Robertson noted that there was much thunder, lightning and rain, but there were other excitements as well. One night the party sprang from their beds 'by a false alarm that the prisoners were breaking out of Gaol'. The ruckus had been caused by one of the officers 'attempting improper freedoms with a Girl'.

Eventually the mission left Richmond, and spent the first few days traversing the Brushy Plains to the northeast of the town, but without success. On 13 January they stopped at 'Hunters Valley, between prossers plains and the Blue Hills', after again having seen nothing of Aboriginal people or their tracks. That night, a morepork owl visited their camp, much to the delight of the 'guides' attached to the party. This bird 'perch'd upon a Tree near to our Break wind began to hoot his evening Note', which gave Robertson a chance, as he put it, 'of observing one of the superstitions of the Aboriginal Natives':

> The two Blacks attached to the party started up and began
> an earnest conversation principally addressed to the Bird who
> occasionally hooted his responses on hearing which they shouted
> with the most extravagant demonstrations of Joy[.] when this
> whimsical Conversation ceased Tom explained to us that the
> Bird (which he called Cocolo diana) was capable of giving any
> information he required concerning his wandering Countrymen.

Kickerterpoller explained the substance of the conversation, but Robertson's only note was that 'we did not put much faith in Mr Cocolos information'. The next day they moved on, heading in a northwesterly direction, further into the interior.

Traversing valleys and lagoons, Robertson was struck by the interspersed forests of 'stringy Bark' eucalypts and 'a great extent of pastoral Ground'. The land was variously inhabited and empty, the abode of native animals or introduced species. It was, his journal captures, in a state of transition.

Occasional stock huts provided shelter and intelligence. At one overnight visit to a settler's hut, Robertson was told that Aboriginal fires had been spotted nearby within the last week. Directed to the location, Robertson's party found an abandoned campsite, discovered some tracks, and followed the trail to what seemed 'a very great resort of the Natives'. This was a 'Barren' area, Robertson noted, 'but abounds with Wallaby'. They soon re-joined a familiar trail, used on that earlier mission that captured Eumarrah and other members of the Stoney Creek tribe. To the roving party's surprise, they spotted 'a Herd of Wild Horses' – further proof of a changing ecology.

As the expedition passed the spot where they had captured the Stony Creek tribe, Robertson allowed the party to be guided by 'Jack', a young Aboriginal man who had been taken during that mission and had since joined the roving party. Jack directed the party eastwards. As Robertson recorded:

> [He] took us over a steep Hill and pointed out to us a large Hollow Tree in which his Tribe had concealed a Number of Spears to be kept in reserve in case of their losing their Arms in the plundering expeditions on which they were engaged at the time Eumarra and the rest were taken.

The tree was in the direction of Tooms Lake, and so Robertson suspected that Danvers' encounter a month or so later in that area concerned 'the remains of Eumarras Tribe'. If he was right, more people had escaped than he had thought. Or he had little idea of what actually occurred on Danvers' mission. Either way, the tree got nicknamed 'Jacks Armoury', and it illustrates how combatants regularly focused on disarming each other.

As the party continued further north, they crossed the Macquarie River, and soon 'fell in with several Native Huts'. Such obviously Aboriginal features within the landscape highlighted the limited extent of colonial control over these so-called 'settled districts'. Although still failing to make any direct contact, Robertson inferred from 'the Number of Old fires and Huts' that he was on the Aboriginal people's 'usual Route'. Furthering this sense of being in Aboriginal territory, Jack noticed the dwindling flour supplies, and suggested careful rationing. He 'cautioned us to be sparing of it', Robertson said, 'as we should not see a white Mans Hut for many nights'.

Eventually, hunger drove the party to carelessness. Seeing a kangaroo, the men disregarded their usual restraint:

> Three or Four muskets were instantly levelled without waiting for any word of Command, one Boomer was brought to the Ground and in a very few Minutes was stewing in our Camp.

If the guns alerted any nearby Aboriginal people, the party no longer cared. About the same time, far to the west, a different Boomer was being shot by soldiers while attempting to escape.

'The Hill on which we killed the kangaroo', Robertson noted, 'is called in the Native Tongue Drially Lualinga lea which I believe literally signifies a Hill abounding with Kangaroo'. He was musing on the fact that kangaroos were usually seen near grasslands, and therefore assumed that there was probably good pastoral land nearby. Notably, a great proportion of Robertson's attention was directed to the quality of the land over which he journeyed. When negotiating with the government about the terms of his mission, he had hoped for a grant of land in return for 'a great Public duty'.[18] Land, he reasoned, 'Costs Government nothing'.

But Robertson's party was travelling under Jack's direction on what he called 'the Black Mans Road'. While writing glowingly about the potential of the land, Robertson was uniquely placed to know that land grants and continued colonial expansion did have a considerable effect on tribal life. After all, he was in daily communication with Kickerterpoller and Jack. In fact, only a few months previously in November 1828 Robertson had, through Kickerterpoller, recorded one of the most detailed accounts of intertribal politics from the period. Commenting on the small numbers in Eumarrah's tribe, Robertson asserted that 'they have either been shot by the stockeepers or destroyed in the wars which are incessantly carried on by one tribe against the other'.[19]

> I learned from the prisoners by means of Tom that three tribes besides the 'Stoney Creek' were assembled in the neighbourhood of Molonys Sugar Loaf[,] Kitby's corners and Black Johnny's Marsh[.] The cause of this gathering appears to be a combination amongst the Oyster Bay tribe, the Swan Port and Stoney Creek Tribes to make war on the Port Dalrymple Tribe – This war originated in two causes – First – To capture wives for the Oyster Bay and Stoney Creek Tribes who had lost nearly all their women and – Secondly – to repel an invasion which the Port Dalrymple Tribe had made on the hunting ground of the Swan Port Tribe which extends from Prossers River to Saint Pauls River – It appears that for some cause they have met without committing any Acts of Hostility and the four tribes I think have made some sort of treaty by which the Swan Port Tribe have given the others permission to hunt on their grounds – From whence each Tribe sends small parties to rob and Murder the inhabitants of the remote huts – I am informed that they are now on their way to Fight the big river tribe for the purpose of compelling them to give up their hunting ground for the common good and make common cause with them in carrying on their warfare against the white inhabitants.[20]

While this reveals some of the ways that traditional animosities continued into the period of active colonisation – and highlights that the Vandemonian War was fought between multiple polities, albeit much of it undocumented – it also illustrates something of Aboriginal desperation and strategy. Many of the tribes of the east coast had made alliances for mutual protection and support. These also turned their animosity against the tribes of the north and west, and targeted the colonial perimeters, probably to attempt to contain colonial expansion. This was no mere piecemeal response to resource competition, but a coordinated strategy for addressing the wider colonial incursion.

Only gradually did some of the leaders of roving parties begin to realise that their Aboriginal 'guides' could be selective about which tribes they tracked more or less effectively. But in January 1829, stuck deep in territory unsettled by colonists, Robertson had become more concerned with rations than either captures or potential land grants. Anxious to find a stock hut so they could replenish their supplies, they made 'a good deal of enquiry' of Jack, who told them of 'a white Mans House on the opposite side of the Hill before us to which he and his Mob had often gone to steal potatoes'. This short piece of oral history again described not just a habit of subsistence opportunism, but also hinted at that wider strategic imperative of economic sabotage and the harrying of a border. And, as it turned out, these hills did form a distinct borderland. From Jack's information, William Grant, one of the convicts attached to the mission, was able to surmise their position in relation to the settlement of Great Swan Port on the east coast. That night they climbed the tiers and spent a hard night with little food but a magnificent view of the sea. Before them lay the fields and paddocks of the truly 'settled districts' of the east coast. The next day they descended towards a rising sun, found farms, and resupplied. Then they again turned north.

Going North and Splitting Up

Like Danvers roughly a month before him, Robertson made towards St Patricks Head. Having fed and washed, Robertson again turned his attention to the quality of the land, quipping on 23 January that they 'saw nothing this Day worthy of remark except a vast extent of Land capable of better occupation'.[21] Robertson's main complaint was that the land was all 'locked up' by Meredith, who just used it 'as Grazing Ground for very numerous but most worthless and badly managed flocks and Herds'.

From this fertile grazing country, the party entered 'a very Barren and Hilly Country', and soon saw 'several very decided traces of the Natives'. But for the most part Robertson turned his attention to the local geology. The hills they crossed caught the sun, and he noted that their light surfaces 'glittered like Chrystal'. As they reached the shoreline, Robertson 'found the Sand on the Beach corresponding with the glittering gravel we had seen on the Hills'. He was building a picture of the whole landscape, acting a bit as a surveyor might. The coast had 'Tremendous Surf', he noted, but in one 'very rocky' spot there was 'an indifferent Harbour'. These mercenaries were advance parties for further settlement.

A nearby supply of 'tolerable fresh water' proved useful, because Jack advised the party they 'should not find a supply of Water for many miles'. Clearly Jack was familiar with the area. The party soon encountered 'a regular beaten Track', which they presumably followed, as it led past 'many places where the Natives had been feasting on Mutton fish and Oysters'. Despite the sand dunes and coastal scrub, Robertson was convinced that 'with judicious management it may be cultivated to advantage by Men of Capital'.

As the party approached the nominal extent of the 'settled districts', where martial law ended at St Patricks Head, they 'fell in with a number of Wild Cattle'. When they saw the 'remarkable Conical Hill about 2 Miles from the Coast', they again met cattle, this time 'belonging to Reynolds and Stanfields'. They 'shot one', and recorded the kill for rationing purposes. Robertson assumed the government would cover the cost. Then, 'opposite St Patrick's Head we saw with much joy what we supposed to be the Native Fires distant about 25 Miles'. Having found their target, the party pushed on 'for some Hours after Dark and slept about 5 Miles North from St Patricks Head'. Robertson had just broached the line of martial law, leaving legality behind him.

The party chased the daytime smoke and night fires for three days, struggling to make any ground on their prey, tracking north towards 'the Settlement at Break o Day plains', a colonial outpost established on the northern part of the east coast. On the last day of January they 'travelled all Day over burning Hills, but could see no recent Places where the Natives had stopt or slept'. But it seemed they may have been led astray deliberately.

> Jack informed us that there was a solitary Native who lived about those Hills and seldom joined any of the Tribes[.] Jack supposed that this Man must have kindled the fires which had drawn us from our Original Route.

Disappointed, the party found the nearest settler's hut to replenish their supplies. But they had great difficulty getting what they needed due to a lack of ready provisions and the large size of the party. To make matters worse, local reports were unclear about which direction the Aboriginal people were headed, so Robertson decided to split his party in two. One group under William Grant would stay in the Break o' Day Plains, and 'watch the motions of the Natives'. Jack would remain with them, while Kickerterpoller would continue inland with Robertson's party. Robertson also took advantage of an offer from one of the settlers:

> Mr Talbot having stated that one of his men was particularly well acquainted with the haunts of the Natives, I agreed to leave James Crawn with Mr Talbot and to take his Man with Grants party for a few Days in hopes that he would lead the party on the Blacks.

Talbot's offer came with a frank opinion:

> Mr Talbot having expressed great suspicion of the fidelity of the Natives who are with us – And in the presence of Jack and Tom – Disapproved of shewing any mercy to those who should fall into our powers even recommending that Jack and Tom should be Shot.

Robertson 'observed with regret that his words were marked by the two natives and excited much apparent uneasiness in their minds'.

The next morning Jack absconded. Getting up a little 'earlier than the rest of the Party', he seemed to feign going to the toilet, and simply did not return to the group. Despite commencing a wide search within minutes of his disappearance, they could not find him. Probably realising they were wasting their time, the parties split up as intended. Robertson took the bulk of the rations with him and told Grant to try to get more fresh supplies from nearby settlers. When they found a party of 'Constables and Soldiers' stationed by one of the rivers, Grant asked them 'not to hurt Jack if they should meet him'.[22]

During the next few days Jack's absence was keenly felt. In a thick fog, they 'could not see 20 yards' while moving 'over Rocky Barren Hills and Scrub' and were reduced to navigating 'by Compass'. They crossed a river by walking over a sandbar 'in about 3 feet water', and then another 'in five feet water carrying our Muskets etc on our Heads'. When they saw fires, they kept a keen watch but could not see who lit them. The Party 'suffered much for want of Water', Grant noted, and recorded that 'we missed Jack very much'.

Grant's Mission Makes Contact

Grant was another convict serving a life sentence.[23] He was convicted for burglary at Aberdeen, and transported to Van Diemen's Land on the *Claudine* in 1821. Grant was absorbed into the field police at Oatlands as part of Arthur's expansion of that paramilitary cohort, but attracted the ire of colonial authorities for various reasons. In 1827 he had allegedly failed to convey two prisoners to Hobart Gaol, but had instead taken them 'to an House of ill Fame in Hobart Town'. While Anstey acquitted Grant, a few months later he was charged 'with indecently exposing his person & using disgustingly indecent expressions'. Anstey dismissed this charge as well, but reprimanded him. A year later Grant was in trouble again, this time for drinking and gambling, and Anstey sought to have him dismissed from the field police. Just a few months after that, Robertson picked Grant to lead an armed roving party through the bush.

Grant's group travelled north towards George's River, well up the east coast. Reaching the bay into which this river flowed, they spent a few days scouting the area, looking for fires and smoke but finding none. Some barking dogs in the darkness provided the only hint of

Aboriginal people, although they suspected it was a wild pack, many of which now roamed the island. Depleting their flour, they turned inland, and headed towards one of the tributaries of the South Esk River. 'We saw a great number of Old Native Huts', Grant wrote of this journey, 'but no recent Traces of the Natives'. The next day they again spotted 'many Native Huts' near various marshes, but were soon stalled in their operations by another combination of 'Dense Fog' and 'Thick Scrub'.

The difficult bushwalking took a great toll on the men and their morale was low. 'They were so exhausted that they were inclined to lie down and Perish', Grant wrote, describing how 'Harry Gunn who is young and of a weakly Constitution was hardly able to move'. Gunn was certainly no stranger to hardship. Since being transported from Edinburgh for life in 1825, he had served time as a shepherd in the midlands and one month in a chain gang.[24] So hard was the tramping, Grant explained in his journal, that even a dog they brought was so weak it was unable to chase a kangaroo they spotted one evening. But, after climbing a hill to see if he could spot any landmarks, Grant saw St Patricks Head in the distance. He could also see 'a Native fire about Half a Mile from where I left the party'. They 'kept watch all night'.

In the morning the party advanced on the location of the fire, but the terrain was so difficult that only John Lightfoot and Ralph Gracie could keep up with Grant. Gracie was another Scotsman, transported for life from Glasgow for forgery.[25] Lightfoot was a farmhand turned poacher from Cheshire, who had been transported for seven years.[26] But the stealth required for poaching had formerly failed Gracie, and did so again. A dog gave the alarm.

Fortunately, the party was close enough to see 'a Black Man start off into the Scrub' away from his fire. The three convicts 'instantly gave chase and enclosed him between us in the Bed of the Creek', Grant reported. 'Dodging under dead Trees and thick scrub with which the place was covered', the man was able to evade capture for some time, but was taken in the end. They led him back to his camp, looking for signs of potential companions, but it was clear that he was and had been alone.

Recovering from the chase, the convicts turned to more closely examine their prisoner, who was 'an old Man he had no spears and only one old Dog'.[27] More curiously, 'he had the under Jaw of a Woman with the Teeth entire worked all over with Cord of Native Manufacture tied round his neck'. Intrigued by this item, Grant described another:

> He had a Bag formed of a thick elastic substance which appeared to be the Skin of a Human head prepared in some peculiar manner – This was full of Grease which appeared to be for the purpose of smearing his Body with.

Beyond these items, the man was naked and destitute of possessions other than a half-eaten possum. Despite his 'Horrid smell and look of his Grease bag' the convicts took him to their own camp, and gave him some hot tea 'as a Token of friendship'. But the effect of this was perhaps unequal to the fact that they shot his dog.

This proved to be a mistake, as hunger and thirst gripped the exhausted party. When they spotted another kangaroo, their own exhausted dog was useless, and Grant regretted having 'shot the Blackmans Dog'. Grant struggled to keep the party together and moving, and failed to elicit any help from their captive to locate water. They managed to make their way back to Talbot's hut. As Grant later noted, Talbot's borrowed servant George Giles returned from the mission cured of any desire 'to try a second excursion with the Native Catchers'.

Upon arriving at Talbot's, 'to our great Joy we found Jack our runaway Guide', Grant recorded, 'who was equally glad to see us'. For three days in the bush alone, Jack claimed to have 'suffered enough to prevent him ever running to the woods again'. He had returned to the point of his departure, and received 'great kindness' from Talbot, despite the settler's earlier suggestion about shooting him. Moreover, Jack was now back on the mission and capable of acting as intermediary:

> Jack told us that the name of the Native whom we caught was <u>Liangla Truighilly</u> – That he had lived by himself for a long time

but could give us no information about the Tribes – Jack from some Cause which we could not ascertain appeared to view his Countryman with great dislike.[28]

Unable to extract anything further of interest, Grant sent the Aboriginal hermit to the nearest district constable to be forwarded 'as Mr Robertson had ordered', presumably to Richmond Gaol.

Once more the party headed inland, travelling between settlers' huts each day and visiting familiar sites in the eastern midlands. They spotted smoke and fires on Ben Lomond, 'Black Boys plains' and other spots, but found no meaningful tracks to follow. They also got word that other parties were operating in the area. At one of their regular provisioning farms, Grant received a letter from Robertson ordering their return to Richmond 'for Shoes and Slops'. On their way south they detoured via a known 'great resort of the Natives' at Kearney's Bog. They found many 'Old Native Huts – but no fresh traces', and continued towards Richmond by way of Ross and Oatlands. Through days and nights of rain the party trudged on, 'mostly naked and Barefooted'. On 13 March 1829 they 'Arrived at Richmond', Grant wrote, concluding his report, 'Ragged and Shoeless after a fatiguing & fruitless Journey of Sixty five Days'.

Robertson was already there, his own meanderings completed without capturing any more people. In fact, when he was still in the midlands, Robertson had unwittingly facilitated Jemmie's escape. Robertson had ordered this member of the Stoney Creek tribe conveyed from Richmond Gaol to join his party, but Jemmie absconded while going to the toilet. The constable in change may also have fallen asleep on the job.[29] The success of Robertson's mission could be measured as one Aboriginal man taken, one lost – a zero net gain to the captive population.

Arthur Reviews the Missions

The Lieutenant Governor was likely unimpressed with Robertson's expedition, especially considering the large salary and promises of success. In response to Grant's account of the capture of the Aboriginal hermit, the Colonial Secretary made just one substantial comment in the margin: 'Why shoot the Black Man's dog?'

In early 1829 the colonial government was quite focused on Richmond. On 27 February – the same day that he learnt of Jemmie's escape, and the same day that Robertson returned to Richmond – the Colonial Secretary wrote to Thomas Lascelles, the Richmond police magistrate, following up on reports of the 'insecure and dilapidated condition of the Jail at Richmond'.[30] While the gaol's condition was central to the fabric of a penal colony, the timing of the Colonial Secretary's letter is a pointed reminder that Richmond Gaol was a place of Aboriginal incarceration.

Arthur was also concerned to maintain and expand transportation infrastructure, essential to economic and military needs. A few days later the Colonial Secretary required Lascelles to 'make immediate preparations for removing the Military and Constables from the Stable and Court House' to make room for an engineer and working party who were going to fix the bridge over the Coal River.[31] This request reveals that soldiers were being accommodated within civic buildings, and they would have to leave for pragmatic reasons, not philosophical ones.

Coincidentally, the machinations of the civil jurisdiction kept Robertson in Richmond, apparently to some local annoyance. By his own account Robertson was 'required as an Evidence before the Criminal Court in three different cases', which 'detained' him in Richmond until late April.[32] Robertson reportedly 'interfered' with 'the interior management of the Gaol',[33] and made a nuisance of himself 'by ordering the Prisoners into the yard, and insisting upon his right as Chief District Constable to communicate with those who are confined for Felony'. After an investigation, Arthur conveyed his disapproval through the Colonial Secretary, who wrote to Lascelles stating 'that it is quite evident that Mr Gilbert Robertson has acted very imprudently, and very improperly', adding that Lascelles 'will express to him His Excellency's dis-satisfaction at this conduct'.

Whatever good opinion Arthur may have had towards Robertson was clearly starting to wane. It was probably made worse by his remaining in Richmond until late April, and then exacerbated by further unsuccessful expeditions through the settled districts in the following months. Robertson 'Sent Grant with a Party towards the Clyde, and the Ouse, with directions to scour about that part of the Country' in late March, and met up with this detachment himself in April.[34] In the Bothwell district, where Grant and then Robertson headed, Arthur had just recently approved the employment of Thomas Standing – a convict with a ticket of leave – 'to go out with a strong Military Party to capture some of the Aborigines', authorising 'a sufficient reward should he succeed in taking many, or in opening a Communication with them'.[35]

Grant followed up reports of Aboriginal people seen crossing the Derwent River during Robertson's absence, and even caught 'one runaway' convict. But they had no luck with Aboriginal people in that area, and turned again to the eastern midlands in May. Half of Robertson's force was stationed under Grant's command 'at a flint quarry which Jack the native, had described to me as a constant resort of the natives at Stated periods'.[36] Robertson meanwhile headed off in a different direction, undertaking various ill-documented excursions.

CHAPTER FIVE

The Oatlands Roving Parties

1829, Winter
The Western Front

Arthur's Priorities

By the late autumn and early winter of 1829 Arthur's overall strategy involved layers of defensive, offensive and diplomatic operations. All were geared towards clearing the tribes from the settled districts. The island had lines of military posts and constables, mobile parties of military and field police, contracted teams of 'Native Catchers', and an increasingly institutional apparatus of Aboriginal detention centred on places like the Bruny Island Establishment and Richmond Gaol.

In response to one reported 'Murder' committed by Aboriginal people, Arthur authorised the formation of 'a Party of four steady Men, to be employed under the direction and superintendence of some respectable Person in pursuit of these Savages'.[1] Despite the continued failure of Robertson's mission, Arthur was willing to offer '200 Acres of Land' to the leader of another 12-month mission, and either tickets of leave or conditional pardons were held out as potential rewards for convicts attached to this expedition. 'The aid of such a Party actively employed,' the Colonial Secretary wrote, 'His Excellency hopes would keep the Carlton district quite clear of the sanguinary Tribe which has been infesting it for some time past.' When one man who was 'not a very trusty Character' was proposed, Arthur thought it would be better to offer 'some pecuniary reward' rather than 'remuneration in land'.[2] Although he was deemed untrustworthy, he was nevertheless 'supplied with Ammunition, and every requisite'.

Less than a week later Arthur received news from Richmond that 'a Tribe of the Aborigines were surprised and routed on Friday last, and that forty Blankets fell into the possession of the Military Party'. He responded through the Colonial Secretary that he 'very much regrets in this instance that the Natives were not captured'.[3] But Arthur's main administrative reaction to the news that the military had 'routed' a tribe was to instruct the police magistrate that 'three or four Men' may be sent to 'strengthen your force', adding that they 'may probably soon have the aid of a Party from Mr Anstey'.

Conciliation and Confinement, Richmond Gaol and Bruny Island

While military actions and locally organised pursuit parties continued throughout the winter of 1829, operational control was increasingly centralised at Oatlands. Arthur, meanwhile, was also concerned with acts of conciliation. As he instructed:

> 'Eumarra' the Aboriginal Chief, who is now in Richmond Gaol may be treated with the greatest kindness, and may be furnished with good Clothing, and all his wants and desires may be liberally supplied.[4]

This overture represents Arthur's hope for a diplomatic engagement between the government and various tribes. By this time, he had received reports that an intertribal confederation was forming. While such a confederation posed a possible military threat, it was also an opportunity to negotiate. But diplomatic overtures were not just about ending conflict or forming alliances with potential intermediaries. They were also about preparing to deal with surviving Aboriginal people once they had been removed from the 'settled districts'.

Conciliation and confrontation were not opposing objectives. They were two sides of the same coin, where captives would become captors in a rolling cycle. Neither approach, however, was unilaterally successful. While 'guides' were being deployed in the field with mixed success, the dilapidated state of Richmond Gaol and the escape of captives like Jemmie highlighted the limitations of conciliatory confinement.

South of the main war zones, the Bruny Island Establishment sought to project a sense of colonial friendliness, while effecting the detention of non-combatants. It took an important administrative step forward in early March 1829 when the government advertised for 'a steady person of good character':

> who will take an interest in effecting an intercourse with this unfortunate race, and reside upon Bruné Island, taking charge of the provisions supplied for the use of the Natives of that place.[5]

The advertisement also announced 'the Lieutenant Governor's anxious desire to ameliorate the condition of the Aboriginal inhabitants of this territory', thereby making the call for applicants a subtle exercise in propaganda. After several men applied, Arthur felt that George Augustus Robinson 'appeared to me, upon the whole, to be the most desirable'.[6] This appointment heralded the transition from ration station to mission centre. When Robinson represented that the salary was inadequate to support his family, Arthur agreed to double it to £100 and provide rations and accommodation if Robinson would expand his duties beyond storekeeping to 'also undertake the instruction of the natives & especially the care of their little children, if they will allow them to be educated'. Arthur also wanted Robinson to focus on 'cultivating a little land for potatoes &c', indicating that the establishment was intended to be a Aboriginal model village.

A cohort of convicts was assigned to assist Robinson in his duties, but Arthur ordered them 'withdrawn' by mid-April because 'Mr Robinson represents that an improper communication has existed between them and the natives'.⁷ Despite this 'improper communication', Robinson settled into his role as provider and teacher. Describing his 'General Plan' for the Establishment in April 1829, he asserted it had two main prongs: 'Civilisation' and 'Instruction in the principles of Christianity'.⁸ He hoped to develop the ration station into 'a general establishment or native village', geared towards helping Aboriginal people 'acquiring habits of industry'.

After several months of communicating with Aboriginal people, moving the site of the Establishment, complaining of unwelcome visits from various colonial men, learning bits of Aboriginal languages and traditions, and communicating with the government over various subjects like the adequacy of rations or alternative sites, Robinson revised his proposals to Arthur for 'conciliating the natives'. He suggested the Establishment 'be forthwith enclosed with a substantial fence, in order to secure such natives as may be captured'. It was looking more and more like an internment camp.⁹ He also wanted all Aboriginal captives sent to Bruny Island, including the prisoners of war taken in the main theatres of conflict, and 'two steady Field Police men be stationed at the Establishment, to prevent the Natives from escaping'.

But these ideas would have to wait. In the long nights of winter, Arthur's attention was mostly directed towards either expelling or capturing Aboriginal people, and he was throwing much more money, men and munitions towards winning the war than administering a future peace.

Centralising and Expanding the Roving Parties

The original salary for the Bruny Island storekeeper was only a third of that paid to the leader of the 'Native Catchers'. Even Robinson's renegotiated rate was still only half as big as Robertson's, but by mid-1829 Arthur's patience with Robertson was wearing out. While Arthur continued to hold out rewards and approve new potential captors, the disappointing results of Robertson's summer and autumn expeditions seemed to inspire an administrative reorganisation.

The Colonial Secretary informed Anstey on 27 May 1829 that it was 'very clear to the Lieutenant Governor' that Robertson's mission 'will not answer, and that a change of measures is essentially necessary'.[10] In part it was probably because Robertson seemed more inclined to follow his own whims than military orders. Anstey was told to take control of the campaign:

> Mr Robertson has now 14 Men, this number will be encreased [sic] to 30, so as to form with the addition of 6 Field Police Constables, 6 Parties of 6 Men each, all of whom are to receive directions from you. Three of the Parties may be placed under Mr Robertson's immediate superintendence, and the other three under some intelligent Man whom you may select.

This expansion of the field police was dedicated to capturing and removing Aboriginal people from the settled districts, with the whole operation centralised in Oatlands. 'One Field Police Man will be in charge of each Party, so that they may act separately,' Anstey was instructed, 'and you can regulate the movements of the whole'. There was no suggestion that military operations would diminish within the various districts.

Moreover, Arthur had clearly already discussed the plans with Anstey, who 'will cheerfully undertake the part'.[11] Significantly, the wording of the Colonial Secretary's instructions to Anstey were mostly verbatim from Arthur's own note on the matter. Both private conversations and written chains of information thereby reveal Arthur's micromanagement of the war – even when delegating authority.

Aware of and concerned with the 'character' of Robertson's men, Arthur was also wary of them being promised indulgences, and wanted close examination of prospective recruits. The Lieutenant Governor even went so far as to propose four convicts for the expanded service whose applications for tickets of leave he was then examining – William Little, John Reynolds, John Boswood and Patrick McGuire. He also ordered clothing and '30 pairs of strong serviceable boots to the storekeeper at Oatlands', having learned from Robertson's experiences, among others, of the need for durable footwear. As some of these new men arrived in Oatlands in June, the town adjutant was ordered to supply them with those 'Arms and Ammunition which may be required' for their duties.[12]

This new phase of convict paramilitary operations expanded from the established methods of the previous few months, but it took time for the new convicts to reach Oatlands, and for Anstey to take complete control of their manoeuvres. In mid-June Anstey reported to Hobart that 'only four men' had arrived, and that based on current projections from Robertson's force and the convict department he anticipated being 'six short of the full number' of the expected 30 men.[13] Moreover, a chunk of Robertson's 'original party' were 'with William Grant, at George's River, or in some other remote part'. Anstey proposed keeping Grant as a party leader, with which Arthur 'concurs', still engaged in managing operations.[14] Anstey also hoped to get 'Charts' to facilitate his orchestration of the missions, and their effective execution, but no suitable maps could 'be procured'.[15]

By the end of June Anstey was still short of his promised complement of rovers, but he had commenced centralised operations, informing the Colonial Secretary 'that all the men comprising the Roving Parties, now under my orders, are scouring the Bush in search of the Natives'.[16] Anstey had Robertson directing two six-men parties 'ranging the Country between the Launceston Road and the Coast'. Anstey thought it was 'to the Eastward that the Natives are most likely to be found during the Winter', and he was prepared to add another party 'to be under Robertson's orders' when he was 'furnished with the means'. But despite giving Robertson some seniority within his centralised system of roving parties, Anstey forwarded some letters from Robertson, one of which provided an early hint that Robertson was struggling to adjust to a subordinate position after his former independence. It was, Anstey characterised it, 'a sort of Protest of Robertson, against the new arrangements'. Anstey also noted that 'Robertson desires that the Captive Chief, Eumarraé, may be sent to him', but felt he 'could offer no opinion upon it'. After the escape of Jemmie, Anstey may have been wary of Robertson's schemes.

Arthur shared Anstey's concerns. In reply to Anstey's letter, Arthur made suggestions for administering the rations because 'Gilbert Robertson, at his first onset, occasioned much perplexity in the accounts'. He also reminded Anstey that Robertson was supposed to make monthly statements to the town adjutant, adding that Robertson was personally responsible for 'every excess over the authorized allowance'.[17] Even though he had centralised operational control with Anstey in Oatlands, Arthur maintained a close watch on how the colonial forces were deployed in the interior, and provided detailed suggestions about how they could cover key territory throughout the settled districts.

Anstey was also preparing to absorb another would-be settler-captor into his operations. 'I have not yet heard from Mr Batman,' he noted in his letter to Arthur, but he expected word soon. John Batman of Kingston farm near Ben Lomond in the northeast midlands had prior experience pursuing Aboriginal people with parties of soldiers and field police. During the winter of 1829 Batman made representations to the government about a 'proposition for the capture and ultimate subduction of the Aborigines', the timing of which meant his scheme received a welcome if slightly conditional response.[18] Batman anticipated 'bringing in alive some of those most injured and unfortunate race of beings', as he called Aboriginal people, by '[taking] to the Bush for a longer period'.[19] After reading the proposal, Arthur 'rejoiced to give effect to the arrangement' if it could 'be conducted as part of the general system' being implemented by Anstey. 'One or two Thousand Acres of Land to such a person as Mr Batman, for such an undertaking', the Colonial Secretary replied to the initial proposal, 'would be cheerfully ordered by the Lieutenant Governor'.

Head Rover Jorgenson and the Potential of Geography

Anstey also had another party in the field. 'Jorgenson, with six men, is gone to the Big River.' Jorgen Jorgenson was one of the colony's best-known figures.[20] This Scandinavian adventurer first visited Van Diemen's Land in 1803 as a sailor aboard the *Lady Nelson,* which brought the first colonists to the Derwent settlement, and he returned again on the *Woodman* as a convict in 1826.[21] According to his conduct record Jorgenson was technically transported for 'Returning from Transportation', part of a rich backstory. Danish by birth, Jorgenson was a friend of luminaries like Joseph Banks, had led an uprising against the Danish Government in Iceland, had been a spy for the British, but was also in trouble in England with debts and political enemies. 'He is a very intelligent man,' the *Hobart Town Gazette* reported when Jorgenson arrived in Hobart, 'and speaks several languages'.[22] That his arrival was even noticed highlights that he was not quite a typically anonymous convict. Jorgenson found early and fruitful employment with the Van Diemen's Land Company, and by June 1827 he had a ticket of leave. Later that year he sought employment with the government.

Jorgenson was certainly known to Arthur. In November 1827 Arthur instructed Anstey to place men under Jorgenson's command, and let him 'apprehend the Robbers infesting the High Road' per a plan that Jorgenson proposed.[23] Within a few months, Jorgenson's role in Oatlands was being put on firmer official footing, with Arthur approving his appointment to the field police in May 1828.[24] A few months after that Jorgenson became Anstey's clerk, gaining an additional allowance of £10 per year to cover the advanced duties expected of him.[25] In this role Jorgenson oversaw the creation of a phenomenal documentary archive. He collated mission reports by parties under the Oatlands field police, documenting the prosecution of the war by convicts like Danvers and Holmes, and soldiers like Ensign Lockyer. From winter 1829 Jorgenson assumed an even greater role administering the midlands roving parties – and with it the amount of documentation dramatically increased.

Among the Lieutenant Governor's suggestions to Anstey for positioning the roving parties, Arthur 'apprehended that Jorgenson would be employed to the Westward and Northward', presumably because Jorgenson had worked for the Van Diemen's Land Company and knew the area. It was the same rationale of regional familiarity that made Arthur and Anstey situate Robertson to the east and eventually Batman to the northeast. But Jorgenson had bigger ideas. On 18 June

1829 he penned a 'plan of operations' to Anstey, articulating that he saw his role as twofold: to protect the settled districts from 'the fury and misguided notions of the Aborigines', and 'to place the Native Tribes in a situation that they may be captured without the parties in pursuit being compelled to shed more human blood'.[26] In phrasing the second of these notions, Jorgenson tacitly acknowledged how operations had mainly worked up to this point: with bloodshed.

Jorgenson's main suggestion concerned operating with 'a steady Eye on the geographical Situation of the Island', pointing out that 'the enemy must be driven from the wide and extended parts of the country into the more narrow parts' if captures were to be effected. The roving parties had to be coordinated and constant to drive Aboriginal people and prevent them from regaining lost ground after the parties moved through. He proposed rationing the parties for multi-week excursions, staggering their returns to base such that only one party was replenishing at any given time, leaving two parties operating in tandem.

He then outlined a series of manoeuvres for his three parties in the western midlands, converging and intersecting among the tiers from north and south, and discussing potential tactics. 'If we find it necessary we will light fires in various places as we pass along,' he indicated, 'so to baffle and confound the calculations of the Natives, and make them believe that they are nearly surrounded and hotly pursued in those parts'.

Jorgenson believed this tactic would drive the tribes south. If the eastern parties under Robertson coordinated with this scheme too, then Jorgenson predicted that Aboriginal people could be 'hemmed in the Southern parts of the Island' where the mountainous country would 'stay their career' because the harsh landscape 'afford[s] no food for any one, and the wandering Tribes could not subsist there'.

In addition to potential starvation, confusion would also work to the colonists' advantage because, as Jorgenson pointed out from direct experience across the island, some of the more disparate tribes 'cannot understand the language spoken by each other'. Denied freedom of movement or opportunities to subsist, they would be captured more easily. Anstey agreed, endorsing Jorgenson's plan. 'To get the Natives into his Decoy,' Anstey enthused, 'and to keep them there "hemmed in" seems a visionary scheme'.

Arthur shared Anstey's sense of Jorgenson's usefulness, allowing Jorgenson an extra shilling a day 'while he shall be employed against the Aborigines'.[27] Meanwhile, Anstey clarified Jorgenson's authority within a chain of command, issuing a set of 'General Orders' on 27 June for Jorgenson's three parties, which Anstey signed but was otherwise in Jorgenson's handwriting.[28] It clarified that Jorgenson was directing the parties' movements, and dealt with matters of rationing, intelligence sharing, obedience and record keeping. With these regulations in place, the parties set off from Oatlands. One party headed west towards Bothwell, followed the next day by Jorgenson.[29]

Jorgenson was accompanied by William Little, one of the convicts that Arthur had personally selected for Anstey's general operations. Unfortunately, Little's 'great toe was very painful on account of a splinter having got into it', which slowed them down on their journey. 'The weather was very cold', Jorgenson added, 'and the frost severe', which probably did not help much either. After overnighting in a settler's hut they ascended into the hills where they admired the snow, which made the slopes appear to be 'perfect Glaciers'. This made travelling difficult, and they 'often slipped down'. Nevertheless, by nightfall they had reached Bothwell and joined the remainder of the party. This included another two of Arthur's picks – Patrick Macguire and John Reynolds – as well as Robert Lee, formerly a member of Robertson's party, and field police constable George James. But Little had to be left at Bothwell, 'his toe being in a very bad State'.

For the next few days Jorgenson and his men visited stock huts, where they sought information on the movements of any Aboriginal people and identified which huts would be suitable for future provisioning. After these investigations, Jorgenson wrote glowingly of Lieutenant Williams' control of the Bothwell police district:

> Provisions are to be obtained in plenty. A party of Soldiers were stationed at Thomson's hut, who were all out scouring the Country. It seems that Mr Williams keeps all the military under

his orders in a State of Activity and very usefully employed in protecting the settlements against the attacks of the Natives.[30]

The ongoing military presence around the Clyde and Ouse rivers reminds us that Anstey's general operations supplemented the military's effort rather than replacing it. Moreover, the field police roving parties learned from the military ones. Having surveyed the strategic situation around Bothwell, Jorgenson took his party up the Quoin, one of the nearby peaks, at dawn on 3 July, gaining 'an extensive view of the circumjacent country'. 'We then fell down on the Soldiers' hut just under the Quoin', Jorgenson added, 'on the road to the Lakes'. There Jorgenson 'found a party of Soldiers', although 'two of them had been sent patrolling to a considerable distance'. This patrol clearly prompted a conversation about the local geography and extent of military coverage, because Jorgenson learned that the soldiers stationed there 'frequently proceed as far as the Lakes' to the north and west, and the officer in charge 'has examined the Country as far as Oatlands' to the east.

Moving towards various stock huts, Jorgenson was pleased that one settler had 'left orders to afford the Government parties every facility, and to pilot them through passes and other places in the neighbourhood', which would aid in the wider project of capturing Aboriginal people. This area had seen much conflict, and Jorgenson wrote obliquely of 'severe and bloody engagements with the Natives which have never been known' conducted by local stockmen. He noted in passing that it 'would indeed be a matter of curious knowledge and useful to mark down' all information connected with the area's recent history. Local knowledge could be used to strategic advantage.

This was especially so because of the limitations of the colonists' geographical knowledge. The next day Jorgenson's party ascended another summit, which he called 'Mount Direction'. Jorgenson's later account frustrated Anstey, who noted in the margin of the report, 'A third Mount Direction!' It was an irritation felt elsewhere in the colony, too: 'Big River' was often used to refer to one of the Derwent's upper tributaries (usually the present Ouse River) as well as what is now known as the Apsley River on the east coast.

After passing this mountain, the party scoured gullies and hills, 'and in the Evening constructed a Breakwind on the Side of a stony Hill'. They spent the night taking turns on watch, no doubt tending a small fire to keep warm, pulling their great coats and blankets close about them. 'The night was stormy', Jorgenson added, 'with much snow'.

It was mid-morning the next day before they could see where to go. The landscape was covered in snow, and a thick fog obscured their view. But when the sun finally broke through the clouds sufficiently to illuminate a potential path, they headed downhill and 'descended on better ground'. Walking round Laycock's Lake, they 'saw numerous native huts, but none of them appeared to have been recently occupied'. That night the party again constructed a shelter, this time augmented with 'Stringy Bark taken from the Native huts', protecting them from another night of snow.

Through Snow and Mist, Highlands Campaigning

They were in thick fog again the following day, and navigated by keeping Mount Penny on one side and Laycock's Lake on the other. After a few hours walking, Jorgenson climbed Mount Penny by himself through 'snow falling down in dense masses', but between the snow and the alpine mist he could not see anything of use. He re-joined his party none the wiser at the foot of the mountain, and they 'passed on over the ridges and rocky ground toward Lake Arthur', skirting one of the inter-lake rivers, and then veering 'in a NW by W direction'. As evening fell they 'descended into some long and large marshes, divided by a small river'. They tried climbing a hill a little to get above the damp, but could find insufficient wood for shelter, and had great trouble lighting a fire in the bitter wind. Their fingers were 'benumbed', but they could ignite some of the tinder and rags that they carried with them.

Jorgenson congratulated himself and the party the next day, when they successfully navigated to the government hut at Patrick's Plains after a two-hour walk. It was an achievement, he noted, because 'none of us had been over the ground before'. When they located the government hut, they found it 'was still in a very good condition, but the stable was tumbling to pieces'. Other huts in the area were in various states of maintenance, one in a 'miserable condition'. Most were 'abandoned', presumably for the winter.

Pushing on, the party now crossed the 'fierce and rapid' Shannon River. One of them was defeated by the river and fell over, 'but got on his legs again' and kept going. The wet men tramped onwards.

As they approached another settler's hut, Jorgenson 'again had a proof of Mr Williams' vigilance; two of his Soldiers had called there in the morning, and speedily went away again.' The roving party was coincidentally shadowing and overlapping with the military patrols operating out of Bothwell.

The men at this hut were able to furnish the party with rations, although the occupants 'had very little' to spare. But Jorgenson did 'obtain much useful information':

> Last Summer and some months since, the natives were seen in all places in this direction. They were frequently seen by the Stock-keepers going down to the River for water. They had been seen in the opening about three weeks since, and last year by this time of the year they robbed the hut.

With fresh intelligence Jorgenson seems to have decided on a rapid strike. Leaving much of their heavier gear behind, including their great coats, the party headed off 'before dawn' the next morning 'for the Big Lake'. They made 'rapid march' through the snow-filled landscape. When they reached the lake after a long walk, they found a stock yard that 'was completely fenced in by a long log fence'. There were two stock huts – the burnt remains of one torched 'by the Natives', and another 'very small one built near to it' as a replacement. They went further, before returning to this spot for the night, and 'could see no native huts, nor tracks, nor any other signs that the Natives had been there recently'.

By morning the lake's surface had frozen. Climbing a hill to observe the terrain and plan their travel, the men spotted 'a native hut constructed of sticks, as there were no stringy bark in the Vicinity'. This was one of the few signs of Aboriginal people. After Lee 'precipitated down a rock, which severely hurt him', they limped back to the hut where they left their coats, 'where we again found another party of Mr Williams' soldiers', which Jorgenson noted with obvious admiration.

But Jorgenson was also disappointed. With the various roving parties still being formed, he did not have any other parties under his direct control, which he wanted to place in the strategic passes in the rear of their positions. That way, Jorgenson explained, he could have pushed on further into the highlands, even into 'the Platform bluff'. As he explained:

> This is one of the strong holds of the Aborigines where they have never been attacked nor disturbed, and a single party pursuing them through one opening might kill some, but could capture but a few, as they would escape through the other openings.

Jorgenson therefore thought that pushing further into this territory would be relatively pointless without more parties to ensure coordinated movements. He hoped to do so on a future mission, having learned from local stockmen that 'for many miles farther to the NW there are innumerable native huts', but beyond the main line of the western tiers 'there is a large extent of country entirely unknown'. They had reached the effective limits of the colony. It was time to turn back.

Due to his injury Lee was left behind at the stock hut to return to Oatlands later, while the party started off again following a cart track towards a safe river ford. Unfortunately, the snow was so thick they lost the trail, although they soon enough found the river. 'Reynolds plunged into the river in a place which was very deep, and where the rapids ran uncommonly strong', Jorgenson noted, leading the party in a hurried but tiresome crossing. As they emerged from the water, their clothing froze 'stiff with Ice', and they had to start running to 'set the blood in circulation' and warm up.

Instead of trying to follow the cart track further, Jorgenson directed the party in a sweeping manoeuvre through 'strong and steep hills' because, he explained to his superiors, 'it is only in such out of the way places that we can expect to find the native huts'. They found 'numerous [structures] of large dimensions where there were nothing but stones', which Jorgenson surmised could not belong to cattlemen, although he did note that a stock hut was only about '2 miles' from this spot. As they wound back into the main settled areas they passed an abandoned stock hut, and 'arrived at the Soldiers hut on Patterson's farm' at sunset, although they pushed on through a snowy and stormy night to reach the Clyde. Clearly exhausted, two more members of the party had to be left at a settler's hut on the way to Bothwell. While they rested, Jorgenson pushed on to Oatlands.

Although no encounters had taken place or captures been made, Jorgenson characterised the mission as a success, at least for proving the concept. 'We have now ascertained that there is one party which can be relied upon,' he wrote, 'and contend against all sorts of difficulties, and by the rapidity of their movements confound the calculations of the Aborigines.' The men held up well, he added, suggesting that 'the natives cannot long escape us'. Jorgenson advanced the idea that Lee would make a good party leader, his injury notwithstanding, because he was 'active, zealous, and indefatigable'. With more parties and coordinated operations, Jorgenson was confident of future victories.

But Jorgenson did have recommendations for Anstey. He complained of the 'inferior quality' of his party's boots, which wore out too easily, and 'wretched knapsacks' that were too small to carry many provisions. He suggested that some boot makers should be brought to Oatlands, and more suitable knapsacks procured. He also commented on the varied distribution of blankets and great coats, which he felt needed standardisation. This was all part of a final mission summary, designed to inform Anstey and ultimately the Colonial Secretary and Arthur of the lessons of the expedition, and benefit the future conduct and management of what Jorgenson characterised as 'a species of flying warfare'.

After Jorgenson signed off this report on 14 July 1829, Anstey read it, made annotations, and forwarded it to the Colonial Secretary, who passed it to the Lieutenant Governor. Within a week Arthur was acting on at least one of Jorgenson's suggestions. 'I should approve of 2 shoe makers with a quantity of leather &c &c being sent to Oatlands', Arthur wrote on the report on 20 July, before handing the document back to the Colonial Secretary.[31]

Meanwhile, having authoritatively designated his party as 'No 1 party of the Western Division', Jorgenson was sent east. 'Jorgenson's men proceeded towards Little Swan Port this morning', Anstey noted on the report as he forwarded it to Hobart, adding that 'Jorgenson follows them tomorrow.' The plan to trap Aboriginal people in the mountain passes in the western tiers was temporarily abandoned and the forces redeployed. 'The Natives have certainly left the Lakes', Anstey affirmed, 'and are now on the Eastern Coast'. The colonial forces were not the only ones fighting a war. The eastern settled districts were under attack.

CHAPTER SIX

Offensive Defence in Reality and Record

1829, Winter
Eastern Front

The Newspapers' War

While the colonists prosecuted their war with soldiers, paramilitary field police and mercenaries, Aboriginal groups raided farms and harassed farm servants. These attacks on civilian targets provided regular stories about fights between stockmen and Aboriginal assailants for the colonial newspapers and subsequent histories, skewing the public perception of the conflict, making it appear something remote and unofficial.

But as Jorgenson found in the highlands, these skirmishes occurred with even greater regularity than the newspapers recorded. Like the operations of the soldiery, distant engagements were so common that they often went unreported in newspapers. A colonist killed or wounded near a town, however, represented an imminent threat to urban readers. As the *Launceston Advertiser* opined after a woman was speared by Aboriginal assailants, '[T]his is indeed a bad state of affairs, when the Aborigines can murder people within six miles of the town'.[1] Distant contestations of hunting grounds and pasture runs were one thing, but the prospect of war in the towns may have seemed increasingly real in the winter of 1829. Attacks on towns would directly affect investors in Hobart and threaten immigration from Europe.

Roving Towards Mr Cotton's

From experience the settlers and government alike knew where to expect trouble, generally where concentrations of settlers crossed Aboriginal pathways and destinations. In Little Swan Port on 22 July, Jorgenson learned that Aboriginal people had raided 'two huts in Great Swan port' in the past few days, 'and in all probability killed one of Mr Meredith's shepherds'.[2] In response to this news Jorgenson immediately manoeuvred to an inland position where he thought he might intercept the attackers. He sent two of the team to Lieutenant Lane, the police magistrate at Waterloo Point, to request 'intelligence as to the route taken by the Aborigines'. He also described his own position, and advised that 'Mr Batman in the Campbell Town district has taken charge of a party in search of the Aborigines' to the north, which was 'the seventh party under the immediate orders of Mr Anstey'. Unfortunately, the two messengers got lost, and had to re-join the party that night before delivering their message.

Lane had sent word of the 'aggressions by the Natives' to the Colonial Secretary the day before Jorgenson even reached Little Swan Port, thereby keeping Arthur abreast of the situation in the area. In reply, Lane was told 'that the Lieutenant Governor trusts you will make every possible effort for the protection of the Settlers'.[3] In another letter replying to Lane, the Colonial Secretary referred to 'the active measures now in operation for the capture of the Aborigines':

> I am directed to express to you in the strongest manner His Excellency's confident hope, that you are calling forth every energy in your power, for the apprehension; in order that the bloody massacres on both sides which are daily occurring, revolting to humanity, may if possible be put a speedy stop to.[4]

OFFENSIVE DEFENCE IN REALITY AND RECORD

Arthur was certainly aware of the intense fighting in this area, and keen for it to be contained.

In the field, Jorgenson was determined to send his letter. He took 'the whole party to Waterloo point', capturing a runaway convict on the way, but had trouble finding any real figures of authority. This left him 'rather at a loss what to do'. So he collected rations and headed off again, leaving town at about 2:00 am, causing much grumbling among the party. But Jorgenson 'shewed them the necessity of the Aborigines in this quarter not being made acquainted that a roving force was about which could be done only by travelling in the night'.

After the sun rose Jorgenson managed to finally meet with Lane, but there was little intelligence to be had other than some vague sightings of 'the native fires', which suggested Aboriginal people were moving 'in a southerly direction'. Tired from their night march, the party slept much of the day, creeping off 'cautiously through the Bush' after 3:30 pm towards Allen's hut. Jorgenson was still unsure what direction to take because 'the natives were in the habit of lighting fires in various places to deceive the white inhabitants'.

With imminent contact and conflict possible, Jorgenson 'examined the firearms', finding that 'Little's musket missed fire, it was filthy and dirty, the Ramrod crooked, and I found that this man had only four cartridges left out of ten.' While the objective was capture, the use of force was clearly part of the operational procedure. After reaching Allen's hut, the party learned of 'a Kangaroo which had been speared by the Natives' some 3 miles away. Being 'no longer uncertain as to what course to pursue', the party crept out of the hut about an hour after midnight.

At dawn on 25 July Jorgenson split his party. He sent three men 'along the Tier to Mr Cotton's hut', while Jorgenson and another man travelled 'by the Seashore' to the same hut. Jorgenson instructed the first party to use the hut for a potential ambush:

> the party should keep close within the hut under cover of a large tarpauline there hanging up, and one to go out now and then without arms and pick up a little wood which might induce

the Natives to pursue him into the hut when the party would
rush between them and the door and receive them with fixed
bayonets, and capture all within.

Unfortunately the men had 'through mere Laziness left their bayonets behind', and arrived too late. As Jorgenson wrote to Anstey:

> You may guess my vexation when Hyatt and I arrived at the point, to learn, that one hour before, the Natives had speared three men at Mr Cotton's, wounded one of them mortally in the lungs, seized their three muskets standing up against a tree within three yards of them, taken away the Dogs, drove the three men into the Saltwater Lagoon, which the unfortunate wretches had to swim across three times.

One of them named Rogers was unable to swim, having been 'cruelly beaten about the head' as well as 'speared in the lungs'. The injured man was helped by the others, 'themselves speared' too, but Rogers' severe impairment slowed the escape. Eventually the others 'were obliged to seek safety in flight and leave Rogers to his fate. Yet he succeeded in running away,' Jorgenson added, 'and flew along the Sea coast, when he happily met with Mr Cotton who stayed the career of the Natives'.

Upon getting news of this affray, Jorgenson 'speedily arrived at Cotton's, and about an hour after in came Holmes and the rest of the party'. Holmes reported that 'Lieut. Lane and Mr Cotton were in the Hut and one of the speared men lay in the Hut very badly wounded'.[5] His party were asked to hold the hut 'until some soldiers should arrive'. While noting the extraordinarily fortuitous coincidence that he had planned to use this hut as an ambush, Jorgenson 'could not help feeling very great regret that we had not come a couple hours sooner to the hut than we did, or the natives a couple of hours later'.

But Jorgenson had even more ominous news for Anstey, reporting that after the attack on Cotton's men, 'the Natives from about 150 to 180 strong moved down on the settlement, and robbed within 1 ¾ mile of it'. This was just the beginning of a series of raids by Aboriginal people now well in advance of the colonial positions. 'Parties of military were sent out in search of the Natives,' Jorgenson added, 'but as none of them proceeded to a great distance, none of them fell in with the Natives'.

Field Plans Amid Disorder, The Peninsula Trap

Believing that a large and hostile group of Aboriginal people armed with guns and ammunition were in the area, Jorgenson wanted to determine whether there were more forces at his disposal. He set off for Oatlands leaving most of his rovers to make a series of ambushes. A team under Holmes was sent 'to proceed along a gully toward the bend of the River (Little Swan port) about 9 miles distant from Buxton's where the Natives can only cross this time of the year for the Blue Hills'. Here Holmes was 'to lay in ambush on the opposite Hill'. 'Another party is in ambush at the Branches,' Jorgenson noted, 'which is the other opening for Prosser's plains'.

En route to Oatlands, Jorgenson met with the disappointing news that no other party had yet 'been formed'. Moreover, while he wanted to give dispositions for some of Robertson's parties to close off the passes in and out of the Great Swan Port district, 'and hem them in', he learned that 'Mr Robertson had left in the morning and Grant could not be heard of'. Full coordination of the various units was being hampered by delays and difficulties in communication. Attempting to remedy this, Jorgenson left Robertson a note at one of the major stock huts. 'The Natives are carrying every thing before them,' he wrote, but concluded that if Robertson followed Jorgenson's instructions, then 'by a proper co-operation the great Tribe of Oyster Bay will be captured'.

When he reached Oatlands, Jorgenson made requisitions for his men, wrote a preliminary report for Anstey, and sent word throughout the settled districts to put the authorities on alert. He also penned a letter to Anstey that was highly critical of Lane's administration of his district,[6] noting poor communication, inadequate deployment of field police, and missed opportunities for capturing Aboriginal people. Jorgenson was also concerned about the administration of the roving parties and conduct of some of its members. This included 'Black Tom and the other Blacks', who Jorgenson and others suspected were 'not willing to bring the parties to where the natives would be very likely to be' on all occasions. While Anstey did not approve of or endorse all these sentiments, he nonetheless forwarded the document to the Colonial Secretary because Jorgenson had made several suggestions that deserved 'worthy attention'.

Of much interest to his superiors, Jorgenson continued to develop his ideas of using the Vandemonian geography for effecting captures, applying them now to the east coast. Coordinated deployments and manoeuvres between Robertson, Batman and his own forces would work particularly well in that area, Jorgenson argued, especially when Aboriginal people moved into the Schoutens. Jorgenson saw a distinct opportunity to close off the 'neck' that connected the Schoutens with the mainland, by placing a line of armed men across it when Aboriginal people were observed within the trap. But this required more men, especially the coordination of the soldiery with the Oatlands roving parties, and perhaps even the arming of some servants. 'I know it is not six nor a dozen of men that will terminate a war against a whole nation,' Jorgenson wrote, recognising that many more men were required for his schemes. But he was convinced it would bring victory for the colony:

> A grand co-operation deduced from a well disported and matured plan alone can produce that effect, and time and expense will be saved by doing that speedily, which otherwise might occupy years.

Jorgenson had even attempted to execute a version of this scheme, without consulting with Anstey or Arthur. When he set off for Oatlands from Cotton's hut, he told Holmes of his plan 'to get as he said, some more men to hem in the Natives upon the Schoutens'. Moreover, the letter Jorgenson left at a stock hut for Robertson actually detailed just such an operation, and effectively ordered Robertson to get military assistance from Lane to close off the Schoutens when feasible.[7] Jorgenson technically lacked the authority to give such direct instructions to Robertson, and to the Colonial Secretary Anstey justified the anomaly of a convict commanding a settler by noting that the 'liberty taken by Jorgen Jorgenson in thus giving orders to Mr Gilbert Robertson' was because they 'have long been familiar and intimate friends'.

But Anstey was misinformed or dissimulating. The pair actually had a growing antipathy that began to affect the operations.

In the Hills above the Coast

The precise origins and nature of the falling out between Jorgenson and Robertson is unclear, but Robertson certainly felt slighted by a letter he received from Jorgenson as well as negative newspaper coverage of his missions.[8] When Anstey investigated their feud, he also heard accusations that Jorgenson drank too much too often, and 'was much deceived by Norah Corbett', a convict woman. Anstey ultimately concluded these accusations were largely unfounded, commenting that 'Mr Robertson is unfortunate in his selection of witnesses'.[9] They certainly seemed suspiciously geared towards the kinds of moral failings that a settler may have levelled against a convict. Lee described Robertson seeming 'very jealous of Jorgenson, and much vexed when his name was mentioned in the Newspapers', adding that Robertson 'did not like his name to be coupled with that of a Prisoner of the Crown'.[10] There were undoubted class tensions at work here, possibly also heightened by rumours about Robertson's mixed Scottish-Caribbean parentage.

In addition to clashing personalities, there were more fundamental issues with communication, and some roving parties were also acting on their own tactical impulses. Robertson, for instance, obliquely recorded that he was 'scouring between the head of the Macquarie and McGill's Marshes' during the second half of July, while his other party was moving relatively independently – and better accounted for their actions, at least in surviving documentation.[11]

William Grant and Jack had been sent by Robertson towards the 'flint quarry' at the end of June. Their mission had a series of dashed hopes. Early in their journey they encountered some of a survey team hunting 'for Kangaroo skins' in 'a place of great resort for the Natives'.[12] Having heard their dogs, Grant first thought he had stumbled into a tribe. He stayed on high alert, despite the early disappointment with the survey team, and found 'evident signs that the Natives had been thereabouts in considerable numbers'.

When a mob of kangaroo started rapidly bounding one evening, clearly evading a predator, the rovers 'immediately started up with our arms'. Stalking about in the dark, they spotted 'one black native almost crawling' but the party lost him in the night. They picked up the trail again in the morning, with Jack taking the lead, but soon again 'lost it'. Grant thought 'that Black Jack on this occasion wished to evade bringing us into the right track', and 'seemed unwilling to proceed farther, and this is not the first time that he has shewn this reluctance'. The party scoured the bush a bit more, and then returned to Oatlands by mid-July, their shoes having disintegrated off their feet.

'During the whole of our journey', Grant reported to Anstey, 'we heard nothing of the other party confided to the Charge of Mr Robertson.' Noting that Jack's behaviour corresponded with reports about 'Black Tom', Anstey forwarded the report to Hobart, complained of Mount Direction being another case of 'duplicate and triplicate names', and sent Grant's party out again 'towards Oyster Bay'.

Grant took his party to Tooms Lake, the same general area where Robertson was reportedly operating.[13] Jack gave local intelligence, revealing 'the different places where the Aborigines used to encamp when he was with them'. They found 'a number of native huts, but none recently constructed'. On 25 July, the day Cotton's men were attacked, Grant's party were 'principally occupied in baking and washing for the party', having just restocked at a settler's hut near the upper tributaries of the Macquarie River.

Despite recent snow, which meant they 'should easily have observed the Native tracks', they found no Aboriginal trails. But while the snow gave some advantage, it also slowed their progress. The party spent 29 July 'behind the windfalls in one of the Old Native huts on account of the excessive severity of the weather'.

The next day they again 'encamped in another old Native hut near a considerable lagoon'. Quite remarkably, Jack 'had assisted in making this hut when he was with the Natives'. Jack also told the party 'where a musket and a double barrelled Pistol had been concealed by his tribe on some former occasion when they had robbed some hut'. As the mission continued, they 'found the musket', but not the pistol. They again visited the flint quarry, 'a large hole dug in the ground by the natives to which they resort in great numbers for the purpose of obtaining the flintstone wherewith to shape and make their spears', which Jack said was used 'frequently' by 'two or three mobs'. For much of late August the party loitered nearby in the hope of ambushing Aboriginal people, while Grant occasionally visited Ross for provisions.

While these expeditions continued, Arthur appraised himself of the overall operational situation. He met with Jorgenson, although the discussion seemed to mostly focus on Jorgenson's salary, which Arthur directed Anstey to resolve.[14] Arthur was also unimpressed with Jorgenson's liberties in speaking ill of Lieutenant Lane. Nonetheless, the Lieutenant Governor generally agreed with Jorgenson's strategic suggestions. 'With regard to the Capture of the Oyster Bay Tribe,' Arthur noted on 4 August 'there can be no question that the Parties must act upon some combined Plan which Mr Anstey will lay down for them.' Probably alluding to Jorgenson and Robertson's feud, Arthur expressed his hope that 'inconvenient interference' between the parties could be avoided.

But mostly he was focused on tactics. Likely reflecting on the missed opportunity at Cotton's hut, Arthur suggested that 'Mr Anstey would also do well to instruct the Parties occasionally to occupy for days together any Huts or Houses which the Natives are likely to attack.' This was an old strategy that soldiers had used throughout the island, and Arthur clearly felt it was still efficacious, thinking that 'if this plan were acted upon the chances are very great that the Natives might be surprised & taken'. But there was more to Arthur's strategy than patience:

> much must depend upon the intelligence of the Leaders of the Parties in tracing out the tracks most frequented by the Natives,

and watching them, taking such a position as may secure them from being seen by the Aborigines.

He was writing in general terms, but also responding to specific circumstances that went beyond Jorgenson. The day before, Arthur had met with the division constable of Prosser's Plains about complaints made against the constable by 'one of Mr Gilbert Robertson's party'.[15] Arthur reckoned 'that the charge is entirely groundless', so it probably served to cast further suspicion on Robertson's men and missions. Moreover, Arthur was possibly starting to give serious thought to the other main expedition leader, John Batman, whose parties were preparing to be deployed into the bush during that August.

Mr Batman's Proposition

Although the Lieutenant Governor had 'cheerfully' responded to Batman's June 'proposition', it was still being organised by 14 August when Arthur had 'just seen Mr Batman'.[16] The delay was partly Batman's fault – he had 'not addressed himself to Mr Anstey' after the government welcomed his June proposal – but things gradually got worked out during the latter part of the winter.[17] When Arthur and Batman met, they discussed the composition of the party and prospective rewards for the nine convicts that Batman wanted to employ. Batman had written in advance, seeking to employ men who were 'strong, healthy', 'patient, quiet', and so on.[18] Arthur agreed on a scheme of service and reward, ordered some convicts sent to Launceston, and instructed they be 'armed and clothed' in readiness for duty under Batman. Arthur also gave detailed instructions about the fitting out of this expedition, including the numbers of camp kettles, tomahawks, blankets and the daily ration of soap to each man. He was, it reveals, particularly focused on the minutiae of Batman's mission. Later in the month, when Batman found that the Launceston stores had only 'yellow' jackets – 'too conspicuous in the Bush' for stealthy operations – less conspicuous blue ones were specifically ordered for him, better suited to blend into fog, rock and mist.[19]

Batman relied on his 'personal experience during the many excursions I have made in pursuit of Aborigines' to argue for his own employment.[20] He tried using this to leverage relative independence of operation, remarking pointedly on 'my own knowledge of the Country and of the haunts and manners of these people'.[21] This was, he avowed, 'such to render me a tolerable judge of the best mode of meeting with and capturing them'. His exploits prior to forming a contract for land with the Lieutenant Governor – like that time in 1828 when he shot dead a man in the act of throwing a spear – are slight but telling. Batman was used to operating in the field, and had been fighting the war for some time before the government made his mission official.

Batman's homestead of Kingston at Ben Lomond fell within the purview of the police magistrate of Campbell Town, James Simpson. Unfortunately, he left far fewer operational records than Anstey. But Batman is one of those cases that highlights that the northern midlands campaigning was similar to that in the better-documented south. Shortly before making his proposal to the government, Batman had been attached to a 14-man military expedition of the 57th Regiment chasing Aboriginal fires under the command of Lieutenant Shadforth.[22]

While they reportedly saw 'two men' flee further into the bush upon the party's approach, the expedition was more newsworthy for its geological discoveries than its military operations. Batman had been part of a small detachment that summited a mountain, finding 'a regular track of the natives', but also an interesting lithic landscape that was described in the newspaper in some detail. The war was normal and under-reported, the rocks new and newsworthy. A subsequent report obliquely but revealingly said that Batman 'has done much for the protection of his neighbourhood from the attacks of the natives'.[23]

While Batman's deployment was administered by Anstey, his operations differed from those of Jorgenson and Robertson in one crucial respect: Batman's guides were not even remotely local. While described in the colonial press as 'a settler, near Launceston', Batman was born in Sydney, and probably took advantage of various connections to augment his roving party with Indigenous men from

New South Wales.[24] The same article mentioned that he had taken 'two of the Aborigines of the Sister Colony' with him. They were frequently referred to as the 'Sydney Natives' or 'Sydney Blacks', although they were not strictly from Sydney itself.

There had been much discussion within Van Diemen's Land about the potential uses of trackers and warriors from the mainland to help win the war. While this did not feature in Batman's main documented correspondence with the government, by August it was clearly relatively common knowledge that this was what he had in mind, suggesting the Lieutenant Governor was likely aware of this part of the plan. The *Launceston Advertiser* reported that 'five or six' indigenous men from New South Wales, along with their wives, were being 'invited from Sydney' to assist Batman.[25] The paper wrote glowingly of these 'most desirable auxiliaries', shortly before mentioning Batman's departure with two who were already in Van Diemen's Land. One of these two, known to the colonists as Pigeon, had apparently learned some of a local language while dwelling in the islands of Bass Strait with a sealing gang.[26]

Armed with fresh convicts and foreign auxiliaries, on 1 September 1829 Batman went 'in pursuit of the Aborigines who have been committing so many outrages in this district', reporting his progress in letters to Anstey.[27] He soon 'fell in with their tracks'. Guided by 'the assistance of the Sydney Native Blacks', Batman's party found a group of 10 huts, which appeared to have been constructed a few days previously, and surmised he was on the trail of a tribe that was 'upwards of 100' people strong. After this, on the eastern side of Ben Lomond, the party found another five huts, even more recently occupied. Going further, they spotted smoke.

Batman 'immediately ordered the men to lay down', reducing their profile. They hid and listened and 'could hear the Natives conversing distinctly'. The party 'then crept into a thick scrub and remained there until after sun set'. In the darkness Batman's quiet and patient men unburdened themselves of their heavier gear, laying their knapsacks and blankets in the bush. As midnight approached, they advanced on the Aboriginal camp. Fanning out as they neared the embers, Batman's party prepared to rush the sleeping figures. Then dogs started barking.

Two of Batman's men had bumped muskets in the dark, which was enough to alarm some dogs. The awakened people commenced a hurried escape, 'running into a thick scrub'. Batman 'ordered the men to fire', after which the party rushed the camp.

One of the expedition team managed to get hold of a woman and child. 'The woman bit his hand in several places severely, but he still held her until another man came to his assistance.'[28] The party did not catch any others that night. Batman recorded that they 'only captured that Night One Woman and a Male child about Two years old', despite searching the area as best as possible in the dark.

With daylight, the impact of the raid became clearer. The party found two more men and took them captive. One was 'very badly wounded in the ancle [sic], and knee', and the other had also been hit. Batman reported that '10 Buck shot had entered his Body, he was alive but very bad'. Moreover, Batman and his party could see that others had also been wounded in their escape, probably mortally.

> There were a great number of traces of Blood in various directions and [we] learnt from those we took that 10 Men were wounded in the Body which they gave us to understand were dead or would die, and Two Women in the same state had crawled away, besides a number that were shot in the legs.[29]

The party also 'shot 21 large Dogs' and took a quantity of blankets and weapons from the abandoned camp. For a few more days Batman pursued the trails of fleeing Aboriginal people, but the guides lost the last clear tracks among rocky ground. The expedition turned back towards their base at Batman's farm with only four captives.

The going was difficult for the two wounded Aboriginal men, who 'found it quite impossible' to walk. One of them was 'a well known character', distinctly lacking two front teeth, who Batman asserted 'has been present at almost every Murder or robbery that has been committed in this district'. Batman tried to push them on, but he could not keep them moving. 'I was obliged therefore', Batman concluded bluntly, 'to shoot them.'

Recordkeeping and the Delicate Politics of Genocide

When the party returned to Kingston farm, Batman wrote a brief account of the mission for Anstey, which he dated 7 September. Tallying their ammunition, Batman could confidently assert that 'the volley we fired at them contained 328 Buck Shot'. He also confirmed that he 'forwarded the Woman to Campbell Town Gaol and have kept the child if His Excellency has no objections I intend to rear it.' Batman congratulated his men and outlined his next series of movements towards the east coast. A few days later he headed off again.

By early morning on 9 September Anstey had Batman's letter in his hands. He hurriedly posted it on to Hobart to the Colonial Secretary, scribbling a short explanatory note on the front page: 'I forward this to Mr Burnett instantly not having suff[icien]t time to read it through myself with attention.' Within another two days the Colonial Secretary had read it and made comments. Beside Batman's account of shooting the captives, the Colonial Secretary pencilled in a brief margin note: 'shoots wounded natives because they could not keep up'. He then wrote a reply to Anstey:

> With respect to Mr Batman's letter of the 7th instant, addressed to you which I duly received by this post, in which you inform me that from the immediate departure of the Messenger after it reached you, that you had not time to read it through with attention, I beg to state that from the very important nature of it's [sic] contents *it does not appear to me proper to submit the letter to The Lieutenant Governor for instructions*, till such time as you have personally seen Mr Batman, and are able to forward to me a full Report and explanation of the extraordinary circumstances to which I have alluded and which probably escaped your observation in your former cursory perusal of the Document which is herewith returned.[30]

But the letter was not so much a rebuke as a political sleight of hand. The Colonial Secretary was drawing Anstey's attention to Batman's execution of a prisoner, while also stating that the Lieutenant Governor had not received the correspondence and was therefore unaware of the incident.

Yet the very next letter in the Colonial Secretary's copybook, also sent on 11 September, suggests that Arthur had seen the letter or been informed of its contents. In a circular sent to officers throughout the colony, the Colonial Secretary reiterated the terms of martial law:

> The obligation of protecting the Colonists, having impelled the Government to adopt more energetic measures for checking the continued atrocities of the Aborigines; I am directed by the Lieutenant Governor earnestly to impress upon you the necessity of acting up to the spirit of the injunctions contained in the Proclamation of Martial Law, promulgated on the 1st of November 1828;- that bloodshed be checked, that any Natives who may surrender or be captured, be treated with humanity and tenderness, and that defenceless Women and Children be invariably spared. It will be your duty, to enjoin the strictest attention to be paid by the parties under your orders, <u>or employed in your District</u>, to these commands, as from the number now employed, it must happen that there will be frequent exercise for their forbearance.[31]

But Arthur had not just vaguely 'directed' the Colonial Secretary to issue such a circular with serendipitous coincidence. Earlier that day Arthur had in fact drafted it. Arthur's written instructions to the Colonial Secretary, and his draft of the circular, survive in a Lieutenant Governor's Office letter copybook dated 11 September.[32] While clearly a response to the specific timing and content of Batman's letter, Arthur turned his government's passive complicity in attacks and executions into an adroit act of propaganda.

While Arthur remained officially unaware of the executions, the colony rejoiced in the encounter. The *Launceston Advertiser* printed the story on 7 September, the same day that Batman wrote to Anstey, believing that '15 or 16 fell' and that 'this will cool their ardour for marauding'.[33] The *Hobart Town Courier* printed the story on

12 September, the day after the Colonial Secretary had read Batman's letter, but this too came from a report in the interior dated 7 September.[34]

Although not entirely identical to the letter sent to Anstey, the overall structure of this report and much identical phrasing and language strongly indicates that it came from Batman himself. Despite describing the capture of the two men, the report was silent on their demise. This all suggests that Batman was actively promoting his success, beyond merely informing the government, although he was a bit selective about who got to know what. Only a week later did the rival Hobart-based *Colonial Times* carry Batman's story, by which time the Aboriginal people had become the aggressors, making 'the first attack with their spears', morphing the story such that Batman's party 'were obliged in their own defence to fire and rush forward'.[35]

This all reflected a wider pattern of newspaper reportage where the war's progress often got distorted by conflicting reports, rumour, partisan politicking and even by the obfuscations of government. Yet the haphazard newspaper reports, and the sense of confused and localised violence historians have generally taken from them, contrast sharply with the generally clear intelligence and lines of communication to and from Hobart and the various parties. A fair degree of autonomy was delegated from Arthur to Anstey to the party leaders to allow tactical flexibility, but also because of unavoidable communication delays. Yet these same delays were nonetheless measurable in days at most, meaning Arthur could keep a relatively close watch over the war's strategic progress.

Following his ostensibly general reminder to the police magistrates about the good care of captives, Arthur also repeated the same injunctions to the military forces in his capacity as Colonel Commanding. But this was not the main sentiment of the Garrison Order of 15 September. Instead, the bulk of this document formally alerted the military authorities of 'more energetic steps' being implemented under Anstey's direction, which were for 'pursuing the native Tribes and of driving them, from the settled Districts, if it be not possible to surround and capture them'.[36] But while the timing and the comment about captives reveals a connection with Batman's mission and report, so too does it hint that Arthur was adapting some of Jorgenson's advice about coordinating forces, insisting that the interior military forces offer 'prompt assistance to the Civil Power' with 'the most zealous cooperation'. It was a reminder of the essential thrust of Arthur's long-term objective that the military was to help effect 'the removal of the Aborigines from the Settled Districts'.

As the fighting near Great Swan Port intensified, and the winter turned to spring, the campaigning continued. The military received their orders, Anstey and Jorgenson directed their field police units, Robertson captured more spears, and Batman crossed the hills from the midlands to the east coast, closing in on more Aboriginal people.

CHAPTER SEVEN

The Methods and Landscape of Settlement

1829, Spring
East and West

Batman's Captives

On 15 September 1829 John Batman and his party were 'on the Sea Coast'.[1] The next evening they came to a farm, where they learned that Aboriginal people 'had attempted to Spear' the occupants earlier that week. Leaving two men behind at this farm with knapsacks and blankets, Batman headed off in rapid pursuit the following morning. Before midday they 'captured one woman that had remained behind the Tribe', and pushed on. After another day and night the party could 'see a number of Natives approaching', so Batman 'ordered the men to lay down and not to fire upon them'. He would give the order 'to rush forward and seize them' at the right time.

By Batman's account the plan worked perfectly. 'I gave the signal,' he said, 'we all ran forward and secured three women, two young children, three Boys, and Two young men,' although six others did manage to 'escape into a thick scrub'. Pigeon then tried to communicate to the captives that the party's 'intentions towards them were most peaceable and friendly'.[2] Seemingly prompted by this, 'One of the women stood upon a Hill, looking down into a thick Scrub' and 'spoke for several minutes' for the benefit of what Batman assumed were hidden friends or relatives. He was unsure of the message, but he recognised that she was 'seeming by her gestures to be earnestly impressing something of import upon those whom she addressed'. Nobody emerged from the bush.

The party 'shot 17 large Dogs' and forwarded the 11 captives to Campbell Town. By 23 September these captives had been forwarded to Oatlands, where Anstey described them as 'The most interesting group of Savages I have ever seen'. When the news was conveyed to Hobart, the Colonial Secretary recorded that 'the Lieut Governor is highly pleased at the capture of the Natives, and the manner in which it has been accomplished.'[3] The same day the Colonial Secretary also advised that Arthur had finally examined the circumstances of Batman's earlier mission, and was now satisfied that 'not the slightest blame attaches to Mr Batman' for its less pacific resolution and the death of the men in Batman's custody.[4] Batman had distanced himself from the executions by a convoluted explanation about his writing style and sense of responsibility for the team.

Meanwhile Batman's party continued ranging, and the new captives were conveyed further south to Richmond. They travelled 'under an escort of a party of the 63d [sic] regiment and constables'.[5] A witness to their arrival on 29 September penned a description for the *Hobart Town Courier*:

> Two of them are very young men, the remainder women and children (some of them at the breast). They halted at the court house. A native man and women taken by a party of the 40th regiment with Mr. Robertson's party in the month of November last, and a woman taken lately by Mr. Batman were sent for from the gaol, immediately on their coming in sight of the newly arrived party, the cry of welcome was evinced, and on coming near each other the feelings portrayed on either side would have done honour to the most civilized – the two women long confined clasped to their arms children and grandchildren each shedding floods of tears of joy.

Then they were put in the gaol and given blankets.

When captured, the 11 Aboriginal people already possessed blankets, as well as jackets and other colonial items. Because these goods were apparently 'robbed' from settlers they were taken away, meaning the group was sent into captivity in a state of practical nudity. This in some ways exacerbated notions of primitiveness and savagery in the public reports. Although probably not deliberate, the contrast between redcoat guards and naked captives was more a product of the process of capture than a reflection of an absolute frontier distinction. Whether choreographed or not, the imagery of gaoling spoke to the paternalism of empire.

In a parallel way, the Bruny Island Establishment encouraged a growing segregation, even though it was ostensibly about 'civilising' Aboriginal people. Only a few weeks earlier Arthur had authorised 'a boat being built' for a 'native youth' as an 'example of industry'.[6] Arthur also wanted to 'confer upon him an allotment of ground' near the Bruny Island Establishment as a 'means of support', hoping that the gardening and boating 'may perhaps have the effect of gradually inclining those Natives who frequent the Establishment at Bruné Island to relinquish their wandering habits'. The youth concerned was 'late in the service' of a settler in the interior, meaning he already lived within the body of colonial society before he was considered for his exemplary potential.

Similarly, in March 1829 Arthur ordered an investigation into two Aboriginal women 'forced away from Bruné Island' by a 'man of Colour, a sealer named Baker or Barker', revealing the ways that the government was looking further than the war in the midlands.[7] Such individual measures were clearly about more than mere protection or vague notions of 'conciliating' combatant tribes. The government wanted Aboriginal people to adopt the colonists' way of life – on the government's terms and under its instruction.

All the while, warfare and frontier violence continued. In September, reports were sent to Hobart of the shooting of an Aboriginal woman by servants of the Van Diemen's Land Company at Emu Bay in the northwest of the island.[8] But even within the long-contested 'settled districts' there were distinctly shifting landscapes of conflict. Settler homesteads and stock huts were not the only sites of contestation, because the roving parties deliberately pushed into the cultural landscapes of various tribes. During late September William Grant maintained his party's close watch on the flint quarry east of Oatlands, for instance, precisely because it was a site of cultural significance.[9] Other parties did likewise to the west. On 7 September, while Batman was writing about executing wounded men, one of 'Jorgenson's parties of Rangers' under the command of Field Policeman George Lucas was at another location of note:

> where the great numbers of Native huts, the Trees marked by the Natives hunting the Opossum, and Trees stripped for bark, sufficiently shew that the Aborigines resort to this place in number at certain seasons of the year.[10]

Only because it appeared to have been abandoned for several months did Lucas move his party on, but he clearly marked its significance for future reference. Some of the parties even left their own cultural relics like 'a very large Bush Hut by the Big lagoon there that had been made by Mr Batman and his party'. One of Grant's supply parties found this structure in an isolated stretch of bush, part of the reformation of landscape effected by the roving parties themselves.

Intense Westwards Roving

While Grant maintained a vigil in the east, to the west the parties were still mainly on the move. After leaving the Aboriginal camping ground, Lucas' party followed the creeks and gullies as best they could, and then turned towards some smoke. But it was only some lime burners, who were 'terribly alarmed at first' because they thought the approaching armed party were bushrangers.

While the war was being prosecuted, the bushranging phenomenon was still real – a threat to colonists and Aboriginal people alike. Lucas got another illustration of the tensions of this period when, a few days after encountering the lime burners, his party was again suspected of bushranging. Mr Clark, a local farmer, intercepted the roving party, and questioned the six of them intently. Covering the exchange were 'no less than sixteen persons under Arms concealed in various places ready to pour their vollies into us', Lucas later wrote. It is a passing revelation of the paramilitary power wielded by some landowners.

Fortunately, Lucas managed to allay Mr Clark's concerns, and was recognised by some of his servants, after which all suspicions evaporated. The party asked about the habits of Aboriginal people in the area, and then moved on to a predetermined rendezvous point a little west of Ross. Danvers met them there and took charge of the party, while Lucas returned to Oatlands to help organise Jorgenson's third party and make his report.

Danvers guided the party into the Western Tiers. From these heights, they 'had a very extensive view of the surrounding Country, and could see a very long way to the Eastward and the Westward, but could observe no signs of the Natives'.[11] Now well-practised in tracking and ambushing, Danvers led his party to Lake Sorell, 'and encamped for the night in a very convenient place for watching Native fires'. But while pressing further into the highlands over subsequent days, the men learned of recent raids by bushrangers, and got on their trail instead as another form of public service. They chased the bushrangers for several days and gradually closed the distance, but other authorities made the arrest before the chase ended. By then in Norfolk Plains, in the northwestern midlands, Danvers and his party spent a few more days out without event before returning to Oatlands.

Although they made no captures, Anstey was impressed with Danvers and his men, commenting that their 'very extraordinary exertions ... have given me the highest satisfaction'. Arthur agreed that Danvers 'deserves great commendation for his conduct.' These notes on Danvers' report were among numerous exchanges between Oatlands and Hobart during the spring of 1829, which detailed all manner of administrative matters from rations and clothing to the appointment of an armourer in Oatlands to maintain and repair weapons.[12] A shoemaker was even attached to Batman's party because of the heavy toll his exertions kept taking on their footwear.[13] Even more men were attached to the various roving parties.[14]

Meanwhile, Kickerterpoller also contributed to the administrative correspondence, raising concerns about the treatment of the captives in Richmond Gaol. He did this through Robertson, who relayed the information to the government.[15] An 'insufficiency of food' was part of the problem, but there was also 'great cause for complaint' with the quality of the meat issued to the captives. 'Tom has also complained', Robertson wrote, that the gaoler 'had confined the Native calld [sic] the Lawyer, handcuffed in a Cell'. Arthur responded by ordering they receive regular visits 'two or three times a week, and see that they are taken good care of'.[16]

While addressing Kickerterpoller's concerns, Arthur was also frustrated with Robertson's general proximity to Richmond, which meant he was clearly not roving. Arthur was 'very glad' when he learned Anstey intimated to Robertson 'the propriety of his leaving the Coal River District'. It was one of a number of signs that Robertson was attracting the Lieutenant Governor's displeasure. When referring the dispute between Jorgenson and Robertson back to Anstey, Arthur thought that Robertson's 'want of success seems to have ruffled his temper!'[17]

Mr Clark's Farm and the Soldier-Settler Reality

In late October Robertson was sent west towards Bothwell, at Arthur's suggestion.[18] The Bothwell district was being pressed by Aboriginal people making attacks around the Clyde River, again shifting the weight of strategic focus from east to west. Seeking help from Arthur in mid-September, Williams was told he might get a party from Anstey, or could raise one of his own.[19] Williams even 'got a party of mounted orderlies and goes out with them himself' one report noted.[20] But while Williams had military forces at his disposal, could expect roving parties from Oatlands, and was forming further parties locally, he was also having trouble with the settlers in his district. Some of them failed to offer much help to the military and roving parties, and took surprisingly little care for their own protection. Arthur was tired of settlers writing in with complaints about Aboriginal raids and repeated calls for help. As the Colonial Secretary advised:

> His Excellency has also desired me to state, that it is only reasonable, that the more respectable class of Settlers, who can afford it, should in some degree provide for the security and protection of their own families, and that it would be advisable for you to ascertain, how far this is attended to throughout your District; not that it should in any way abate the activity of the Military.[21]

Clearly some settlers took more precautions than others. Mr Clark, who had surrounded Lucas' roving party with armed men, certainly did. He wrote a short treatise for the *Colonial Times*, detailing strategies for making properties safer.[22] Clark basically suggested siting huts in cleared ground, so there was no cover for approaching raiders, and advocated using a 'stockade' to provide a defensive firing position. But other settlers were less active in this regard. In a subsequent letter the Colonial Secretary told Williams to 'see every Settler of any respectability, and animate all to take precautions for their own preservation'.[23] Far from discouraging frontier violence, the government was actively encouraging settlers to be prepared for it.

Unsurprisingly, given these sorts of concerns, Arthur helped military men to settle in the colony. In 1826 the British Government had issued instructions seeking to encourage 'Officers of the Army, more especially those on Half-pay, to become Settlers in New South Wales and Van Diemen's Land'.[24] Shortly after receiving this instruction in early 1827, Arthur forwarded to London a testimonial of a 'late Captain of the 6th Regiment of Foot'.[25] This man had 24 years of military experience, sold his commission to settle in Van Diemen's Land, and was what Arthur characterised as 'the kind of Settler that deserves encouragement'. This 'faithful old Soldier' was William Clark, Justice of the Peace in the Bothwell district, and by 1829 commander of a private militia capable of surrounding and outnumbering a field police roving party.

The scheme for encouraging soldier-settlers expanded relatively quickly.[26] The British Government allowed soldiers to keep their half-pay, and gave them a stepped scale of financial advantage, freeing them from quit rents on a sliding scale based on length of military service. In effect, soldiers were given significant financial incentives to settle in Van Diemen's Land. This would, it was thought, 'secure to the public the Services of a valuable and intelligent class of persons'.[27] In December 1827 a scheme for encouraging naval settlers was also implemented.[28] Soon, immigrant soldier-settlers were taking advantage of these schemes, acquiring land during the Vandemonian War, and seemingly getting deployed by Arthur for strategic ends. Typical of the phenomenon, in 1828 Arthur ordered land surveyed per terms of 'the Regulations of the General Military Order' for a 'Capt Spotswood, late of the 98th Foot'.[29]

These grants were part of the process of occupying Aboriginal territory. John Spotswood's grant particularly highlights this, because he came to occupy part of the Tasman Peninsula on what was, in his own words, 'commonly known as Blackman's plains' and bounded in part 'by Blackman's river'.[30] Spotswood was not alone in his post-military frontier deployment, with several other soldier-settlers immigrating during the late 1820s and attracting the Lieutenant Governor's personal attention.[31]

In November 1829, during a time of considerable hostilities, Arthur also authorised the construction of huts at government expense for 10 discharged members of the Veteran Company.[32] Such moves went beyond merely rewarding old soldiers. These policies were also about populating the settled districts with militarily experienced civic leaders. Like the police magistrates, the civilian settlers were not quite what they seemed.

This militarised settlement was not just about the war as such. It was also a defence against bushranging and any potential convict uprising. While soldiers protected chain gangs from Aboriginal harassment, they also guarded the convicts against escape. But as more settlers occupied ground, they thereby also denied its occupation by others, specifically Aboriginal people.

Similarly, while the roving parties were mainly directed for military action against Aboriginal people, they were sometimes diverted to other ends. This included more regular police duties, and Danvers briefly attracted public notice during October 1829 for such a mission. 'Two parties of black rangers under the direction of constable Danvers and Richard Tyrrell closely pursued the murderer,' reported the *Hobart Town Courier*.[33] Convict James Brown had absconded from custody, was recaptured but escaped again by striking a constable. The constable regained consciousness enough to report the assault, but died of his head injury. When Danvers and Tyrrell's chase failed, the government offered £20 reward for Brown's recapture, and within a few weeks he was caught trying to cross the Derwent in a small boat.[34] Brown was later sentenced to be hanged, but was apparently reprieved.[35] But by then Danvers and Tyrrell were prosecuting the war again.

The Rangers and Aboriginal Relics

In response to the hostilities near the Clyde River, during October and November 1829 several parties of 'black rangers' from Oatlands operated throughout the Bothwell district, and their overlapping movements reveal Jorgenson's operational mechanics were maturing. On 20 October Richard Tyrrell reported to Bothwell for instructions, and Williams sent him 'to proceed over the River Ouse, and to remain in that part of the country three weeks'.[36] Over coming days Tyrrell learned from local stockmen 'of the continual attacks by the Natives on the neighbouring huts', proof of which was found on 24 October when his party found some blankets taken from one of the earlier raids.

As Tyrrell's party examined the blankets, Danvers was leading a party westwards from Oatlands.[37] The next day they arrived at Bothwell, before heading up into the tiers. On 27 October Danvers' party 'found a tolerable good blanket and a number of broken spears' at a place he called the Gibraltar Marsh. They also located a 'a Bag marked GT. which the Aborigines had carried off full of Flour'. Like Tyrrell's find, such artefacts of raiding showed Aboriginal people were in the general area, although neither party had yet seen fires or tracks.

Meanwhile, Tyrrell was gaining information. He spent some of 27 October in conversation with Mr Young, who told him about various battles in the district:

> They had attacked Clark's hut three miles from the River, had speared a woman in the breast and side, and set fire over her. The poor woman came out of the hut her clothes all a fire. She was met by one of the Native chiefs. She held her hands up to him and said to him 'Oh spare my life for God's sake.['] He ran to her, put out the fire and shook her by the hand, and led her away from the other natives who were in the act of throwing Spears at her. I believe the woman was in the last stage of pregnancy. The Tribe then turned their attention to the hut, murdered a man of the name of Clark, and cut his head off, and then put the head and body in the fire. ... On this same day the natives met Constable Williams from the Clyde, conveying a female convict servant of Mr Triffitts, to some other place. The natives murdered this woman and speared Two other men.

The district was, as one report put it, 'in a state of considerable alarm'.[38] Many settlers and servants suffered from raids, and reports and rumours circulated throughout the districts, sometimes even reaching the colonial press. Earlier that month, for instance, another of Mr Triffitt's servants was the victim of a tale of frontier woe. This man 'was found dead in the bush', made more interesting for the press because a sheep dog had kept a two-day guard over the body.[39]

But not all reports were accurate. Captain Clark was surprised to read an account of his own house being attacked when no such thing had occurred, which is what prompted him to write the detailed account of his defensive arrangements – proof that he could take care of himself.[40] The roving parties were sometimes thwarted in their operations because of such incorrect reports. On one mission Tyrrell spent several fruitless days chasing what turned out to be 'a false hood'.⁴¹ But unless they saw fires or found tracks, local reports were still often the rangers' best leads.

Up near Lake Echo, Danvers gradually got on an Aboriginal trail, finding two butchered kangaroo, areas of burnt grass, and 'three very large Natives huts' built by the lake only days earlier. But Danvers found nothing else and turned back.

On 1 November Danvers received orders from Williams to proceed towards the Shannon River. Over the next few days Danvers' party remained unable to see any Aboriginal fires, despite routinely camping on high ground and keeping night watches. As Danvers shifted directions in accordance with orders, Tyrrell heard of another attack. Aboriginal people apparently 'attempted to rob a man's hut named Burn, who most manfully, with the assistance of his Dog, beat a Tribe off'.

By now Robertson was also in the district, and he too was listening to local reports, including one 'that the Natives had attacked Mr Clarke's shepherd's hut'.⁴² Courtesy of Jack's guidance, Robertson managed to find their tracks and their campsite, and was met there by Grant's party, which had also heard of the attack and diverted to that direction. The two parties combined, and most of them headed up towards the lakes, while a few remained behind to defend the settlers. On the way, they met one of Danvers' men, who had diverted to the chief district constable for further orders while Danvers headed to the 'Soldiers Marshes'. A few days afterwards, on 9 November, Tyrrell's party 'fell in with one of Mr Gilbert Robertson's parties'.

While these parties scoured the tiers, watched for fires, followed rumours and were led astray by 'false reports', another party led by Peter Scott was detached from Oatlands. This party headed towards the tiers and lakes, scouring the country while veering towards Bothwell. Two of Jorgenson's three parties reached Bothwell, made their reports, and then returned to the bush on 19 and 22 November respectively. In the meantime, Danvers' party returned to Oatlands on 20 November. Just as Jorgenson had instructed, two of his parties were always in the field, in addition to the various parties directed by Robertson and others.

Soldiery on the Western Front

The Oatlands rangers and local Bothwell parties were not the only forces in the field. They were just the best documented. Even before learning the outcome of these roving missions, Arthur was sending further reinforcements to the Bothwell district. As well as encouraging settlers to defend themselves, authorising the formation of locally raised roving parties, and sending in forces overseen by Robertson and Jorgenson, Arthur sent in more of the army. On 13 November the Colonial Secretary wrote to Williams at Bothwell, and his counterpart in New Norfolk:

> The Lieut Governor having learnt with extreme regret that repeated outrages of the most barbarous nature, have recently been perpetuated in your District by the Natives has been pleased to direct that Lieut Gibbons and a Detachment of Military, should proceed tomorrow morning to Hamilton at the Lower Clyde, there to encamp, in order to check the atrocities and expel the Aborigines from that, and the surrounding Country; you will therefore be pleased to co-operate by every means in your power, with the Officer commanding the troops, for the attainment of these very important objects.[43]

Details about the military operations are scarce, but Arthur's orders were clearly followed relatively swiftly. 'A detachment of 100 strong' left for 'the Clyde station' within a week.[44]

A week later, a report mentioned some of the dispositions of soldiers stationed at Bothwell:

> Besides the parties of rovers sent in pursuit of the natives, four parties of military composed of six men each, set out from Bothwell this morning to scour the country. A number of soldiers are now stationed in various stock huts from under the Western tier, down the Great river, and the Shannon.[45]

This was the type of 'decisive, combined, and simultaneous exertion' that the Colonel Commanding demanded.[46]

Military operations were further strengthened in November 1829 when Captain Vicary replaced Lieutenant Williams as Bothwell police magistrate. It was not intended as a slight to Williams (he was being transferred with his regiment to India), but the appointment of a more senior officer as a replacement likely reflects intensified conflict in the foothills of the high country. Vicary was a recent promotion, and a relatively new arrival in the colony, but had already demonstrated a fighting spirit. One correspondent commended his 'measures adopted' against Aboriginal people.[47] Another praised Vicary for parties under his command in the midlands, because 'nothing could exceed the alacrity with which they performed their disagreeable duty'.[48] The experience of combined operations to protect and clear the central midlands were now being turned more fully towards the western high country.

The immediate impact of Vicary's new force is hard to discern. Certainly, it bolstered defensive arrangements. This increased the colony's capacity for offensive operations to clear the area of Aboriginal people, and freed the rangers to rove further from the settlements. Moreover, it probably helped regional morale. While some settlers appeared recalcitrant and lax in their own defence, others enthusiastically joined the war effort. Incensed by his son being speared, one settler went 'to join a party of military under the command of Capt. Vicary, with a determination to scour the hills'.[49]

New Norfolk and the Southern Flank of the Western Front

The Bothwell district was not the only theatre of conflict. Further south and west, the adjoining district of New Norfolk was also under attack. Earlier in the year Arthur had instructed the police magistrate that the 'deep gully' was an 'important station for the residence of a Military Officer'.[50] There was a convict chain gang there, guarded by 'a strong Military Party', but Aboriginal people could still raid with impunity. In late October there were reports of a series of attacks, including the spearing of a stock-keeper among 'the hills behind Lieut Fry's house' near Macquarie Plains.[51] While Lieutenant Fry took 'a party of soldiers

THE METHODS AND LANDSCAPE OF SETTLEMENT

in pursuit', Aboriginal people attacked his house. While 'a soldier stationed there fired upon them', they broke in, and 'plundered it of every thing they had time to carry off'. A correspondent noted that '[t]hey escaped notwithstanding a party of soldiers quickly arrived from the Gully' and that '[t]he greatest promptitude was shewn by every settler in the district on the first alarm. No less than ten different parties, well armed, have been scouring the bush.'[52] But the results of these sorts of scouring missions were rarely reported in the colonial press.

While military forces and police magistrates had to contend with a general state of conflict that spilled over district borders, and an enemy that was exceedingly difficult to track, coordinated military and paramilitary action had clearly become the main colonial strategy by the spring of 1829. About the time that Vicary replaced Williams at Bothwell, Arthur also replaced the police magistrate at Richmond. When James Gordon confirmed his arrival and assumption of office, Arthur advised him of his responsibilities:

> to consider in what manner, with the force at present at your disposal, the extensive District under your care can be protected from the attacks and aggressions of the Aborigines. It will be necessary for you, to look to all the distant stock huts, animate the Settlers generally, to adopt judicious measures for their defence.[53]

Jorgenson opined that good reconnaissance was crucial to such strategies:

> Our knowledge of the Country, the Mountains, the passes, and fording places, render us in these respects a match for the Aborigines and I hope that by patience and perseverance we shall before the end of the Summer put an end to the war.[54]

But despite his optimism, Jorgenson still wanted more help. He drew Anstey's attention to the way that he had organised a party under

Robert Hyett 'to remain in ambush' and 'if occasions require it, receive assistance from the military and the Shepherds', among other cooperative manoeuvres with various groups of soldiers. This plan was done 'in conformity with some suggestions offered by His Excellency when I was last in town', Jorgenson noted, again highlighting Arthur's intimate knowledge and very personal direction of the war's prosecution. Jorgenson also made a point of drawing Anstey's and therefore Arthur's focus to a strategic request 'in a separate letter dated the Clyde', where Jorgenson 'expressed my hope that my parties may be supplied with the assistance of one Native at least'.

In this letter Jorgenson described his expectations of imminent success, but also mentioned that 'we find it extremely difficult to continue in the tracks of the Aborigines when having moved over rocks or grass'. It was this inability to track Aboriginal people effectively that made the rangers so reliant on local intelligence, or reduced to climbing hills and looking for signs of smoke or fire – albeit now with the aid of a telescope in Jorgenson's case. Asking Anstey if he could 'obtain for me some clever man or lad of the native race to accompany that one of my parties which shall be most actively engaged in pursuit', Jorgenson observed that both Batman and Robertson has such auxiliaries attached to their parties.[55] Anstey ultimately agreed, suggesting to Arthur that augmenting Jorgenson's force with Aboriginal men would increase the chances of his 'falling in with the predatory Hordes'. Arthur approved the effective conscription of a captive, and Jorgenson was authorised to take one of those held at Richmond.[56] Accordingly, a young man known as Mungo was attached to Jorgenson's rangers.

As the army moved into the high country in November, Jorgenson assessed his parties and prepared for further roving operations.[57] Noting that Tyrrell's party 'has been found useful in protecting the settlements', Jorgenson sent Tyrrell and his men 'to his former station' by the Ouse River, and Peter Scott 'to scour the Abyssinia Tiers, the hunting grounds, Cockatoo Valley etc.'. Both of these parties were strengthened by Hyett and John Reynolds, previously occupied with ambush missions, but now freed from that duty because 'the Soldiers are roving'. James Hopkins was brought in to temporarily take over

Danvers' party, who Jorgenson commended as 'indefatigable'. Danvers was redeployed to make 'preparations for a long and arduous journey from the Extreme Western Bluff, down along the whole line of demarcation as far as the Peak of Teneriffe'. As Jorgenson explained:

> The Black native Mungo and myself will accompany Danvers on this journey, and our party will then be eight strong. We have hitherto found it impracticable to spare a detachment for the purpose of taking a great circuitous route, so to get the Aborigines between the parties and the settlements, but now that a number of military is roving over the Country we shall be able to accomplish our wish.

Now that his complement of roving parties was growing in strength and operating in a coordinated fashion across multiple districts, Anstey was aware that the gaze of the Colonel Commanding and the wider colony were upon his missions. 'The time is now nearly arrived,' Anstey informed Arthur about a month earlier, 'for trying the real merits of the present system'. But by the end of the year Anstey opined that '[t]he want of success of the Roving Parties is much to be deplored.' In late November Anstey threatened the roving parties could be disbanded, which had what Jorgenson described as 'very salutary effects' upon the rangers.[58] But the roving parties continued to go out, and auxiliaries like Mungo proved to be often enthusiastic and good at what they were increasingly employed to do.

CHAPTER EIGHT

Aboriginal Auxiliaries

1829–30, Spring–Summer
Southern Frontier

Robertson's Contract Ends

Anstey was not the only person to express misgivings about the roving parties in late 1829. The Colonial Secretary also conveyed to Anstey 'that the Lieut Governor feels much discouraged at the total want of success'.[1] These records of similar sentiments were seemingly unconnected, but probably reflect a wider discussion about the campaigning to be undertaken in the weeks and months ahead. Arthur wanted Anstey to provide 'observations or suggestions' for a potential 'alteration in the system'. While Anstey replied that 'I do not think that the present plan is capable of improvement,' thereby tacitly backing Jorgenson as the key theoretician of the plan, he also implied that there were potential issues with some roving party personnel, probably a coded comment about Gilbert Robertson.[2]

After tensions between Jorgenson and Robertson escalated, the Colonial Secretary increasingly queried Robertson's success and diligence.[3] For a considerable part of the spring, Robertson had been out of action with what he described as a 'chronic distemper', failing to fully report his or his parties' movements with any frequency or reliability. Eventually the Colonial Secretary directly asked for Robertson's missing 'Quarterly Journal', which was needed 'in order that it may be deposited as Record in my office'.[4] The government was preparing to archive Robertson's missions, which would have been a simple task but for Robertson's evasiveness. As 1829 drew to a close there was little serious suggestion that Robertson's contract would be renewed.

In December Robertson recognised that he was unlikely to be employed again. 'I do not expect His Excellency will consider it expedient to require an extension of my Service beyond the present year,' he informed the Colonial Secretary.[5] But he nonetheless advocated that the men attached to his mission should receive their various rewards. He explained that Grant would 'petition for his conditional Pardon, And wishes to be employed again, with a view to obtaining his Absolute Pardon'. Grant was, Robertson explained, 'heir to a small property' in Aberdeenshire and was 'anxious to earn his liberty to visit his native Country'. Engaging in warfare was a chance to escape the sentence of transportation, and possibly even leave Van Diemen's Land. Most of Robertson's rovers wanted to be transferred to the field police, or otherwise engage in future missions with the prospect of further reward.

But even the transfer of such men proved complex, in part because Robertson kept them from reporting to Hobart, but also because the bureaucracy was inflexible. Sam Robinson, for instance, wound up stuck in the Hobart Prisoner's Barracks.[6] Infuriated by his situation, he wrote to Anstey, thereby giving a subordinate's close and unique perspective on Robertson's mission, noting that Robertson's 'chief object was in looking for good Land for he seemed more interested in that than natives', and that Robertson did not maintain daily field journals but composed them later. All these assertions likely reinforced Anstey's suspicions, and he annotated the letter with the comment that 'a number of the men belonging to Mr Gilbert Robertson's late Parties are kept idle at the Coal River'. With his superiors against him, Robertson's roving missions were effectively over.

Preparatory to Further Colonisation, the Port Davey Mission

The process of terminating Robertson's mission left convict servants like William Grant and Sam Robinson in uncertainty, but the situation was clearer for the Aboriginal auxiliaries. On 1 December 1829 Arthur gave orders to Anstey:

> give the necessary instructions for causing one of the 'Aborigines' who is at present with Mr Gilbert Robertson, to be delivered to the charge of Mr G. A. Robinson, who is proceeding to Port Davey, for the purpose of endeavouring to effect an amicable understanding with the Natives of that quarter.[7]

Later that month the captives in Richmond Gaol were also 'placed at the disposal of Mr G. A. Robinson' for his diplomatic mission to the tribes of the south.[8]

The notion of a mission to the Port Davey tribes had been around for some time. In June 1829, for instance, the *Hobart Town Courier* 'wished that the present peaceable Blacks in the neighbourhood of Port Davey could be brought in before any contamination of the murderous habits of those in other parts of the island.'[9] The paper advocated that George Augustus Robinson, with his 'black family' at Bruny Island accompanying him, was an ideal candidate for such an endeavour.

Port Davey, at the most southwestern edge of Van Diemen's Land, was effectively separated from the settled districts by mountainous terrain. One reporter described the Aboriginal people living there as 'a degree above those in the interior', which mainly meant they appeared less inclined to fight the colonists.[10] This 'Port Davey mob', as the Aboriginal people of the southern coast of Van Diemen's Land were often collectively termed, had long been in contact with colonists right up as far as Bruny Island. As already seen, the Bruny Island Establishment gradually grew from the government's efforts to utilise a location of regular coastal contact to encourage Aboriginal people to remain out of Hobart and its surrounds and gradually become sedentary agriculturalists.

The Port Davey people's notional friendliness, however, reflected the colonists' limited incursions into their territory. Port Davey itself was a stopover on voyages between Hobart and the Macquarie Harbour penal settlement, and timber cutters had begun logging along the Huon River. But where the midlands had been aggressively occupied by the British over two decades of colonial expansion, southern Van Diemen's Land had far fewer settlers and soldiers, and so the Vandemonian War had not really extended to that part of the island.

Yet even while trying to maintain a line of demarcation between settled and unsettled districts, the colonial government was looking to a broader geographical future. Several months before Robinson's expedition to Port Davey, efforts were being made to explore the territory in greater detail. In March the *Hobart Town Courier* briefly described a preliminary mission:

> A small party, with two native guides, is we learn to be
> dispatched with the next vessel that sails to Macquarie harbour,
> in order to be landed at Port Davey, and to explore from thence
> the country up to Hobart town.[11]

Immediately below this, the paper contains a glowing account of the 'little colony, or home for the Blacks at Bruné Island'. That Aboriginal people were guiding reconnaissance expeditions while others were being encouraged to farm potatoes, highlights a complex spectrum of inter-cultural interactions that has too often been overlooked in Vandemonian history.

But cultural exchanges often went two ways. During a different mission to Port Davey, for instance, one colonist apparently feigned a snake bite so that he could learn about traditional medicinal practice. He reported the treatment upon returning to Hobart:

> The Black immediately took two pieces of bark with sharp points
> which he lighted, and rubbed, or rather drilled into the wound,
> until he had made a considerable cavity. He then plucked some
> of the soft wool of an oppossum [sic] and stuffed into it, singeing
> the projecting fur smooth off with the skin, which process he
> declared was sufficient to prevent evil consequence.[12]

While there may have been more to this story than appearances suggest – as it sounded a lot to bear for the sake of curiosity – this account of a field dressing shows colonists learning about Aboriginal practices with a certain enthusiasm. While not all such reports were documented, Aboriginal people revealed parts of their cultures to travelling companions across the colony and beyond. At the Bruny Island Establishment, Robinson was able to learn and record snippets of Aboriginal cultures. In the winter of 1829, for instance, he learned from one group 'that they had some idea of a good spirit whom they called PAR.LER.DY, and that he stopped in the sky'.[13] A few weeks later he might have seen or heard about another medical procedure when Boomer's widow, again at Bruny Island after her husband's tragic demise, treated herself for an illness. She reportedly cut gashes in her flesh and bound the wounds with plant matter.[14] Although Robinson only learned second-hand that she died from the affliction, he was nonetheless relatively well placed to observe and describe some Aboriginal practices. The Bruny Island Establishment gave him access to a greater proportion of Aboriginal people than most other colonial agents. Only the Richmond gaoler rivalled him in this regard.

But in preparing to go to Port Davey with Aboriginal companions, Robinson was following a broader colonial agenda that went beyond acculturation. The early 1829 exploratory expedition returned to Hobart with reports that 'there is a considerable quantity of good land in that direction'.[15] Robinson's mission was therefore part of a land grab.

The Convenience of Committees and the Results of Patronage

Arthur authorised Robinson's Port Davey mission on 28 November 1829.[16] It came as part of a set of instructions to concentrate all Aboriginal captives at the Bruny Island Establishment, fence them in, and provide field police to guard against their escape. The expedition to Port Davey was intended to 'effect an amicable understanding with the Natives in that quarter, and through them, with the Tribes in the interior'.[17] Robinson was provided with 'five steady men', one of the men currently with Robertson, and 'one of those in the Hospital'.

Like Richmond Gaol, the colonial hospital in Hobart was another institutional site where Aboriginal people were confined. In early November, five of the 14 captives at Richmond were 'conveyed in a cart to the Hospital in Hobart town' to help stop the spread of an illness among the rest.[18] Colonisation brought new diseases that afflicted Aboriginal people, particularly when they were confined. These patients from Richmond reportedly 'shed tears at parting' as they were taken away towards Hobart.

With the gradual development of a more centralised concentration of Aboriginal captives at Bruny Island also came questions about the conditions of such detention. After Robinson raised concerns about the rations at the Establishment being 'insufficient', Arthur formed a small committee to investigate the scheme of provisions and make recommendations.[19] Formed in October, it was composed of the chief police magistrate, the port officer and 'An officer of the Commissariat Dept'. A few weeks later, Arthur formed another committee to review the site of the Bruny Island Establishment.[20] It was considered 'objectionable principally from the proximity of the whaling parties at Adventure Bay'. Ironically, the very thing that made Bruny Island appealing to begin with – a locus of habitual association – had seemingly become a problem. This committee, which was composed of the Colonial Treasurer, the chief police magistrate and the Colonial Surgeon, was then asked to suggest new locations on other islands or mainland Van Diemen's Land for an 'Aboriginal Establishment'.

In December, Arthur added two new members to this committee, both ministers of religion. Increasingly concerned about fraternisation between whalers and Aboriginal people, Arthur tasked this expanded committee with overseeing 'the care and treatment of the Captured Natives and for suggesting such measures of conciliation as shall appear to them calculated to bring about a permanent friendly intercourse between the native tribes and the Colonists'.[21]

One of the two new members of this 'Aborigines Committee', as it came to be known, was the colonial chaplain Reverend William Bedford of the Church of England. Bedford was an obvious choice for Arthur. As a moral leader, he had already shown an interest in the treatment of Aboriginal people. Earlier in the year, for instance, Bedford staged an experiment where 'an Aboriginal youth' was exposed to an organ recital in Launceston to gauge his response.[22] More particularly, Bedford was already connected to the administration of the Bruny Island Establishment through Robinson.

Bedford and Robinson had a close relationship. One of Bedford's duties as colonial chaplain was to attend to the spiritual needs of prisoners in the Hobart Gaol, especially those sentenced to death. Before his appointment to the Bruny Island Establishment, Robinson also regularly visited the confined and condemned.[23] Both were committee members of the Auxiliary Bible Society, where Robinson was also a collector of subscriptions.[24] It seems very likely therefore that Bedford advocated for Robinson in his application for the job at Bruny Island. Certainly he actively supported Robinson thereafter, acting as an intermediary between Robinson and the Lieutenant Governor on several occasions, and even directly relaying Robinson's scheme for an expedition to Port Davey. Arthur's own instructions replicated ideas and phrases from one of Bedford's letters, including the suggestions to fence the Bruny Island Establishment and send a mission to Port Davey, which the Reverend noted was the result of 'much conversation with Mr Robinson'.[25] Bedford was, in effect, Robinson's patron – giving the former bricklayer relatively direct access to the highest level of government in the colony.

The Politics of Conciliation

Government concerns about the treatment of Aboriginal captives overlapped with a broader focus on the moral improvement of colonial society. While having a rapidly expanding cohort of free settlers, Van Diemen's Land was still a dedicated convict colony, where the government's systems of punishment, training and rewards aimed at the rehabilitation of those often considered a degraded criminal class. But Hobart was also a busy port servicing sailors, sealers and whalers from a diverse range of classes and places. With that developed a seedy side that undermined the image of colonial respectability fostered by genteel settlers and urban professionals.

In their own ways, the Auxiliary Bible Society and the Bruny Island Establishment both sought to save body and soul from sin and ignorance. But there was a sense of growing urgency about Aboriginal people's futures as the continued prosecution of the Vandemonian War made their total extermination seem ever more likely.

The Bruny Island Establishment and the Port Davey expedition therefore served as useful political counterpoints to the Vandemonian War. Both were visible signs of the government's paternalism. The money expended on them, however, was only a tiny fraction of the costs of soldiers and roving parties. It is telling that their oversight was delegated to a committee, while Arthur personally oversaw strategic combat operations.

Although Robinson's expedition was represented at the time as a major turning point in government policy, they were equipped with a supporting crew of armed servants and Aboriginal auxiliaries who had formerly been stationed with Robertson. The Port Davey expedition was never called a roving party, but it rather looked like one.

By late 1829 and early 1830, elements within colonial society were becoming increasingly uncomfortable with the war. Typifying this was a meeting of 'upwards of a hundred of the most influential individuals of the colony' in the Hobart Court House in January 1830.[26] Styled the Van Diemen's Land Philosophical Society, it reveals some of the ways that the ambiguities of British colonialism were played out in public discourse, with much attention to science, discovery and colonial improvement. 'Our very residence in this island may be termed the offspring of science,' one speaker announced, framing the occupation as a direct result of navigational advancement and maritime exploration. 'The amelioration in the state of those nations of India, which have become subject to England,' he went on to add, 'is perhaps the most beautiful illustration of the practical effects of science that can be cited.' This supposedly pacific control of India was, however, then contrasted with Van Diemen's Land where 'the brutal inhumanity of white men' had, the speaker argued, left Aboriginal people hostile to the colonists. He hoped the Philosophical Society would focus on 'acquiring to more intimate acquaintance with this much wronged people, with a view of ameliorating their condition, and of saving them from being extirpated'.

In part, this was a colonial narrative that had developed about the war and its origins, which borrowed heavily from Christian theology and scientific notions about humanity. This placed the cause for conflict with the distant sins of white forefathers and regretted its continuation as a function of a child-like animosity of uncivilised peoples. It was a narrative sequence later made official by the Aborigines Committee, which investigated 'the origin of the hostility displayed by the Black Natives' in early 1830, and came to much the same conclusion as the January speaker.[27]

But the deponents quizzed by the Aborigines Committee, like the members of the Philosophical Society, generally had compromised positions. Even that speaker at the Philosophical Society was deeply involved in the ongoing work of colonisation. He was Surveyor General George Frankland, who had helped survey the good land of the Huon Valley between Hobart and Port Davey.[28]

In early February the *Colonial Times* carried two adjacent advertisements that further illustrate these compromised ambiguities of colonialism. The Aborigines Committee requested 'communication and suggestions' from members of the public, while Frankland advertised the new 'road having been opened and completed from Hobart Town to the River Huon', which meant 'parties in search of land for location, have now the power of penetrating with facility into the heart of the unexplored country in the south-western portion of the Colony'.[29]

Robinson's Friendly Roving Party

Robinson's expedition was transported into that southern country not by Frankland's road, but rather by boat. Just as Frankland's mapping was part of the process of colonial expansion, so too was Robinson's expedition. While framed as a diplomatic mission, and tied to general narratives of the war, it was also clearly about opening new territory for more intensive colonial occupation. As he approached the territory occupied by the Port Davey peoples, he 'Served out six rounds of ammunition to the party'. Robinson was more than prepared for his party to fight if needed. Such expeditions could have more than one purpose, after all. War and diplomacy are not necessarily opposites.

Accompanied by Kickerterpoller and Eumarrah – veterans of the roving parties – as well as his armed servants, Robinson started his overland journey from the area around Recherche Bay.[30] On one of his first days out, some of his party found an Aboriginal woman's body. As one of Robinson's companions explained:

> [She] had been attacked with sickness and left here by her tribe to linger and perish, as is their custom when overcome with sickness. The natives informed me that plenty of natives had been attacked with RAEGERWROPPER or evil spirit, and had died.[31]

Illnesses had killed many of the Aboriginal people at Bruny Island, and Robinson now surmised disease was 'general among the tribes of aborigines', perhaps explaining away the impact of confinement – in which he was highly complicit – in fostering infections.

After a week of difficult travel and diminishing provisions, Robinson lost part of his team. 'The civilised aborigine Robert absconded without permission,' he noted. But nonetheless, through his travels he learned various local words from his companions, and saw cultural practices from boating to the preparation and consumption of seal meat. Like many colonial explorers, Robinson named features of the landscape, including one range of mountains after Arthur. He also saw many unoccupied huts, much like the roving parties of the interior, and similarly climbed mountains for the heightened views, turning towards signs of smoke.

In the middle of March, Robinson found the skeletal remains of three escaped convicts laying near a small flag that had failed to attract the attention of passing ships. It was a reminder of how far from effective colonial occupation the expedition had travelled. And it was here, on that day, that members of Robinson's party made contact with the Port Davey tribe. Four of the members with Robinson's expedition 'stripped themselves of their European clothing', went ahead and established the terms of a meeting for the subsequent day. One of them, Dray, having met her relatives, spent the night with them.

Over the next few days there was periodic contact between Robinson's party and various Port Davey people, sometimes involving Robinson himself. It all seemed peaceable enough, helped by the fact that some of Robinson's companions were clearly related to the people they met. Moreover, the coast of Van Diemen's Land had been a place of regular contact with outsiders since at least the 1790s, so there was much precedent for polite and curious exchanges in the area. However, Robinson noted that some of his team were 'anxious to make captives', and this even extended beyond the colonial servants. 'The blacks were as eager to make capture', Robinson added, noting that one of them named Woorrady 'bore a mortal hatred to these people'.

Nonetheless, the mission continued, negotiating difficult terrain and complex social relationships. Over subsequent months Robinson travelled to Macquarie Harbour, then up the west coast of Van Diemen's Land into the territory occupied by the Van Diemen's Land Company, a sweeping circuit of those least settled coastal areas of the island. Robert returned to the party, but Eumarrah later absconded. A number of Aboriginal people joined the expedition. All throughout this journey Robinson kept a journal, detailing bits of local history, cultural traditions and providing a record of various human encounters, albeit often one-sidedly. But he was not the only colonist to have such opportunities.

Richard Tyrrell's Wartime Ethnography

While Robinson wandered the wild and rocky southern coast, the colonial government was weighing up other strategic options and still waging war in the settled districts. Just as some of the men formerly associated with Robertson joined Robinson in the largely uncolonised south, so too did some of Robertson's former rovers join Jorgenson's operations in the contested interior.

On 7 January 1830, the same day he sent Kickerterpoller to Hobart, Robertson dispatched four of his rovers to Oatlands.[32] The small party included the young Aboriginal man Jack. Within a week they had arrived at Oatlands, and were sent into the field under the command of Constable William Wilson at Jorgenson's orders.[33] Their excursion was relatively short and uneventful. When the report of the mission reached Hobart, the Colonial Secretary even annotated it for Arthur that 'There is nothing in this report deserving of notice'.

But the same day the Colonial Secretary forwarded another report to Arthur. 'The parts of this Report which I have marked with pencil,' he noted, 'appear to me well deserving of notice.'[34] It detailed a mission conducted over the turn of the new year. This concerned operations in the highland lakes area by a party headed by Richard Tyrrell.[35] The first of the Colonial Secretary's annotations concerned a report by Tyrrell of 'a number of native huts: some so large that one would easily shelter sixty persons'. The Colonial Secretary underlined the text, as one of the government's key reconnaissance questions concerned the size of the island's Aboriginal population. Robinson's mission similarly sought to answer that question in relation to the under-settled districts. Yet there was more of interest about these huts that the Colonial Secretary thought worth the Lieutenant Governor's notice:

> Some of them, by their appearance, could not have been constructed more than six days. On the inside of the Bark within the huts were drawn striking likenesses of Kangaroo, Dogs, several men in the attitude of fighting, and the moon.

About a month later the Aborigines Committee received a similar report detailing imagery found on trees and within huts, from a convict servant named Francis Browne, who had also served on parties pursuing Aboriginal people on the east coast.[36] Browne described a series of 'hieroglyphical representations (drawn with Charcoal) of Men & animals' and even drew pictures of some of the images as he recollected them.[37] One of them, he noted, bore a striking resemblance to the broad arrow that was stamped on colonial government property. When Frankland learned of such images, he made a representation to

Arthur proposing to use pictures to help communicate with Aboriginal people.[38] Reportedly, some pictures were subsequently painted, albeit with a slim documentary trail suggestive of relative strategic insignificance.[39]

But drawings were not the only marks Aboriginal people made on the landscape of Van Diemen's Land, and Tyrrell's mission encountered a number of other examples. At 'Native Corners' the expedition found many spears 'that had been thrown at trees', and came to the conclusion that this was a place where 'the natives is [sic] here frequently practicing the Spear Exercise'. This did not particularly attract the Colonial Secretary's attention, nor the 'fresh fires' or the site where the group 'found one spear and seven waddies', or more weapons near a butchered kangaroo: 'one spear twelve feet long, and one waddy, the largest I have even seen', according to Tyrrell. Of more interest was the party's observation of 'a pile of Stones most curiously arranged', which they 'were induced to remove'. Digging underneath, the rovers discovered 'the head of a woman, carefully wrapped in fine grass, and the whole remains of a child'. The party 'took the head with us'.

Burial customs were also revealed through the correspondence to the Aborigines Committee. Browne, for instance, described quite a different practice on the east coast:

> The Blacks appear to burn their dead. I am credibly informed, that when one of their companions is killed, or dies, they put the Body, into a hollow tree, and pile a quantity of Brush Wood round it, to which they set fire on their next visit; shouting and dancing round, as it burns.

But the war was disrupting Aboriginal cultural practices even while it provided the means and incentive for recording them. While Brown also detailed how 'the full of Every moon' was a significant time for 'a general Corroboree by Moon light', he also added that 'of late they change their rendezvous etc frequently, that it is not known where or how to find them'. This was the great irony of the newfound interest

ABORIGINAL AUXILIARIES

in studying, documenting and understanding Aboriginal people – their society was changing faster than it was being documented.

And it was also being effaced from the landscape. Shortly after exhuming the woman's remains and that of the child, Tyrrell's party finally made contact with Aboriginal people near the highland lakes:

> we came suddenly up to the fire. We saw twelve Kangaroo roasting by the fire, and several dogs by it. To our astonishment we could only see two natives, although by their gestures and manner we easily knew that others were close by, but the Scrub was so high and heavy that we could devise no means for capturing any. I was thus reluctantly obliged to fire at the Two, and the ball struck one of them in the breast and he dropped down instantly and expired on the spot.

Beside the report, the Colonial Secretary again underlined a key phrase, and simply wrote a word in the margin: 'why?' Further down the page he also queried why they had put the dead man's body 'on a pile of wood ... and burned it'.

With his attention duly drawn to these key passages, Arthur thought Tyrrell 'might have made greater exertion to have captured the two natives in place of firing at them', and wanted Anstey to remind his men 'to act with the utmost possible humanity towards these wretched people'. But such platitudes were fairly light reprimands, and rare in the documentary record.[40]

Tyrrell wrote an earlier description of the event, which also ended up in the file that contained his formal report. This was a letter to Captain Vicary at Bothwell, who in turn forwarded it on to Hobart. 'Sir,' Vicary addressed the Colonial Secretary:

> I have the Honor to enclose a letter addressed to me by a person named Tyrrell stating his having killed One Native and Fourteen Dogs.[41]

It echoed Tyrrell's own words, who wrote that:

> I with Mr Espies Overseer followed them up and shot 14 Dogs
> One Native ten Miles the other side of Lake Eccho, this happened
> the 11th.⁴²

Mr Espie was one of the settlers who had earlier irritated Arthur by not adequately supporting the war effort. But by loaning his servant to the roving parties, Espie had certainly now joined the campaigning, even if prompted by personal attention from the Lieutenant Governor. The lowly 'person named Tyrrell' was doing the fighting, but a whole social hierarchy was supporting and watching him.

Amity and Animosity in the Midlands

While scouring in the hills a few days after Tyrrell's attack, Danvers had come to a spot where 'we found some spears from which circumstance we thought that the natives had lately been disturbed'.⁴³ This became another report which 'does not contain anything worthy of notice' for the Lieutenant Governor. Forwarding the reports of Danvers, Tyrrell and Wilson, Jorgenson suggested that if Tyrrell's party had 'been stronger, he might have done more good', a sentiment that the Colonial Secretary queried, but on which Arthur made no comment.⁴⁴

Aware that the roving parties could still be disbanded, in January 1830 Jorgenson provided a report on Aboriginal activity in the area to demonstrate how he was gradually learning to predict their movements. Providing information on the activities of Aboriginal people in the Clyde area, Jorgenson described one stock-keeper fleeing before a group, who was saved when a 'Shepherd most providentially fired at a kangaroo' nearby, clearly scaring them away.⁴⁵ He also described a bloodier incident in greater detail, capturing the sorts of exchanges also taking place within the Oatlands district:

> On Saturday afternoon the 2nd of January, Fisher's hut on the
> Big Lagoon near Oatlands was attacked by a hostile tribe of
> the Aborigines. One of Fisher's men was dangerously wounded
> by a Spear, but he had sufficient strength to extricate it. At that

moment a stout native came up saying 'Give me that Spear you white _____: you die!' The man, although wounded, and weak from loss of blood, had sufficient strength of mind and courage to thrust the Spear into the Black man: the latter staggered and was assisted by some other Blacks in getting away. The wounded man, according to Dr Hudspeth's report, cannot live many days longer, and if possible, will be removed to the Hobarton Hospital.

Jorgenson continued his list of robberies, attacks and 'great ravages amongst the sheep', but also noted that these 'movements on the part of the natives have in great measure been anticipated'. While the Colonial Secretary made no comment on Jorgenson's self-confessed prescience, he nonetheless considered that 'This Report detailing various outrages of the Aborigines is worthy of the perusal of Your Excellency.'

As the senior officials read and corresponded, the missions continued. But the parties were now tired. 'Danvers as well as Tyrrell look like Two Skeletons,' Jorgenson said, and Peter Scott's men 'are all barefooted and ragged'. Jorgenson gave Danvers some rest, while the others were mostly sent out shortly after their return to Oatlands. Tyrrell's party was, for instance, preparing to head towards the Ouse River, now augmented with what Jorgenson described as 'the Black boy lately sent me from Richmond'. But down in Hobart, the day after Jorgenson mentioned this, the Colonial Secretary wrote to Anstey with a different plan in store for Jack and Mungo:

> I am directed by the Lt Governor to request, that you will cause two aboriginal lads who are at present attached to the parties under Mr Gilbert Robertson and Jorgen Jorgenson to be immediately withdrawn ... for the purpose of being restored to their distressed relatives under the care of Mr G. A. Robinson at the Aboriginal Establishmt.[46]

But the Lieutenant Governor met with a remarkable piece of insubordination. Jorgenson explained the situation to Anstey in his reply to this instruction:

> I communicated on Saturday last to Jack, the Black Guide, (lately arrived from Mr Gilbert Robertson's parties) that it was necessary he should proceed to Hobarton there to join his relations. He flatly refused to leave his party, stating that his father was killed, and that his mother lived with a white man. He said he could and would trace the Blacks, and frankly confessed (how true I know not) that he had often been on the traces of the Aborigines, but did not choose to trace them as he had on several occasions been severely beaten, but if he was not beaten he would trace the Natives with great fidelity.[47]

Jorgenson explained that Mungo was still out in the field, and that Jack had gone out with one of the parties. 'This may perhaps be considered deserving of perusal,' the Colonial Secretary noted for the Lieutenant Governor.

A few days later the Colonial Secretary learned of another Aboriginal person being attached to an expedition. John Batman, ranging throughout the east midlands and east coast in January, acquired 'an Aborigine Native, brought up by James Cox Esqr ... by permission of Mr Cox'.[48] This elicited little official notice. Instead it was changes in Aboriginal behaviour that probably attracted most attention, like the fact that the Aboriginal people seemed to use 'decoy' fires to distract the rovers, had 'forsaken their old hunting grounds and other places they used to resort', and perhaps most worryingly had stolen 'Ammunition, and Two Guns'. Such things probably prompted the Colonial Secretary's written reaction to Batman's letter, summarising things for the Lieutenant Governor. 'There is little in this report deserving of notice,' he wrote, 'except that it tends to confirm the opinion which I had formed of the great intelligence & sagacity of the Natives.'

Among his travels, Batman also tracked an Aboriginal group but 'considered I could not follow them' when they were spotted in territory 'where Martial Law does not exist', and so headed in another direction. Arthur disagreed with this decision. He annotated the report, mentioning that he had an 'earnest desire still to conciliate' if communication was possible, but also declaring that Batman 'under the circumstances he states, may follow the natives into the Territory where Martial Law does not extend'. The message was clear that hot pursuit trumped technical legality. Batman need not fear prosecution for engagements beyond the line of martial law.

The Colonial Secretary duly conveyed to Anstey the Lieutenant Governor's quiet but tacit support for roving beyond the designated settled districts as limited by martial law.[49] Moreover, he did it within days of Robinson's departure for his ostensibly conciliatory mission to Port Davey. Few coincidences revealed how much diplomacy and warfare were not mutually exclusive options, and how the government publicised some measures and was discreet in others. The divergence highlights that while conciliation was an aspiration, clearance and capture were still the main policy objectives, and the law of the land was no barrier.

CHAPTER NINE

Pushing Further while Debating Peace

1830, Summer
Western Front

From Hills to Highlands

During late January 1830, Sam Robinson led his rangers through the southern midlands.[1] Departing Oatlands on 18 January, they headed towards the Jordan River, 'but saw nothing of the Natives' on their first day out, and nothing again on the second day as they travelled towards the area known as 'the Hunting Grounds'. The same continued as they moved further south into some hills, scouring as they went, making for 'the Dromedary Hill' and then 'the Black Hill', tracking the settled areas a little north of Hobart. The party then turned 'in a Direction of Jerusalem' to the east, in the Coal River Valley, before heading north again towards Oatlands. It was a typical expedition, crossing ranges and valleys, scouring those areas 'much frequented by the Natives'.

In the Coal River Valley the party came across a stock hut solely occupied by 'a Boy about 16 years old'. This lad recently heard that Aboriginal people were in the area. Because 'the Boy had neither Fire Arms, nor Ammunition and no one but himself', Sam Robinson explained, the armed rangers spent a day and a night at the hut.

Two other servants nominally stationed at the same hut had the only guns, and they were out with the livestock, leaving the boy inadequately protected. Sam Robinson recognised it was the sort of situation when huts were often attacked and therefore hoped to ambush some Aboriginal assailants. But no raid came, so the following day the party continued. As they headed further north they met a man who 'reported he had been chased by the Natives on Saturday', but 'seemed to prevaricate in his Story' too much for the party to divert its mission. That afternoon, on 25 January, they again reached Oatlands. The report of the expedition was annotated 'Nothing worth notice'.

Sam Robinson's return to Oatlands did align with things that were noteworthy. It was the same day that Jorgenson explained Jack's refusal to go to the Bruny Island Establishment, as well as the renewed push into the highlands. In late January Anstey and Jorgenson planned a coordinated operation beyond the western part of the line of martial law. The neat distinction between settled districts and nominal Aboriginal refuge territory was getting decidedly blurred. Numerous colonial agents were pushing beyond the limits of martial law, increasingly guided by Aboriginal people and with centralised governmental acquiescence and orchestration. As part of this wider strategic push, three parties of Jorgenson's rangers headed to Lake Fergus.

Operation Lake Fergus

The Lake Fergus operation was designed to address several concerns. It was ostensibly a reaction to Aboriginal incursions. They, Jorgenson asserted, seemed to have 'changed the system of warfare and depredations which they have for some length of time past carried on against the White Colonists'.[2] The regularity with which Aboriginal groups raided huts, rather than just attacking isolated stockmen, might have indicated a new dependence on the provisions of the colony. Citing 'numerous reports transmitted to Mr Anstey', which provided 'strong and decided proofs', Jorgenson asserted:

> instead of resorting to their usual mode for obtaining subsistence, they had closed in upon the settlements, robbing the huts of flour and other provisions, in very large quantities, thus in fact that food which was formerly disregarded by them, had now become to them actual necessaries of life, scarcely to be dispensed with. Flour and Sugar seemed to be the Chief articles sought by them.

It was certainly plausible that ongoing colonial expansion, military harrying and territorial scouring had pushed some Aboriginal people out of their regular hunting grounds, and that raiding was potentially necessary. It is also probable that economic sabotage was a strategy adopted to contest colonial occupation. Either way, Anstey and Jorgenson certainly saw the recent aggressions as a shifting phenomenon, one that matches Batman's comments about the same time. Aboriginal people had not been seen about the highland lakes in recent weeks, which was very unusual. It was at least worth checking out.

Assessing 'the number and strength of the Aborigines to the Westward of the River Ouse', exclusive of 'Blacks at Cape Grimm, the Western coast, and Port Davy', was the core mission objective. Jorgenson was clearly frustrated by 'the delusion kept up by the public prints, limiting the number of the Aborigines of this island to about two hundred or three hundred'. He suspected that attacks, when made long distances apart, were not necessarily the same group, even if they appeared to be in succession. He recognised that the newspaper reportage could create false realities, turning a weird mix of reality, rumour and retrospection into narrative structures. Like Clark's desire to write in to set the record straight, this was another indicator that the war as it appeared in the newspaper could be quite different from the one fought on the ground.

A related concern was determining a firmer sense of the demographic profile of Aboriginal Van Diemen's Land. If they had indeed concentrated within the settled districts, it could be a worryingly new development, indicative of wider strategic alignments. That 'women and children were also carefully concealed out of harms way' in so many attacks exacerbated the difficulties in coming to sensible population figures, but also highlights that attacks were deliberate acts of warfare, not mere incidental engagements. Taking this logic a step further, Jorgenson wanted to learn whether the tribes 'have suspended among themselves their mutual jealousies and animosities, and directed all their hostile intentions, movements, and operations, against the white inhabitants'.

Jorgenson and Anstey were concerned that the increased hostilities of the summer may have reflected a new confederation of tribes engaged in coordinated warfare against the colony.

Reconnaissance aside, going to Lake Fergus was also an opportunity to start turning government policy away from partition and containment. The notion of dividing the colony into settled districts and areas of 'native liberty' had, Jorgenson intimated, essentially failed to restrain Aboriginal people. Explaining his mission to Anstey – undoubtedly knowing that it would be forwarded to the Colonial Secretary and thereby Arthur – Jorgenson noted that 'doubts had arisen' about a policy that provided a secure base for launching 'murders and depredations'. Whose doubts he did not say, although it was relatively unlikely they were his alone.

The Lake Fergus incursion beyond the line of demarcation was, therefore, an expression of the 'established principle that an invading enemy may, even in the most legitimate warfare, be attacked and followed into the Country of a neutral power, should the invading enemy seek refuge within such territory'. It was one thing to fight Aboriginal people within the settled districts to discourage their return, but it was another thing for 'the humanity of Government' to become an encumbrance to the colony's combatants.

Three parties were readied. Each was to head to Lake Fergus by a different route, aiming to arrive at the lake on the same day. After meeting up, the parties then intended to shift from reconnaissance to offensive manoeuvres, and 'fall down along the River Ouse', which Jorgenson characterised as 'the greatest stronghold of the Aborigines of this island'. Danvers, 'the most active Leader in the Colony', was to take Jorgenson, 'a Black guide' and six men. Tyrrell, also 'accompanied by an able black guide', and six more men were 'to penetrate from Mr Espie's hut'. The third party, led by Peter Scott, was redeployed before the operation to deal with a reported Aboriginal sighting, and an incident where 'a black woman had been captured'. Nonetheless, in early February, 15 men departed Oatlands in two teams led by Tyrrell and Danvers, intending to regroup on 14 February at Lake Fergus, allowing a few extra days in case of mishap.

A few days after Tyrrell's party headed out, Danvers' team headed to Bothwell.[3] They arrived in the evening, and 'learned that Capt Clark's and Piper's huts, had on the preceding Thursday been robbed by the Aborigines'. This was particularly remarkable because, as Jorgenson knew, Clark's property was well defended. He decided to investigate further, especially because Vicary advised that 'a small Tribe of Aborigines were continually ranging between the Blue Hill, Mr Howell's hut on the Shannon, and Captain Clark's farm.'

While Jorgenson gathered rations from the Bothwell storehouse, Mungo explored the town. His reactions to the settlement went unrecorded, excepting for one incident. As Jorgenson wrote:

> for the first time in his life [Mungo] saw a monkey, and on seeing it, some indescribable emotions of wonder and disgust, seemed to cross his countenance. Not understanding English perfectly, and not being able to distinguish clearly between the sounds of 'Mungo' and 'Monky' [sic] – he began to imagine that we compared him to the latter creature, and called him by the name. This gave him great offence, and we avoided calling him Mungo ever since.

To his face they called him Jack, like the other guide, but to make their reports intelligible they persisted in using Mungo. This was likely intended to prevent confusion with the guide attached to Tyrrell's party, and perhaps also because it was Anstey who had named him Mungo and who read the reports. Nonetheless, it was a remarkably sympathetic act on the part of the rangers.

A Potential Reconciliation

When the rangers finally reached Clark's, the captain-turned-farmer confirmed the attack happened on Thursday 4 February 1830, a few days before the rangers left Oatlands. As Clark described it to Jorgenson:

> a small Tribe attacked Piper's hut on a farm closely adjoining Capt Clark's farm, and the huts not above 500 or 600 yards apart, Capt Clark, with two armed men lost no time in proceeding to Piper's assistance. After Capt Clark had arrived at Piper's hut, some of the Blacks came to the Captain's hut, and robbed it. Two or three went up to the principal dwelling [and] forced Mrs Clark and one of the Servant maids to fly across the fields to Piper's, whilst another servant maid with a child in her arms, came to the outer door near the kitchen. A stout black man appeared, and the woman said 'Do not kill me and my babe.' The man replied – 'No I'll not kill you, but come along with me.' The woman said 'I cannot go with you, for there are four or five gentlemen in that room (pointing to the parlour) who I must attend upon,' and then she rattled about a parcel of plates, knives, and forks, as if she was very busy in her attendance.

The woman was left unharmed, and became a minor colonial celebrity. When the *Hobart Town Courier* carried the story a bit over a week after the event, the man had become a 'chief':

> though at first disposed to be hostile, [he] was pacified by the adroitness of a female servant, who with a child in her arms, came out to him with a curtsey, which induced the black to come forward and shake hands in a friendly manner, and after receiving a few cakes peaceably to retire.[4]

Jorgenson's take on the event was that the man was compelled to leave the woman alone by the necessity of raiding quickly, the proximity of armed men, and the apparent nearness of several gentlemen in an adjacent room. He thought the invitation to the woman was suspect at best, and may have led to her death. Either way, he argued that 'the subsequent outrages perpetrated by the Aborigines sufficiently prove that their hostile determination' was continuing.

Jorgenson gave this incident particular attention when writing up his report because he knew it had attracted the Lieutenant Governor's notice and caused a new policy development. With the woman and child ostensibly spared, Clark was 'inclined strongly to the belief that the Aborigines were not adverse; in future, to pursue towards the whites a system of humanity and conciliation'. Vicary notified Arthur of this 'conduct of the Natives', leading the Lieutenant Governor to think 'that a very favorable opening has presented itself for conciliating that unfortunate race of beings'.[5] As Arthur informed Vicary:

> with the view of further conciliation, directions have been given to send Twenty five Blankets and some Tea and Sugar to the Commissariat Store at Bothwell for distribution among the Natives. The Above Articles, together with some Flour and Potatoes, would seem to His Excellency to be all that the Natives are likely to wish for.[6]

Arthur was clearly hoping to use Clark's farm as a ration station like he had successfully done at Bruny Island.

In his first government order for the year, Arthur officially adopted the view that 'a reconciliation may be opening'.[7] This view was predicated on the 'moderation ... with which a mob of natives have in one instance lately conducted themselves in the neighbourhood of Bothwell'. Arthur promised settlers a 'handsome reward' and convicts 'an immediate pardon' if they could 'effect a successful intercourse with any tribe'. But while enjoining the colonists to attempt diplomacy, and treat captive or vulnerable Aboriginal people with 'tenderness' – especially 'women and children' – the government order was also a realistic reflection of the current situation. 'No opportunity should be lost to draw any Tribe into terms of conciliation,' the injunction concluded, 'and no effort should be spared to expel those who will not be conciliated.' It was good politics that gave the appearance of change while changing relatively little. If the peace failed, it would not be the government's fault.

With Mungo-Jack to Lake Fergus

Jorgenson, however, rejected the premise of such passive conciliation. 'I thought it my duty to afford the settlement some protection for a few days,' he stated. The rangers went a few miles on from Clark's farm to 'Mr Howell's on the Shannon'. Some of the party guarded the hut 'in a state of quietude', hoping to ambush an attack, while Danvers and Jorgenson 'searched the scrub and gullies' for signs of the Aboriginal people. On Friday 12 February the rangers continued their advance towards Lake Fergus, hoping to make their rendezvous with Tyrrell's team. They headed towards Patrick's Plains, using the 'unknown and unfrequented paths' and 'side creeks', where they thought they would be more likely to find Aboriginal people.

As they crossed one of these creeks, Mungo-Jack smelled smoke and roasting kangaroo. He alerted the rangers, and told them to hide near the water, because the people making the scent might come to drink after their meal. He also 'prohibited the use of Tobacco', warning that Aboriginal people 'could smell the smoke of it for a considerable distance'. The rangers were taking orders from their guide.

Eventually Mungo-Jack guided the party away from the creek. He led them 'over stony and rocky mountains' and then 'down to a thicket', instructing the rangers 'to be on the look out'. It was hard going, but Jorgenson was deeply impressed by Mungo-Jack's ability:

> We should never have thought of roving over these places, and the thicket or scrub would certainly have eluded our search. Although Mungo had never been here before, he forms a perfect conception of the places where the Aborigines are likely to shelter themselves.

Then:

> All at once, Mungo ran swiftly round the scrub, three of us followed him, and four remained on the other side with their pieces cocked, and their bayonets fixed. Mungo heard something in the scrub, and presently rushed out a native dog. On entering the scrub we found it to be a place where the natives found woods from which to make their spears and waddies, and from the prints of womens [sic] and children's feet in the ground, it was clear that this was a place of concealment for the Females and children, when the men went out on their predatory excursions. From the marks of the feet, it could only have been very recently that some Tribe had been here.

With Mungo-Jack on their side, the rangers were learning how to see the landscape in new ways. The tactical imbalances of bush pursuits were shifting, as Aboriginal people began to lose some of the advantages they had previously enjoyed.

In part this shift was not simply about the presence of Mungo-Jack, but rather one of attitude. Jorgenson may have wondered about a tribal confederation, but he also knew about continuing animosities and recognised that Mungo-Jack's enthusiasm for pursuit was 'particularly useful to us':

> [he] is at present infected with a deadly hatred and an ardent desire of revenge against the Big River Tribe. He belongs to the Tribe of Limaganny (Ben Lomon [sic] Tribe), and some of Mungo's nearest relations have been murdered by the Big River Tribe.

After searching the thicket, the rangers spent the night at a stock hut in Patrick's Plains. The next day they carefully traversed some of the plains, but knowing that they could be easily spotted in the treeless landscape, they stopped and waited until after nightfall. About an hour before midnight, when the moon rose, they continued and 'crossed the plains in stormy weather, and by an extraordinary and rapid march succeeded in getting in under the northern mountains by daybreak'. Exhausted, they lay beside a clutch of fallen logs for several hours, and were drenched by rain as they slept.

Awaking mid-morning they 'ascended the heights' taking in a magnificent view of Van Diemen's Land's many peaks. But they were unable to see any signs of fires, which may have provided an early concern, because they were looking for 'indications that Tyrrell's party, had arrived at, or was hovering over Lake Fergus'. Still, they proceeded with the mission, circuiting through plains and 'wooded hillocks' before making a direct northwesterly line for Lake Fergus. While crossing some of these plains the rangers found 'a spear greatly decayed', which seemed perplexing. As Jorgenson wrote:

> On asking Mungo what could have brought it there; he explained to us that this was the precise place where all the native Tribes met once every year for the purposes of general deliberation, and at the same time to display their warlike exhibitions in throwing the Spear and the Waddy: Mungo had been here with his Tribe last year, and it was only now that I learned that he had been all round Lake Fergus with his Tribe, but no farther in a Southern direction.

While the information about intertribal gatherings was notable, Jorgenson was not interested in local nomenclature. Closing in on the lake, the rangers encountered a river, and Jorgenson slavishly named it for Anstey. With a thinly veiled compliment, he noted in his report that Anstey River 'is fierce, rapid, and deep'.

But Lake Fergus proved immediately disappointing. As the rangers reached the lake, which was surrounded by hills and clear territory, they could see all around its shores. There were no Aboriginal people, and no signs of Tyrrell's team. They walked around it, just to be sure, but the site was deserted of people. Danvers' team was only one day later than initially planned. Hoping to alert Tyrrell to their location, the party 'lit a conflagration' and waited. Tyrrell failed to arrive.

On 16 February, two days after their planned rendezvous, the rangers departed. Guided by Mungo-Jack, the party climbed 'some very high, and rocky mountains', towards a fresh water source. He also led them 'to the native huts' that were nearby, but these had clearly been abandoned 'for <u>moons</u> past'. From here the colonial navigators took over, and the party wasted the remainder of the day searching out a lake inscribed on their map, which they failed to find. At the end of their fruitless search, the rangers 'encamped in a Gulley for the night'.

The next day they reached 'Mr Espie's hut', where the rangers heard of Tyrrell's team getting 'rations for ten days'. But they also 'learned that Twenty of Mr Espie's sheep had been speared on the preceding day'. Three of Espie's men 'were out in pursuit of the Aborigines who had been seen a few hours before over a fire roasting oppossums'. The rangers quickly forgot about Tyrrell:

> At daybreak we started and speedily got upon the traces of the natives, and Mungo pursued their tracks with an eagerness which can scarcely be accounted for unless being actuated by the most ardent desire of revenge. He led us over rocky and difficult summits, through Gullies, and on the edges of precipices. We crossed the River Ouse several times in deep places, and had to climb up almost perpendicular places of great height.

Astounded by Mungo-Jack's capacity to track Aboriginal people by footprints, small tufts of possum fur, or 'by fires which had dropped on the ground from firesticks', Jorgenson described how the party was very close behind their targets: 'We every moment fell in with their fires yet warm; one was still burning, we saw kangaroo speared which had been left hanging on the trees.' Fleeing fires and dropping their food, these Aboriginal people were clearly in full flight from the rangers.

Hobart's Humanitarians and an Extermination Debate

With each stock hut the rangers visited they learned of various 'outrages' perpetrated by Aboriginal people while they had been away at Lake

Fergus. They stopped at Thomson's hut for a few nights, using it as a base 'to rove about the heights'. But they were probably also slowed because eventually it was clear that 'Mungo had fallen ill'. Unable to continue close tracking, and with 'many alarming accounts of murders' coming in from various settlers and their servants, Jorgenson had to give up his pursuit. He also wanted to get information to Anstey, and to better orchestrate the movements of multiple parties out in pursuit in this immediate district, so he and Danvers headed to Bothwell.

'When I arrived at the Police Office,' Jorgenson later reported, 'Capt Vicary placed in my hands the Gazette of that day's date, containing the Lieutenant Governor's proclamation, promising a reward to any one who should be able, by some means or others to effect a proper understanding and reconciliation.' His mind immediately strayed to Mungo-Jack, and the propitious coincidence that this reward was being advertised just as the lad was demonstrating such enthusiasm for the colonial cause.

But Vicary also had another piece of news from Hobart, which amused Jorgenson. 'Capt Vicary also placed in my hands an address to Mr Davies, signed by a number of highly respectable and humane gentlemen in Hobarton.' The address, signed by Reverend Bedford and other members of the Aborigines Committee, promoted conciliation and prevailed upon 'resident settlers of similar humane feelings ... to adhere to a system of self-defence and not of wanton aggression'.[8]

Reading these sentiments of well-fed and safe urban gentlemen, Jorgenson admitted that 'a transient smile crossed the features of my face'. He probably recognised that they were projecting an image of the war at odds with reality, where bad servants caused and perpetuated the conflict, and that the committee itself held out the best hope for its peaceful end.

The address had been printed on page three of the 19 February *Colonial Times*, the day before Jorgenson and Danvers reached Bothwell. Vicary's attention may have lingered on this page because it also contained another letter from 'A Settler', which detailed a series of attacks by Aboriginal people in the Bothwell district.[9] It described an incident where, on Friday 12 February, 'the whole of Mr HOWELL's premises and property burned to the ground before his eyes' after being ignited by an Aboriginal man flinging a firestick upon the thatched roof. 'The rapidity of conflagration was such,' the settler wrote, 'that Mrs Howell and three small children escaped with difficulty from suffocation and destruction.' The family was apparently reduced to 'living under a break-wind', but at the time of writing had not yet received some blankets that Vicary had forwarded to them.

The settler also had another, similar tale. 'While writing this', he stated, 'a messenger from Mr SHERWIN' arrived with information that Sherwin's hut had also 'been burned to the ground'. Pointedly reacting to press reportage of Clark's female servant, the settler concluded that these events are 'very unfavourable omens of friendly terms with the blacks, and instead of opening an amicable alliance, in presenting them with sugar and sugar cakes, we would recommend more severe measures than has hitherto been adopted'.

Other news in the same paper described Aboriginal people having 'killed two men, one a man of colour', mentioned the remarkable story of Aboriginal people moving by torchlight through the night despite their reportedly traditional fear of darkness, the burial of another young spearing victim, and vague reports about two or three more servants killed in the Clyde district. At least one seven-man party went in pursuit after one of these raids, the newspaper noted, mentioning also that 'the report of several guns has been heard in the direction they had taken', conveying the immediacy of the conflict through the sound of gunfire in the hills.

The report about Sherwin's house proved both wrong and prophetic. Sherwin's property had not burned down. But, in the middle of the afternoon of Sunday 21 February, Sherwin's property was attacked. As he described it a few days later:

> I was sitting in the front Room when the Servant called out 'Fire – Fire – the Natives' – I immediately ran for Water, and to alarm the men who were in the Hut at the time – soon after which a Fire broke out from the back of the Men's hut – We then endeavoured to save the house, but, seeing this was impossible we began to get what things we could from the house.[10]

During the crisis, Sherwin saw various Aboriginal figures moving around the perimeter of the property, setting fire to fencing, while others directed the operation from a large rock. From this rock some of them yelled to the settlers: 'Parrawa Parrawa – Go away you white B__g_rs – What business have you here.' A series of moves and countermoves followed in a tense confrontation. These Aboriginal people disappeared shortly after Sherwin aimed to shoot.

Sherwin told his story to the Aborigines Committee in Hobart on 23 February, two days after the attack.[11] He asserted that the attackers were all young men, and from the 'Abyssinia Mob'. Arguing that 'the lives and property of every white inhabitant in the Colony are endangered', Sherwin suggested the colony deploy 'Sydney Natives' and 'blood hounds' to capture them. He also commented that he 'had heard' that 'decoy huts' filled with 'flour and Sugar strongly impregnated with poison' could work as a remedy against these sorts of attacks. Sherwin, the scribe noted, 'Conceives they must be captured or exterminated'.

The committee took evidence from two other settlers that day. George Espie, brother of the settler on the Clyde, described how Aboriginal people slaughtered sheep as a means of harming the colonists: 'none of the carcasses were used by the Natives for food,' he noted, 'nor were the Sheep touched after they had been speared'. They were clearly slaughtering the stock for effect, not for food. Espie too felt the war had reached 'such a crisis that no other remedy appears to me but their speedy capture or extermination'.[12] He recommended the deployment of 150 prisoners given promises of pardons for making certain capture quotas, but he also 'believes they would shoot more than they would capture'.

After Espie, the committee heard from John Sinclair Brodie, a settler on the upper Clyde who had survived four spear wounds received at the start of February when Aboriginal people raided his hut.[13] He survived, he stated, by running for the military hut which was within sight of his own. 'On a former occasion I gave them bread & to my knowledge my servants never ill treated them.' They were actuated by desire for 'our luxuries & comforts', he felt, 'not from motives of revenge & retaliation'. But he too argued 'that some very strong and decisive measures must be adopted either for their capture or extermination'.

Like Sherwin, he advocated the deployment of 'Sydney Blacks' to assist in their capture. 'The Country must either belong to the Blacks or the Whites', he argued, concluding that 'the assigned servants have become very much afraid of the Natives'.

The minutes were written up in full, although with some details excluded from the official testimony. The decoy huts were included, for instance, but the idea of using poisoned flour and sugar was discreetly omitted from the official record. This doctoring of evidence – most likely by Charles Arthur, the committee's secretary and the Lieutenant Governor's nephew – was one of a number of ways by which Arthur seems to have managed the formal record and public perception of the Vandemonian War.

Committee Recommendations and Settlers Militant

Political machinations aside, after hearing from Sherwin, Espie and Brodie on 23 February the Aborigines Committee offered Arthur three strongly recommended 'measures':

> 1st That Sydney Natives be obtained from N.S. Wales to trace the Aborigines & thereby effect their capture. 2nd That pecuniary rewards be offered for each Native captured. 3rd That Tickets of Leave should be granted to Prisoners of good character for the capture of some given number of Natives.[14]

These suggestions were simply extensions of the systems currently in place with the roving parties. Two days after the committee took evidence from the settlers of the Clyde, Arthur issued a second government order.[15] 'The destruction of the whole of Mr Sherwin's properties on the Clyde', 'threats and vindictive feeling', and 'other outrages' became official facts that 'demand an instant simultaneous and energetic proceeding on the part of the settlers'.

But the government order also provided for an incentive scheme to get the settlers to act 'with vigour and perseverance' for the protection of themselves and the colonial community:

to stimulate them to increased activity, the Lieutenant Governor has directed that a reward of five pounds shall be given for every adult Aboriginal native, and two pounds for every child who shall be captured and delivered alive at any of the Police stations.

Such rewards were a common part of the Vandemonian economy. These bounties for Aboriginal captives had precedents in rewards for the capture of bushrangers and runaway convicts. But while this reflected a new policy initiative, it was not the sum of the government injunction. Arthur also announced that he would soon 'make a tour' to examine the implementation of defensive measures which he 'expects to be universally adopted'. Moreover, the order was transparently addressing a misconception, carried 'out of the colony', that Aboriginal people constituted a militarily capable 'horde of savages', which Arthur asserted was clearly at odds with the reality of 'an inconsiderable number of a very feeble race, not possessing physical strength, and quite undistinguished by personal courage'. This sentiment served to modify perceptions of the war abroad, while working as another jab at settlers who left themselves 'almost defenceless'. He closed the order by reiterating calls for humane treatment of Aboriginal people 'consistent with the overruling necessity of expelling them from the settled districts'.

Although Arthur had initially delegated oversight of conciliation to a committee, two other government notices helped give a public impression that he was becoming increasingly involved.[16] One of them advised that Arthur lent a room at Government House for the Aborigines Committee, and requested future correspondence 'be addressed to Charles Arthur'. The other announced that the committee would meet 'every Tuesday at Government-house'.

His close management of conflict operations continued. On 25 February, after writing the government order, Arthur instructed the Colonial Secretary to forward 'a Circular to all the Police Magistrates', drawing their attention to the new order.[17] As he wrote:

[success] depends upon their exertions in their Districts, by ascertaining at all the remote Stations what measures for defence

are taken; whether the Settlers are arming all their Sons who are able to carry a Gun and further, whether any effort is making for surprising and securing the natives.

The Lieutenant Governor was advocating for the settlers of Van Diemen's Land to become militant: armed, active and ready to turn to paramilitary duties when required. While the bounty was new, Arthur's tone increasingly echoed his early plans for a local militia.

Further highlighting this growing government-sponsored settler-militarism, the next day Arthur followed up with the Colonial Secretary about sending a specific letter to Vicary. Ordering 'a working party from Bothwell ... to render every possible assistance to Mr Howells in erecting a shelter for his family', Arthur also took the opportunity to again impress upon the police magistrate the necessity of the settlers becoming militant:

> it is in vain for the Settlers to expect that the Government alone can afford them protection, and that the most strenuous efforts must be made by the Colonists themselves.[18]

Also that day, Arthur instructed the Colonial Secretary to forward a notice to the government printer about a new 'Act to facilitate the apprehension of felons or other offenders illegally at large'.[19] It was a short Act, allowing settlers or their servants to 'apprehend without a Warrant' anybody reasonably suspected of being 'a Transported Felon or other Offender then illegally at Large'. While seemingly directed at convicts, the Act was also applicable to the capture of Aboriginal people.

The timing of the announcement of this new law is also telling. It was included in the *Hobart Town Courier* along with the government order about bounties for Aboriginal captives, and is another example of the way that the politics of the war infected many other elements of government business.

The publication of these notices is anything but coincidental, and to read them in isolation would be wilfully naive. They were highly collaborative elements of a government agenda to motivate frontier settlers to arm themselves and act with fortitude, while also placating humanitarian qualms in Hobart and beyond. They also serve as hints of a regime focused on the important business of protecting the Lieutenant Governor's reputation. Arthur steered the committee away from the present to the past, distracting generations of historians in the process.

CHAPTER TEN

Roving Still

1830, Autumn
Southwest and Northeast

A Political Twist

On the first Tuesday in March 1830 the Aborigines Committee met in Government House.[1] The new Archdeacon, Reverend Brompton, was elected chair after being appointed to the committee by Arthur. The new member coincided with a shift in focus, turning the committee from a mainly advisory body into an investigative one.

The Lieutenant Governor was, the minutes detailed, 'anxious to obtain a detailed account of the rise & progress of the hostility displayed by the Natives'. Particularly interested in the situation 'previous to his assumption of the Government', Arthur was clearly setting up a fact-finding mission largely designed to deflect blame into a deeper past. The committee obliged. A preliminary conclusion was recorded that, while generally treated well by colonists, the Aboriginal people of Van Diemen's Land had 'a lurking spirit of cruelty & mischievous craft in the native character' that was evident well before Arthur arrived. This, the committee suggested, was the reason for their various 'acts of mischief and barbarity'. But the committee also sought further proofs, so they developed a nine-point questionnaire to put to various settlers. Eight of the questions pertained to the cause and history of Aboriginal enmity and hostilities, only one to the prospects for peace or protective measures.

Over subsequent weeks, the committee quizzed various men in the colony, starting the following day with the former roving party leader Gilbert Robertson. Their ultimate conclusions strayed little from their preliminary thinking. The committee submitted a report of their findings to Arthur, which cast his government as humane and measured in its response to the situation.[2] The committee's ostensibly impartial fact-finding mission became the first official history of the Vandemonian War. With politically charged arguments predicated on selectively recorded evidence, it established key parameters for subsequent versions of the conflict.

While the Aborigines Committee came to represent Arthur's government as humane – just as he had probably hoped – it was in sharp contrast to his ongoing and active role in the war. In fact, on the same Tuesday that the Aborigines Committee met, the Lieutenant Governor personally instructed the Colonial Secretary about some war-related minutiae. Some of this was aimed at helping Sherwin, the man whose house fire was the catalyst for the introduction of cash bounties for Aboriginal captives.[3] Arthur wanted 'to afford him the assistance' for three months of two sawyers, two stone masons, and a 'Joiner or Carpenter' to help rebuild his house. A blacksmith would also be useful, Arthur noted, before reminding the Colonial Secretary that Sherwin was owed two assigned servants. Like Howell before him, Sherwin was compensated for Aboriginal attacks. For these two settler families, the apparatus of the convict state worked to put right some of the damage done by Aboriginal people, as it had for many before them.

But any theoretical line between home front and frontier was thin. Take, for instance, John Sherwin Junior, who was preparing 'to go out with a party' in retribution for the attack on his family's house.[4] For some of that Tuesday the Lieutenant Governor helped arrange for three convicts to be attached to the expedition. The bounty system certainly 'augmented' military options and roving parties, but it did not replace them.

While the Aborigines Committee deliberated at Government House, out in the field, operations continued under the supervision of government. On 4 March 1830 news reached Hobart that 'some of the native women who were under the charge of Mr Robinson, this morning made their escape into the Bush'.[5] The Lieutenant Governor wanted parties to attempt to recapture them without violence. But he was also still active in orchestrating a larger war strategy.

The same day, the Colonial Secretary informed the police magistrates of Richmond and Oatlands to expect trouble. 'Fires of the Aborigines, have been observed ... and sticks stuck in the ground at regular intervals have been found'. As Danvers had learned, such sticks indicated directions of movement.[6] They were heading east. The following week the police magistrate of Richmond was given another prompt to 'pay every possible attention to the protection of your Station', and the police magistrate of New Norfolk was told that 'a strong roving party, in charge of Mr Sherwin's son', was operating near the Clyde River.[7]

Ranger Roving Continues

Jorgenson was also busy in the area around the Clyde River, although his parties left an unusually slim documentary trail during February and March. Having reported his Lake Fergus expedition, he detailed the dispositions of his forces, but some of this was contingent upon Tyrrell, who had still not returned.[8] When he did, he was supposed to join Danvers, who was 'sent over the Big River to rove on both sides'.

While the Aborigines Committee was established to deflect attention from conflict in the interior, the increasing politicisation of the war provided opportunities for some colonists, which in turn enhanced the public's awareness of the roving parties. In response to the recent attacks in their district, 32 settlers of the Clyde area petitioned Arthur for more protection, asserted that 'conciliatory measures will be ineffectual', and requested reduced taxation.[9] When the Colonial Secretary acknowledged receipt of the petition, the leader shared it with the press. Among the signatories were Sherwin, Howell and Brodie, revealing a complex interplay between government advisors and loyal critics of government policy.

Clearly hoping to further the cause of increased force in the Clyde, one anonymous writer parodied the roving parties and advocated that bloodhounds should be used instead.[10] This elicited a response from 'A Settler', who called the anonymous writer 'ignorant', before detailing some of the activities of two of Jorgenson's parties, which both 'rendered the greatest services to the community'.[11] This 'Settler' described the parties 'as the best disciplined regular troops of the line', before giving more details about their recent operations:

> Since the 17th February last, John Danvers and his party have pursued the Aborigines with the most indefatigable perseverance, he has not suffered them to rest any where; he has driven them from their places of rest and their food, prevented them from robbing the stock huts, and killing the whites. When the Aborigines made their appearance at Mr. Young's on the Big River, and were repulsed by Mr. Young and his people, Danvers came up an hour after, having driven them down the side of the Big River. Without stopping at Mr. Young's, he immediately went in pursuit, followed the blacks at death's door, and in crossing the Derwent in hot pursuit, Mungo, the black guide, fell off the tree on which the party crossed, and would infallibly have drowned (as he had his knapsack over his shoulders), had not Danvers jumped into the river, and disengaged the knapsack from his shoulders, but in so doing Danvers had nearly shared a similar fate, for although he is an expert swimmer, his knapsack was very heavy.

While this description reveals Danvers broadly following the operations detailed by Jorgenson, it also captures a growing closeness between the men and Mungo-Jack. The image of a roving party leader diving into a river to save a guide was a long way from the soldiers shooting at Boomer in the same district just a year earlier.

'Settler' also noted that the expedition had a close encounter. Mungo-Jack guided the rangers 'on the native fires':

> the party came within 200 yards of a tribe, then in the act of cooking kangaroo. The party proceeded along a gully through a scrub, but when approaching the tribe, two blacks watching on the hills on both sides of the gully, gave the alarm, and the tribe fled. Some of their blankets, arms, and other things were taken.

The other party that 'Settler' described had more luck. This was led by Peter Scott, a relatively new addition to Jorgenson's rangers. It was the second encounter in as many days, at least according to the reports of newspaper correspondents. One account described Scott's party arriving at Espie's house on 8 March, just in time to meet some sawyers who had been accosted 'and chased':[12]

> [Scott], immediately accompanying corporal Jackson of the 63d [sic], went in pursuit and came upon the Natives, whilst in the act of cooking kangaroo. The Party, in endeavouring to cross the bed of a creek which divided them from the Blacks, were discovered, and they immediately discharged their pieces at them, and followed so quickly, that the Natives left behind them a number of spears, 13 blankets and other things. The party killed one dog, and must have wounded several of the Natives as blood could be traced for a considerable distance.

Both Jackson and Scott attracted enthusiastic praise 'for their perseverance on this occasion'. As 'Settler' mentioned, Scott had 'several times come up with the Aborigines', and one of these encounters occurred the following day when Scott's men attacked another Aboriginal camp:

> At sun-set he came on their fires, and managed to get through a scrub, on hands and feet, within forty yards of them. At that moment, when he thought himself certain of capturing some

of them, his party was assailed by a number of ferocious dogs, and seeing that the tribe was about to decamp, he had no other recourse left than firing a volley among them. When disengaged from the dogs he set out in pursuit, but coming on dark he lost the tracts [sic] of the Aborigines, the traces however of blood were seen for a considerable distance, which left no doubt that numbers had been wounded.[13]

The takings from this tribe included '15 blankets, 63 waddies, a number of spears' and various colonial implements like coffee-pots and a teapot. With 'sufficient parties', the writer claimed, 'the Aborigines will not be able to reign many months'.

The exact movements of the rangers over these and coming weeks are a little unclear, perhaps because Jorgenson was distracted by the new politicisation of his missions. On a visit to Hobart in March, he penned a lengthy report that was likely in response to rumours that the roving parties were to be abandoned. A Commissariat Office notice of 25 March called the public to put in their receipts if they had furnished Robertson or Jorgenson's parties with rations before 24 April, which likely gave Jorgenson the impression that his parties were going to be disbanded like Robertson's had been.[14] In his report, therefore, Jorgenson defended the conduct of the rangers and called for the full implementation of his earlier suggestions to coordinate the parties across the island.[15] He advocated 'sending into the Bush an adequate and imposing force as that none of the Tribes should dare to invade the settled districts', pointed out that his roving parties were 'becoming more perfect' with each mission, and that Mungo-Jack could become 'a negotiator' in due time.

Internecine Tensions and Conciliatory Opportunities

Mungo-Jack was not the only prospective negotiator in the colony. While Jorgenson finished his report in Hobart, Robinson's mission in the south was chasing after some Port Davey people. These were, Robinson diarised, 'poor forlorn creatures, who were fleeing before my approach as clouds fly before the tempest'.[16]

But through the agency of his Aboriginal companions, Robinson eventually managed to meet two of the Port Davey tribe. After being introduced by 'the young woman accompanying me who belonged to their tribe', Robinson was well received, and later spent the evening in the tribe's company. There was 'great conviviality, singing and dancing until a late hour, making the woods to echo with their song'. In the far south, away from the Vandemonian War in the interior, the hoped-for conciliatory overtures were showing signs of success, at least as Robinson recorded it. He even named the place Friendly River.

Nonetheless, the continued enmity between tribal groups troubled Robinson.[17] While he made overtures about coming 'to do them good', he also noticed the way that a woman had 'pointed out the knapsack that contained three pistols' among his baggage. The mission was effectively making contact, but the nature of the relationship was still being worked out. Far from the main theatres of conflict, ancient tensions and colonial armaments reveal the ways that the diplomatic expedition was also experienced as a threatening incursion. Woorrady, one of the Aboriginal men attached to the expedition, thought the Port Davey people 'were no good and he wanted them sent to Hobart Town'.

Back in Hobart, Robinson was being involved in another attempted diplomatic mission. A week and a half earlier, on 16 March, the Lieutenant Governor approved a recommendation from the Aborigines Committee:

> that the black Native women, now captive in Hobart Town, should be permitted to join their Tribe on the northern side of the Island with the view of endeavouring to conciliate, by pointing out the kind treatment they have experienced from the Whites.[18]

These women had 'been living at Mr Robinson's', and were sent to Launceston in the custody of Charles Stirling, a convict servant who 'resided with them' at the Robinson residence.

While these diplomatic missions were represented as a change in direction, the prosecution of the war continued as before. On 16 March, Captain Vicary reported to Hobart that he was unable to provide 'a Military Party' to escort one of the government surveyors, because his forces were already fully deployed to deal with 'the present disturbed state of the District'.[19] Moreover, diplomatic endeavours tended to be directed through existing operational mechanisms. When these Aboriginal women arrived in Launceston on 26 March 'to be set at liberty and allowed to return back to their former haunts', as one report put it, 'Mr Batman happened to be in Town to meet His Excellency, and prevailed upon the Commandant to keep them until the Lieutenant Governor arrives'.[20]

The Roving Parties Are Nominally Decentralised

Arthur's departure from Hobart was observed in the press. The *Colonial Times* mentioned that he left 'at an early hour' and was 'attended by a considerable retinue'.[21] The report mostly focused on the fact that Archdeacon Brompton also travelled with Arthur, and that they expected to dine with Anstey en route to Launceston. Before leaving Hobart, Arthur arranged for the smooth operation of government in his absence. The Colonial Secretary was authorised to deal with 'business of the Government of ordinary occurrence', while an itinerary ensured that more pressing business could be sent by the quickest route to the Lieutenant Governor if needed.[22] The town adjutant was 'directed to dispatch Troopers whenever necessary' to ensure the smooth and safe movement of such important intelligence.

On schedule, the party reached Anstey's homestead Anstey Barton on the evening of Monday 29 March, and stayed there for the night before continuing. 'His Excellency and Mrs. Arthur were much pleased with the improvements that have taken place all along the road,' the *Hobart Town Courier* subsequently noted.[23] While Arthur likely informed Anstey directly, part of his preparatory memorandum to the Colonial Secretary had concerned 'the Roving Parties'. Arthur wanted Anstey to receive 'my thanks for the trouble he has taken' in overseeing the roving party operations, but also to know 'that it is my intention to make some change in the present system'.[24] Arthur intended to decentralise the roving parties, making each police magistrate again 'answerable for the Security of his respective District'. Later in the week, by which time Arthur was already in Launceston, the Colonial Secretary prepared a letter to Anstey detailing the new arrangements and requesting 'a nominal return' of Anstey's current force and projected requirement.[25]

Because Robertson's forces had already been disbanded and redistributed, and therefore no longer required Anstey's supervision, the new arrangements made little difference to the *status quo*. Jorgenson's rangers worked across districts, but were presently operating out of Bothwell. Batman continued to operate relatively independently, simply reporting his movements to Campbell Town and Oatlands between missions to and from his farm. With the addition of more settler-led roving parties like Sherwin Junior's, the prospect that police magistrates would soon be occupied dealing with bounties, and more parties proceeding past the lines of martial law, Arthur may just have felt that the war had outgrown the pretence of a police operation that could be administered from Oatlands alone.

Even the Aborigines Committee acknowledged that the interior was in a 'state of warfare'. Their recommendations likely contributed to the decision to decentralise the roving parties,[26] but they had also suggested that a 'system of mutual cooperation' – where 'each band should have a particular portion of the District assigned to it', become familiar with the main Aboriginal tracks and places of resort, regularly patrol their area, and have access to 'Magazines of provision' – would obviate the need for supply runs to the towns.[27] With this the committee mildly criticised Anstey's administration of the roving parties:

> notwithstanding the exertions of that highly respected individual who has had the superintendence of these parties, an error has been committed by them in extending their march over too wide an extent of Country, whereby the Natives have been either chased before them, or they have passed the Natives unperceived, and have left them unmolested to ravage the Country in their rear.[28]

The committee also criticised the conduct of the parties, 'carelessly running backward and forward, talking, shouting, smoking' and thereby generally giving warning of their movements. But these concerns reflected more the opinions of a few agitated settlers than any real engagement with the evidence.

In the end, the committee made the Oatlands-centred roving party system the political scapegoat for the government's failure to end the war, and so Anstey was asked to step aside.

An Indigenous Roving Party

The Lieutenant Governor and his retinue reached Launceston in the late afternoon of 1 April, arriving with much military fanfare. 'A salute in their honor was fired from the battery in the Barrack yard,' the *Launceston Advertiser* noted, and 'the troops were under arms at Government House to receive them.'[29]

After this display of loyalty and force, Arthur focused on 'surveying and planning various improvements' to the civil infrastructure of the town – at least according to the *Launceston Advertiser*. But Arthur was not occupied solely with bridges and wharves. While in the northern part of the colony Arthur had a discussion with Batman 'respecting the Black Women'.[30] After this discussion these women were sent to Batman's property, which they reached on 5 April.

The evening following their arrival, an infant died. This baby accompanied one of the women, and was otherwise undocumented. Batman explained that he buried it 'in my Garden' in accordance with the wishes of the distraught mother. 'At sun rise,' Batman noted, 'I found her crying over the Grave.' This subsequently attracted the Colonial Secretary's attention, who annotated 'Grief!' in the margin, seemingly to alert the Lieutenant Governor to this sign of humanity. Nonetheless, despite being visibly distraught, the woman went on her mission.

The women, accompanied by two of the 'Sydney Natives', left Batman's farm with 'as much as they could carry of Bread, Sugar, Tobacco, Blankets, &c' – just like other colonial forces. Before they left Hobart, they were also supposed to have been given 'some Trinkets', presumably to offer Aboriginal people they met.[31] Batman asserted that the women 'promised most faithfully to return here with all their Tribe'. This was probably because he promised them he would try to get their 'Boys' back from Robinson's custody. Return meant reunion.

After the indigenous roving party departed, Batman 'despatched men in different directions to inform the settlers and stock-keepers' of the mission. The women planned to 'make signal fires' to attract the attention of their tribes, so it was important that they were not mistakenly ambushed. Batman stressed this, requesting his neighbours were '<u>not</u> by <u>any</u> means to <u>fire</u> upon any Natives they should see until this plan had been tried'. The warning was a testament to standard practice among the settlers of his region.

But Batman also hedged his bets. His kept his men 'scouring round the Settlers Farms and runs', while he waited to see if the women would return. Conciliation may have been a hope, but capture was still the main objective.

With his parties deployed, Batman dealt with his correspondence. Still communicating with Anstey about operations, especially those concerning Danvers, Batman stressed to Anstey that 'in case He [Danvers] should fall in with the Natives, not to fire upon them, that is, until I hear further about the Black Women, and my Two Sydney Natives'.[32]

Batman also wanted to 'know where the Stoney Creek is He Names', referring to advice from Danvers, because 'Two or three bears [sic] that Name'. The confusion of names was continuing to trouble coordination between districts. Batman supposed that his indigenous roving party would head towards St Patricks Head on the east coast, and was worried that if Danvers' party went in that direction 'it would have a bad effect'. Batman hoped to communicate directly with Danvers, to 'more fully explain to Him the different routes &c I intend to take from time to time', but also to 'give him a <u>Pass Word</u> in case we should meet at Night'.

Anstey received this correspondence from Batman on 14 April, two days after it was penned. He 'Dispatched Danvers to Mr Batman', and forwarded Batman's correspondence to Hobart. Anstey noted that he thought Batman took 'a very prudent view of the matter'. The plan for Danvers to coordinate with Batman was reviewed and approved by Arthur the same day. It was then forwarded to the Aborigines Committee, and returned to the Colonial Secretary a week later. All such correspondence was now, potentially at least, politically loaded.

As Batman's letter was conveyed from Ben Lomond to Oatlands to Hobart, Batman's indigenous roving party was disintegrating.[33] At 'about 9 A.M' the two men from New South Wales left the women, apparently 'unwell', and returned to Batman. The men told the women 'they would get more flour, Tea, and Sugar and meet them again', while the women promised the men 'that if they fell in with their Tribe they would be down to my [Batman's] Farm in five days'. The women also promised to 'make smoke every day' as a signal, which would guide the returning men to their position. The men reached Batman on 15 April, retrieved provisions, and headed out again.

Danvers also arrived at Batman's farm on 15 April.[34] Batman thought Danvers would 'be of mutual benefit to us, and to the Service', and planned to meet him again soon. Now holding a ticket of leave – approved by the Colonial Secretary while the Lieutenant Governor was on his tour of the interior – Danvers could have found other employment, at least theoretically.[35] But clearly, he remained active on roving duties, agreeing to Batman's request 'to keep from St Patrick's Head for a few days', and again being warned 'not by any means to fire'.

At that time, over a week into the mission, Batman was 'anxiously looking' for the return of his indigenous roving party. He promised to inform Anstey as soon as they arrived, especially because it was of interest to Arthur. 'The Governor promised', Batman wrote, that if the indigenous roving party was successful and 'brought a Tribe', then Arthur would 'ride up immediately to see them'. By a remarkable coincidence, the two men from New South Wales returned to the farm only '10 minutes' after Danvers left, prompting Batman to send word calling him back.[36] It was particularly important that Batman and Danvers had another discussion because the men reported that the Aboriginal women 'threw away their brass Plates &c' and 'went off unknown to them' one night.

Anstey received three of Batman's letters on the same day, which detailed plans, anxieties and apparent failure. Numbering each to clarify the order in which they arrived, Anstey alluded in a comment to the failure of conciliatory measures. The information contained in one letter revealed 'the defect of all these hopes', he wrote, before forwarding them to the Colonial Secretary 'for His Excellency's information'.

Batman was incensed that the women had thrown away the metallic symbols of government protection and absconded. 'I am now at a loss to know what to think of their wretched race of People,' he wrote to Anstey. 'I now think they are not to be reconciled by any means,' he added, before asking Anstey 'what you think had better be done'. Then he added a seemingly innocuous but clearly coded comment: 'Danvers had better now take His own plan'.

Old Roving Grounds

Close to a week later Danvers left Oatlands on another of his missions, gradually heading to the northeast.[37] He made for Major Grey's farm in St Paul's Plains south of Ben Lomond. Moving into this area seems to have prompted some recognition from Mungo-Jack, who told Danvers 'that when very young he had been last on the East side of Ben Lomond'.

When Danvers reached Grey's property, there was a letter waiting for him from Batman. '[He] wished me not proceed any higher until he (Mr B) heard something respecting his 2 Sydney Natives'. Batman had sent these men out again in search of the women, and gave Danvers a time and place to meet a week later, in order for them to exchange information. In the interim, Danvers kept roving, noting how at 'every part as we went Mungo pointed out a number of places where the Natives had stopt and said he had been the same way before'. The rangers started looking for a 'Flint Quarry', and even Mungo-Jack struggled to locate it. When he was 'with the Tribe', and they 'stopt to build huts', 'the women went for the Flint' so he did not know its exact location.

While they were tired by their continued marching, dry weather helped the rangers, at least in revealing signs of earlier habitation. They were able to follow 'several old tracks of the Natives' beside dry creeks and across the marshes, and as they scoured the valleys 'Mungo pointed out many places where the Natives had been some time back'. But then the weather turned against them. As they camped on a high tier, it 'snowed hard the whole night', and kept up the following day as they 'beat to' a settler's hut for provisions and shelter.

As the conditions eased, the rangers went out again, sleeping on hills and in valleys, as they scoured the country. They found 'several old Native Huts' at one location and Mungo-Jack identified another spot 'where the Natives had slept' which, 'by the number of Huts', he estimated 'there had been upwards of 30' Aboriginal people.

Danvers made his rendezvous with Batman, but neither had much to report to the other. Batman had still not heard anything 'respecting the Sydney Natives', and 'strongly pressed' Danvers to refrain from heading north just yet. Danvers certainly wanted to head that way, because there was a 'place where Mungo wished to go', but agreed to delay again until another pre-arranged meeting at Batman's farm. So, after a night at Grey's, Danvers took the rangers to the hills again and 'scoured every likely part'.

By 4 May, 'Mr B. not having yet heard any thing of the Sydney Natives', both Batman and Danvers wrote to Anstey. Danvers 'forwarded them down to Campbell Town by one of the party and ordered him to wait for an answer'.

Despite the nominal change in the system of roving parties, Anstey was still active in administering operations beyond his own district, possibly because they particularly interested the Lieutenant Governor. But Anstey may have tired of this.[38] Referring to 'the many Letters lately addressed by Mr John Batman of Ben Lomond to me', Anstey suggested on 4 May that Batman 'should be directed to put himself in communication with Mr Simpson the Police Magistrate of the District in which Mr Batman resides'. Arthur readily approved this recommendation, and the Colonial Secretary informed the police magistrate of Campbell Town, James Simpson, that he was now in charge of giving orders to Batman.[39]

But Simpson was also told that 'from the proximity of your Situation to the scene of his [Batman's] operations it is expected that you will be better able to detect and check any irregularity which may prevail than the greater distance will allow Mr Anstey to do'. Like Robertson before him, Batman's failures were becoming political liabilities. Anstey informed the Colonial Secretary that Batman's 'whole Party have ceased to take any active measures against the hostile Aborigines', and intimated that it was possible that a 'trick is now playing by this Party'. That any such 'imposture' needed close surveillance became Anstey's main argument for passing responsibility to Simpson, and quite a reasonable one, but it also reflected the way that senior figures were distancing themselves from Batman's failed conciliatory overtures. Besides, Batman's letter-writing had caused Anstey trouble before.

Danvers waited a few days for a response from Anstey, travelling to Campbell Town to consult with Simpson after hearing nothing. Simpson suggested a direction to scour, so Danvers returned to Batman's farm to collect his team of rangers. Upon arrival at the property on 8 May, Danvers 'found the Sydney Natives had returned', but the women had not. Batman, still unaware that Simpson was now supposed to be directing Batman's operations, wrote to Anstey with the details:

> My Two Sydney Natives returned here Yesterday Afternoon after walking from George's Bay, round the East Coast to George Town, during the whole of the time (21 days) did not see a single Native neither did they fall in again with the women that left this [sic] nothing has been heard in any quarter of the women. I now think they have no thought of returning back again and have entirely forgotten their promises.[40]

Batman also explained that he was going 'with the whole of my party in pursuit of the natives and will endeavour to capture more'. Anstey forwarded the letter to Hobart, for the information of the Lieutenant Governor, adding his own comment that Arthur 'will receive with regret, the certain intelligence, that force is our only resource'. Arthur forwarded it to the Aborigines Committee.

Batman informed Anstey that Danvers' rangers would 'act in conjunction with me for some time', and Danvers' report bears this out. On 10 May the combined parties left Batman's property to 'scour round Ben Lomond'. By the evening of the following day they had reached the place where 'Mr. B. first fell in with the Natives'. The parties, Danvers remarked, 'found a number of the Bones of those who were there killed'. After his failed attempt at conciliation, Batman had gone to the place of his greatest victory.

Attitudes of Animosity

Danvers did not record how Mungo-Jack reacted to seeing the Aboriginal people's bones, although over the following days he apparently began 'to complain of being unwell'. But Mungo-Jack still took the lead, guiding the parties through 'some very steep and rocky Hills', and showing Danvers 'a place where he had slept when with the Tribe'. The parties camped that night by a river which Batman was convinced was the South Esk, before Mungo-Jack led them the next day to a remarkable place. This was 'a clear spot of ground where 6 Tribes met and fought'. There Mungo-Jack 'picked up a Waddie which he said was his'.

The forces divided after reaching this former battleground. Batman crossed a river, and Danvers' rangers took a different direction. But while theoretically freed from travelling at the speed of a larger force, the rangers slowed down. 'Mungo complaining,' Danvers noted a day before the party 'Proceeded slowly Mungo being worse.' By 15 May, Danvers was facing a real problem: 'Mungo so very bad this day that we were obliged to carry him up almost every little rise and all the Hills.'

Yet even while the party was still 'going very slow' the next day, Mungo-Jack continued to illuminate Danvers, showing him 'a place where the Natives cut waddies within the last fortnight', and taking him 'to a musket in very bad condition'. This weapon had been left in this spot 'by Humarraa'.

After finding this artefact, the party spent the night nearby at Dr Henderson's farm. Danvers then split his force. He took most of the party and 'went to the Creek pointed out to me by Mungo called Stoney Creek and laid by there'. Danvers intended to camp out for four or five nights, hoping to make an ambush. Tactfully, he left Mungo-Jack 'in charge of one of the party' at Henderson's.

When no Aboriginal people showed, Danvers returned to the farm, 'in hopes that Mungo was better but found he was worse'.[41] Moreover, Mungo-Jack had been at the centre of a minor dispute. 'Mr Steele a New Settler', temporarily occupying Henderson's hut, would not have Mungo-Jack in the same building. Henry Thompson, the ranger left with Mungo-Jack, 'was ordered to put a berth or bedstead in an old deserted Hut' for Mungo-Jack's use. Thompson examined the hut, but found it was so dilapidated that 'if 2 men were employed for 3 days they then could scarcely make it fit for any person to stop in there not being a door, window, or one sherd of the roof to it.'

Thompson appealed to Steele, informing the settler 'how very bad the lad was', and pointing out 'the service he was to the party in forwarding the views of Government'. Eventually, after much pushing, Steele relented and Mungo-Jack was brought into the hut, but Thompson had more trouble. Steele 'had never afforded the lad the slightest nourishment and delayed upwards of 20 minutes giving an Onion to put in soup for Mungo'. It was, Thompson reported to Danvers later, the only bit of food Steele shared with him.

The rangers were not the only visitors to Henderson's hut about this time. Thompson told Danvers of 'a Man named Ford who had pretended illness' and had arrived 'under pretence of being assigned to Dr. H.'. The feigned illness and illusory service were revealed when Ford snuck away after 'robbing' the hut of many of its contents. He took the men's 'rations of Tea, Sugar', 'a shoulder of Mutton', a spade, a pot, a kettle and the like. More ominously, he also stole off with '1 Butchers Knife' and 'a pouch belonging to a Soldier containing 10 rounds of Ammunition and 12 Balls'. A pursuit party forced him to abandon many of the stolen goods by a campfire, just like Aboriginal people. After Danvers returned, and for the remainder of the month, the party of rangers chased after him towards the east coast.

Failing to catch the runaway convict, Danvers' rangers soon turned back to scouring for Aboriginal people. Although Mungo-Jack was 'a little better', his health did not greatly improve. Describing him as 'reduced to a near skeleton and still unable to walk without assistance', Danvers 'left him in charge of one of the party to take to Oatlands by easy stages'. The remainder of the party continued roving in the east for another week before also heading back to Oatlands and reporting to Anstey, still clearly if discreetly taking some control over operations crossing over multiple districts. While disappointed that the 'villain' Ford escaped capture, Anstey nonetheless praised Danvers' exertions to the Lieutenant Governor. He also drew Arthur's attention to the way that Mungo-Jack 'appears to have been treated with much unkindness by Mr Steele', but could report that 'The Lad is now at Oatlands and fast recovering from his late illness.' Anstey also alerted Arthur to Mungo-Jack's 'exhibiting a new feature in the Aboriginal character', referring to the cause of the boy's illness. Mungo-Jack had told Danvers 'that the cause of his illness was the sight of some bones of the men who were shot the first time Mr Batman fell in with the Natives'.

'This is remarkable indeed!' Arthur inscribed on this letter, before forwarding it to the Aborigines Committee for their information. Hidden in the folds of the letter were a few last-minute pieces of information from Anstey: 'Danvers is on his way South,' he stated, and 'the Boy Mungo is very ill.'

Black Rangers

With Danvers' return to the midlands, the press got vague reports of his close encounter with Ford, where his roving party attracted an incidental but telling mention:

> Francis Ford, the bushranger ... has been lurking a fortnight and upwards at Dr. Henderson's farm, at St. Patrick's Head, where he committed a felony. He fled from thence on the approach of Constable John Danver's [sic] party of black rangers.[42]

While the *Hobart Town Courier* detailed Ford's escape, and mentioned that 'notification of his being in this quarter may do great good by putting people on their guard', on the same page was a police notice that Ford had been apprehended.⁴³

But this small reference to 'black rangers' was not the only one printed in Van Diemen's Land during June 1830. The same paper had only the previous week contained a story about 'Peter Scott's party of black rangers' leaving a settler's hut 'a short time before the natives appeared'.⁴⁴ Aboriginal people 'speared two men', one of whom 'ran away, with the spear sticking in his back'. He did this, the paper commented, 'instead of running into the hut for guns'. It was meant to be read as an act of foolishness or cowardice. Normally men kept their guns handy, but this time they had placed them inside because of 'a shower of rain'. But the particulars of the incident aside, the report captured the fact that multiple roving parties were still ranging the interior. It went on to describe the directions of roving of three separate parties, including Scott's.

Peter Scott had been formally appointed to the field police in mid-April, with retrospective effect from late March.⁴⁵ Three days before this authorisation was gazetted, the Colonial Secretary wrote to Anstey naming five convicts 'to be placed under the charge of Peter Scott'.⁴⁶ The formalities of colonial governance often ran behind the realities of wartime operations.

In a similar disjuncture between reality and formality, Arthur may have seemed to have acted upon the Aborigines Committee's advice by decentralising the roving party system, but he in fact continued to give Anstey considerable responsibility and increasing resources. The notion that Anstey had administered the system was, after all, only ever half true. He delegated much of the operations to Jorgenson, and through the Colonial Secretary Arthur was often aware of missions and intimately involved. Highlighting this is a small annotation by Arthur on one of Anstey's reports concerning the runaway Ford. Arthur instructed the town adjutant to 'make some inquiry respecting the Soldier alluded to in the letter', referring to the soldier whose pouch Ford had stolen. The chain of command during the Vandemonian War had always led to and from the one figure, at once both Lieutenant Governor and Colonel Commanding.

As the autumn turned to winter in 1830 there was limited talk of conciliation. Instead, the bulk of correspondence from the period points to a continued focus on capturing or repelling Aboriginal people from the settled districts. After meeting with Vicary in Bothwell on his inland tour, for instance, Arthur remained 'quite convinced that the Settlers themselves make no effort of their own', and advocated that Vicary take 'active and energetic measures'.[47] But while maintaining pressure on settlers to defend themselves, and having parties continually scouring the colony, Arthur was also beginning to contemplate even more dramatic measures.

CHAPTER ELEVEN

Beyond the Limits of Law and Documentation

1830, Autumn and Winter
Settled Districts and Northern Front

Men of Justice in Ambush and the Proxy War

While Danvers and Batman stalked about the northeast, Jorgenson's reconnoitering beyond the frontier was abandoned in favour of defensive patrols in the central and southern midlands. Then the strategic focus gradually again shifted from west to east.

Returning to Oatlands from a patrolling expedition during late April 1830, Jorgenson provided Anstey with a brief update, which gives some information about an otherwise poorly documented period.[1] Ranging southwest of Oatlands and staying east of Bothwell, Jorgenson 'fell in with Peter Scott and his party'. This meeting between parties meant that Jorgenson could report to Anstey that Scott 'in conformity with your directions had passed through Davis's bottom, and Michael Howe's marsh'. Jorgenson also updated Anstey about Scott's proposed movements, so that orders could be sent if needed, and because 'some boots will have to be sent to his party'. Anstey annotated the letter before forwarding it to Hobart, letting the Colonial Secretary know that Aboriginal people were moving eastwards towards the 'Little Swan Port River' and that he had ordered Scott to go in that direction.

Scott's movements provided Anstey with strategic and political intelligence. 'Mr Hone has a sheep hut in Davis's bottom', Jorgenson related, 'where he has placed four men, all well armed, and form a very excellent protection in that part of the country.' Joseph Hone's armed men reflected the sort of settler-militancy that the Lieutenant Governor so often advocated, and may have been inspired by Hone's own economic misfortunes. In early March his hut 'at the Black Marsh' had reportedly been robbed and set on fire while the servants were absent.[2] As a nearby resident wrote to the *Colonial Times*: 'They are hovering close round us. I live in constant anxiety, fearing some murder or other dreadful accident.'[3]

Jorgenson's observations about Hone's servants highlighted that Hone's men were prepared for a fight and determined to protect their master's interests. This was useful information for Anstey to relay, not least because Hone was a well-connected part of the Vandemonian ruling establishment.

While his men were fighting in the midlands, Hone served as a Justice of the Peace in Hobart. He also chaired the Committee of Papers in the Van Diemen's Land Society, and was chair of the Mechanics Institute.[4] Hone was demonstrably connected to the Lieutenant Governor, the Colonial Secretary and other significant figures in Vandemonian government and commerce. His armed servants at 'Davis's bottom' therefore offer a peculiar image of the operation of civil law and civil society during the Vandemonian War. Rather than the uncontrolled violence of convict servants and stockmen of the official narrative promoted by the Aborigines Committee, the war was frequently fought by servile proxies.

But while praising this group of private servants, Jorgenson also pointed to problems within the public service. He was 'not so well acquainted' with the 'disposition of John Danvers' party' as Anstey, but this was of no real concern. The most pressing matter was that Richard Tyrrell was still missing.

Class, War and Richard Tyrrell

Unlike the gentleman-rovers such as Gilbert Robertson and John Batman, or even the relatively famous and well-connected convict Jorgen Jorgenson, the subordinate rangers attracted relatively little press attention unless their exploits seemed particularly newsworthy. When Hone's hut was attacked in March 1830, for instance, a letter published in the *Colonial Times* mentioned that Aboriginal people were 'closely followed by one of JORGENSON'S parties'.[5] This might have been all the information available to the correspondent, but that in itself highlights how press reports tended to reflect class realities. There were noteworthy people, and everyone else. Tyrrell's disappearance, like most of the roving operations, attracted little public notice.

But Tyrrell's whereabouts certainly agitated Jorgenson, already concerned about the politicisation of the roving parties. Moreover, Jorgenson was clearly annoyed because Tyrrell 'left us in the lurch on the Big River', when Tyrrell was supposed to join with Danvers in sweeping down both sides of the river towards the settled districts.[6] Writing on 13 April to Francis Aubin, the Hobart town adjutant, Jorgenson admitted that 'I have not transmitted his [Tyrrell's] late reports to His Excellency, nor do I send you the Copy of his requisitions, as his conduct will undergo a most particular investigation by Mr Anstey'. It was an acknowledgement, albeit made in passing, that Jorgenson forwarded his reports knowing they were seen by Arthur. In this instance, at least, Jorgenson also confessed to being selective about the documentation forwarded to the Colonial Secretary and therefore the Lieutenant Governor. It was an admission that the archive was sanitised even as it was produced.

Jorgenson only mentioned the content of Tyrrell's reports to Aubin in passing, noting that Tyrrell 'only sent in two or three reports, which bear every stamp of imposition and falsehood'. Because the rangers took rations from settlers, and issued them with receipts, these could be used to track the parties later. These receipts were the subject of Jorgenson's letter to Aubin, after all. While complaining that Tyrrell claimed unusually large rations, Jorgenson also pointed out that through this supply and accounting mechanism Jorgenson could track

Tyrrell's movements, 'and sufficiently point out where he has been loitering':

> This man with a party of six men has been prowling about the Country for 10 or 11 weeks, kept himself out of the way, acted in defiance of the most positive instructions, went to a part of the Country as you will see by his receipts, whence he could have no manner of business, and whence for the greater part he has actually been loitering beyond the limits whence martial law does not extend.

This became Jorgenson's main fixation, telling Aubin about his last intelligence from Tyrrell. In a letter dated 22 March, Tyrrell 'states that he intends leaving the Western river for Port Davey', which Jorgenson thought meant that 'were he to kill a single black, he would be guilty of murder'. Two weeks later Jorgenson informed Anstey that 'I fear that these men have proceeded to attack some of the peaceable Tribes either on the Western Sea coast, or without the limits where martial law is not in force'.[7]

Jorgenson had sent word to Launceston and Bothwell to instruct Tyrrell to return to Oatlands, 'but he always eludes our search'. Aubin passed the letter to Arthur, who ordered the police magistrates to forward Tyrrell to Oatlands if he appeared in their district.[8] When Jorgenson communicated with Anstey about Scott's party and Hone's servants, he also mentioned that Tyrrell 'has not been heard of for thirty-eight days'.[9] While worried that Tyrrell was engaged in warfare beyond the settled districts, Jorgenson also contemplated the possibility 'that some fatal dispute or quarrell [sic] may have arisen amongst the men'. He may also have wondered if Tyrrell or his men had absconded to become bushrangers.

Alerting Arthur to Tyrrell's absence, Anstey declared himself 'seriously alarmed'. Despite having 'entertained a good opinion of Tyrrell', Anstey asserted his 'determination to put them into Oatlands Gaol'. With access to Tyrrell's conduct record, Anstey might have known that Tyrrell had absconded once before, prejudicing his opinion.[10] Tyrrell, transported for highway robbery like many other rangers, had managed to remain at large for about five months in 1824, getting 50 lashes in return. Moreover, Tyrrell's disappearance would have been an embarrassment for the master he served for five years, and who advocated his appointment to the field police in August 1829 – Alfred Stephen, a founding member of the Mechanics Institute and the Solicitor General of Van Diemen's Land.

Venting his frustration, Jorgenson characterised Tyrrell's party as 'a dead weight, of no use to the district, and useless altogether'. He stated that this 'loose and disorderly band is the worst in the country, and of no manner of service to the government'. But Tyrrell had not absconded and had not, as Anstey feared, 'been Murdered'. Illustrating the centralisation of information, Arthur knew by 12 May that Tyrrell 'has been heard of to the Westward', and was acting under instruction from 'Capn Smith', police magistrate of Norfolk Plains. Tyrrell's party, which included the Aboriginal man Jack, was engaged in ranging duties in the northwestern midlands and potentially further west.

Despite the widespread worry about his potential behaviour or misfortune, when Tyrrell returned he was quickly exonerated. The circumstances are a little unclear, but later in the year Anstey endorsed and forwarded a petition from Tyrrell to the Lieutenant Governor, incidentally giving some extra details about Tyrrell's movements in the process.[11] Anstey mentioned that he had made 'due enquiry' about Tyrrell's absence, discovering that Tyrrell 'went with his Party to Norfolk Plains and the Country to the Westward', which 'was occasioned by the Police Magistrate at Norfolk Plains'. Tyrrell himself, writing a lengthy explanation to Anstey after his return, apologised for a false report about having killed an Aboriginal person, and mentioned that part of the cause for his lengthy absence was directed towards the capture of a bushranger.[12] While Anstey admitted that Tyrrell's unexplained departure 'gave me great offence', and probably some embarrassment, Anstey nonetheless declared to Arthur that 'Richard Tyrrell hath zealously exerted himself to the utmost of his ability, in pursuit of the Aborigines'. As so often in the war, the actions of servants reflected upon their masters and patrons, but fortunately scandal and disgrace could often be effaced from the record after the fact.

Hunting and Gathering in the Southern Midlands

While Tyrrell zealously pursued Aboriginal people in the Norfolk Plains district – not long after some reportedly 'beat to death with their waddies' a flock of Smith's sheep – rangers continued to patrol the southern midlands.[13] Peter Scott led a party towards Jerusalem, and on 1 May 1830 'Crossed the Coal River and ranged round the tiers', finding 'several native Huts' in the process.[14]

Ten days later Scott's party was still ranging, and needed to resupply. But on applying for rations at one stock hut, the rangers were rebuffed by Pennington, the overseer, who told Scott 'that his Master – Mr Hobbs – told him not to give Rations to any party'. In need of supplies, Scott tried to pay for flour and bread, but was again denied food. Despite being under-supplied, with 'every Reason to believe the Natives were in the neighbourhood', Scott led his rangers on further.

Yet, not for the first time during the war, the party of rangers were seemingly shadowed. The next day, with Scott's party away, Hobbs's hut was attacked. Aboriginal people 'speared Pennington and one man more slightly, and struck Pennington's Wife with a waddie', and then 'Burned down an unfinished Hut'.

Another party of rangers left Oatlands the day after the attack on Hobbs's hut, led by George James, with some of Tyrrell's formerly wayward team, including Jack.[15] This young man was, Anstey noted on this mission report, now 'about 16 or 17 years of age'. Although unaware of the attack at Hobbs's hut when they left, within a day these rangers were on the assailants' trail.

Only one day out from Oatlands, the rangers established contact. As James reported:

> about eight Oclock we herd [sic] the noise of dogs and the natives rising from their fires[.] Black Jack the guide seemed very pleased and told me the direction they would make[.] we went a bout [sic]

four miles and got a head of them[.] we could distinctly here [sic] them a hunting all the way.

Having got ahead of this group, James decided on an ambush. The party hid 'behind a dead tree' in the path of the hunt, and waited.

Secreted, the rangers watched a kangaroo getting chased towards them by three dogs. But, detecting the hidden force, the dogs suddenly abandoned their hunt. They 'went back about two hundred yards and began to bark'. With his opportunity for an ambush slipping away, James 'wanted Jack to pull off his clothes and go and meet them'. Jack undressed, and started moving forward. The rangers followed, shadowing him from behind, trying to remain hidden. But the young man 'appeared very frightened and would not keep any distance from us', James reported, making the new plan of using Jack as a decoy ineffective. The rangers 'lost all trace of them' as the Aboriginal people escaped.

The rangers then temporarily abandoned their pursuit, and headed off in search of provisions. Over the next few days they prowled around hills and swamps. Then, as they descended 'a small rise' near McGill's Marsh – in the general area of Hobbs's hut – the party came 'close upon the natives as they were hunting'. There was no time to hide and ambush the tribe.

Seeing the rangers, one of the Aboriginal man 'called out "Riely" to the rest', a word which Jack explained meant 'white man'. The group fled, dropping 'several blankets knives and different articles' to expedite their escape. The rangers gave chase, 'but could not overtake them'. The pursuers were also hindered by the 'kangaroo dogs', which rounded on the rangers 'like a pack of Foxhounds'. As James's men killed 13 of these dogs, the Aboriginal people made their escape.

The rangers gave further chase without effect, so they returned to the scene of the encounter. James hoped that some Aboriginal people might have hidden in the bush rather than run. After a quick search, James took his party to a prominent rock. They climbed up, carefully hid, and then James 'told Black Jack to call same as the natives do when they are lost'. Jack obliged, cooing and whistling, and within a few minutes, as James described it:

he was answered by a woman and boy which came direct up to the rock that we were laying on the top and I am certain they must have smelt us for they ran back[.] I fired at them but mist [sic] they dropped another pot and Blanket[.] we run them into a creek and all-though the ground was burnt on both sides and we saw them fall behind the logs we could not find either of them[.]

The rangers continued the search, but the woman and child had disappeared. Jack tried calling again, 'and a dog came to him' which he killed 'with a spear'. That night, the party looked for fires but saw none.

In the morning the party 'proceeded by the lower part of Hobbs Lagoon through some fine hunting ground and stopt in a deep gully'. The following day they 'came to the pine creek and followed it down', noting that 'there are a great number of native huts and it is a fine place for them to make spears', but they did not encounter any more Aboriginal people. A few days later they returned to Oatlands with news of their contact, and a report that the Penningtons had fled to Hobart.

Vermin Traps and Fresh Appointments

While the Penningtons escaped the war zone, other representatives of the colony continued to contest the region. In late May, two shepherds living 'at the Swan Port River' found their hut plundered.[16] 'There was a blanket on the floor, with about 30 lbs. of sugar scattered upon it,' showing that Aboriginal people had learned how to avoid being maimed by traps, which stockmen and settlers left to inhibit raids on food supplies. In this instance, 'the man-trap that had been left set, was found let off, showing that the former disaster by the same instrument had been remembered'. A month earlier these shepherds had laid such a trap, and found their 'large vermin trap' a little distance from the hut with 'the hand in it', which had been crudely amputated by the victim or his companions.[17]

Finding their trap had failed on this second use, the shepherds 'then set off towards Mr. HOBBS'S hut, in the Eastern Marshes, to give the alarm'. Along the way they 'heard two guns fired' and 'saw two soldiers and a constable in full pursuit of a large number of the blacks, two of whom it appears were wounded'. While these people escaped, the shepherds reported that the constables and soldiers had another skirmish the next day, where one was speared before the force 'fired upon the Aborigines, who instantly retreated into some scrub, and were lost sight of'.

While soldiers and constables pursued and harried Aboriginal people, Arthur continued advocating the use of military forces in the police districts for operational support, but also for 'civil' administration. Hobart town adjutant Lieutenant Francis Aubin, for instance, was made a Justice of the Peace in early May.[18] He was subsequently transferred to Oyster Bay on the east coast to replace Lieutenant Lane as the new police magistrate.

A few weeks later Arthur also appointed Major Sholto Douglas a Justice of the Peace, prior to being sent on duty into the interior.[19] Douglas was well known to Arthur, having married a daughter of John Burnett, the Colonial Secretary.[20] As with most of Arthur's appointments – indeed, the civil administration of Van Diemen's Land more broadly – there were networks of patronage and personal connection at work.

Prior to commissioning Douglas as a Justice of the Peace, Arthur even prepared a memorandum aimed at explaining his decision to the new appointee.[21] Douglas, Arthur noted, 'will necessarily be involved in Duties with the Civil power which will render it highly advantageous to the Service that he should be enabled to discharge the functions of a Magistrate.' Arthur even made it explicit that Douglas's objectives were military, instructing the Colonial Secretary that he should:

> Notify to Major Douglas that the great alarm which the Inhabitants in the Interior continue to labour under from the sudden attacks of the natives has induced me to order all the Military that can be disposed of to be employed in the Protection of the Settled Districts.

Arthur wanted Douglas to deploy 'active measures', but also to act with 'prudence in their adoption'. The Lieutenant Governor wished Douglas to ensure Aboriginal people were treated with 'the utmost humanity' – intimating thereby to avoid killing women and children or mistreating prisoners – but he also told Douglas that 'he will receive detailed instructions through the Military Department'. This meant that Arthur would relay specific instructions through his capacity as Colonel Commanding rather than Lieutenant Governor. But while the specific operational strategy was not recorded, Arthur added one core detail to the memorandum: 'I have felt it important,' Arthur asserted, 'to place all the outstations generally under his [Douglas's] command.' Shortly after making a public show of decentralising the nominally civil roving parties, apparently in accordance with a recommendation of the Aborigines Committee, Arthur discreetly centralised the administration of the military frontier. Once again, this command structure centred on Oatlands, where Douglas was soon stationed.

While Douglas's instructions passed through military channels, Arthur continued to communicate with his police magistrates via the Colonial Secretary. The correspondence for May 1830 reveals several continuities. Arthur was 'extremely pleased' with one of Smith's servants after an encounter with Aboriginal people, and there was a proposal to Anstey from a convict to 'take Tyrrell and others' in search of a bushranger named Bevan.[22] A proposal 'from "John York" of the River Isis' from Campbell Town was also being considered, highlighting a continued focus on new roving parties, but Arthur wanted more details on the proposal first, 'stating the number of Natives he would undertake to capture to entitle him to the Land and the men to indulgence &c &c'.[23] This expedition was subsequently rejected, because it was 'not judicious'.[24] Moreover, highlighting a growing focus on the northern parts of the settled districts, Arthur informed Smith at Norfolk Plains:

> that it is certainly quite within the range of your Duty, as Police Magistrate, to <u>request</u> the Officer commanding, to station the several parties in the situations, which you may deem most eligible.[25]

Smith was also told that if 'the Officer Commanding' had 'any objection to the arrangement which you propose', then it had to be put in writing and 'may be referred for the decision of the Lieut Governor.' Against all of this was a situation of open warfare between the colony – represented by settlers, servants, field police and soldiers – and any Aboriginal people not obviously engaged on the colonial side.

In this incendiary situation, the bounty system of cash rewards for Aboriginal captives was also beginning to have an effect, and this too came to occupy the Lieutenant Governor's attention.

A Bountiful Harvest

In the far north of the colony, beyond Launceston and east of George Town, 'Three Native Black Women and One Boy' were captured at the farm of William Gee. They were taken to George Town and then forwarded to Launceston, where they were put into the custody of William Jones, overseer of the prisoners' barracks. These captives were known to authorities, having disappeared from Batman's indigenous roving party some weeks earlier. Their recapture was noteworthy because, as a memorandum from Jones explained, 'the Man that took them has made affidavit at the Police Office and Claims a Reward'.[26]

Although evidence for the northern midlands is less comprehensive than for the southern midlands, Gee's hut had been a site of previous conflict between settlers and Aboriginal people. In March, a few days before Smith's sheep were slaughtered, Gee's hut was raided while being guarded by a single servant, James Spangle.[27] When the rest of Gee's men returned, they 'found the hut had been robbed of a quantity of flour and sugar, a fowling piece and ammunition, together with a young kangaroo dog'. Finding no sign of Spangle inside, the men searched around the property, finding him 'lying on his back' dead. His body had 'several spear wounds in the neck, one through the hand, and another had entered about the region of the heart.' The wounds told a story of attempted self-defence, serious wounding, and a killing strike. The men returned with news of the slaying of their companion. Some time after that 'a cart and four bullocks' was sent for the body, but by the time they arrived Spangle's body was 'so much mutilated by wild animals and so decomposed' that 'they buried it where it lay'.

The report in the *Launceston Advertiser* that detailed this March raid also related the attack on Smith's sheep. But as the editor quipped: 'What measures do the Aboriginal Committee recommend on this occasion?' The newspaper also told of 'a party of volunteers busily employed man-catching in the neighbourhood,' as well as the Lieutenant Governor's imminent arrival in Launceston as part of his tour of the interior. The editor also made comment on the bounty system: 'Five pounds a head is a tempting sum, but our accommodations in this quarter are rather too limited to furnish board and lodging for these sable gentry.'

A few months later, when the women from the indigenous roving party were captured at Gee's hut, reports reached Hobart that their excursion was fruitless and that they were badly treated. As one correspondent from Ben Lomond wrote:

> One out of the five had died, another had been shot, and the three that came in had been very shamefully treated. During the whole of this time, these poor creatures could not meet with a single individual of their own tribe.[28]

Another writer reported from Launceston that the Women 'complain of having met with a different reception to what they expected'.[29]

The circumstances of the capture, and the condition of the captives, became clearer upon their arrival in Launceston. As Jones the overseer affirmed:

> These women and Boy, are of the number that was sent from Hobart Town in the Month of March and were taken away by Mr Batman to Benlomond in April, when His Excellency the Lieutenant Governor was in Launceston[.][30]

He also recorded their version of events:

> The account the women gives is nearly as follows, That they in Company with two other women that left Launceston with them (one of which they say is dead the second left in the Bush) left Benlomond in quest of their Tribe reached Pipers River and came to the Hut (Gee's Hut) when three white men took them into a Hut and fastened the Door, beat the women with Muskets, took from them their Native Passes, Knives, Tom hawks three Blankets and destroyed their Dogs, and then took them into George Town.

Batman arrived in Launceston on 24 May, and recorded the story in a letter to the police magistrate of Campbell Town, which was subsequently forwarded to Hobart. The captives were, he asserted, 'very ill treated'. He was incensed that the lead captor had 'gone to Hobarton to get the reward for bringing them in', and wanted an investigation. 'I understand they were brought in from Pipers River by some settler's men that live there,' Batman noted, adding that 'it appears that one of the women died and another was shot by those men'. 'The women state to me,' Batman elaborated, 'that when they went to the Hut they cryed out The Governor, Mr Batman &c.'

When the news reached Hobart, Arthur ordered an investigation into 'an outrage committed on the Female Aborigines recently at liberty'.[31] He wanted the police magistrate of Launceston to take statements from two of the servants and compare them with each other, while the chief police magistrate in Hobart 'has been instructed to deal with' Arthur Maynes, the man heading to Hobart for his reward. Arthur was alerted by the police magistrate at Campbell Town that Maynes was formerly a servant employed by Roderic O'Connor, which might have reminded the Lieutenant Governor of O'Connor's statement to the Aborigines Committee in March that 'Stock-men used to hunt them [Aboriginal people] on horseback & shoot them from their horses,' and his advocacy that 'every settler should protect himself'.[32] Certainly, Maynes was examined once he got to Hobart, but the chief police magistrate found that 'it was impossible to detain this man in custody'.[33]

A small note to the Colonial Secretary, dated 10 June, records the substance of the chief police magistrate's investigation:

> I have the honor to report that Arthur Maynes asserted here yesterday, that no one article was taken from the black Native Women by him or his companions, except for protection, but that they were well treated, and their whole property delivered by him to the Gaoler at George Town.[34]

Further information about the investigation's outcome – including whether Maynes received his bounty – seems not to have survived. But punishment certainly appears unlikely. The investigating chief police magistrate had formerly been stationed at Launceston, and may have known Maynes and the other men concerned.

Nonetheless, the women and boy remained in the Launceston 'Penitentiary' until early June, when Arthur 'directed' authorities in Launceston 'to cause the Aboriginal women ... to be delivered into Mr Batman's charge'.[35]

Curiously, this episode prompted an unusual note in the book of memoranda and instructions from the Lieutenant Governor to the Colonial Secretary. Lodged between two entries from early June 1830 is a memorandum dated 15 March 1830.[36] This detailed the representations made by the Aborigines Committee to Arthur, 'recommending the native women now in Hobart Town should be allowed to join their Tribe on the North side of the Island'. It seemed that after the indigenous roving party mission failed, someone made sure to formally acknowledge that it was not originally the Lieutenant Governor's idea by documenting the original suggestion well out of sequence and normal conventions.

Batman's Plans amid Administrative Nuisances

This was not the only bounty capture that attracted Arthur's personal attention. Overseer Jones had also reported that 'two Youths were taken at South Down Beach by Mr Rosvere and Charles Thorp on

12th of May', who were soon in custody in the Launceston prisoners' barracks.[37]

The boys were apparently about 13 and 15 years old. Their captors had allegedly 'treated them kindly, and supplied them with food and clothing'.[38] As one correspondent noted:

> one of them is supposed to be a chief's son; his hair is besmirched with red ochre, and hangs in graceful ringlets down his shoulders. I understand they were alone and without food when captured.

But while they had been forwarded to Launceston, at least one of the boys appears to have been removed back to the place of his capture. 'Mr Rosvere wishes to have one of the Boys,' Arthur noted on Jones's memorandum in late May, 'to which I have no objection.'

Yet while these boys, like many other Aboriginal captives, passed into relatively obscure custodial situations, the case for the women returned to Batman was clearer, precisely because he was still an active agent in the Vandemonian War. Batman's own file segment in the Colonial Secretary's records ends with the women's recapture, but other correspondence reveals that his and their war continued. On 1 June 1830 Simpson wrote to the Colonial Secretary detailing Batman's 'future operations'.[39] Batman was ordered to take 'one of the Native Women' and some of his own men through the tiers to Pipers River:

> and there endeavour to ascertain how the aggression complained of by the Women took place and if possible to discover the body of the woman said to have been shot; then to take an easterly course along the coast to Ringarooma so to proceed to the southward along the coast.

At this stage the investigation was still ongoing, but Simpson was also clearly concerned to know for certain that the woman was indeed dead, and not otherwise still at large. Moreover, his plan for Batman clearly went well beyond the lines of martial law, signalling that the northeast – still technically an area of Aboriginal sanctuary – was now being routinely scoured. The remainder of Batman's force, in company with the other Aboriginal woman, was directed to travel east and then north along the coast until meeting the other party in a classic pincer movement.

Simpson also had a plan for when the two groups rejoined:

> Mr B. shall build a hut to the East of Ben Lomond between the Mountain and George Bay, and there post his party secreting their arms and appearing abroad as little as possible from this hut, the women and Sydney Blacks to make excursions for two or three days together lighting fires to attract the notice of the Tribe and endeavouring to open a communication with it[.]

This prospective communication between Aboriginal rovers and the tribe was still possible, Simpson and Batman thought, because 'both the Women and the Boy Mungo fully comprehend the wishes of the Government and are anxious to assist in bringing about a friendly intercourse'.

These sentiments, however, differed between tribal groups. Mungo-Jack, for instance, had earlier conveyed his 'deadly hatred' for the Big River tribe. But according to Simpson, Mungo-Jack was apparently 'the Son of the Chief of this [Ben Lomond] Tribe, by one of the Women now with Mr B.', meaning he was probably more open to the possibility of becoming a negotiator in the northeast with his own people. While noting that Mungo-Jack was then out with Danvers, Simpson wanted to place him under Batman's charge. It was a notion to which Arthur agreed in the margin of this letter, before then approving the whole of the plan.[40]

A week after Simpson informed the Colonial Secretary of this scheme, but before receiving his approval from Arthur, Simpson forwarded another report to Hobart.[41] Simpson and Batman had met, the latter expressing that he 'naturally felt much annoyed by the impediments thrown his way by the Commandant', presumably over the custody of the recaptured women. Moreover, Simpson wished 'to suggest the propriety of <u>one person</u> being visited with full authority to act in all cases which have reference to the proceedings against the aborigines in this quarter'. Simpson may have hoped to be vested with similar responsibilities to those previously held by Anstey, or perhaps he might have hoped for Anstey to again take charge. Either way, Simpson's prescient complaint seems to suggest he was unaware of Douglas's new role in the midlands, set in train in the previous few weeks.

Simpson's complaints – and his apparent ignorance of a newly centralised military command – reveal how delays in communicating throughout the colony sometimes affected the prosecution of the war. But distance was not the only obstacle to effective communication. Simpson and Batman had both alluded to bureaucratic pedantry, and Jorgensen too had complained of the delays with forming parties and the problems of adequately equipping and rationing them. Fighting a war through civil departments made for convenient politics, but brought its own problems.

Nonetheless, the police magistracies and colonial secretariat were more efficient than their complaints would suggest. Their concerns were real, but they tended to be directed at the Convict Department specifically. In a postscript, for example, Simpson worried about Mungo-Jack's ill health. Believing the boy was still at 'Dr Henderson's Farm on the Coast', Simpson 'acquitted Mr Batman to send immediately for him and obtain every possible assistance to further his recovery'. Showing that the police magistrates in the midlands were sharing their intelligence, the following day Anstey wrote to Arthur that 'Batman will send for him [Mungo-Jack] and atten[d] ... to his wants.' Anstey, Simpson and Batman were clearly coordinating messages and all demonstrably had the same understanding within a day of each other. Such cooperation was important and timely over the following months, because while there were hopes for a winter lull in raids and attacks, the winter of 1830 would be anything but peaceful.

CHAPTER TWELVE

Keeping up the Pretence and the Pressure

1830, Winter
Western Front and Midlands

A Pastoral Moment

All was relatively quiet on the western front in early winter 1830, at least as reported by Captain Vicary on 8 June. 'I have the Honor to inform you,' he told the Colonial Secretary, 'that the Aboriginal Tribes have not been heard of in this District since my last Communication.'[1]

Vicary then went on to detail a report of 'questionable a shape' concerning an incident from late May, which he had 'altogether discredited' at the time and therefore not reported immediately. But, on closer investigation, this encounter proved worth sharing. 'Mr Franks' shepherd was out with his flock at a place called Stoney Hut Valley near Cross Marsh,' Vicary stated, when 'he found himself suddenly surrounded by Eight or Nine of the Blacks'.

Edward Franks wrote an account of his shepherd's adventure for Vicary, and this too got passed to the Colonial Secretary.[2] Franks detailed how George Bagshaw, the convict shepherd concerned, 'was passing through Stoney-Hut Valley' in the middle of a Saturday morning, chasing after strayed sheep, when he was 'intercepted' by an armed party of Aboriginal men. Alone and outnumbered, Bagshaw noticed that there were '10 or 11' of them, 'each armed with three spears and a waddy'. Bagshaw had 'a fire-lock' musket, which he immediately 'pointed towards them'. He probably knew that he was safer with a loaded gun than a discharged one. Nonetheless, the men 'approached sufficiently near to demand Tobacco'. In reply, Bagshaw threw some forward, and a pipe too, but when the men 'asked for a knife' Bagshaw told them that he did not have one.

According to Bagshaw's information, 'they then insisted upon having a sheep, and upon the obtaining of which they allowed him to depart'. Bagshaw herded the remaining sheep away, repeatedly and nervously turning to watch the Aboriginal people behind him, anxiously noticing that he was followed for some distance. When Bagshaw reported this to Franks, the settler 'sent [word] to Flexmore and Ashton – who promptly raised a party of eight, which were joined by my Shepherd and another, making 10'. Francis Flexmore and George Ashton were district constables in the Cross Marsh, men holding the same position that Gilbert Robertson had held in the Richmond district.

The pursuit party met with little success. As Franks reported:

> They were out all night but without overtaking any of the
> Savages – My man says they discovered indications of their
> having recently been in a part he described, and that it appeared
> they had gone towards the source of the Koyn Creek.

While thinking it would arrive too late to be of use, Franks nonetheless forwarded this account of these movements to Vicary. The police magistrate in turn forwarded it to the Colonial Secretary, and three days later Arthur had read it. 'Is the Shepherd a man of good Character' Arthur wondered, 'if not, I should be indisposed to credit his statement & rather suppose that the Blacks never got his lost sheep.' The Lieutenant Governor clearly suspected that Bagshaw had concocted a story, intimating that the convict might have pilfered and possibly eaten the lost sheep himself.

Arthur's laconic response to the Bagshaw incident seemingly reaffirms Vicary's assertion the fighting had calmed, especially when matched by Arthur's willingness to quip about convict criminality. The war may indeed have seemed to be slowing as the days shortened. But the colony was about to be shocked.

Raiding Renews, Roving Continues, But the Documentation Diminishes

The *Hobart Town Courier* called it 'one of the most appalling murders that has yet been committed by the misguided and benighted blacks', and the *Colonial Times* related the tale as a 'painful duty'.[3] Slightly different versions of events reached Hobart, but they had the same context and the same end. The attack occurred at a place called 'the Den' in a hut owned by Captain Wood, occupied by Richard and Mary Daniels and their two infants. Situated north of Bothwell, this was a place that one account described as 'perhaps one of the most remote and exposed situations in the island'. The couple had married in the area during the last spring, and had two young babies only 'weeks' or 'months' old.[4]

On the day of the raid, Richard was occupied some distance from the hut but still in sight of it, when he noticed something awry at the hut door. He went to investigate. Opening the door and peering inside, he 'beheld the mangled corpse of his wife and infant children'. Mary was 'sadly disfigured, being speared and beaten with waddies in a dreadful state', while the children appeared to have been strangled because 'their faces were discoloured and their mouths bloody'. A window frame was also broken, some geese were slaughtered, and 'a few trifling things' had been taken.

When informed of this raid, Arthur expressed 'the deepest concern'[5] and suggested that 'the sagacity which the Natives have displayed … may prompt you to adopt some system of decoy, which may prove very beneficial.' As the Colonial Secretary instructed Vicary: 'His Excellency has no doubt that it will stimulate you to make still greater efforts to capture the bloodthirsty tribe, by whom it has been perpetuated.'

Nevertheless, by late June the *Colonial Times* referred to the killing of Mary Daniels and her children as an isolated tragedy that heralded a period of relative quietude:

> Since the late murders committed at the Den, Regent's Plain, on the family of Daniels, Captain Wood's Overseer, the country seems to have enjoyed some respite from the natives. A man was chased two or three days since, at Jerusalem, by a small tribe, and Mr. Evans's shepherd, on the river Ouse, was hard run last week, by another tribe, but both succeeded in escaping.[6]

Alert newspaper readers may have connected this 'respite' with another report, higher up the page, quoting from 'a letter, from Oatlands'.[7] In the absence of Jorgenson's mission reports, it captures some of the only information about the rangers for these weeks:

> The Oatland's [sic] party, under the charge of Peter Scott, has been scouring the country about the Little Swan Port and Eastern Marsh Rivers, the Blue Hills, McGill's Marsh, and Sam the Butcher's Marshes, and all that neighbourhood, since the 15th May last. The party often fell in with recent native fires, and lately built huts. Notwithstanding the threatening appearances of the Natives in this direction some time since, the party under Scott, and one headed by James Hopkins, in the vicinity of Malony's Sugar Loaf, with another under Benjamin Allinson about the Big Lagoon, have succeeded in checking the atrocities of the Natives, who much frequent those parts at this season of the year. The men attached to these parties are compelled to stay in the bush, and not allowed to go to the stock-huts, except absolutely in want of rations, or for the purpose of procuring intelligence. John Danver's [sic] party is moving about the Quoin, Green Ponds, and is directed occasionally to have an eye to the Hunting Ground and the Black Marsh. The cold and frost have lately been very severe in this part of the island.

Few people were placed to have such a good knowledge of the movements of the rangers, so it is likely that the unnamed correspondent was Jorgenson, or at least an associate.

But Jorgenson was on the cusp of freedom. This, as much as any other factor, probably slowed the compilation of records and disrupted the regularity of correspondence to and from Hobart and the fronts. While there had been earlier times when rangers returned to base after short or inconsequential missions, at least in the Oatlands district there tended to be records stating as much. These were usually compiled as mission reports detailing daily movements, which Jorgenson then perused and forwarded. Because of this, a surprising proportion of the CSO1/1/320 (7578) file derives from Jorgenson's diligently recorded administration of the roving parties. Other districts did not lack for fighting, but they did lack a committed record-keeper.

Jorgenson's good service had earned him some powerful friends. In early June, following advice from London, Arthur ordered the preparation of Jorgenson's conditional pardon.[8] This was gazetted on 16 June.[9] On 28 June Jorgenson, being 'restored to the freedom of this country', wrote to Anstey about his resignation from the field police.[10] Jorgenson wanted to stay on until 1 August because, as he put it, 'there are many little matters to arrange'. Anstey made the recommendation to Arthur, who approved an August resignation.

Jorgenson then offered to run combined roving operations between the Oatlands and Bothwell districts, 'in occasionally leading out the bands, and looking after them in the bush, and perfecting their accounts'. Jorgenson also hoped, through this service, to 'complete a proper, and I hope a most useful history for the reference of the Government'. In reply to this request Arthur simply advised that Anstey should inform Jorgenson 'not to delay employing himself in any way that may be most advantageous for his own interests'. But the Lieutenant Governor also told Anstey that 'Should the Government hereafter require his [Jorgenson's] services, you will no doubt be able and kindly disposed to communicate with him.'[11]

Curiously, a few weeks before Jorgenson's departure, the Aborigines Committee corresponded with Anstey about Robertson's roving parties. Anstey informed them 'that <u>all</u> the information which Mr Robertson thought fit to communicate to me, is in the hands of the Colonial Secretary' and that Robertson's reports were 'on the whole, very meagre'.[12] The same can be said for the committee's own records. While there is evidence for the continued provision of some mission reports to the Colonial Secretary from police magistrates, not all survive in the CSO1/1/320 (7578) file, further highlighting the diminished documentation of this period. In late June, for example, Simpson forwarded a report from Batman to the Colonial Secretary. The cover letter survives, but the report itself was not archived in this file.[13]

Winter Fighting and Snowy Outposts

The winter lull in Aboriginal raids was a small respite but not a truce. In early July the *Colonial Times* expressed a general agitation at 'attacks and depredations', illustrating the war's continuance.[14] It asserted that attacks 'within a few miles from the townships and Military stations, assume a regular and alarming consistency'. The newspaper detailed a five-hour battle at 'Mr. Evans' hut on the Big River', followed by the dispatch of 'a party of the military in search of the Aborigines, although the weather was wet, and the rivers swollen'.

In another incident 'a man was dangerously speared by some of the Aborigines at Mr. Nicholl's stock-run, on the River Ouse.' A group of 'men in the employ of Lieutenant Betts of the Big Lagoon' were cut off from their guns and hut while chopping wood, and only escaped by using a cart as protective cover as they fled to a nearby neighbour. As they armed and set off to their own hut, they found it robbed and abandoned. While they surveyed this scene, the neighbouring hut they had just left was also robbed by Aboriginal people who also attempted to burn it down. In yet another raid 'upon Captain Wood's hut, in Poole's Marsh', a raid was beaten off with gunfire. 'Six or seven shots were fired,' it was reported, 'but all missed.' One of the Aboriginal men was 'recognised as having twice before been at the hut'. A few days later another hut was robbed nearby. It was all evidence, the *Colonial Times* argued, of 'a cunning and superiority of tactic which would not disgrace even some of the greatest military characters'.

These reports were followed by a lengthy 'Extract from a Letter from Green Ponds, dated July 12', which railed about 'the apathy which exists so visibly amongst some of the settlers'.[15] Like the earlier anonymous letter from Oatlands, this too has more than a whiff of Jorgenson about it. Pointing out how close each of these locations were to 'roving and military parties', the writer then went on to detail 'the utmost exertions' of several parties. This included Peter Scott, who 'with a full party are incessantly roving in the Eastern Marshes, Rushy Lagoon, the Blue Hills, sometimes debouching towards little Swan Port, but within the District of Oatlands'. The letter also detailed Anstey's dispatch of a party 'into the Oyster Bay District', composed of 'five of the Police Constables' under James Hopkins, George James and 'a black guide'.

The Green Ponds correspondent also described an attempted ambush scheme being conducted by another party:

> Benjamin Allinson with a small party, all but one or two concealed within a recently constructed hut, a few miles from the Big Lagoon, are erecting a small sheep-yard with a brush fence, so as to try if this scheme will not decoy some of the Aborigines into the hut, and thus make capture certain.

Within a week of the letter from Green Ponds being published, the Colonial Secretary relayed Arthur's enthusiasm for such tactics to Smith in Norfolk Plains:

> It having been represented to The Lieutenant Governor, that the Aborigines commit frequent depradations [sic] upon the house or dwelling of a person of the name of 'Bonally' who resides in the immediate neighbourhood of Mr P Minnitt on the Liffey, I am directed to suggest, that if some stratagem were used to surprise the Natives there, it is very probable that the capture of some of them would be effected.[16]

Just as he knew the Lieutenant Governor disliked settler apathy, Jorgenson also knew of Arthur's inclination towards using huts for ambushes. The letter from Green Ponds therefore, like the one from Oatlands before it, was perhaps a sign that Jorgenson was attempting to win popular support for the roving parties in the last stages of his control over them.

But the information was not just political posturing, because a surviving report from Danvers – the last forwarded by Jorgenson that survives in the Danvers section of CSO1/1/320 (7578) – matches one assertion in the letter. As the correspondent from Green Ponds reported:

> John Danvers with another full party are roving near the Quoin
> beyond the Cross Marsh, stretching sometimes across to the
> hunting ground, and ranging along the Jordan within the District
> of Oatlands.

Danvers' report, dated 19 July, refers to a mission commenced in the middle of June 'to scour the Bush between the Road to Green Ponds and the Road to Jerusalem for a fortnight'.[17] Danvers initially obeyed these instructions, but soon moved the party's patrolling area.

> After that we somewhat diverted our roving positions, and
> chiefly confined our operations between the Quoin and the
> Black tier, taking care to send occasionally to the Cross marsh
> to learn if any instructions or orders were transmitted to us from
> headquarters.

On 12 June, the same day the letter from Green Ponds was written, Danvers 'heard that some of the Aborigines had robbed two huts on the Big Lagoon, and had threatened and robbed two huts in and near Poole's marsh in the district of the Clyde, closely bordering the Oatlands district.' This timing further suggests the association with Jorgenson.

'Knowing' where Allinson's party was stationed, 'and that the Natives would not venture to remain in that neighbourhood', Danvers planned an ambush:

being very certain from the situation of the numerous native huts that I had seen lately, and their general route, from the sticks placed in the ground, that they would not be long before they returned in this direction, we kept on the top of the mountains whence we could have a good sight of the country for many miles round, as well as tracing in the Snow the traces of their feet.

Danvers also established a more permanent forward operating base for these operations:

I have now formed a hut in a thick Scrubb at the source of the Quoin rivulet, in a Gulley, whence no smoke can be seen, and whence we cannot be observed unless coming within a few yards of the place. Two of the party alternatively ascend the hills to keep a strict look out.

The party had been isolated from other colonists, including stock huts, for eight days at the time of Danvers' report. This isolation was made starker by 'the unexampled Severity of the weather, the snow lying many feet deep on the ground, and the floods very high and the streams rapid'. A subsequent report described this snowstorm as 'unprecedented since the establishment of the Colony'.[18] Indicative of the extremely bad conditions, Danvers mentioned the fact of 'upwards of sixty Kangaroos in the bush, which laid dead in the bush from cold, and probably also for want of food'.

A few days later, the *Colonial Times* reported on the dead kangaroos and described some of the extremity of regional flooding.[19] Probably sourced from the same informant, the newspaper also reported that Allinson's party closed in on an Aboriginal group, who 'went into a scrub, and disappeared'.

With this report and its newspaper synopsis, Danvers' mission drifted into documentary obscurity. One of the last things Danvers appended to his report, although not surviving with this letter, was a description of 'the Quoin rivulet ... which fixes the Boundaries between the Oatlands and Richmond Districts'. It shows him engaged in geographical reconnaissance as well as a combat mission, nominally well within the settled districts, but clearly still very disputed territory. After scribbling a report to Anstey from his hideaway hut, Danvers largely disappears from the historical record. He was 'in hopes to come on the traces of the Aborigines in the Snow'.

Mercenaries on the Western Front

Although mainly occupied with the field police rangers operating out of Oatlands, the Green Ponds correspondent also had intelligence for the *Colonial Times*'s readers about the situation in the Bothwell district.[20]

> In the District of the Clyde, independent of the numerous military parties so judiciously distributed by Captain Vicary, Mr. Sherwin, junior, an active and indefatigable young man, is roving with a party between the Rivers Ouse and Clyde, under the more immediate instructions of Captain Vicary. Doran with another party, is ranging in another direction, within the same district.

John Doran's father had been speared some time back.[21] Like John Sherwin Junior, his family had been attacked, and now he was leading a roving party sanctioned by the Lieutenant Governor, potentially mixing revenge with the promise of a reward of land.

Such mercenary operatives were useful for Vicary, whose district was one of the most hotly contested in the colony. Unable to provide Vicary with more soldiers, the Lieutenant Governor informed him in late July 1830 that 'it will be necessary to supply the deficiency of numbers by superior address'.[22] Moreover, the Colonial Secretary made it clear what such 'active measures' entailed, and typical of most of Arthur's instructions, the word 'conciliation' did not appear:

> The Lt Governor desires it to be repeated, that His Excellency's only hope of putting an end to the warfare with the natives, is founded in the plans which may be put into operation by yourself and other Gentlemen holding similar situations, you mention

that the Aborigines have <u>been seen</u>, now, as The Lieut Governor considers it to be well known that they always move very leisurely, the moment they were got sight of, some arrangement should have been made for pursuing them.

To further assist pursuit parties, Arthur mentioned a scheme which some of the settlers in Vicary's district had advocated to the Aborigines Committee some weeks earlier. As the Colonial Secretary wrote:

I am further directed to enquire, whether it has occurred to you to train some small dogs to trace the Natives, so that when once seen, they might be followed, at least until they were dispersed.

Through this hypothetical musing Arthur tacitly encouraged the use of hunting dogs.

About a week after this missive was sent to him, Vicary reported an encounter.[23] He mentioned that during the last two weeks of July Sherwin's force was divided, apparently ready to ambush Aboriginal people. With two of his men, Sherwin was 'stationed at Mr Espie's Basham Plains'. The rest of the force were 'concealed at Weasel Plains'. Then, on 29 July, Sherwin learned 'that fires were seen about five miles higher up near the River Ouse'. Sherwin 'proceeded immediately in the direction with one of his Party and John Tobin Ticket of Leave, in the Service of Mr Espie'. Tobin's sparse convict conduct record has only one offence noted, which, although concerning misbehaviour in September, is nonetheless probably quite telling about this man's usefulness to Sherwin's party only a month prior. Tobin's technical offence concerned having 'a Dog unlicensed named "Wolf" on the premises of his master at Bashan Plains'.[24]

With Tobin's aid, Sherwin soon got 'within two hundred yards of the fire' of Aboriginal people. But, as so often, the advancing colonial force was spotted, and the intended targets fled:

one of the Blacks gave an alarm and about ten others were seen running away, the Party did not succeed in taking any of them, they disappeared in an instant, and the nature of the ground afforded them ample concealment, they however destroyed Seventeen Dogs, burned Eighteen Spears and as many Waddies, and they brought away a Drawing Knife, parts of Sheep Shears, some bags of Ruddle [i.e. ochre] and a small quantity of lead ore[.]

After despoiling the camp, the men resumed their pursuit. While 'ascending a steep hill, two Spears were thrown at them from above'. One of these 'passed close to Mr Sherwin'. One of the assailants was spotted just as he 'disappeared'. Vicary concluded his brief for the Lieutenant Governor by noting that 'all their further search proved unavailing'. Arthur's response was to 'Express my great disappointment that none of these men were captured', and to advocate for the 'utmost possible precaution' when in pursuit. Greater stealth was required by parties 'engaged in this arduous warfare'.[25]

A Lucrative Capture Brings Good Publicity

Only minor elements of Sherwin's operations were described by Vicary in his brief letter to the Lieutenant Governor. The failed pursuit – like so many across the colony – was not reported in the newspapers.

But the details of another mercenary operation in the field during late July are captured in much greater detail. One of the members of the party was Sam Robinson of the Oatlands field police, who was used to writing such reports for Jorgenson.[26] There are also corroborating statements about the composition of this party, and the timing and effect of its mission, because Anstey wrote to the Colonial Secretary regarding 'the reward of £17 for capturing on the 28th ultmo [last, July] 3 adults and one Child, of the Aboriginal Natives, according to the Government notice'.[27] Unlike Sherwin's mission, this pursuit was a success.

The mission was also a victory for Anstey. The leader of the party was Anstey's son, George Alexander Anstey, who 'relinquished … his share of this pecuniary reward' to the prisoners and employed men that constituted the party. Other than Sam Robinson – the only ranger on the mission – the men were all drawn from Anstey's own pool of assigned convict servants and employees. Within two days of the capture Arthur presented this mission to the public as a model of good service. Government Notice 146, dated 30 July, conveyed some details of the capture as well as crafting a message of settler activity for the public:

> The Lieutenant Governor having received information that, on the 28th instant, Mr. George Anstey, accompanied by a party of six men, with great perseverance traced out a Tribe of the Natives, and succeeded in capturing a Man, two Women and an Infant, unhurt. His Excellency has great pleasure in marking his high approbation of the conduct of respectable young Men, who thus step forward, and are the means of carrying into effect, with humanity and kindness, the Orders of the Local Government with regard to these benighted People, by conferring upon Mr. George Anstey, a Grant of Five Hundred Acres of Land.[28]

This notice also mentioned that the convicts on the party may receive tickets of leave 'if their characters in the Books of the Police, shall not preclude the indulgence'.

But George Anstey's 'humanity and kindness' in taking captives 'unhurt' was little more than propaganda, designed to encourage settlers to go out in pursuit in the hope of reward. None of the prisoners received their tickets of leave that year. Moreover, Sam Robinson's report of the encounter, written the day it occurred, reveals elements of the story were left out of the government notice:

> Yesterday afternoon (27th July) one of Mr Anstey's Shepherds observed a fire in the direction of the Table Mountain, the Man lost no time in giving information to Mr Anstey, when a party was instantly sent off in that direction supposing the Natives to be there ... The party left Anstey Barton about 4 o'Clock [sic] in the afternoon, and travelled until about 10 at night passing over some very bad ground, as we supposed we must be near to the place, where the fires had been seen, we agreed to halt for the night, and as we was upon high Ground to look out at Day

Break next morning for smokes, we accordingly arose a little before Day Break examining the Ground very careful as we pass'd along, when we had proceeded about one Mile from our Nights [sic] encampment all of a sudden we observed smoke, and instantly a number of Dogs began to Bark when we perceived the Natives beginning to run away, the party then Discharged their pieces rushing towards the Natives at the same time the Ground being so bad gave the Natives a great advantage[.] However the party succeeded in capturing one male two females and an infant (in all four) and killed 14 Dogs, the party also took five spears upwards of Twenty waddies, thirteen Blankets, a great number of knives, and several other Articles, the Natives who escaped was [sic] left destitute of every thing of which a few minutes before they had been possessed of.

Sam Robinson's report of this encounter was likely forwarded immediately to Hobart. A small annotation was pencilled on the last page, stating that 'this was sent with Major Douglas' letter', meaning that the military authorities in Oatlands were probably also informed. Yet despite this probably being one of the key sources of Arthur's understanding of the event – in part because Anstey only wrote about the reward after the government notice was published – Arthur's public pronouncements made no mention of the captors having fired upon fleeing Aboriginal people. All documentation and correspondence studiously avoided the topic of casualties. But Sam Robinson's letter did have one final detail he felt worth recording, which also failed to attract public notice. 'One of the men belonging to the Tribe', he said, 'endeavoured to carry the infant child with him but being so closely pursued he left the child which was picked up by one of the party and given to its mother who was then captured.'

Systemic Harassment
While such stories point to individual trauma, the collective pressures of the Vandemonian War on Aboriginal people are impossible to

accurately assess. Broader Aboriginal tactics, strategies, alliances and enmities can only be partially deducted though inference. Even with all the surviving mission reports, letters and replies, queries and answers, newspaper stories and country correspondents, the documentable history of the war is but a small fraction of it. Only one side in the war is comprehensively documented.

Sometimes, however, well-placed colonial informants record tantalising hints of intertribal war – or wars. One such case came from Jorgensen, when on 6 August he wrote to the Colonial Secretary about a range of mostly financial matters.[29] In this letter he noted that 'I have the honour to inform you that a most sanguinary [i.e. bloody] battle has been fought amongst the Native Tribes in which one whole Tribe has been killed except six'.

Within a week the *Colonial Times* also had a snippet of news about 'a sanguinary battle', which 'has been fought between four of the Aboriginal tribes'.[30] The paper gave no other particulars except to mention 'that a number were killed'. It was perhaps another indicator that Jorgenson or someone in the Colonial Secretary's Office shared bits of information with the press. It could have been a true report of a major realignment of tribal power structures; it could have been mere rumour.

Either way, the story of a 'sanguinary battle' was just one of many unverified and unverifiable reports conveyed from the battlefields of the interior to the administrative offices in Hobart – and sometimes also to the printing presses. With this intelligence also came news of the transfer of Aboriginal captives to Hobart. 'The four blacks captured by Mr George Anstey', Jorgenson informed the Colonial Secretary, 'are now on their way to town in charge of Special Constable Richard Tyrrell and Police Constable Holmes'. Jorgenson was in Hobart at the time, so the letter was sent and received on the same day. But unbeknown to Jorgenson, one of the captives was planning to escape.

CHAPTER THIRTEEN

Captivity, Qualms and Escalation

1830, Late Winter
Towards Hobart

The Captive's Poor Health

When Richard Tyrrell and William Holmes left the convict settlement at Green Ponds (now Kempton) for Hobart, the Aboriginal man seemed well. But as the group walked on he 'was taken ill', and looked to be 'in a Dangerous State', struggling with the journey.[1] As they 'arrived near the Crown Inn Bagdad, he then fell on the Ground and appeared quite senseless'. But they pushed on. 'Tyrell took him up in his Arms and covered him with a great Coat,' and the two custodians 'took it [in] turns to carry him'. They wanted 'to get to the Public Works at the New Bridge Bagdad, in order to procure a Government Cart to Convey him to Bridgewater'. Yet the man's condition appeared to be worsening.

'He lay down and appeared dying', so the constables 'covered him with Blankets and a Great Coat', and a nearby spectator 'fetched some refreshment for him'. But the man resisted, and they 'could not put any thing into his mouth'. Being now within a mile of the convict station, Tyrrell went ahead and asked the overseer 'for a Government Cart to

Convey the Native to Hobarton'. The overseer 'refused saying he had orders not to let any person have a Cart', telling Tyrrell the constables 'might go and hire one'. Not for the first time in the war, bureaucratic inflexibility and a lack of inter-departmental cooperation stalled even relatively straightforward tasks.

The overseer at least agreed that Tyrrell could take 'a Couple of Men to assist in placing him in a Wheelbarrow to Convey him to the Hut' where they intended to stop for the night. The man was wheeled down the road and taken inside, where 'A Good fire was made and he was placed in Blankets, and every attention paid to him the Two Women and Child'. But the infant was 'crying so much' that the overseer's wife 'came and examined it, and found it in a bad state for want of proper treatment'. She 'washed it, and put it on [sic] some clean clothes'.

'As we knew it was the Lieutenant Governors [sic] order to treat the Aborigines with Humanity,' Holmes and Tyrrell noted in their report, 'and as the man appeared to be in a Dying state we did not Hand cuff them together'. They also noted that the assistant surgeon from the Richmond district 'came, and left some Medicine to be given', but 'The Man refused taking any thing'. Then the party settled in for the night. Holmes and Tyrrell 'sat up until about Twelve'. When 'the Natives appeared quiet and as if asleep' the two constables also readied themselves for sleep. They 'had not had any rest for Two nights previous'. They then 'lay down taking care to fasten the Door, Tyrrell lay across the Door way'.

Then, after a few hours of sleep, the constables 'awoke and found the Door open and the Natives gone, it appeared one or more of them had gone up the Chimney'. As they raised the alarm, they discovered the overseer's wife had only just heard the baby cry. Holmes and Tyrrell were convinced that they only 'miss'd them before they had been gone a quarter of an hour'.

Apparently 'a hue and cry was raised' in the area, 'but in vain'.[2] One of the pursuers 'discovered one of their fires, where they had thrown aside the clothing which had been given them at Oatlands'. After the publicity given to the capture of these four people, their escape was a source of considerable embarrassment.

Fisher's Triumph and Peletega's Subjugation

Yet even while some Aboriginal people were escaping from colonial confinement, more were being captured. After reporting the Bagdad escapees, the *Hobart Town Courier* described an encounter in the Bothwell district the following evening:

> A party of the blacks have for these last few days made their appearance in the neighbourhood of the Clyde and Shannon, and on Sunday night Constable Fisher with a small party overtook some of them at the Shannon and had a skirmish, when one woman was shot, a boy wounded (who escaped) and a noted chief taken prisoner of very large and athletic frame named Peletega.[3]

This incident instigated an ideological contestation between the hawkish and dovish elements of colonial society, at least as captured by the press following Peletega's arrival in Hobart a few days after his capture. The *Colonial Times* gave its readers an extended account of what it characterised as a 'farce' and 'a ridiculous and degrading scene':

> It appears that some days back an engagement took place up at the Shannon between some Constables and a tribe of the Aborigines, two of the latter were killed and one taken prisoner ... and the prisoner of war was led in chains to the capital – and something in a similar manner was he brought to town as a dancing bear is led by his master. A large and heavy cart chain was twisted round his neck, and the other end of it was in the left hand of one of the conquerors, who most manfully, fearlessly, and courageously stepped out, being defended only with an unsheathed long sword in his right hand, and on either side a man under arms with loaded musket and fixed bayonets; in this manner was the poor creature led to the gaol, where, on his arrival, he was heavily ironed.[4]

'Nothing would have given us greater pleasure,' the editor concluded, 'than to have seen His Excellency witness this degrading scene, and we venture to assert it would have been the last of the kind.' But the editor was probably quite wrong. Upon receiving word of Peletega's capture, Arthur had given Vicary clear instructions: 'The Native Chief who has been captured should be sent under a <u>very sufficient</u> and <u>secure</u> escort to Hobart Town immediately.'⁵ Arthur's main concern was to avoid any further escapes.

Nonetheless, the *Colonial Times* used Peletega for much effect. By presenting this captive in contrast to his situation – 'grinning and laughing' while being marched into town, nonchalantly smoking a pipe while 'the irons were being put on his legs' – the episode worked as a means of criticising the prosecution of the war, at least regarding the treatment of prisoners. The *Colonial Times*'s 'farce' dripped with editorialising.

On the same page as the story about Peletega was a glowing report of 'the expedition sent by government under Mr. Robinson to conciliate the native tribes', which had reportedly resulted in much 'friendly intercourse'. Diplomacy and hostility were thereby contrasted, without the connection having to be made too explicit. Even while recognising the need for 'catching and gaining them [Aboriginal people] over to civilisation, or else effectually to deter them from continuing their ravages', the paper was speaking to current politics. Hoping to 'tame and instruct these poor people to habits of useful industry' constituted a political argument unrelated to the war itself. The *Colonial Times* advocated that using Aboriginal people as labourers would be better for the colony than the 'attempt now making to introduce Chinese labourers amongst us', a reference to the recent importation of Chinese mechanics into Launceston by the *Nimrod*.⁶

The *Colonial Times*'s concern with the importation of Chinese labour went mostly unnoticed and unremarked, but the rival *Hobart Town Courier* took the opportunity to respond to its war commentary:

> We have received several letters from the neighbourhood of the Clyde, complaining of the observations of a contemporary, the *Colonial Times*, on the conduct of Constable Fisher who happily succeeded the other day in securing Peletega, the powerful and

crafty chief of the tribe of blacks, which has of late been so troublesome in that quarter. We trust, however, that neither Fisher nor any other person will be deterred by any ill natured remarks of the kind from strenuously doing his duty. Had Fisher not used the means he did to secure his captive with a chain, he would have been subjected to the same reproach as those who were lately allowed the blacks to escape at Bagdad. The greatest circumspection is indeed necessary to guard against the cunning of these poor but at present very dangerous people, and no possible means should be neglected which common sense and humanity will dictate, to keep them safe when in custody or to guard against their cunning attacks when at large. In this case Peletega, whose tribe consisted of about 100 blacks, and who had shewn himself on former occasions a most determined enemy of the whites, was conducting by Fisher from Mr. Howell's farm on the Shannon to Bothwell, when on the road he made a daring attempt to escape, which had nearly proved fatal to Fisher before he was aware of it. He had placed one finger in his mouth, and was endeavouring to force out his eye with his thumb, until after a desperate struggle he was overpowered.[7]

Peletega's case was one of the few public reports of Aboriginal people being conveyed into custody. While there were contested presentations of the sequence of events, they are generally not mutually exclusive at the level of descriptive detail. The difference in the way they were presented says more about divergent attitudes – not over conflict, capture and expulsion, which all agreed on – but on the treatment of the captives.

The Politics and Economics of Capture

The captivity of Aboriginal people was even treated with some literary flippancy. One story of 'a very active and determined young man' catching 'a wild woman' while on a morning walk is a case in point. The woman struggled by biting her captor 'severely' on the hand, but 'he would not relinquish his prize, and the wood nymph has, by this time, probably rewarded his virtue'.[8]

The *Colonial Times* also received letters complaining of their coverage of Fisher's chaining of Peletega. The editor of the *Colonial Times* referred to one of these, a 'Mr. A____'s letter, dated Clyde', which clearly reflected a very hostile attitude towards Aboriginal people.[9] The editor was 'sorry to find in him a supporter of such a system as the one alluded to', and suggested that the writer's 'very vindictive feeling he seems to manifest, is the only real cause which prevents a unison between the Aborigines and ourselves'.

But while intimating shock at Mr A's views, the *Colonial Times* had certainly stoked enmity. It was this paper, after all, that in February had reported the burning 'of the whole of Mr. Howell's premises and property' by Aboriginal people, putting before the reading public the image of his wife and children fleeing the burning building, leaving a destitute family dwelling under a bark shelter dependent on blankets from the local police magistrate.[10]

Arthur was impressed by Howell's efforts to capture Peletega and their propagandistic potential. As the Colonial Secretary wrote to Vicary:

> I am to request that you will have the goodness to inform
> Mr Howell that The Lieut Governor has heard with the greatest
> satisfaction of the energy and enterprise he has evinced, in
> following up the Natives, after their recent attack upon his
> premises, and that he may rely upon it, His Excellency will not
> permit such conduct to pass without marking it with some strong
> testimony of his approbation.[11]

A few weeks later a public notice was gazetted, drawing the public's attention to 'the indefatigable energy which has been displayed by Mr. Humphrey Howell, of the Clyde, in pursuit of the Aboriginal Natives'.[12] Arthur was, the notice affirmed, 'much gratified to observe, that notwithstanding the severe losses which he has suffered from their frequent attacks he has invariably acted towards them with humanity, as well as firmness'.

Howell's efforts were rewarded with a grant of 1000 acres. Another government notice of the same date publicly rewarded John Batman with 2000 acres of land for his 'twelve months, in pursuit of the Aborigines'.[13] One of Batman's men was rewarded with a conditional pardon, and four more with tickets of leave. There was a strong culture of public reward and recognition – for certain types of people at least.

Fisher also received a ticket of leave for his services in capturing Peletega and conveying him to Hobart within days of the capture.[14] But greater rewards were held out for continued service. 'A Ticket of Leave will be immediately prepared for Constable Fisher,' the Colonial Secretary told Vicary, 'whom you will be so good as to inform, that if he is disposed to continue his services in the Police, and shall be further successful in capturing the Aborigines, The Lieut Gov will be happy to reward him with some further mark of His Excellency's approbation.'[15]

It was a considerable turnaround for Fisher. Initially sentenced to death, he was transported as a reprieve, and held the sort of conduct record that might normally have mitigated against reward.[16] His track record in the convict system included refusing to work, assaulting and beating someone, possessing stolen goods as well as various absences, for which he received two 50-stroke lashings, was sentenced to work on a chain gang, and at one stage was reduced to a diet of bread and water. One of his cases was even referred to Arthur, who might have noticed on Fisher's record that the convict sported a tattoo of a 'Naked Woman'.[17]

Nonetheless, Fisher was appointed to the field police in 1827, initially at New Norfolk.[18] When caught 'Illegally retailing Spirits' while a field police constable, Anstey recommended that he 'lose his prom[ise]d TL for all his former serv[ic]e'. Only a few months prior to capturing Peletega, Fisher was sentenced by Vicary to serve another three months in the field police for an unspecified 'Neglect of duty & pretence of illness'. Yet a single capture had dramatically advanced him through the convict system. He may not have become a public example like George Anstey, Humphrey Howell or John Batman, but within the system there could be little doubt that Fisher's conduct in this matter brought him reward and made him an exemplar for other convicts. Moreover, Fisher got a further reward when he received a bounty for Peletega's capture. A page from the accounts of the 'Aboriginal Department', which now survives as a stray relic of a much larger body of accounting, records that £5 was paid to a party led by Fisher for 'Apprehending one male Aborigine' at the 'Blue Hills'.[19]

Two other disbursements on this page of accounts were for 'apprehending one male and one female Aborigine' (£10), also taken at the Blue Hills, and for 'one male Aborigine' (£5) taken at 'Abyssinia'. One of Howell's assigned servants from the Peletega capture led the other 'Blue Hills' success, which suggests there was another dedicated roving party. This stray page also referred to a 'Receipt attached', pointing to yet more records originally produced during the war. But while the bounty system appears to have operated relatively smoothly, the Lieutenant Governor seems to have felt the need to respond to the negative press concerning Peletega's treatment.[20]

Government Notice 161 from 20 August was a carefully worded response to the *Colonial Times* issue of the same date, and stated that 'The Lieutenant Governor has learned with much regret' that the system of rewards 'appears in some recent instances to have been misapprehended'. Using 'any sort of violence or restraint to such of the Aboriginal Natives as may approach the European inhabitants with friendly views' was, Arthur declared, against 'the spirit' of the system or any previous government proclamations or notices. Rather, he clarified that 'the reward was offered for the capture of such natives only as were committing aggression on the inhabitants of the settled districts ... no violence or restraint shall be offered to the inoffensive natives of the remote and unsettled parts of the territory.' The notice effectively asserted the humanity of government policy past and present, without specifically mentioning the means of capturing hostile Aboriginal people or detaining them once they were prisoners of war.

Despite this public gesture, the means of capture remained a political sore point, as highlighted by another story in the *Colonial Times* referring to events in late August 1830:

One day last week a servant of Captain Wood, of the Clyde, brought into Hobart Town an Aboriginal prisoner which he had captured. It appears, from what we have heard, that a mob of these misguided wretches rushed on the man in question, who took shelter in a stock-hut, where fortunately for him there happened to be some fire-arms ready-loaded, which he put immediately into requisition, and in the course of a short time, as we are informed, killed several of the Natives, and took the one in question prisoner. On arriving in Hobart Town, Captain Wood's man conveyed the black to the Police Office, of course expecting to be immediately paid the reward … but he was there desired to leave the man, and his case would in due course be laid before His Excellency. The man was apparently not very well satisfied in his own mind about the time which might elapse before his reward would be forthcoming, and he therefore refused to deliver over his prisoner without payment there and then. Ultimately a letter was written to His Excellency by the Magistrate, and handed to the man, who attended at Government house accompanied by his prisoner.[21]

With the aid of one of the Aboriginal men dwelling at George Augustus Robinson's property in suburban Hobart, Arthur interviewed the captive, learned 'that the white men had destroyed several of his companions' and authorised payment of the bounty anyway.

Mobilising Political Will

As the colony endured another winter of warfare, August 1830 became something of a month for rallying cries and hardening public attitudes. 'The country about Bothwell is in a sad state,' the *Colonial Times* stated, because attacks 'on the Settlers … are every day getting more and more frequent'.[22] Referring to reports 'that Captain Wood's men have had several skirmishes with the different mobs', the newspaper also carried other stories about fighting, including the case of a settler who Batman found with 'an axe stuck in the back of his skull'. The

CAPTIVITY, QUALMS AND ESCALATION

Launceston Advertiser reported Aboriginal people stealing guns from shepherds, as well as the marriage of a 'domesticated' Aboriginal couple. The overall picture was of intense combat across the settled districts, and little hope of reconciliation. 'Something must be done!', the *Colonial Times* argued, because 'the plan at present adopted will leave no other chance of obtaining peace than the annihilation of the whole race'.

> Parties of the old inhabitants, with persons who are acquainted with the country as well as the Natives themselves, would be the right kind of men to employ capturing them, and in the end these must be the persons fixed upon; not one party but scores be regularly appointed, who would be able to watch all the different passes at once.

The *Hobart Town Courier* shared a similar sentiment that something 'bold' was required.[23] Claiming that 'the record of the truth is the duty of the public journalist', the editor argued that the colony must 'plan and act upon a uniform system' and take 'a more stern and defensive posture' within the settled districts. It too offered examples of violence, like the case of 'a horde of the Aborigines' who stole some shepherds' guns, and successfully speared one of them who 'had his arm completely transfixed by a spear; and received a tremendous blow between the shoulders from a waddy'.

The depth of the crisis was indicated by the account of a woman firing at Aboriginal assailants in her husband's absence, successfully frightening them off, while her 'youngest son, a little boy about 4 years old', brought a second gun while she 'maintained her ground'. They reportedly lay down to avoid her shots, before heading off and robbing a different hut. Dozens of other reports followed, filling most of the page, and providing a growing list of colonial victims from settlers and shepherds to 'old John York's horse'.

In response to 'the repeated and very distressing Outrages which are still daily committed by the Aborigines' – but also seemingly to address the public agitation on this issue – Arthur called for the

Aborigines Committee to reassemble.[24] Their first point of business was to determine whether Arthur's most recent government notices were contradictory. Where Government Notice 160 outlined a bounty system for the capture of Aboriginal people, Government Notice 161 cited the 'friendly intercourse' with tribes achieved by George Augustus Robinson and Captain Welch beyond the settled districts, and requested 'that all Settlers and others will strictly enjoin their Servants cautiously to abstain from acts of aggression against these benighted beings, and that they will themselves personally endeavour to conciliate them wherever it may be practicable'.[25]

Obligingly, the Aborigines Committee met on Saturday 28 August and declared there were no contradictions. The committee also considered 'Whether more vigorous measures should be adopted to repel the Aborigines from the Settled Districts', and 'What measures they would recommend should be adopted towards the disposal of such of the Aborigines as should be captured.' Determining that Aboriginal people 'have been actuated by the most rancorous animosity', the committee agreed that they should be removed 'by every means that can be exercised'. The committee suggested sending captives to Maria Island, which had a convict station and military presence already in place.

Such conclusions were hardly surprising as on Friday 27 August, the day before this meeting, Arthur had taken a couple of decisive actions. He issued another government notice, which repeated that numbers 160 and 161 had been 'misinterpreted':

> the measures which are indispensable for the defence and protection of the settlers should be tempered with humanity, and that no means of conciliation should be spared; but it was not intended to relax in the most strenuous exertions to repel and drive from the settled country those Natives who seize every occasion to perpetrate murders, and to plunder and destroy the property of the inhabitants.[26]

Arthur further used this notice to instruct police magistrates to check defensive arrangements in their districts and urge settlers and servants 'to keep their arms in good order'. He forbade aggressions beyond the settled districts or upon surrendering people, but gave broad sanction to much else. 'They are,' he clarified, 'by every possible means, to be captured, or driven beyond the settled districts.' The Aborigines Committee subsequently reached similar conclusions, which they expressed with similar phrasing.

At midday on that Friday Arthur also turned his Executive Council to the issue of the war.[27] They were presented with evidence sent from the interior of 'various outrages committed by the Natives', and requests from Anstey and Vicary for firmer measures and greater military support. Arthur then presented the earlier report of the Aborigines Committee, which asserted that conciliation had 'proved quite ineffectual' and affirmed 'it had become essentially necessary to adopt the most vigorous measures'.

The council then concluded that the present crisis pointed to the necessity of strong measures. Aboriginal attacks 'on men armed and unarmed, and on defenceless women and children, can be considered in no other light than as acts of warfare against the settlers generally'. The council recorded their collective belief 'how absolutely necessary it is that the settled districts at least should be freed from their presence', and recorded their misgivings about further attempts at negotiation. According to the minutes of the meeting:

> In such a state of things, it appears to the Council that the time is now arrived when it has become absolutely necessary that some vigorous effort, upon a more extended scale than has hitherto been practicable, should be made for expelling these miserable people forthwith from the settled districts. ... even if it should cost more lives than the Council anticipates, it is a measure dictated not less by humanity than by necessity, since it is calculated to bring to a decisive issue a state of warfare which there seems no hope of ending by any other means, and which, if much longer continued, the Council fears will become a war of extermination.

By this political reasoning, a massive act of ethnic cleansing was a logical necessity, required to prevent an extinction. But the rationale was less important than the cover. With the support of his Executive Council and the Aborigines Committee, and apparently encouraged by public calls for action, Arthur had sufficient demonstrable political support for a massive military operation.

General Mobilisation

Preparations for mass military mobilisation within the colony were soon underway. On 9 September 1830 Arthur issued Government Order 9, calling for 'a general and simultaneous effort'.[28] Arthur asked 'every settler' who could join the effort 'to place himself under the direction' of the police magistrates, which would form a 'volunteer force' to manoeuvre in conjunction with the military and field police. Urban volunteers could join adjacent rural districts. Furthermore, to 'augment to the greatest possible extent' the roving parties, 'all the prisoners holding tickets of leave, who are capable of bearing arms' were required to report to the police magistrates. The settled districts were divided into seven military zones of command, headed by five captains and two lieutenants, with Major Douglas taking overall command of the military per prior arrangements. While clarifying that 'no individual is to expect any specific reward', Arthur nonetheless mentioned 'that a service rendered to the public is never overlooked or forgotten by the colonial government.' The 'general movement', as the operation was termed, was designated to start on 7 October.

But such an operation did not simply spring forth from the ferment of a weekend in late August 1830. As the prior appointment of Douglas to overall command illustrates, Arthur had been contemplating such a manoeuvre for months. A clue to this is in his increasing focus on defences in the north of the island, just as Robinson's diplomatic mission rounded from the west coast into the north.

A letter from the Colonial Secretary to Smith at Norfolk Plains reveals that orders were issued 'to detach a party of Four men to

CAPTIVITY, QUALMS AND ESCALATION

Foulger's Hut, at the back of the Van Diemen's Land Establishment, provided the building is entirely given up for the use of the Military'.[29] A few days later Smith was asked 'whether you feel yourself able to afford any protection from the Police of your District to the Settlement at Port Sorell', further indicating a focus on the defences of the north coast.[30] As already seen, Arthur's focus in the western settled districts at this time mostly concerned capture missions and captives, but he was also irritated by 'learning that the Assistant Surveyor's hut has been robbed and the Arms taken from it by the Natives' in the Bothwell district.[31] Arthur wanted it 'minutely and carefully investigated'. As the Colonial Secretary expressed it to Vicary, 'His Excellency cannot permit, either by carelessness or negligence, that the Blacks should be suffered to possess themselves of Arms'. Although Aboriginal people still mainly attacked with spears and waddies, the prospect of their wider adoption of firearms terrified colonists. But while offering another instance of that worrying trend of Aboriginal people taking guns, the incident also highlighted the continued surveying of that district, despite being so hotly contested.

While having already laid some of the groundwork, Arthur began mobilising men as soon as the decision for a general offensive was made. One of the first groups to be directed to this cause arrived in Hobart on the *David Lyon*, a convict transport that reached Hobart from London on 19 August.[32] Aboard was a guard, consisting of a captain, an ensign, a sergeant, and '38 rank and file' from the 17th Regiment. The male convict transports generally brought military guards with them, who often then got deployed on duty within the colonies. But Arthur also wanted to use the convicts for the war effort. The Colonial Secretary informed Anstey that 20 of the *David Lyon* prisoners were being sent to his district, 'whom, you will have the goodness to assign to such settlers in your District (being in want of Servants) as appear to you to be the most exposed to the attacks of the Natives'.[33] Vicary was also sent 20 prisoners and a similar letter. The convicts had been conscripted to the war effort. They would help bolster the defences at huts, but they would also provide settlers with a larger pool of servants to co-opt into the General Movement when the time came.

Private capture missions did not cease with the General Movement, but the publicity associated with bringing captives to Hobart probably encouraged more captors to simply apply at their nearest Police Office, which is what Arthur had originally envisioned anyway.

During September Vicary asked the Colonial Secretary whether bounties were to be paid to the principal captor or to 'all the persons present and assisting', which at least suggests bounties were being presented in his district.[34] Arthur determined that the reward should be shared, although the documentation of this process has been mostly lost. Even the captives arriving from Robinson's mission are relatively poorly documented. Among the August shipping arrivals in Launceston were 'four Aborigines' from Circular Head on the northwest coast. Robinson had sent them, along with letters for the Reverend Bedford and the Lieutenant Governor, aboard the schooner *Friendship*.[35]

Yet while the bounty system survived its bad publicity, some of the roving parties did not. In late August Simpson forwarded 'Mr Batman's last report of his proceedings'.[36] The report itself is no longer with the covering letter, but annotations overleaf by Arthur reveal his frustration: 'Mr Batman's Services have ended, as most of the other Expeditions have done, unsuccessfully!'

Like Robertson before him, Batman's failure to take sufficient captives to end the hostilities was an embarrassment for the Lieutenant Governor, especially considering their publicity. But despite this misgiving, Arthur did not give up on roving parties altogether; he just became more discreet about their establishment, and clearer about their contractual terms.

CHAPTER FOURTEEN

Agitation and Armament

1830, Spring
Hobart, and Command HQ

Deflecting and Recruiting

The decision to mobilise the colony changed the way that the Lieutenant Governor dealt with applications from would-be roving party leaders. On 14 September 1830, a few days after issuing the first government notice of the General Movement, the Colonial Secretary replied to Simpson at Campbell Town about one such application that had been forwarded to Hobart:

> I am directed to request that you will communicate to the Messrs Darke, that The Lieutenant Governor is very much obliged by their offers to take charge of parties in pursuit of the Aborigines, and that His Excellency would have taken their propositions into consideration, but that the Government has come into the determination to make a vigorous and general effort, in which the Settlers will be called upon to join in the month of October next (as they will learn from the Gazette); His Excellency however trusts that they will unite their exertions, with the Police of their District, in the combined movement which will be directed against the Natives.[1]

It was the second such application from the Campbell Town district rejected that day. 'Mr J W Massey' was also informed that 'the general measure about to be adopted ... prevents The Lieutenant Governor accepting his services in an especial manner but His Excellency will most gladly avail himself of them in furtherance of the above more extended operations'.²

Throughout the Vandemonian War the Colonial Secretary received a significant volume of correspondence from settlers offering their services against Aboriginal people. Some reached Hobart directly from settlers, others via police magistrates or various patrons either writing on an applicant's behalf or forwarding their proposal.

The September 1830 application from the Darkes was at least the second from this family. A year earlier, in August 1829, Assistant Surveyor John Helder Wedge wrote to the government on behalf of 'Willm Darke, a relative of mine', who was offering to lead a roving party for 12 months.³ 'In the Absence of Sydney Natives', Wedge noted, likely referring to Batman's party, Darke could field a team drawn from 'the Sealers in Bass' Straits'. Wedge was sure that these men 'would gladly lend their aid' if they were 'remunerated'. 'The fact of their having a number of native women with them, whom they take by surprise and force,' he added, 'is a proof they would be efficient if they were employed', noting also that Darke was 'ready to cooperate with these men'. While this application was politely rejected, it did not stop the Darkes trying again in 1830.

The prospects of land and salaries seem to have inspired many applicants and a range of schemes. Andrew Barry, in his August 1829 application, drew attention to his prior experiences:

> having had much experience in his native Country, in assisting to capture the Indians, would gladly render every possible aid in capturing the Aborigines in this Colony for which he feels himself fully competent.⁴

He hoped for 'a moderate Salary with Rations, and a location of Fifty Acres of Land'. Arthur's response at the time was blunt: 'Refused.

It will be better, I think, to take prisoners'. Among surviving papers is a wealth of documentation regarding the selection and appointment of convicts and servants to the various field police and roving parties, including assessments of their characters and the terms of their promised indulgences.

These applications have become the only means of documenting many of these schemes. While plenty were rejected by Arthur, others were approved, or went through a series of discussions, which reveal something about their implementation. One example is the case of Edward Wilson Hodgson, a convict who responded to Arthur's February 1830 government notice that promised a reward for any person willing to undertake a reconciliation.[5] Hodgson proposed taking two men with him:

> to look out for their fires by night, and when so done lay by till day break then make towards them, and give my fire arms to the men who I should wish to remain in the rear, and then if possible go amongst them and leave my fate to him above who is always ready to assist in a good and just cause. I should then by motions, signs, and little trifling presents endeavour to gain their friendship.

Forwarding Hodgson's letter, Anstey noted that 'Hodgson is one of the best behaved Convicts that I have met with in this Colony', adding that 'I shall be very sorry if the poor man's life should be forfeited by his temerity', clearly unimpressed with the idea of such a pacific approach.

Arthur's response, however, was to instruct Anstey to see this man, 'hear what he says, make any suggestion that occurs to him, & then forward him on to Hobart'. Arthur also promised Hodgson 'a Pardon' if he was successful, and thought that 'Capt Clarke's at the Clyde' was 'The best situation for making the attempt', where the woman had been spared during a raid. Anstey ordered Hodgson to head to Hobart in early March 1830 'to get furnished with the Beads, Trinkets, &c'.

Personnel Overlap and Tactical Continuities

This body of correspondence connected with applicants and their parties also reveals some of the networks among the convicts and settlers as well as insight into the workings of the roving parties and how they continued into the general mobilisation. Successful applicants generally had some personal connections to people in positions of power, and then could draw on their own networks to form teams, thereby providing a pool of experienced men upon whom Arthur could call in the spring of 1830. Back in April, for instance, both Danvers and Scott made formal representations about their parties, each highlighting Arthur's ultimate oversight. Danvers wrote to Anstey on 2 April:

> With reference to His Excellency's orders that I should be permitted to select some prisoners of the crown to proceed with me on a particular Service I beg to recommend the four undermentioned prisoners of the Crown. James Hewitt is keeper of a very few bullocks belonging to the Government at Oatlands. Henry Thomson and John Oliver belong to the Public Works at Oatlands. Francis Cains is assigned Servant to Mr McLeod at Campbell Town, but has his master's permission to join my party.[6]

All were approved for the mission, excepting John Oliver 'on account of the number of Offences he has committed'.

In forwarding Danvers' letter to Hobart, Anstey mentioned to the Colonial Secretary that Arthur and Danvers had conversed about the roving parties and rewards for service, referring to 'The conditions of Peter Scott's and Danvers' appointments, which His Excellency ment[ione]d to Danvers verbally on Tuesday last'. Anstey also mentioned that 'His Excellency said he had ordered, previous to his leaving Town, a Ticket of Leave for J[ohn] Danvers.' It meant that Arthur's tour of the interior involved discussion with some of the convict roving party leaders, as well as the police magistrates and gentlemen rovers like Batman. It points to that wider phenomenon of verbal communications and orders, now largely invisible.

While Danvers called his mission a 'particular Service', Peter Scott's April letter claimed he had 'been given to understand that His Excellency has been pleased to signify that I should proceed on a special Service'.[7] Scott listed five convicts, including one 'sometimes employed as a Shoemaker to the roving parties at Oatlands'. As with Danvers' letter, an annotation by Anstey reveals the Lieutenant Governor personally directed the operations just at that moment when he seemed to decentralise them away from Anstey. Scott's nominated men were 'ordered to place themselves under his orders, at Miles's Opening and places in that vicinity, agreeably to His Excellency's suggestion on Tuesday last'.

Anstey also noted on Scott's letter that 'Most of the men now employed under Jorgenson have nearly completed their period of Service'. The abandonment of the roving parties may have appeared intentional, but it all fitted within a larger frame of personnel shifts – much of which related to convict service and punishment.

So while individual rovers came and went, the roving parties continued. Even the determination on the General Movement in the spring of 1830 did not see the end of individual roving missions. One case particularly illustrates the continuities with perfect timing. On 16 September 1830, two days after rejecting proposals from the Darkes and Massey on the grounds of an imminent 'general measure', the Colonial Secretary finalised arrangements for a 'proposed expedition against the hostile Aborigines' led by Nicolas Fortosa.[8]

Fortosa's Special Force

When Arthur visited the interior in March and April 1830 he met with the police magistrate of Campbell Town. In late April, Simpson noted that 'The Lieutenant Governor ... authorised me to raise a Band for the purpose of capturing the native Tribes.'[9] Simpson's correspondent was not the Colonial Secretary, who normally dealt with such matters, but Arthur's private secretary William Parramore. Explaining that he had told Arthur he 'could procure an intelligent active person to head a party', Simpson nominated Nicolas Fortosa, who would soon be in

Hobart. Simpson suggested 'that [Fortosa] should be furnished with all the necessary supplies of Slops, Bedding, Arms &c for himself and party'. But lacking 'His Excellency's authority to enter into particulars' with Fortosa, because the terms of service involved the promise of 'Land', Simpson hoped Fortosa could 'wait upon His Excellency' to work out the full details of his contract in person.

Fortosa, or Turtosa as he was also sometimes called, had been in the colony for about two decades. Born in Rome, Fortosa was an Italian ex-convict who had been transported for life from Malta on the *Indefatigable* in 1812.[10] He was 37 years old when he arrived in Van Diemen's Land, had dark hair and eyes, and a very slim convict conduct record. In 1816 he was acquitted on a charge of 'Cutting & maiming'. Evidence from New South Wales reveals Fortosa was shipped to Sydney to act as a witness in a criminal trial in late 1819.[11] The following year he was conditionally pardoned. After that, his record is silent. In early 1830 Fortosa was presumably known to Simpson, but on paper he was the closest thing to a ghost of any of the expedition applicants. As well as being an ex-convict, Fortosa was also an ex-soldier. He served in the Royal Sicilian Regiment, and was in Malta towards the end of the Napoleonic Wars.[12]

By the end of June Arthur was supportive of Fortosa's appointment. 'This proposal is from a man who I think is more likely to be useful in the bush than any I have yet seen,' he wrote on the back of another note from Simpson.[13] Fortosa wanted 'a party of Crown Prisoners (nine) under his orders', with a scale of rewards for them after 12 months of service. The government should supply 'Arms, Ammunition and Blankets', but Fortosa wanted 2 shillings per day instead of government rations and clothing. He probably hoped this would avoid some of the problems previous roving parties had with getting provisions and the administration of receipts, but it would also facilitate their operations throughout the island, including beyond the prescribed limits of martial law. In addition to these conditions, Fortosa wanted 'Five pounds reward for <u>each</u> native captured', to be shared by the party, and further rewards for Fortosa including a large land grant.

'Nicholas Fortosa is ready to start,' Arthur informed the Colonial Secretary, authorising most of the convicts who volunteered for this

AGITATION AND ARMAMENT

service to join the party. A list of the proposed roving party reveals that among the volunteers was at least one other ex-soldier, a deserter by the name of Samuel Duffield.[14] Yet despite the apparent readiness of the leader, a month later the formalities were still being worked out. On 30 July Arthur minuted that he had seen Fortosa 'and approve of his services'.[15] Fortosa was engaged for 12 months largely as he had proposed. The scaled rewards were agreed, as was the size of the roving party. The daily pay of 2 shillings in lieu of rations was raised by sixpence. Arthur stuck to the bounty scale by clarifying that while adult captives would earn the party £5, children were at the rate of £2 each. The Lieutenant Governor also modified the terms of the reward of land, noting that Fortosa 'for his personal services, will be allowed One Thousand Acres of Land, unrestricted provided the Party captures 20 adult Natives'.

Arthur delegated the selection of convicts to Simpson, who could organise their appointment with their respective masters. By 16 September the arrangements for Fortosa's party were almost complete. The convicts attached to the mission had been formally approved and the Colonial Secretary advised Simpson that the 'Arms, Ammunition and Blankets for the party will be, immediately forwarded.'[16] Moreover, Arthur gave a further piece of advice to Simpson about how Fortosa's rewards were to be calculated:

> The Lieut Governor has approved of the Reward of One
> thousand acres of Land, to Fortosa, being increased in quantity
> or diminished, according as the number of Natives captured
> shall exceed or fall short of Twenty, as, also should the party be
> unavoidably compelled to use violence, and loss of life ensure, that
> the Capture <u>thus</u> made, shall be admitted a claim for reward.[17]

With that, Arthur approved paying bounties for Aboriginal people killed by Fortosa's party. The Colonial Secretary concluded his letter by advising that 'The Lieutenant Governor expects Nicholas Fortosa will speedily take the field.' Arthur clearly wanted this mission underway before the General Movement began.

Veterans and Preliminaries

Fortosa was not the only man being picked for service in advance of the forthcoming operations. Jorgenson's retirement from government service was relatively short-lived. The *Hobart Town Courier* ran a short piece in early September about Jorgenson having 'a narrow escape ... from the furious attack of a bull, who is said to have gone mad near Bothwell'.[18] The story was among others about Aboriginal hostilities. They had 'pillaged' a supply cart on its return journey after it 'conveyed the baggage of a detachment of the 17th regt', and the 'same horde attacked' another hut 'and were beaten off by Constable Lawrence and others'. They had also 'crossed from the westward into the district about Ben Lomond, from which', the newspaper stated, 'we had hoped the late exertions of Mr. Batman had effectually removed them.' Finally, 'a party of the blacks robbed Lieutenant Hill's shepherd's hut on the Elizabeth river'. The message was simple: they were all over the place, and they were still dangerous.

While the story about Jorgenson was more about the bull than the former roving party leader, it highlighted his continued association with the Bothwell district. A few weeks after resigning from the field police, Jorgenson was charged at Bothwell 'with being drunk and disorderly' and fined 5 shillings.[19] Curiously, the same day, Norah Corbett – the woman with whom Jorgenson had previously been accused of associating – was also fined 5 shillings in Bothwell for the same offence.

By mid-September Jorgenson was back in the midlands. On the morning of 16 September he and Anstey had a conversation, most likely at Anstey Barton. Jorgenson followed this with a letter explaining his decision to quit the field police, and offering his services for the 'levy en masse' as the mobilisation of the soldiers and settlers-militant was sometimes being called.[20] Jorgenson went on to offer some advice for the operations:

> It strikes me that amongst the multitudes that will be called into the bush there will be some well qualified to perform the duties required of them, and others less so. I would therefore undertake

Colonial Van Diemen's Land in the 1820s. Hobart (above) was the largest settlement, the main seat of government, and a military base. *Allport Library and Museum of Fine Arts, Tasmanian Archive and Heritage Office: Watercolour of Hobart Town Van Diemen's Land by George Frankland.*

Further inland, like this spot on a tributary of the Derwent River (below), the landscape was called 'settled' but was still contested. The tree markings were made by Aboriginal people hunting possum. *State Library of New South Wales: [IE1955124], Thomas Scott's Sketches of Van Diemen's Land.*

Contemporary depictions of conflict during the Vandemonian War remain rare. The war was often represented as a contest between Aboriginal aggressors and civilian settlers (above). *State Library of New South Wales: [IE1656866] 'Pencil drawing entitled The Aborigions of Van Demondsland endeavouring to kill Mr John Allen on Milton Farm in the District of Great Swanport on the 14th December 1828'.*

But roads like those near New Norfolk (below) served military as well as civil needs, highlighting that colonisation was far from militarily passive. *National Library of Australia: The new road leading to the northward from New Norfolk, Van Dieman's Land.*

rub their cheeks against it until they have thoroughly imbibed the stench. As soon as the opossums were singed and well heated on one side our cook turned them on the other, and then dragging them by the leg from the fire, he scraped off the fur, and with a sharp flint cut out the inside, and again threw it on the fire, from which it was soon after taken and eaten, without the trouble of

(An Aboriginal Dinner Party.)

knife or fork, in a half raw state. Occasionally they would take a short walk to the lagoon, and laying themselves on their breast, and dipping their mouth into the water drank without cups or chalice the pure element of nature. They then returned to their rural hearth, and sitting or reclining on the ground they dozed as deliciously as if they had reposed on a velvet couch.

The colonial press had a complex relationship with the Vandemonian War. It provides an important record of events, but was frequently partisan and inaccurate. An 1830 description and illustration of 'An Aboriginal Dinner Party' (above) is part ethnography, part parody, part propaganda. *Tasmaniana Library, Tasmanian Archive and Heritage Office: Page from the Hobart Town Almanack for the year 1830.*

Farmsteads (above) in the so-called 'settled districts' served as strong points and ration stations during the Vandemonian War. *National Library of Australia: June Park, Van Dieman's Land, the general appearance of the country in its natural state, perfect park scenery [Augustus Earle].* Colonists strategically used landscape features while harassing Aboriginal people, for instance utilising narrow peninsulas like the Schoutens (below) to try to trap Aboriginal people. Many settlers were in fact ex-military. *Allport Library and Museum of Fine Arts, Tasmanian Archive and Heritage Office: Joseph Lycett, View of the south end of Schouten's Island, 1825.*

The Vandemonian War helped document what it destroyed. Colonists recorded many Aboriginal cultural practices during the war years, including these rare manuscript depictions of colonial-era Aboriginal tree art (above and below). *Tasmanian Archive and Heritage Office: CSO1/1/323.*

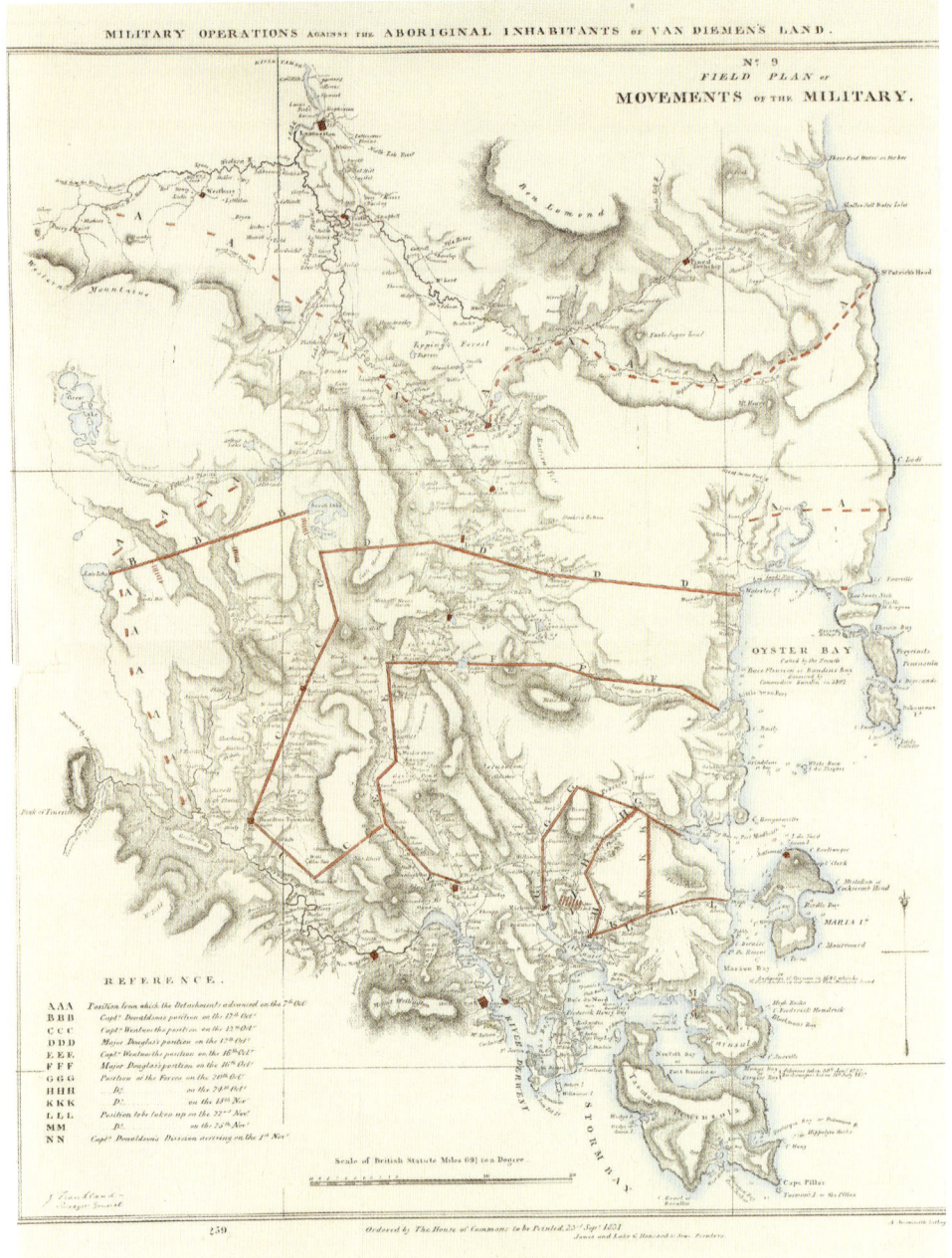

The General Movement of late 1830 was a massive military campaign designed to sweep the midlands clear of Aboriginal people (above). *W.L. Crowther Library, Tasmanian Archive and Heritage Office: Surveyor General George Frankland's 'Field Plan of Movements of the Military'.*

The General Movement of late 1830 was Australia's largest domestic colonial military campaign. A list of volunteers contains a sketch of a mounted participant (above). *Tasmanian Archive and Heritage Office: POL35/1/1.*

After a series of driving movements, the colonial forces established a fortified line (below) to contain Aboriginal people while they were harassed by dedicated skirmishers. *Tasmanian Archive and Heritage Office: CSO1/1/324.*

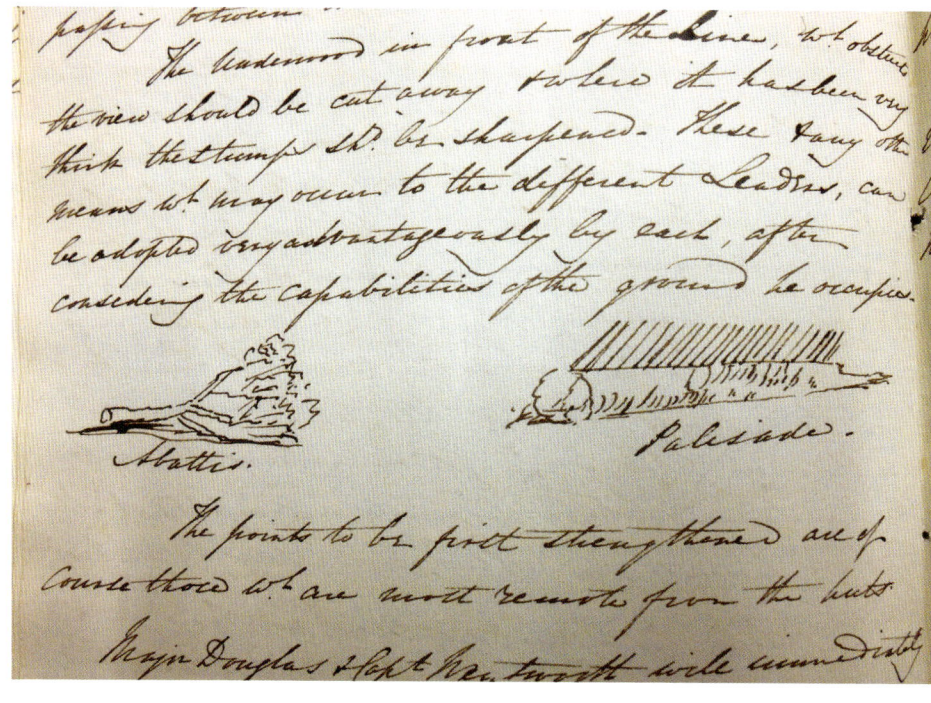

There is overwhelming evidence that Aboriginal tribes were systematically cleared from Van Diemen's Land. This account from 1830 (above) records colonial government payments to men who captured Aboriginal people. *State Library of New South Wales: DLADD 83, Item 3: 'Tasmania Aboriginal Department - Return, dated 16 May 1831 and signed by D. Wentworth, listing recipients of reward for apprehending aborigines'.*

to place those less qualified in the very spots where they might do good service, whilst the more active and experienced men should take another range.

Pointing out that good rations and accessible provision depots were crucial to the smooth running of operations, Jorgenson also highlighted that many knapsacks would be needed and suggested someone issue 'authority to purchase Kangaroo Skins' so the parties could make their own. Jorgenson also suggested that if he could have 'a horse' then he could rapidly lead parties to 'their cruising grounds'. He asked to 'be gazetted as a special constable'.

Anstey forwarded the letter for Arthur's attention, recommending Jorgenson 'to His Excellency's favourable notice', adding that 'Jorgenson is eminently well qualified to take the lead' in either a field or administrative role during the operations, and agreeing with Jorgenson's ideas about 'Depots being established'. Then Anstey added one final message: 'Thinking that the Lieut Governor may wish to see Jorgenson before the meeting at noon today, I now send him to Oatlands for that purpose.'

This highlights that Arthur, Anstey and Douglas were already coordinating in advance, meeting in the geographical heart of the operations weeks before they were due to commence. With them were members of the survey department, drawing lines on maps in readiness for Arthur's campaign.

The Plan of General Movement

The final plan of operation was gazetted five days after this meeting in Government Order 11, dated 22 September 1830.[21] The main targets were 'the Oyster Bay and Big River tribes, as the most sanguinary'. The general plan was to form lines of soldiers and militia at the fringes of the settled districts and manoeuvre them in advancing sweeps before coming together into greater concentrations as the lines joined together. By this Arthur hoped to drive Aboriginal people south and east into the Tasman Peninsula. While the operation came to be called 'the Black

Line', it was really a series of units operating in conjunction. Their positions in relation to each other formed sweeping or stationary lines at different points in the campaign.

While the plan was essentially simple, its execution was as complex as the campaign was massive. Government Order 11 had 29 numbered clauses, which detailed only the most general movements that the wider public needed to know about. There were two main divisions of troops, one under Major Douglas that extended east to west across the north, and another under Captain Wentworth which curved north to south along the west, basically shadowing the old line of martial law. These two major fronts were supported by supplementary divisions. On 7 October all forces were to move into their starting positions, effectively sealing the settled districts. They were then to commence advancing towards another predetermined position, which formed a secondary line, by the afternoon of 12 October.

Individual elements within these divisions were given geographical targets deserving of minute examination. In the north, part of Major Douglas's left flank was directed to 'thoroughly examine the country between their first stations and the head of the Macquarie'. This encompassed Tooms Lake and the nearby upper waterways that had previously been sites of contact and conflict. The military units were 'strengthened' by the addition of 'roving parties under Mr. Batman'. On Douglas's right flank, to assist in the movement across the midlands, the soldiers were supplemented by over 40 parties of settlers which were supposed to be formed 'into parties of ten'. At 'Major Douglas's extreme right', the division was 'supported' by a mixture of 'roving parties', 'police', and 10-man 'volunteer parties' from the Oatlands district. Douglas's combined force was ordered to move south into its secondary line, which the soldiers could identify in relation to key landmarks. Where there were multiple peaks which could cause confusion, large fires were supposed to be lit as guidance beacons.

Meanwhile, a supplementary operation in the east coast district aimed to trap Aboriginal people on the Schoutens. The constables and settlers normally situated on the neck of land connecting the peninsula to the mainland were to 'withdraw before the 7th October, in order that nothing may tend to deter the native tribes from passing the Isthmus'. Then, with a large force of military, settlers-militant, police and 'whatever force can be collected', Lieutenant Aubin was directed to move in, sweep the coast and seal the peninsula:

> Between the 7th and 12th of October, Lieutenant Aubin will thoroughly examine the tier extending from the head of the Swan River, north, down to Spring Bay, the southern extremity of his district, ... On the 12th, Lieutenant Aubin will occupy the passes in the tier which the Natives are known most to frequent, and will communicate with the extreme left of Major Douglas's line; taking up the best points of observation, and causing at the same time a most minute reconnaissance to be kept upon the Schoutens, in case the Natives should pass into that Peninsula, as they are in the habit of doing either for shell-fish or eggs, in which case he will promptly carry into effect the instructions with which he has already been furnished.

Those instructions, presumably, were to seal the neck.

On the western front, the situation was more complex. Captain Wentworth's western line was really an arrangement of forces which pushed up the rivers and high country plains. He was instructed to:

> push a strong detachment, under the orders of Lieutenant Croly, from Bothwell towards the Great Lake, for the purpose of thoroughly examining St. Patrick's Plains and the banks of the Shannon, extending its left on retiring to the Clyde, towards the Lagoon of Islands, and its right towards Lake Echo.

This detachment was 'assisted by the roving parties under Sherwin and Doran'. Another detachment of soldiers from Hamilton, led by Captain Vicary, were to take up positions 'across the Clyde, to occupy the western bank of the Ouse'. It was similarly supported by parties of settlers and field police. A third detachment under Lieutenant Murray was 'to scour the country on the west bank of the Ouse' from the north bank of the Derwent River. They were to be supported by 'volunteers and ticket-of-leave men from Hobart Town and its neighbourhood'. Between 7 and 12 October these three detachments were supposed 'to drive towards the Clyde whatever tribes or Natives may be in those quarters', joining up with 'Major Douglas's extreme right'. Supplementary elements of the volunteers and ticket-of-leavers were to be kept in reserve and posted on key passes to help further seal this complex riverine and mountainous front.

A major reserve line was to be occupied by Captain Donaldson, who was directed to advance from Norfolk Plains in the northwestern midlands into the central lakes area, 'driving in a southerly direction any of the tribes in that quarter'. By 12 October he was supposed to occupy a line from Sorell Lake to Lake Echo. 'In this important position he will remain, with the view of arresting flight of any tribes towards the west, which might possibly pass through the first line.' Donaldson was to be supported by settlers and whatever forces could be deployed by the police magistrates of Launceston and Norfolk Plains.

By 12 October all the mobile detachments were supposed to have reached their secondary positions, collectively forming a single line. From Waterloo Point on the east coast to Sorell Lake to Bothwell and Hamilton, the southern midlands were supposed to be sealed. Two days later, on 14 October, another advance was to commence with the northern front pushing southeast and the western front pushing east, both reaching their next positions to form another line by 16 October. Once again hilltop fires would help guide the advances. They were to rest on Sunday 17 October.

On Monday 18 October the northern front again pushed towards the southeast, while only the northern flank of the western front pushed forward to maintain a cordon. They were all to halt on 20 October at another predetermined line, and await 'further orders'.

The remainder of the government order dealt with rations and ration stations, the equipment that volunteers and servants should bring, the number of guns required for each party and the responsible allocation of weaponry to prisoners. Settlers were advised 'not to make any movements against the Natives within the circuit occupied by the troops, until the general line reaches them'. The settlers were also advised 'that the object in view is not to injure or destroy the unhappy savages ... but to capture and raise them in the scale of civilization'.

War Fever and Extermination Debated

Arthur's attempt to represent the General Movement as a humanitarian endeavour stands in striking contrast to the public's sentiment and to Arthur's own private instructions. There was much enthusiasm for this combined military offensive. A public meeting was quickly advertised in Hobart after the General Movement was first announced.[22] Nominally it was about planning for 'the Inhabitants of Hobart Town, to undertake a portion of the Military Duty in the Town' such 'that as many Soldiers as possible shall be at the disposal of the Government, for duty in the Interior'.

The government may have had a hand in organising or at least encouraging the meeting. On the same day the public meeting was advertised, the Colonial Secretary wrote to the police magistrate at Launceston:

> any arrangement which you can make for the performance of
> the duties in the Town of Launceston, by which all the Military
> may be enabled to take the field, will be extremely desirable and
> meeting with the entire approbation of The Lieutenant Governor.[23]

Within a week of this letter, a public meeting was advertised in the *Launceston Advertiser* seeking volunteers 'to perform the duty of a TOWN GUARD'.[24] Like the Hobart meeting, it was scheduled to take place in the town court house.

The Hobart meeting was held on 22 September – the same day the government order detailing the General Movement was gazetted.[25] Described by the *Hobart Town Courier* as 'one of the most numerous meetings which has yet been held in the colony', the proceedings commenced with the election of Mr Hone – the settler who kept servants in discreet ambush on his rural property – as chair.

The first speaker, a former soldier, spoke of the necessity of the military action, and moved the first resolution of the day, which insisted on 'the duty of every man cheerfully to contribute to the common cause, every assistance in his power'.

The second speaker, called upon to second this motion, was Joseph Gellibrand, a former Attorney General of the colony who Arthur had removed from office some years previously. Gellibrand seconded the motion, but also took the opportunity to question the legitimacy of the operations if violence was to be deployed. He stated that 'a great legal question arises upon the subject', and suggested 'that before the proposed operations are commenced, some change in the existing law should be effected'. Gellibrand acknowledged that if an Aboriginal person was known to have 'committed the dreadful atrocities' but could not be caught, then 'it might be justifiable to shoot them'. But he was concerned that such killing could constitute murder in other circumstances.

Solicitor General Alfred Stephen stood up to reply to Gellibrand's commentary. He pointed out that the substance of Gellibrand's comments had no clear relation to the purpose of the meeting, and turned the discussion back to the question of a town guard. The resolution 'was passed unanimously'. But the distraction pointed to tensions within the crowd, as the dovish and hawkish elements of society tussled during what was intended to be a highly scripted event.

The second motion concerned 'personal service'. Those able to leave Hobart were requested to head into the interior, while those unable to leave Hobart were asked to fill in for the military for a few weeks. The town was, after all, full of convicts, and there was a genuine concern for order and safety. Thomas Horne, local lawyer and proposer of this motion, also took the opportunity to react to Gellibrand's commentary:

> surely he forgets, when he speaks of the indiscriminate slaughter of the blacks, how indiscriminate have been the slaughter of the whites. Surely, he cannot have forgotten that the grass has hardly yet grown over the graves of the two children who were recently so barbarously murdered!

Horne went on to talk about the significance of wool to the colonial economy and the dangers for shepherds in the interior, before addressing the substantive question hovering over the meeting: 'If therefore extermination is necessary, horrible as is the alternative, I do not see what other means of protection exist.'

Clearly Gellibrand's comments had caused some agitation. After this motion was seconded and recorded, another speaker got up and proposed a third motion, in which the townspeople effectively agreed to undertake town military duties for five weeks. This too was seconded and recorded. But the proposer, a medical doctor from Hobart, also took issue with 'what fell from Gellibrand', as he put the lawyer's qualms.

Dr Adam Turnbull had served as assistant surgeon in Richmond before taking to private practice in Hobart. He was therefore well placed to comment on the effect of the violence in the interior, more than the lawyers and jurists of Hobart. He argued that the proposed general operations were necessary, and that it was not the place of the public to query their execution. He advocated putting trust in the executive, and like others framed this as a lesser evil to allowing the war to continue as it had been:

> The present plan will strike them with dismay – they will be either taken or destroyed, or driven into some of the recesses of the interior. The present warfare of the stock-keepers is infinitely more one of extermination than the proposed one will be. The simultaneous movement will excite terror, not rage.

The next speaker advocated modifying their resolution, such that the town guard was in place earlier than first proposed, so that the soldiers had more time to get to their starting positions.

A fourth resolution followed, addressing the technicalities of the formation of guard units. Because it dealt with 'mere detail', the proposer – Alfred Stephen – gave it only brief attention. The guard needed to be about 200 men, cycling every four days, and volunteers had options to choose their preferred place of service. With this formality addressed, Stephen turned to broader issues, taking care for the second time during this meeting to make it clear he was speaking 'individual sentiments' rather than as Solicitor General. But as most of the listeners and later readers likely knew, the commentary of such a leading figure of colonial society and government carried great cultural weight. As he went on:

> I agree with Mr Horne that the slaughter of the whites has been as indiscriminate as any which can be the result of the proposed operation, and I say, that as they have waged such a war upon the settlers, you are bound to put them down.

He then presented a legal argument, basically suggesting that the colony held a duty of care towards convict servants who were 'involuntarily sent here' and exposed to danger. Speaking 'with much animation', Stephen spoke directly to Gellibrand's qualms, picking up on one word in particular that had echoed in the court house over several speeches. 'I say, sir,' he declaimed:

> that you are bound upon every principle of justice and humanity, to protect this particular class of individuals, and if you cannot do so without extermination, then I say boldly and broadly exterminate!

Stephen then turned to particularities. He stated that he would try to capture Aboriginal people, but admitted that if he could not then 'I would fire upon them'. He closed by reiterating this point: 'I am of opinion – capture them if you can, but if you cannot, destroy them.'

Gellibrand tried to push his point, but Stephen waived the concern off as 'totally inapplicable to the subject before us'. Like many meetings, it drifted into tangential particularities, debated minor points of fact and changed topics. The discussion reflected a community divided about the cause, conduct and proposed termination of the war – divisions that were also reflected in the divergent ways that different newspapers presented the meeting, emphasising or glossing various elements of the proceedings.

AGITATION AND ARMAMENT

But claims for loyalty and necessity carried the day. Eventually the meeting ended after two further resolutions – one forming 'a standing Committee of fifteen gentlemen' to oversee the town guard arrangements, the other about reporting the meeting's resolutions to the Lieutenant Governor. The following day a deputation from the meeting 'waited upon His Excellency', and read him their resolutions after a very brief preamble. Arthur replied that their efforts gave him 'great gratification'. He accepted their assistance, which he characterised as arranged in 'patriotic a manner', and looked forward to their 'vigilance' in securing the town. He then informed them of the 'proposed arrangements' contained in the government order issued on the day of their meeting.

Operational Details, Enlistment and Recruitment

Over the remainder of September and into October Arthur gave directives for the General Movement, much of it recorded by the Colonial Secretary. A 'Most important' message to the police magistrate of Richmond was about 'keeping up a very large fire on the Brown Mountain', which 'must be kept up both by day and night'.[26] Anstey's attention was similarly drawn to a fire in his District, 'on the Blue Hill Bluff', which also had to be kept up constantly during the allotted period. The Colonial Secretary advised Anstey: 'have the goodness to send a very careful man on whom you can confide, in charge of a sufficient number of Convicts, to collect wood.'

A horse was also available for Anstey 'should you require it, in aid of any of Major Douglas's operations'. A few days later Anstey was sent a letter marked 'Immediate', also revealing a key focus on horses:

> I am directed by The Lieutenant Governor to request that you will be good enough to purchase for the service of the Government, at the Sherriff's sale of Darby's property at York plains, Five Horses which it is understood are for sale, should you consider them suitable for the Mounted Police and should they be sold at a reasonable price. If purchased, the Horses may be

handed over to Major Douglas for the purpose of mounting some persons in his division who are not provided with Horses.[27]

This special purchase was a little unusual, which explains the fact of the correspondence. It unfortunately turned out that there was only one horse for sale from this property, which Anstey called 'an unsound little animal, utterly unfit for the use of Government', so he did not buy it.[28]

In a letter explaining this, Anstey mentioned that the horse was 'bought by Solomon the Jew', before going on to describe a few attacks by 'A Horde of Natives' who 'robbed' one hut, 'sacked' another and killed two servants. This sort of continued aggression in part explains the generally positive response to the government's call to arms, and some members of the community were certainly willing to offer their animals for the aid of the operation. When a lieutenant in the Bothwell district applied to the town adjutant for a horse, the Colonial Secretary noted:

> the Settlers have come forward in other Police Districts, and offered to assist the Government on the present occasion with Horses, Carts, &c, and The Lieutenant Governor therefore trusts a similar spirit will induce some of the Inhabitants at the Clyde, to afford the use of their horses for the service of the Government.[29]

Another letter reveals that in New Norfolk a settler 'kindly offered the Government four Horses ... for the use of the Military and Police, during the approaching movements against the Aborigines.'[30] It is only recorded because the Colonial Secretary advised the police magistrate that 'Saddles and bridles for these Horses, will be forwarded to you by the Ordinance Storekeeper', to whom they had to be returned after the operations were complete.

There were other procurements. When 'two of the Government Bullocks' at Great Swan Port were found to be 'unfit for use', Arthur authorised the local assistant police magistrate to purchase two

AGITATION AND ARMAMENT

replacements, and 'cause the two unserviceable ones to be slaughtered and turned into store'.[31] In the west, 'provisions for the Clyde District' were going to be temporarily stored at a settler's residence while the police magistrate arranged 'to procure carts, to convey them from thence'.[32]

As well as food, Arthur also replied to requests for weaponry and ammunition. In fact, as the commencement of operations approached, there were some concerns that the transportation of armaments and ammunition from Hobart to Bothwell and Oatlands had actually taken such precedence that food provisions had been delayed.[33]

Arthur was intimately involved in authorising much of this weaponry. He approved 'four pairs of Pistols and Ammunition' to New Norfolk although 'desired that they shall not be issued ... to any person who has the means of providing Fire Arms for himself'.[34] Fortunately many of the men did arrive already armed. In the Launceston district, most ticket-of-leave men reportedly came with their own guns, although many of these may have included 'fowling pieces', which formed the majority of guns held by some 320 men nominally from Launceston and Norfolk Plains that were eventually attached to Captain Donaldson's force.[35] When the Richmond police magistrate applied for 'a large supply of Ammunition', Arthur approved the request but cautioned 'that it must be very sparingly issued, and that not more than five rounds at the very utmost must be given to any individual employed in pursuit of the Aborigines'. Guns and ammunition were expensive, after all, and had to be accounted for later. But this fact also makes it abundantly clear that the General Movement was very well armed.

The post-operation accounting reveals much about the operational arrangements of the General Movement. A subsequent 'Nominal Return of Persons to whom Arms were delivered' from the Richmond district, for instance, details 24 men receiving 36 guns.[36] As remarks in the margin explained, 'Those to whom more than one were delivered were Leaders of Parties'. Among these party leaders was John Stewart Spotswood, son of the soldier-settler, who received three guns. Other settler-leaders named Lloyd and Irwin each got two, and Currie and

Long took five. Considering that Arthur encouraged settlers to have guns – as did living in a war zone – and he urged them to bring their own for the operation, even these neat accounts only reflect a small proportion of the total number of weapons used.

Another post-operation document, a 'Return of Arms issued from the Ordinance Magazine for Service against the Hostile Aborigines', tallies the armaments delivered between 27 September and 6 October.[37] On the day before the main fronts began moving, 52 Pistols and 490 'Muskets with Ramrods' were issued. Of these, 32 were for the 'Provisional Committee Town Guards'. The remainder were delivered to various centres in the southern midlands and western front including Oatlands, New Norfolk and Bothwell. Douglas's northern volunteers were accounted elsewhere, so are not included in these figures. A further 89 muskets and four bayonets were issued from this magazine during the following weeks.

Giving a sense of the scale of the operations in the north, the commissariat officer complained of the difficulty in getting adequate assistants to issue rations when he reported the requisitions he had received at Launceston for the establishment of depots.[38] He itemised five stations each preparing to supply '200 [men] for 30 days', which in total was 'equal to about 60,000 lbs Biscuit & Meat'. There were another two coastal depots which he did not detail.

Attaching a requisition for 'probable' requirements for the operations, the commissariat officer listed a token amount of tobacco, 'Two thousand pounds of Tea', 'Eleven thousand pounds of Sugar' and 'One hundred thousand pounds of Salt Beef and Pork'. Making arrangements in response to this, Arthur noted that 'Capt Donaldson's Division consists of about 450 Persons'.

So massive was the drain on colonial resources that some families of ticket-of-leave men conscripted to the operation were left without support, and the government stepped in to provide assistance by putting them on ration.[39] 'Mary Ann the wife of John Eagle', for example, had 'a Boy 8 years' and three daughters aged seven, two and nine months. 'Elizabeth wife of Thos Hubbard' had a five year old daughter and an infant. 'Margaret wife of James Boxall' was 'An infirm aged woman'.

The Colonial Secretary flagged at least 13 women and nineteen children for such aid.[40]

Meanwhile, convict women who were still under sentence were co-opted to the service of the campaign. In the 'House of Correction for females' – the Cascades Female Factory near Hobart – arrangements were underway almost as soon as the operations were announced to have the women prepare 'Clothing for the Soldiers going into the bush'.[41] The output was considerable. 'No less than 640 pair of trowsers [sic] were made by the women in the Female House of Correction last week,' the *Hobart Town Courier* reported on 2 October, 'for the use of the men employed in the expedition against the blacks.'[42]

But not all preparation went completely smoothly. On the evening before the movement was supposed to commence, a provisional constable stationed at Bagdad in the southern midlands wrote a hurried and apologetic letter to the Lieutenant Governor.[43] Having just 'this moment received' a letter detailing 'your Excellencys [sic] wish that the Parties from this quarter should be forwarded to Bothwell as quick as possible', the constable advised that he had sent 'a Man on Horseback' to the fringes of the district to urge outlying settlers to 'get their parties ready by the time appointed', but the messenger had not yet returned. He had sent a cart in the middle of the night to a settler named Murdoch, where the arms and ammunition were supposed to be deposited, but they had not arrived, so the carter left and had to be ordered to go again. The constable blamed the weather for the 'delay', which 'must have arisen from the violent Wind blowing so hard all this Day', which stalled the carter's second run. The constable hoped to press some other carts into service, and meet the Lieutenant Governor in Bothwell 'early on Friday'.

While some of the settlers straggled to join the main divisions of soldiers, a few others absconded. Sailing off the northeast coast of Van Diemen's Land in late September, the crew of the *Nimrod* spotted a large congregation of Aboriginal people on the coast near Swan Island.[44] The captain reported 'immense number of Natives close to the Beach', which he estimated to comprise 'from Six to Seven Hundreds'.

When this news reached Launceston it 'occasioned considerable apprehensions in the minds of some settlers at the Eastward' that were supposed to join Captain Donaldson.[45] The *Launceston Advertiser* suggested the region was 'left unprotected' by the resource demands of the general operations, and complained that 'we of Launceston are always behind the Hobartians'.[46]

The police magistrate reported to Hobart that 'many of them' had 'withdrawn their Services for the purpose of protecting their own Neighbourhood'. Arthur read this news on 11 October, by which time the General Movement had commenced. 'With regard to the Natives to the Eastward', he wrote, 'observe that the same endeavour to capture them will be made as is now in progress in the County of Buckingham'. The Colonel Commanding was so confident in his trap that he was already contemplating future operations to clear Aboriginal people from other parts of the island.

CHAPTER FIFTEEN

Propaganda and the Preliminary Manoeuvres

1830, Spring
South, West and North

Arthur's Campaign

The General Movement began, but few of the hundreds of participants recorded it. There are also curious gaps among the many letters in volume CSO1/1/320 (7578). For instance, there is practically no inbound correspondence from police magistrates between late August and late November 1830. Batman's and Danvers' reports had already ceased being filed with the others, and there is nothing from the usually prolific Jorgenson for the entirety of October. Even the volume's largely miscellaneous section on 'Reports & Journals of Various Roving Parties' is silent about Arthur's campaign.

The clean copy correspondence files of the Colonial Secretary's Office only capture a small part of the action, and the Lieutenant Governor's own memorandum and letter copy file goes quiet on the subject after 28 September when Arthur directed the police magistrate at Richmond to send various batches of volunteers to their prescribed positions.

A whole volume in the Colonial Secretary's archive was dedicated to the campaign, and contains Arthur's letters while in the field,

Douglas's reports and those of commissariat officers, as well as a few other bits and pieces.[1] These capture the upper command elements and provide insight into Arthur's overall strategic view, but they are slight on many frontline details. The colonial press did follow the campaign with great interest, albeit often a week or so behind the action and with its almost habitually questionable reliability. But there were some volunteers who diarised their participation or later shared their experiences.

Emmett's War: Departing Hobart

One such volunteer was Henry James Emmett. His family compiled a manuscript account of what was titled his 'Reminiscences of the Black War by Leader'.[2] While ostensibly his own writing, it was completed some 40 years after the war and shows signs of editing and improvement by another author, probably Emmett's son. 'I have deemed the subject of sufficient interest to the public,' the editor admits, 'to rewrite them, and to add to the reminiscences from personal recollections so as to render the narrative less fragmentary'. What survives then, is a complex and argumentative document, reflecting and addressing the concerns of the 1870s as much as the actualities of October 1830. But, these caveats aside, it is still a valuable account.

Styled 'Commander of The Black War party' in his reminiscences, Emmett was a clerk in the Colonial Secretary's Office when Arthur's campaign was announced, and 'being desirous of seeing the whole country' volunteered to join the General Movement. His acquaintance, a young man named Groom, also volunteered with him. They 'were ordered to start away on the 1st October'. Other members of the department remained in Hobart 'to mount guard'.

Emmett's experience was also played out in Launceston, where documentation survives showing Arthur encouraging recruits: 'any clerks in the Public Offices ... whose services can be dispensed with may volunteer to lead parties of Ticket of Leave men'.[3] In Hobart such instructions were passed verbally, so it would seem likely Emmett and others were encouraged directly. After volunteering, Emmett was asked to lead a party. It comprised himself, his friend Groom, his own assigned servant, his father's assigned servant and six others, totalling 10.

Emmett then enthusiastically 'made arrangements for my departure and my outfit'. He got fitted out in 'a complete suit of dark Moleskin', but regretted it later as inadequate to cope with the weather. The winds that bothered the Provisional Constable in Bagdad heralded a cold front, which brought snowfalls to parts of the island. Emmett also acquired 'a pair of Stockkeeper boots', 'a canvas knapsack', and a compass. Completing his kit was a 'double barrel Percussion gun costing £20'. Volunteering was not cheap, especially as Emmett had to see to the servants as well.

At '6 in the morning of a most lovely day', 1 October, Emmett and his team met at the Hobart Police Office 'with two days provisions in our knapsacks'. He reported that about 300 men 'formed a square facing inwards' in the yard, with 'a large number of persons assembled including the merchants Public Officers & others' in attendance as spectators. An hour later Arthur arrived with his staff. As Lieutenant Governor and Colonel Commanding, he was entitled to an armed guard, no doubt heightening Emmett's sense that he was participating in something significant.

From the centre of the square, Arthur 'addressed us in a most feeling speech of upwards of an hours duration giving us an outline of our intended duties, every thing being done in Military Style'. Even more pleasing for Emmett:

> At the conclusion of the speech His Excellency spoke to me in the most friendly & fatherly manner thanking me for what I had undertaken. He also requested me to take charge of thirty more men so far as New Norfolk.

Several hours later, after preparations had been completed, Emmett's volunteer force 'marched off'. Shadowing the force as it left Hobart was a large gathering of spectators, many of whom were upset by the departure:

> It was pitiable to observe the sad state of the poor women & children who followed a considerable way sobbing with their aprons to their eyes & others with plates of food & mugs of Tea, as if it was the last meal we should ever partake of, or that we should never meet them again.

Despite this scene, Emmett noted he 'would not allow the men to fall out of the ranks'. He marched the volunteers a few miles out of town before he ordered them to halt and 'allowed the men to take an affectionate farewell of their wives & sweethearts'.

Emmett faced what he called 'a fresh trouble' when he had 'to get the men past the public House' – the Black Snake Inn at Bridgewater. While seemingly an amusing aside, it really addressed a larger concern for the young leader. Emmett 'stopped for a short time on the road side and allowed some beer to be brought down but would not suffer the men to enter the Inn'. He was worried that some of the men might use the opportunity to abscond from the party of convict conscripts and volunteers, especially the extra 30 men that Arthur had asked him to oversee. These were 'perfect strangers, men holding tickets of leave and who were compelled to serve', Emmett noted.

After their break he marched the party a further 2 miles on before stopping for the night 'in a very pretty valley'. As they slept in the open around their fires Emmett attempted to stay awake, worried some of the men might try to slip off and retrace their steps to the inn.

In the morning, Emmett counted his own team, and then used the muster roll to check the others. Despite his night watch one had managed to escape in the dark, 'leaving his musket & knapsack behind', who Emmett remembered years later as 'Paddy Something'. Paddy's disappearance, Emmett admitted, 'very much grieved and annoyed me, fearing that I should be blamed'. Nonetheless, that afternoon they reached New Norfolk and Emmett transferred responsibility for the 29 men and the missing Paddy to the police magistrate. He at least had the satisfaction that when Paddy was caught, he 'would have been severely punished as his conduct set a bad example to the others'.

Law, Facts and Politics

The conduct of the parties was a topical concern. On the day that Emmett marched from Hobart to New Norfolk, Arthur formally extended martial law to the whole of the island:

> against all the Black or Aboriginal Natives ... excepting always such Tribe or individuals of Tribes, as there may be reason to suppose are pacifically inclined and have not been implicated in any such outrages.[4]

The announcement neatly answered and dismissed Gellibrand's public concerns and the debate it instigated at the meeting at the court house: Aboriginal people were fair targets unless other conditions were met. The Proclamation enjoined that 'the actual use of Arms be in no case resorted to, by firing against any of the Natives or otherwise, if they can by other means be captured'. So shooting at Aboriginal people was sanctioned if they could not be captured or if there was reason to believe they were not 'pacifically inclined'. Basically anything other than peacefully surrendering meant they were fair targets. That captives 'be treated with the utmost care and humanity' was the only injunction without such a logical inversion or a subjective loophole. Arthur's Proclamation therefore had the overall effect of mostly protecting colonists from Gellibrand's theoretical murder charge.

But this legalistic sleight of hand also contained a major public lie. Following convention, it articulated the cause and effect of the previous declaration of martial law and the partition of the colony in 1828, before turning to an explanation for its extension:

> And whereas, by reason of the aforesaid exceptions, so contained in the said Proclamation, no Natives have been hitherto pursued or molested in any of the places or portions of the Island so excepted; from whence they have accordingly of late been accustomed to make repeated incursions upon the settled districts with impunity, or having committed outrages in the settled

districts, have escaped into those excepted places, where they remain in security.

This was nonsense and Arthur knew it. When Batman had raised the issue of the extent of martial law, Arthur had personally given instructions to pursue Aboriginal people beyond its technical limits. Jorgenson had been sent beyond the line of martial law to assess the extent and impact of Aboriginal people in those areas, and he concluded it was not used as a raiding refuge. The Proclamation followed ancient legislative conventions and prerogative convenience by writing legal fictions into its own preamble – thereby making them facts at law.[5]

Arthur's Proclamation ensured the legality of what it called 'an active and extended system of Military operations against all the Natives generally, throughout the Island, and every portion thereof, whether actually settled or not'. The public got behind it, and the press continued their obsession with the Aboriginal atrocities.

Even the frequently critical *Colonial Times* – which opined that Arthur's campaign would likely meet with 'bad success' – ran several stories of Aboriginal attacks in its last edition before the campaign commenced.[6] In one ambush on a sawing pit, a badly wounded sawyer succeeded in grabbing a musket from an Aboriginal attacker and firing it at his assailants as they fled. The sawyer's companion, though only slightly wounded, suffered horrible side effects of the strike: he contracted a 'brain fever', lingered a few days, and 'died raving mad'. Another case concerned the killing of 'a soldier of the 63rd, stationed at Boomer Creek', who was 'beat about the head and horribly disfigured' when alone in the bush. Two fellow soldiers were reportedly too scared to leave their hut, and only found the body in the morning. Moreover, 'a runaway from Hobart Town, has likewise fallen a sacrifice to the inveterate feelings of the Aboriginal inhabitants', and there was 'a very horrid murder of some of Major Gray's men'. Again the story dwelled on the desecration of bodies, reporting that the attackers 'afterwards disfigured them in a most shocking manner, cutting the heads off of three of them, and placing them between their legs.'

PROPAGANDA AND THE PRELIMINARY MANOEUVRES

The *Hobart Town Courier* contented itself the next day with reproducing just one of the 'letters from the interior', which it claimed to be receiving in volume. It referred to some of the same incidents, revealing the way that news of attacks clearly spread by word of mouth:

> Benlomond, Sept. 27, 1830. – Dear Sir, I have just time to say that the natives, last Thursday week, murdered two men at Oyster bay; and on the next day they beat a sawyer almost to death. On Sunday after they murdered a soldier. On last Wednesday they attacked the house of Mr. Boultbee, when he was absent, and if it had not been for a soldier who happened to be there they would have murdered Mrs Boultbee and all their children. On Friday last, they murdered three men at a hut in which eight men lived, belonging to Major Grey, and left a fourth for dead who is not yet out of danger. They robbed the hut of 4 guns, 12 blankets and other things, they had come direct from Oyster bay. Your's [sic] Truly, JOHN BATMAN.[7]

Curiously, the *Hobart Town Courier* also carried letters from two speakers from the public meeting at the court house, rejecting the newspaper's coverage of their speeches. 'If the expressions you have dared to impute to me are read in other countries,' Adam Turnbull wrote, 'what will they think of us?'[8] He went on at great length about many points, but all connected with his own reputation.

> You make me speak of extermination as if it were a household word, and contained nothing awful in its meaning, at the very time that I was advocating the interests of the Aborigines and insisting upon the necessity of saving them as it were from themselves.

Concerned at being thought of 'as an exterminator', Turnbull went on to reject reports that the meeting's resolutions had been passed unanimously. But he nonetheless admitted his real position in support of the campaign, as being for the greater good of Aboriginal people:

> I would not with an affectation of mawkish sensibility, unregulated by reason, shrink from the shedding of blood, if that alternative be necessary, for the only means of preserving the Aborigines is, in my opinion, to dismay them, so that revenge may be drowned in terror; and if this terror cannot be excited without bloodshed, then some must suffer that the rest may be saved, and the Whites secured.

Turnbull ended by quoting Ovid in Latin, literally presenting himself as against the hawks. In reply, the editor reproduced Turnbull's second and third speeches in full, omitted from the earlier reporting. 'The blood you shed will be the means of ending the war,' Turnbull had claimed in one, posing the campaign as a means to save Aboriginal people from 'the occasional murders by the stock-keepers'. It was a real sign of the moment that the ones who saw themselves as the peacemakers were so willingly advocating terror.

Turnbull's letter and speeches took up most of that page, but a short letter from James Thompson also rejected any inference 'that I advocate the destruction of the native tribes of the island'. These gentlemen, whose names were known abroad, were concerned for their reputations back in Europe and into posterity. Turnbull's repeated references to the Spanish in Mexico highlight his sense that history was being made, and his reputation was at stake as an advocate of strong military action.

The fallout from the public meeting at the court house and the tension between an aggressive military campaign and concerns about Britain's humanitarian image continued into the following week. The *Colonial Times* came to its rival's defence and parodied Turnbull's obsession with his reputation, declaring simply 'that on that day the extermination of the Aborigines was considered by several as advisable and expedient'.[9] But it also queried the policy of conscripting ticket-of-leave holders into the campaign, 'compelled to belong to a band of guerrilla warriors after the Blacks'; referred to the commencement of operations by quoting an old rhyme about a king and soldiers marching up a hill and 'down again'; and poked fun at the enthusiastic but coddled young heroes of town who were spoiling for adventure in the interior, who each had a:

> poor pack carrier who follows his young master, the juvenile leader of a legion, to the field, charged upon no account to let the dear boy get his feet wetted, but to be sure to carry him safely through whatever streams they should have to pass – to let him have a cup of warm tea the last thing at night, and the first in the morning – and to sit by him when asleep to keep the mosquitos from biting his darling cheek.

Reunions Near the Western Front

Once in the New Norfolk district, Emmett's party camped for two nights before moving on towards Bothwell on 4 October. Surprisingly, just as the party was making plans for departure, the runaway Paddy 'turned up'. He 'begged so hard to be forgiven' that Emmett took pity on him and allowed the 'penitent' fellow to escape punishment. But there was another surprise in store. 'On reaching the punt to cross the Derwent river,' Emmett wrote, 'to my astonishment I met my youngest brother George.' A clerk like his elder brother, George worked in the chief police magistrate's office in Hobart, and 'had obtained permission to join' Emmett's party, although he took a few days to catch up and find Emmett's trail. George had another of their father's servants in tow, bringing Emmett's party 'to twelve persons'.

Emmett was ordered to travel 'along the dromedary tier about halfway up keeping the beautiful Macquarie plains in view, and then to make my way across the country to the township'. While the General Movement was yet to properly commence, operational tactics were already being deployed and the country scoured, perhaps intended as a mix of genuine reconnaissance but also impromptu field training for these civilian militiamen. 'There were other parties above and below mine', he added, 'though we did not meet'. The party stayed on alert as best they could. 'The Natives had been very troublesome in that quarter,' Emmett noted, although adding that 'I did not see any signs of them during my route'.

The journey to Bothwell was incident-free. Upon arrival Emmett reported to Captain Wentworth of the 63rd Regiment, the current police magistrate. Emmett thought him 'a most gentlemanly man, with whom I got on very pleasantly'. But their sojourn in Bothwell was brief. Emmett's party was directed to leave camp before dawn the next morning and march to the farm of 'a retired soldier residing at Cluny', Captain Clark. Together they 'would proceed ... to the foot of the Blue Hills', but first they enjoyed a 'most sumptuous breakfast which Mrs and Miss Clarke [sic] had prepared for us'.

On the subject of food, Emmett recollected:

> The provisions we drew from the settlers was generally very good ... but the Commissariat Tea & Sugar was abominable. The tea was at once christened Posts & Rail, consisting in fact of black sticks an inch long (black tea in those days was not thought of). The sugar was of a dark color [sic] and quite wet like a lump of putty.

Emmett also noted that he 'was compelled to draw' the full ration of Tobacco – despite the fact that he and two others in the party did not smoke – because 'the Commissariat Officer said it would make confusion in the accounts'. It was good fortune for the smokers in the party, but the bureaucratic pedantry, like the food, clearly stuck with Emmett into later years.

After breakfast, the parties headed off towards the hills. On the way they 'crossed a long narrow marsh, pretty clear of timber except here & there a fallen tree', which would have made for pleasant walking except it was 'swarming with large black snakes'. Emmett claimed to see 'between 20 & 30 which slowly crawled out of the way'. He was unable to 'stop to kill them, or call out for assistance, as the men were at least 300 yrds [sic] distant on each side'. They were already marching in a dispersed formation.

Upon reaching the base of the hills, the plan was 'to extend and make one long line each man keeping as far apart as possible, & then quietly to ascend the mountain, which was a resort of a very Savage Tribe of

PROPAGANDA AND THE PRELIMINARY MANOEUVRES

natives'. Two hours into their climb, which Emmett characterised as 'a most arduous task', they heard a sound which put them on alert. But it was 'Mr Champ a Leader of a party, dipping up water with his pannican' [sic]. Champ 'had accidentally been separated from the rest by proceeding along a gully which branched into two, his men taking one, while he took the other'.

Emmett commented that Champ was woefully under-equipped, carrying 'neither a blanket, or an ounce of food, nothing but his tin pot'. Emmett made a point of noting that 'I always carried the same as my men, or rather more, with chart, Journal, Compass &c'. But Emmett was big-noting himself: Champ was actually a lieutenant.

The party reached the summit in the evening, finding it 'quite flat and of considerable extent of fine grassy land, swarming with kangaroos'. Emmett added that 'not a shot was fired'. While the prospect of kangaroo meat may have been tempting, the men had managed to maintain a quiet profile. They went to sleep in the open after 'a beautiful and warm day'.

Emmett's movements reveal that he was operating according to the instructions in Arthur's Government Order 11, clause 13:

> The parties of volunteers and ticket-of-leave men from Hobart Town and its neighbourhood will march by New Norfolk, for the purpose of assisting Captain Wentworth's force in occupying the Clyde; and they will be rendering a great service by joining that force in time to invest the Blue Hill, which will be about the 10th of October.[10]

Emmett's party was also on schedule. He and the other auxiliaries were supposed to take and hold the high ground, denying Aboriginal people the protection afforded by these hills as the main forces swept through. If the instructions were being implemented elsewhere in the district, then another detachment of volunteers was probably heading towards 'the pass which runs from the high road' to take another key landmark. Meanwhile, the main military detachments of the western division, assisted by roving parties, were likely starting to scour parts of the high country and river valleys in preparation for the main drive.

Preliminaries at Midlands HQ

As these preliminary movements began, Arthur was in the midlands, reviewing his strategy and the disposition of the colony's forces. By 5 October he was at Ross, having travelled up from Hobart the day previously. Arthur corresponded with the Colonial Secretary at various points en route, getting arms and convicts sent into the interior, and giving the Colonial Secretary authority to deal with certain administrative matters in the Lieutenant Governor's name and absence.[11] These campaign memoranda were recorded and numerated in a subsequent copybook, but this is not a complete record of events. Some further correspondence – referred to in surviving letters – remains missing.

Nevertheless, Arthur gave a series of instructions from Ross as the force prepared for the first drive.[12] His focus that day was Major Douglas's northern front, forming in the northern midlands. There were several considerations, mainly concerned with lines of march and the 12 October positions 'to occupy, when the line is formed'. Douglas had 'carefully examined the whole of the ground' that was going to form the 12 October front. The 10-man parties each had a specific part of that line as their main objective. Arthur wanted Douglas to 'take care to appoint to each party a guide who is competent to lead it in the proper direction'. Once in their 12 October positions, each party guide was supposed to then receive instructions about 'what bearing he is to observe on the march' from Assistant Surveyor Thomas Scott.

Scott's role in preparing the campaign was significant, as was his role in recording it. Like Emmett, Scott left a manuscript devoted to the campaign, in his case a volume of collected 'Papers – Connected with the Campaign after the Natives'.[13] 'NATIVE WAR' is heavily penned in bold on the cover. In this is an almost miscellaneous collection of documents, including drafts of Arthur's Government Order 11, memoranda, various lists of men and dispositions, and even some short letters from Arthur asking Scott to dine with him and attend a meeting in the midlands to prepare for the campaign. As well as attending the Oatlands planning meeting and helping to chart the lines of movement, Scott had published a map of the colony, which went on sale in early September in Hobart and Launceston in readiness for the campaign season.[14] 'Copied from a Map, in possession of His Excellency The Lieutenant Governor', the map contained 'the several police districts ... the roads, townships, most of the settlers dwelling houses and stock huts'. It was available for 10 shillings and sixpence, or 15 shillings 'in a Case for the Pocket'. It was likely the chart carried by Emmett and other volunteers.

But for all the talk of maps and bearings, Arthur believed that men familiar with the country were critical to the success of the military operations. The Colonial Secretary informed the police magistrates of Oatlands, Campbell Town and Bothwell in late September 'that one of the most important services you can render in furtherance of the measures against the Natives, will be to form a Corps of Guides in your District to be attached to Parties'.[15] Thanks to Scott's collected papers, a small part of one guide's preparations are preserved in a letter, dated 5 October at Oatlands, from John Danvers. He had just returned from the east coast, having guided one of the bonfire teams to their station while also running messages:

> On the 1st October the wood gatherers with myself reached the mountain. On the same day I went part of the way to Waterloo point with Willoughby, and arrived there next morning.
> I delivered my dispatches, and on the same day proceeded to Little Swan port. ... The Officer commanding at Great Swan port will send men to relieve and assist the fire gatherers, in case it should be wanted. There can be no doubt but that the fires will be well attended to.[16]

In a similar way, the final section of 'Miscellaneous letters and Reports' in the Colonial Secretary's volume on the campaign contains a few documents capturing the final preparations in the Oatlands district. Anstey advised Arthur on 4 October that 'the Oatlands levy en masse will exceed 200', adding that 'I have fresh offers of assistance every hour'.[17] An enclosed report from Jorgenson contained the names of four settlers who had volunteered their assigned servants but not themselves, several who could not volunteer because they had no servants, and detailed a few settlers yet to advise their contribution or who were otherwise recalcitrant in coming forward.[18] One had reportedly refused to participate 'upon principle'. Jorgenson only mentioned in passing that the force included some of 'the Field police Constables'.

Anstey's militia became part of 'The Civil Force which is to reinforce Major Douglas's Line', as Arthur described them after receiving this news from Oatlands.[19] Arthur's own figures on the military deployed along Douglas's northern front were split into five divisions, totalling 367 rank and file. Three of these divisions were drawn from the 63rd Regiment, and one each from the 17th and 57th. Intending that they would converge into a line on 12 October covering the country at the northern midlands from the east coast towards the central highlands and lakes, Arthur ordered Anstey's whole levy of some 200 men to 'be distributed along Captain Mahon's Line'. This was the 'Right Wing', the westernmost part of the front covering the edge of the midlands and highland lakes. Here Arthur was still following his established plan, so it is likely the Oatlands field police were sent there too.

At the same time, Arthur gave orders regarding the remaining midlands volunteers. He ordered 'Nine parties of 10 from Mr Simpson's levy' at Campbell Town to support the 'Right Centre', a further 70 from Campbell Town and 50 from Richmond were attached to the 'Left Centre', while the 'Left Wing' leaning towards the coast was to receive 60 men from Campbell Town and 50 from Richmond. Among the named party leaders in this district was John Batman.

None of the midlands volunteers were sent to Lieutenant Aubin's division on the coast itself. A letter from Aubin in early October confirmed for the 'Colonel Commanding' that he had established a provision depot 'on the Oyster Bay tier', but this is a rare instance of documented activity.[20] This crucial flank remains one of the least-documented parts of the campaign.

Lawrence's Party and the Launceston Volunteers

The forces preparing to form a reserve line among the lakes under Captain Donaldson were slow to gather. On 5 October, in fact, one of the volunteer parties going to join Donaldson in Norfolk Plains was only just leaving Launceston. Like Emmett, Robert Lawrence was a young volunteer leader, only in his early 20s when leading nine other men off to war.[21] Like Emmett, he too had an assigned servant attached to his own party, and two others were former servants of his father. A wealthy landowner's son, Lawrence was a keen botanist and diarist, and kept a daily account of his experience of the campaign. Knowing that he was potentially engaged in a history-making event, he made a distinct break from the remainder of his journal, subtitling the new section 'the expedition against the Blacks'. In this he may have been influenced by the *Launceston Advertiser*, which suggested in late September that it would be good if 'each leader of a party will take pen, ink, and paper with him, and note down a journal of each days [sic] transactions'.[22]

The *Launceston Advertiser*'s suggestion highlights the peculiar nature of the relationship between the colonial press, the conflict and its record.[23] Launceston's small size, its distance from the seat of government and the proximity to major landowning settlers produced quite a different dynamic from that in Hobart. The public meeting held in Launceston, for instance, had a completely different outcome.[24] Having learnt that Launceston's civil commandant had initiated a voluntary town guard without consulting those who styled themselves 'community leaders', the *Launceston Advertiser*'s editor published an open letter to the Lieutenant Governor complaining of the commandant's actions. Presumably the editor was unaware that the commandant had been ordered to 'secure the Town' a day beforehand.[25] That the commandant had also withheld the key to the court house, thereby stalling the meeting, only added to the editor's fury. During the delay in retrieving the key, many would-be attendees supposedly left, and so the perceived attempt to prevent the meeting became the scandal rather than a debate about extermination.

But on the issue of extermination the *Launceston Advertiser* was obliquely clear: supportive of the mobilisation, wary of hoping for captures 'if they were bound to catch them alive', and of the opinion 'that the result will be beneficial to the settler and the country generally, but it cannot be achieved without bloodshed'.[26] The day before Lawrence's departure from Launceston, the newspaper printed reports of multiple victims of Aboriginal people's supposedly 'base and bloodthirsty passions'. 'To capture them will be very difficult,' it noted in reference to these attacks. The forthcoming campaign 'will be very difficult, but to visit them with condign punishment, will be not only easier of performance, but will far better satisfy the friends and relatives of the fallen'.[27] In Launceston, the campaign was a chance for revenge.

The *Launceston Advertiser* had long been hostile to any pacific language or government injunctions, so its less than subtle hints were unsurprising. But like many local publications its editors often failed to grasp the bigger picture of which the newspaper was a part, and frequently failed to recognise the nuances of some of Arthur's political posturing through government notices and orders. In advocating that 'there is very little chance of preventing their deadly incursions, except by shooting a few of them', the newspaper saw the general mobilisation as a chance to move on from misunderstandings about one tribe's reported 'peaceableness at George town'.[28] This was a reference to Arthur's Government Notice 183 of 16 September, reporting that the Lieutenant Governor had learned 'that a tribe of Aboriginal natives which has recently visited George town, has evinced the most friendly and amicable disposition in their intercourse with the European Inhabitants'.[29] Arthur had encouraged colonists to treat 'this tribe, or any other which may manifest similar feelings ... with tenderness and kindness by such parties as may happen to fall in with them'. But, situated in the area beyond his imminent campaign, the order was conveniently vague, a general reminder about humane conduct certainly, but also a formal record of the government's humane intentions that would be carried on departing ships throughout the empire just as a major military operation was about to commence.

Government Notices 182 and 183 of 15 and 16 September probably better reflect Arthur's priorities. Through these Arthur made a member of the 63rd Regiment a Justice of the Peace and appointed one 'Sholto Douglas, Esq. to be Chairman of the Quarter Sessions at Oatlands, and Campbell Town'.[30] Even Arthur's systems of public reward highlighted a strong focus on catching over conciliating. Closely following these was Government Notice 186 of 17 September rewarding three men for their efforts 'in pursuit of the hostile Aborigines' with land grants of 100 acres each. They were two 'Aboriginal natives of New South Wales' and one 'Aboriginal native of Van Diemen's Land', Pigeon, John Crook and Black Bill respectively, all men attached to Batman's party.[31]

In the first week of October when the campaign commenced, Arthur issued a government notice and a government order which neatly reveals his publicity machine at work.[32] In Government Notice 193 Arthur very publicly rewarded a convict servant of Captain Smith with a conditional pardon for capturing three Aboriginal people. This was supposedly achieved by laying down his gun, and then giving them bread and blankets, whereby:

> he soon succeeded in so completely conciliating all three as to induce them to go opossum shooting with him, by which stratagem he led them voluntarily to the military party.

In publishing this, Arthur encouraged 'other prisoners to act with equal humanity and forbearance', but was also reminding the conscripted prisoners that captures would bring hopes of reward.

Arthur's propagandising continued with the government order of 7 October – the same day of the major drive. This ordered the police magistrates of the colony to:

> use their utmost exertions to obtain the most ample accounts which can be derived from authentic sources, of all such outrages as may have taken place, within their respective districts during the last five years, and, that they will forward with the least possible delay, a very minute and particular report, not only of all persons who may have been murdered or wounded by the Aborigines, but also of all houses which have been attacked or plundered by them.

While his further request for information about 'the numbers, movements and habits of the savages' could be construed as being useful military intelligence, it also reinforced the idea that Aboriginal people were the aggressors and the strong colonial response justified.

CHAPTER SIXTEEN

Necessity Has No Law

1830, October
Northern, Western and Reserve Divisions

The First Drive, 7–12 October
The day before the main advances commenced, the Colonel Commanding was at Campbell Town making final arrangements. He directed that certain deficiencies in the forces needed to be filled, and gave instructions about guides, fires, the occupation of key river crossings and so on.[1] Dressed in his military finery, he was admired by many of the young men who felt honoured to be serving under him, although others mocked what they saw as the Lieutenant Governor's militaristic pretensions exceeding his civil responsibilities. One observer described Arthur as 'cased in glittering steel', wearing 'a military coat' and 'claret coloured trowsers', and sporting 'a well-burnished and effective sword, secured by a gold embroidered belt'.[2] This was not intended to be a flattering account: a sequence followed that had Arthur wielding his sword aloft like some caricature of an ancient hero. Unsurprisingly these anonymous observations were recorded in the *Colonial Times*, which continued to treat the campaign with greater and greater flippancy once it commenced.

Claiming ignorance of the campaign from official sources, the *Colonial Times* took to parodying the experience of the volunteers by publishing a series of letters from the interior, ostensibly written by a George Augustus Widlikens to his 'Dear Mumma'.[3] Widlikens 'had not walked three miles before my feet were so sore that I wished myself at home again'. He 'made Thomas take off my shoes and stockings and then putting on a bit of plaister'. This dynamic between the pampered and privileged Widlikens, who 'missed our nice soft cushions very much', and his long-suffering if sometimes 'impudent' servant Thomas, was played for mild comic effect. Similarly, Widlikens' pretensions to military service were contrasted with an innate cowardice, as he worried about 'nasty spears' and carried a book 'borrowed from Captain _____'s wife, about fortifications, assaults, &c.' Moreover, the fictional youth became a means to poke fun at Arthur, 'riding about, and looking after every thing'.[4] The Colonel Commanding reminded the young leader 'of Alexander the Great or Socrates' on one occasion, and of 'Pompey or King David' on another'.[5] Over subsequent editions, the letters and reports of other members of the Widlikens family furthered the running jokes.

Whether the *Colonial Times* was playing off genuine reports or not, the volunteers in the field did have a difficult start to their campaign. Camped on the top of the Blue Hills, Emmett faced a dramatic shift in the weather which threatened the success of the whole campaign. 'Very soon after dark a fearful storm of thunder & lightening came on,' he wrote, 'quite as severe as any hitherto experienced in the colony'. While his perception of the ferocity of the storm was possibly influenced by his relative inexperience of the bush, there are corroborative reports of bad weather at the beginning of the campaign. The *Colonial Times* itself, in a column next to one of Widlikens' letters, noted seriously that:

> A Correspondent in the interior writes, that on Thursday, the 7th instant, the weather in many parts of the country was more severe than had been experienced at any time during the past winter. It was exceedingly cold, accompanied with squalls of wind, rain, and hail.[6]

Further north of Emmett, Lawrence similarly diarised the shift in weather. In fact Emmett's description of the storm allows for some means of assessing the relative timing of his actions. While sometimes covering day-to-day action, Emmett's narrative was hardly written with calendrical accuracy, but his remembrance of 'that memorable night' highlights it had a major impact on the campaign's opening manoeuvres. Parties were exposed to extremely difficult conditions just as they were intending drives among the highlands and hills, and potentially quickly became exhausted and demoralised. As Emmett recalled:

> torrents of rain, accompanied by a terrible gale, stripped the forest in all directions of large branches & small limbs, but fortunately we all escaped injury, though [we were] soon wet through to the skin.

Emmett 'sat on a log throughout the storm with a rug over my shoulders'. During the wet and windy night he watched Champ laying motionless beside the fire 'though a stream poured off him during his profound repose'. Emmett had given him a blanket, and this seemed sufficient to ensure a good night's rest, irrespective of the tempest. While at first amused by the soldier's lone wandering, he seemed to have developed some respect for the lieutenant's ability to cope with the trying conditions. Having now lost his own party, the soldier decided to stay with Emmett until they returned to Bothwell, 'where he found his men'.

The morning after the storm they looked for 'signs of natives' but found nothing. At some point they heard 'that two dead blacks had been discovered in a tree'. Whether they had died naturally or were the victims of some misfortune, or perhaps simply rumour, the report highlights the difficulties of ascertaining exactly what took place in the hills, gullies and forests during Arthur's campaign. It was hard to know the truth of things then, and remains far harder nearly two centuries later.

Because he was among those Hobart volunteers fulfilling support roles in the Clyde district, Emmett's movements do not reflect the usual experience of the drive to form the first line between 7 and 12 October.

The Blue Hills were a little northwest of Bothwell, and according to Arthur's plans, some of the military detachments under Captain Wentworth should have been further westward, actually making towards Emmett's position. This is partially borne out by Emmett's following remarks. After taking the Blue Hills, Emmett's party seems to have been given over to roving duties within the district, heading for other places associated with Aboriginal people, before then joining the line proper as it formed from the detachments of soldiers sweeping through the district:

> We crossed the Country in a different direction, making for the Big river, another place where the natives had been committing depredations and a favourite resort; we reached a Station at Capt Young at noon, he was however absent making a bridge at the Big river to cross some soldiers.

This means the soldiers were in fact west of Emmett's position, just as they should be, and moving eastwards as expected. Nevertheless, despite capturing one of the few firsthand reports of military manoeuvres, Emmett's story turned to other things. Emmett received rations for his party at Young's station, and 'a nice dinner for the Leaders'. Not for the first or last time his narrative gave over to food at much greater length and detail than manoeuvres. 'The Settlers were all extremely kind to the various parties, feeling that while close to them, they were safe from the attacks of the Blacks,' he noted.

While at Young's Emmett received orders to return to Bothwell. On their way, the party approached another farm, but were initially mistaken for bushrangers. This was, Emmett admitted, 'a very natural impression from our general appearance'. But the misidentification was soon resolved, the embarrassment forgiven, and the party fed with 'a second supper'. With full stomachs they moved on and reached Bothwell the following day. As Emmett put it:

> we joined the Line which extended to the Sea coast from the Westward – All the Parties before we joined had been driving the

natives towards the centre some 3500 men being placed along the Line, each 320 yards apart. It was astonishing to see the manner in which the Settlers had turned out with their own servants leaving their homes for an indefinite time.

It was, Emmett recalled, a magnificent display of force. But, writing 40 years or more after the war, Emmett also noted: 'There are not many left now who can recollect the trying occasion. Mr Bonwick says there were 119 Parties but I imagine there were more.'

Explicitly responding to James Bonwick's *The Last of the Tasmanians; or, The Black War of Van Diemen's Land*, published in 1870, Emmett's recollection was certainly influenced by versions of the campaign that had formed subsequently.[7] His account is extremely valuable for the level of experiential detail, but on individual events and sequences he is much weaker. His understanding of the campaign's progress was greatly influenced by the stories he had later heard and histories he consulted.

Further Drives, 12–20 October

Emmett's sometimes vague memories contrast with the precision of Arthur's centralised command. While the various parties throughout the colony were advancing towards their 12 October positions, in the midlands Arthur continued giving directions about a range of matters, tweaking forces and strategy. He was certainly micromanaging elements of the manoeuvres. Thinking it 'extremely important that the Blackman Tier should be thoroughly examined', Arthur ordered 'two very smart parties' to scour it.[8] Arthur even gave instructions about the formation of one of these parties, which was to be led by a settler but supported by a non-commissioned officer 'and eight men' from Douglas and 'two good guides' from Anstey. Both parties were reminded to be in position on their part of 'the Line on the Evening of the 12th October'. Arthur also gave explicit directions for the movements of 'The Volunteers from Richmond under the charge of Chief District Constable Robertson', lightly reprimanded Major Douglas for not having fully reconnoitred the proposed line positions, and gave instructions for guiding the whole force and its constituent parties.

In all this, Arthur was clearly focused on using the military for the most important missions, and using volunteers for back up and peripheral duties. 'As all the best Guides are now selected for the Military', the Colonel Commanding told Douglas, 'it will not be necessary to mix any of the Civil Force with them unless you wish it.' The soldiers that civil leaders like Lawrence and Emmett only mentioned in passing were the ones really doing most of the campaigning.

On 12 October, Arthur dealt with complaints about the lack of tobacco and arranged for 500 pairs of shoes to be sent to various depots.[9] That same day Douglas forwarded petitions from some of the officers asking about a field allowance.[10] That evening Douglas's northern front was due to merge with Wentworth's western front, forming a relatively continuous barrier from a sequence of parties of soldiers and civil militiamen connecting the hills beside the Derwent to the east coast.

But in the morning, it was clear that the mission had already partly failed. Referring to 'Several Reports brought in by the Parties employed under Captain Wentworth' on the western front, Arthur was convinced 'that some of the Native Tribes have been left in the Rear' in the southwestern part of the combined right flank near the Derwent.[11] Arthur instructed Donaldson to 'Detach some strong patrols' from the reserve line towards the area while the remainder of the operation continued as planned. Then, on 14 October, the great line moved toward its 16 October second line position.

'All being declared ready,' Emmett later recalled, 'orders were given to start and on we went, over plains, mountains & rivers ... constantly keeping up a discharge of musketry which I assure you was well done.' The idea of this massed shooting was to terrify Aboriginal people, thereby driving them before the colonial forces.

William Coventry, another volunteer party leader who was later interviewed about the operation, also remembered this part of the drive, saying that 'all day long they fired Blank cartridges all down the line'.[12] This musketry served the same function as beating the bush for a giant hunt. As they crossed the country, Coventry added, the parties shifted their composition:

> The plan was that never less than three men were in a party – but in thick scrub they rose to 50 or 60. In open country they were at times 200 yards apart – but in the Bush not more than 50 yards.

All went well in the beginning. 'For several days this march was carried on and the natives were known to be in front of us', Emmett recalled. The newspapers were certainly optimistic about the early stage of the campaign:

> On Wednesday [13 October], dispatches were received in town from His Excellency the Lieutenant Governor, stating that the parties about Oatlands were in pursuit of a large body of Natives, report says three different tribes amounting to above 200; the account goes on stating that the Natives were retreating exactly in the direction intended, and that the parties have most sanguine expectations that the termination of the measures will be most fortunate.[13]

But, despite the reportedly smooth start, both Emmett and Coventry focused on reports that the line was almost immediately broken. With the benefit of hindsight and an established narrative, Emmett thought the idea so impractical as to make failure inevitable. Aboriginal people could never have been contained, he argued, 'in consequence of so many obstacles in the way of a given progress, Gullys [sic] and rocky hills, were continually met with, rendering the task an utter impossibility'.

Correspondence from Arthur to Donaldson in the rear line dated Sunday 17 October, the day of rest at the second line position, reveals that Arthur too believed the cordon had been breached:

> Captain Wentworth's line reached the Jordon [river] yesterday, and as there is reason to fear that the Tribe in question may have passed through it, I have pushed four parties back towards

the Quoin hill which they are now roving. If you can dispatch an active party to search the Country between Table Mountain and the Quoin, and the Caverns about the former, it may be the means of capturing this most dangerous Tribe.[14]

He then gave more particular information about where he expected the tribe might be hiding.

Accompanying his instructions, Arthur also sent Donaldson a report of an encounter between a farm servant and an Aboriginal group. The report was subsequently gazetted in a lengthy government notice, narrating an encounter between a servant named Thomas Savage and a group of Aboriginal people who were accompanied by a shotgun-wielding 'White Man' named Brown.[15] With a convoluted series of explanations, the gist of the story was that Savage was surrounded and threatened, but was saved by Brown, who was part of the tribe. 'Brown told me he had been with the Natives about 3 years,' Savage explained after the group departed, 'and said he was surprised at so many parties being out.' Savage saw some of this tribe bringing in a sheep for their dinner before hurrying away when they heard a gunshot. Once Savage got news of the encounter to the authorities, Arthur was swift to act:

> By the time this information was given it was nearly dark, but the Lieutenant Governor descended the tier with all dispatch, and in the course of an hour and a half four parties were sent off, with orders to proceed during the night ten miles beyond the Lagoon, as far as the Quoin, and then to spread themselves out and scour the bush thoroughly; and supposing the natives to be tired with their long march the previous night, and especially so the woman with child, it may be hoped that they will be surrounded, or at least driven to the southward and eastward, if that has not been already effected by the parties which came over the tier at day light this morning [18 October].[16]

In response to this intelligence that 'the Natives are headed by Europeans', as Arthur put it, he ordered increased use of fires along the line during the night camps, and instructed that men had to camp in threes.[17] He also instructed Douglas to initiate 'a constant Patrol by Day as well as by night' once the parties arrived at their third line positions on 20 October.

Emmett described the night-time arrangements in some detail. He noted that the line:

> was generally made up to its proper state at the halting hour, and the Sentries fixed for the night, three men from each party the Leader being in the centre, who had himself to keep watch half the night, marching up and down the line to the adjoining party on his right and left and every half hour or so calling out the number … of his party No. 1 <u>Alls Well</u>. Six fires were kept up by each party all night, one in front of each Tent and three others fifty yards in front, which in some places where search of wood kept the men well employed. It was an exceedingly pretty sight to see the fires for miles, especially on the tops of hills, and hearing the Sentries Watchcry, coming down the line at intervals helped the effect.

Another participant similarly wrote of the line of campfires giving 'rather a fine effect', while also giving an illustration of how alerts were dealt with:

> From one of our stations we could discern fifteen or sixteen of them, and they caused a blaze which illuminated a great extent of forest. In the event of the blacks attempting to force the line, or if, during its advance, they shewed any inclination to give battle, orders were given to fire, and drive them back, but unless absolutely necessary in self-defence, not to kill them.[18]

This linesman then described his section readying their arms for action on their second night out, until 'hearing the cry of "All's well," denoting, of course, that we had put the enemy to the route' [sic]. He also gave an anecdote about a convict who 'was mistaken for a native and fired at'.

Contemporary commentators generally observed that Aboriginal people were frightened of travelling at night, and did so only in the most extreme circumstances. Their attempts to get through the line of men, fires and gunfire was therefore a telling illustration that the movement did in fact have some success. Emmett mentioned that 'the natives on several occasions tried to get through at night', and gave one instance of his party taking on guard duties:

> We were camped on a saddle tolerably clear country with a gully below, in which the natives were heard moving about, though we did not see them. The night was lit up by a full moon & was frosty & exceedingly cold.

Emmett also gave an anecdote of when 'the natives threw a spear at a Sentry, who was putting some wood on a fire, but missed him'.

While accounts of particular skirmishes along the line remain relatively rare, it is nonetheless clear that it was a common enough experience along the volunteer sections of the main line. Of the area where the soldiery formed the main front, the records remain almost eerily silent. But highlighting the extent of shooting during the operation is one of Arthur's memoranda after the divisions reached their 20 October positions. On Saturday 23 October he wrote to the Colonial Secretary:

> Be so good as to direct the Ordinance Storekeeper or Town Adjutant to send over to Kangaroo Point, without delay, Four Thousand ball Cartridges, and Two thousand blank Cartridges for the use of the Forces in pursuit of the Aborigines. I will send a pack horse to Kangaroo Point to convey this ammunition to the Bluff Ferry at Sorell. I bear in mind that tomorrow is the Sabbath, but necessity has no law.[19]

The Reserve Line

Lawrence's movements formed part of the rear-guard division. As he moved into the mountains in readiness for the first drive, having 'to crawl on our hands and knees, in some places', Lawrence entered a snowy alpine environment with the appearance and 'air of extreme barrenness and bleakness'.[20] Nonetheless, they got immediately to work scouring country and keeping 'look out for fires'. Hearing gunfire to the east, Lawrence may have assumed other parties were already at work too, and the fires he saw 'appeared to me to be fires belonging to parties of the line'.

As Lawrence neared one of the highland lakes he saw smoke on the other side and identified the fire producing it as a potential target. He determined to 'sneak upon them before morning'. In the early hours of the morning, 'when the moon rose which it did about 3 O'Clock', his party 'started cautiously'. Lawrence sent the constable ahead to reconnoitre, who returned claiming there were two fires looking similar to Aboriginal ones. Lawrence divided his party to flank these campfires on three sides, using the lake as a fourth barrier, and waited for daylight. But his stratagem was wasted:

> Upon closing upon them however, we found to our great disappointment, that our labour had been thrown away upon a party of the line, who were bye the bye, quite out of it, all fast asleep.

Lawrence was disgusted that they had not even posted a sentry, and had been firing their guns hunting the day beforehand.

Lawrence continued to send out small reconnaissance parties from his own, scouring for prospective targets, hearing shots, and encountering a lost party. A team of surveyors helped direct Lawrence towards the main camp at Sorell Lake. On his way there he found some Aboriginal huts and 'picked up a piece of old blanket'. The party found the wrong lake, spent an 'exceedingly rainy' night in the field, and overshot their target considerably. 'This day we ought to be stationed on the line,' Lawrence wrote on 12 October, 'but we are still at fault'. It took another two days before his party 'arrived and took our station' where they were supposed to be. While there were soon reports of a large gap in their line, there were also reports 'that the parties to the westward have been successful'.

NECESSITY HAS NO LAW

This rumour may have been a reference to parties on the far west of the reserve line. A letter to the *Hobart Town Courier* by 'H.R.' described the adventures of one such party chasing 'a large Mob of the Blacks' in the area around Lake Echo, albeit a week after Lawrence's news.[21]

> We counted forty two. They were proceeding in a direction for the Big Lake; they crossed the Shannon. We wrote upon a piece of bark, which we nailed upon a tree, that we had seen this mob, and intended to follow them, and requested Mr Collins, the leader of a party, to inform Captain Donaldson of our movements. We tracked the Blacks in a north-east direction. On the same day of our pursuit we saw 13 Native huts, and we found a tomahawk, a part of a woman's chemise, and part of a child's frock, and several other trifling articles, evidently part of the plunder of the Blacks. Their tracks led us round the north-east side of the Big Lake for 3 days, and then to the westward; and we continued upon their track until yesterday morning [24 October], when we were obliged to make for Mr. Leith's, at the Retreat, for provisions.

The newspaper added that Aboriginal people committed an attack in this area about that time, killing a settler.

Lawrence's adventures were less newsworthy. While the main western and northern fronts moved, he remained occupied with reserve duties. He divided his party into three smaller ones, received various minor orders, recorded occasional rumours, endured snow and dined with settlers and military officers. 'Our principal occupation is still walking to and fro, between the stations, to prevent our passage of the Blacks', he noted on 19 October, well into the main campaign. Lawrence's journal certainly captures his feelings that reserve duty quickly became tedious, and that the adventure rapidly waned. Slight remarks of passing soldiers were the only comments of real significance about the campaign he recorded, seemingly too preoccupied with his own troubles to care much about the broader strategic situation. Lawrence's war was not really all that far from his fictional equivalent, Widlikens.

But finally, on 22 October, the reserves began to move. Donaldson ordered Lawrence to march towards Bothwell. On his way he saw a pack of dogs, sketched some mountains, was rained upon and dissected an echidna. After going to bed on 27 October he was roused from sleep with new orders hurrying him to Bothwell. He added some commentary on his current situation and rumours of the wider campaign:

> Report says that this movement is in consequence of several large tribes of natives having made their appearance in the neighbourhood of Richmond, to which place we are to march I believe, from Bothwell. Several murders have been committed during the week. I understood that one man has been killed in front of Major Douglas's line.

The next day Lawrence reached Bothwell, which 'consists of about 80 or 100 houses and can boast of a very comfortable inn.'

Major Douglas's Northern Front Advances

While Lawrence patrolled the reserve line in the high country and Emmett and Coventry pushed eastwards with the western front, the northern front also contracted towards the southeast. Because Douglas wrote a series of brief letters to Arthur about his movements, these can be observed in some detail. On Sunday 17 October, when the line was resting in position after its first push, Douglas provided Arthur with a schematic drawing of how the line was constituted along the northern front.[22] By this point the line was supposed to run west to east, basically sealing the valleys and floodplains of the Little Swan Port and Coal rivers. It ran through the farm of a settler named Hobbs, which Douglas included as a reference point on his illustration. With this visual aid Douglas could explain the movement to Arthur.

Douglas had staggered his parties along the line, creating a formation of alternating parties of volunteers and soldiers. Douglas told Arthur that 'the left centre I know are just as described and are all present except those marked', which referred to two parties of the

63rd Regiment on the far left wing of the centre. 'The right centre I believe to be if any thing more correct than the left.' He was satisfied that the first drive had gone according to plan, and unfazed by the two missing parties of soldiers, simply assuming they were delayed getting rations.

Douglas also told Arthur of a reported Aboriginal attack on a settler's hut, which was being investigated. In passing, he mentioned that 'The Coal river parties are exceedingly alert and willing'. As his schematic explained, while drawn from the Coal River these were charged with scouring the other flank of his line, the Little Swan Port River area closest to the coast. Here there were no named parties of 10 men or so, just a small explanation: '100 men reported all present by Gilbert Robertson'. The former rover was leading a large cohort of men charged with covering the scrubby eastern tiers.

Other old rovers were also out there, their special missions lost among the generalisations and the scarce documentation. One surviving letter from Douglas about the drive to the third line reveals at least one of the former rovers acting as a guide.[23] Douglas requested a subordinate 'to return with Peter Scott for the purpose of shewing the road through the Scrub to Prosser's Plains'. While highlighting that the advance did not always maintain a line formation, it also reveals the special role that former rovers played in facilitating the series of manoeuvres.

The public knew little of the early stages of the campaign, but as the force approached closer to Hobart, more news reached the town and its press. While George Augustus Widlikens continued to write home – thanking his 'Dear Mumma' for 'the rhubarb tart', detailing 'what the book calls a flank movement', relating how he 'just missed falling in with a large party of the nasty blacks' and explaining 'that Thomas has gone after them along with another party' – his parodies were made richer for playing on actual news as well as experiential complaints.[24] After the forces had reached their 20 October third-line positions, the *Hobart Town Courier* corrected the 'wholly unfounded' reports of Aboriginal people breaking through the line, before giving its readers some general information about the state of the campaign:

> To give a full narrative of their proceedings at large would be impossible, suffice it to say that, the original plan of the campaign has been followed up almost to the letter. ... The several Police Magistrates and commanding officers are continually on horseback visiting every part of the line of their respective forces, while His Excellency, regardless of all personal fatigue, and with unwearied perseverance takes in, in rapid succession the general sweep of the whole, at one time to be seen extending the lines and infusing a portion of his own ardour into the parties.[25]

Yet while going into detail about guard duties and praising the campaign leadership, the newspaper had little else to say. A week later the same newspaper reported 'one general spirit of cheerful and determined perseverance pervades the whole', despite the recent weather making the ground wet and boggy and many rivers difficult to cross.[26] It also carried reports of 'attacks made by the Blacks round Pittwater and the Carlton', which seemed to indicate there were hostile Aboriginal people within the cordon. 'The general opinion,' the newspaper claimed, 'is that, the bulk of both the Big River and Oyster Bay tribes is now hemmed in.'

Hold and Skirmish, 20 October

Arthur's original plan was that when the line contracted to its 20 October position, the force would halt and wait for further orders. With Arthur approaching his endgame, the volume of surviving documentation increases. On 19 October Arthur reprimanded a lieutenant of the 63rd Regiment who 'occupied with a party the Isthmus', because this act of initiative threatened the whole scheme if it stopped Aboriginal people from fleeing into the Tasman Peninsula.[27] He ordered the lieutenant 'to withdraw the party immediately & by water'. Arthur's scheme relied not only on pushing Aboriginal people before the line, but giving them room to flee.

To ensure the line was adequately provisioned, such that parties could remain in place, Arthur gave a series of instructions about rations, including ordering 'a cart or pack horses' to be used to transport supplies.[28] But even as the line came to a halt, Arthur gave new orders for manoeuvres. On 20 October Arthur ordered both Douglas and Wentworth to made an advance the following day, carefully scouring their paths.[29] On 22 October Arthur ordered '5 Skirmishing parties' to detach from the main line to advance and 'thoroughly scour the Country'.[30]

The next day, 23 October, Arthur dealt with reports that parts of the line were 'insecure', and followed up on information that one of the skirmishing parties under the settler Edward Atkyns Walpole 'had not proceeded on the duty in question'.[31] As Arthur noted:

> the part of the Country appropriated to Mr Walpole is the most likely for the concealment of the Natives, & should be most thoroughly examined and if Mr Walpole has not proceeded on this duty, & is not prepared to do so, another party must be immediately selected. Mr Gilbert Robertson would be a proper person for this duty.

With the overall strategy in place, the line turned its focus to containment while the skirmishers went out front. Correspondence from Douglas dated 23 October reveals that he gave specific instructions to 'five roving parties' that had been personally approved by Arthur the day beforehand.[32] Walpole's delayed departure turned out to be related to the rationing arrangements, and Douglas agreed that if he was not soon out then Robertson would be sent in his place. In reply to Arthur's queries about the line being secured, Douglas affirmed his belief that most parties were in place, although 'there is a party under a person called Fortosa that I believe has not yet crossed the river'.

Aware that these skirmish missions could encourage Aboriginal people to attempt to break the line rather than flee into the peninsula, Arthur issued a circular on 24 October encouraging the linesmen to maintain their vigilance, because 'the slightest relaxation in any one party may have the deplorable effect of disappointing the hopes of the whole Community'.[33] Arthur now ordered the lines to maintain a relative silence, avoiding bugles or unnecessary gunshots. He wanted quiet sentries out front to listen for approaching Aboriginal people. Over the coming days he made several other orders regarding the improvement of the line, tinkering with certain parts or practices.[34] He insisted that 'every leader will exert his ingenuity in creating obstructions to the sudden passage of the Natives through the Line':

> It is impossible to point out any one mode of strengthening every post, as the means of fortifying them must vary with the variations of the ground, but it may be sufficient to explain that the object in view is to form a chain of obstructions immediately in rear of the Sentries, so that should the Natives rush past the post, they will be entangled in the artificial obstacles w[hic]h will have been prepared for them.

If any Aboriginal people managed to get past the forward sentries or ingenious obstacles, then Arthur also wanted an area of clear ground in front of the line to deprive Aboriginal people of cover. He also suggested the construction of a 'palisade' of forward-leaning sharpened sticks and logs, providing illustrations by way of explanation. Finally, the Colonel Commanding wanted a line of sharpened branches arranged behind the line just in case.

Some of these instructions were likely inspired by attempted breaches of the line. On 25 October Major Douglas informed Arthur of an encounter at about 2:00 am that morning:

> One of Mr Batmans [sic] party states that a Native attempted to pass through the scrub close to his post … he ran up to him … the Native made his escape towards the Marshes and Mr Batmans man fired at him … further that more were seen with fire sticks and this man says he heard a rustling noise as if more were close to him. A good many unnecessary shots were fired along the line.[35]

When Douglas heard shots in the distance the following morning he laconically informed Arthur that 'no doubt the ammunition has arrived at that place'.[36]

By this time Arthur was convinced that he had 'enclosed within the Lines the Big River & the Oyster Bay Mobs', and ordered Donaldson's reserve line to now advance to reinforce the line.[37] That would free up more parties for skirmishing duties out front. Moreover, with the timely arrival of two convict transports from England, Arthur also now had more troops to deploy. He relieved the Hobart volunteer town guardsmen of their duties and was still able to order 25 soldiers and a non-commissioned officer to join the main camp at Sorell.[38] But as these arrangements were being made, the campaign was on the cusp of its most public success. Within the cordoned territory, the slow-starting Mr Walpole had spied a group of Aboriginal people.

CHAPTER SEVENTEEN

Harass Them if They Cannot Be Taken

1830, October–November
East Coast

Interception

Walpole's skirmishing party left the stationary line on Sunday 24 October just as the Colonel Commanding had ordered.[1] Arthur had given up any pretence that Sundays were for rest. On what he described as 'the extreme left of Lieut Aubin's division', Walpole's party made their way toward the coast, as far as the Sandpit River. There Walpole temporarily based the party at Captain Glover's hut. This was about halfway between the line and the small neck of land that connected the two peninsulas to the mainland. On the other side of this neck was the Forestier Peninsula, then the Tasman Peninsula after another small neck of land. Through local intelligence Walpole learned that some Aboriginal people were further south, near Bream Creek, but were heading in a northwesterly direction – away from the peninsula and back towards the line. He decided to try to intercept them.

'I stationed half my party at Capt Glovers Hut', Walpole later explained, 'where the Natives are in the habit of appearing, and with the remainder, went on the tiers to reconnoitre'. After travelling for about 5 miles Walpole's party 'heard the Natives hunting' in the early afternoon. Creeping closer, the party soon saw their target. They watched the Aboriginal group for a few hours and waited till they had made camp for the night. Walpole then got the rest of his men from Glover's. During the night the team returned to the campsite and advanced to 'within 300 yards' of the Aboriginal huts.

At dawn Walpole 'crept to one of the Natives without being perceived'. He grabbed the sleeping figure by the leg, who immediately gave alarm. Four more men, Walpole said, 'rushed out through the bark while some of my party were stooping to catch them. One of these was caught while jumping into the Creek and two others shot.' As Walpole explained later, there were other escapees from this raid:

> There were five other huts across the Creek in the centre of a
> very thick scrub. I had fully intended to attack the main body but
> I found it impossible to get near enough with[out] being heard.
> The hut with the 5 Men appeared to have been a look out, it
> being in a clear spot about two yards from the creek and scrub.
> The Natives in the other huts fled on hearing the shots and left
> most of their plunder and property the greater part of which
> I destroyed.

In addition to the mostly colonial items that Walpole listed were '30 Spears'.

A few days later a correspondent penned an account of the raid for the *Hobart Town Courier* which offered some details not included in Walpole's own account to the Lieutenant Governor.[2] In this version, Walpole's captive 'tried to make his escape by twisting his legs and biting:

> [He] would have succeeded had Mr. Walpole not drawn a small
> dagger from his belt and inflicted a slight wound, which so
> frightened him that he was secured. The other taken, was a boy
> of about 15 years of age, and appears to be the son of a chief
> from the ornaments upon his body, cut with flints or some sharp

instrument into the skin. ... The boy, when taken, wished them to let him go, as he said there were 'plenty more black fellows in the scrub,' pointing to it.

The differing versions again highlight that events could be told in different ways for different audiences. As with many conflicts, the affray reveals the limitations of descriptive documentation in wartime, which is generally written after the fact and not always for the public record. Walpole's encounter was relatively unusual in this regard for being a subject of public notice. While Walpole was later remembered for 'only' having caught two people, at the time the information was most likely taken as an early signal to future accomplishments. The line had closed, attempted escapes had been thwarted, and the first skirmishers were having some success.

Skirmishing Auxiliaries and a New Insurgency

But there was more to the story. Returning towards Camp Sorell with his captives, Walpole 'met a civilized Black Boy in Kirby's party'. Kirby's skirmishing party had been sent out at the same time as Walpole's. Unlike the main line with its daily reports to headquarters, these skirmishing parties mostly engaged in remarkably ill-documented activities in front of the static line. This unnamed 'Boy' enabled Walpole to extract useful intelligence about the movements of the escapees, which he passed on to headquarters:

> their number consists now of Twenty six Men, Nine Women and six lads and children ... their intended course was through Prossers Plains to the Lake, but the name of which I am not able to inform Your Excellency.

But while this intelligence was tactically useful, it is probably Walpole's passing mention of Kirby that is of most historical significance, for it highlights an element of Arthur's campaign almost entirely forgotten – the deployment of Aboriginal people with colonial forces. Although claiming he personally 'never saw a Black all the time he was out', William Coventry also asserted that 'they had a Black who was forced to help them'.[3] And, among the lists of parties, there was at least one 'Black Jack'.[4] He was the only 'free' man attached to a party of prisoners from the Richmond police district led by one 'G. Robinson', almost certainly George Robinson, the son of George Augustus Robinson.[5]

In fact, only a few days before these skirmishers were deployed, Arthur arranged for Eumarrah to join the campaign.[6] As it turned out, the 'Boy' attached to Kirby's skirmishers enabled Walpole to better interrogate his captives, thereby learning that Eumarrah's tribe was among their enemies:

> they belong to the Oyster Bay and Big River tribes which are united ... they have been at Pittwater and speared as well as stealing knives and Blankets ... five of the tribe have been shot by White Men ... they have fought the Stony Creek tribe and killed a great number.

These passing remarks again point to the complex political realities within and between the tribes, and hint at the possibility that Arthur was knowingly utilising intertribal enmities to prosecute the war. The more captives the colony held, the better its leaders understood these animosities. Early in the campaign, Arthur had recorded that his goal was to target specific tribes, in part to stave off political developments among his enemies:

> I determined not to employ any Force to the North East until a great effort had been made to capture the Oyster Bay and Big River Tribes w[hic]h are by far the worst & have evidently endeavoured to excite the other Tribes to cooperate with them.[7]

This unusual explanation was part of a longer letter, ordering the settler James Cox to call back a party led by his son, which he had sent eastwards on his own initiative. Arthur was worried such a mission could compromise his broader strategy. Cox's son's party had arrived at St Patricks Head in mid-October, while the line was still moving.⁸ Cox's idea was that they could range northwards instead of joining the southward-moving divisions.

Arthur explained to Cox that his plan for those tribes beyond the area of the line was to try negotiation before force, which was by then being deployed in the main settled districts. Referring to the mission of the Aboriginal women sent out from Batman's farm and the extended peregrinations of George Augustus Robinson, who was now focusing on the far northeast, Arthur explained:

> By the time the movements against these Tribes to the Southward had taken place the period would have fully expired during which the women had engaged to bring in their mob & Mr Robinson would have had a reasonable period allowed him for negotiating, & failing in the attempt then my arrangements were made for proceeding with the whole force & occupying the Position from George Town to Ben Lomond & from there to St Patricks Head, preparatory to advancing towards Cape Portland, for altho' one or two parties may fall in with the Tribes & destroy some of them nothing, we know from experience, but a very large force is capable of <u>capturing</u> them w[hic]h is the object every one must have most at heart.

While stating that his plan was technically to remove Aboriginal people by capture rather than destruction, Arthur's explanation also made it plain that he was prepared to order another line to clear the northeast of the island after the southeast was clear. By this point his objective was clearly to extirpate the tribes from the entire colony, one region after the other.

Unfortunately for Arthur, Cox's retrieval party got co-opted into serving the colony en route.⁹ But this brought good news for Arthur, because the retrieval party 'were on their calling at Mr Batmans Farm detained by Capt Grey to assist taking care of some Natives who had surrendered themselves'. The women sent out from Batman's farm on a second excursion had met with success. Reporting the news only a few

HARASS THEM IF THEY CANNOT BE TAKEN

days before Walpole's raid, the *Hobart Town Courier* captured details of intertribal warfare when describing the women's return to Batman's farm:

> bringing with them 9 men, the whole that now remain of their once numerous tribe excepting one man, who was in so bad health as to be unable to accompany them. They however returned with some men dispatched by Mr. Gray, then at Mr. Batman's, who found the man lying sick by the fire, and carried him home, where proper attendance it is hoped will restore him to health. None of these poor people shew any inclination to return to the bush, at least at present, though closely watched. They state, that their tribe has suffered much of late from the cruel and hostile attacks of the Oyster bay tribe, led on by their sanguinary chief Neumarrah, who has succeeded in reducing them to the present small number, with the exception of Eumara, who has for some time been domesticated at the Aboriginal establishment formerly at Brune island, but latterly on the New town road.[10]

Apparently once they learned of Arthur's campaign, they welcomed 'the idea of a stop being put to the attacks of their enemy'. The report suggested that it was this intelligence that encouraged Arthur to send for Eumarrah 'who has readily joined the levy and is now assisting the parties in their movements.' The newspaper then went on to inform the public that Robinson 'with his domesticated Blacks is now exploring the region round George-town and Cape Portland with the same conciliatory views'. It was classic division and conquest.

The captivity and cooperation of some Aboriginal people even seemed to herald a broad colonial success. During that phase of the General Movement when it had little news from the front to report, the *Hobart Town Courier* gave a long description of 'Peletega, the chief lately apprehended at the Shannon', whose chained journey to Hobart had caused such controversy.[11] Peletega, confined in the Hobart Gaol, supposedly 'displays the most perfect good humour and cheerfulness':

for a small reward of sugar or other desirable food [he] will sing and dance to entertain the donor. He has a method of clapping the palms of his hands and soles of his feet simultaneously on the ground, and immediately making his frame rebound in a perpendicular position 4 or 5 feet in the air, and then dancing and singing round and round in a rotary motion.

The report continued by giving two examples of Peletega's spear-throwing abilities, one of which was undertaken with 'an old broom stick'.

But the colonial command of its captives was not entirely secure. All seemed well when Batman was detached from the line to head home and oversee the Aboriginal people at his farm. They initially 'seemed quite at home, enjoying every comfort', but quietly left the property in the early hours of 24 October.[12] The departing group comprised 'eleven stout men, three women, and one child'. Naturally the story caused some alarm, especially because they reportedly took 'about twenty knives and tomahawks', and some 'had learned the use of a musket, and as might be expected from the keen unerring eye of these savages, were excellent shots'. Almost more worrying, this group now included 'the lad Mungo who has so long been domesticated with Mr. Batman, and was in a great measure inured to civilized habits'. Mungo-Jack apparently discarded his shoes as he left.

The departure of Mungo-Jack was a particular setback for the colonists, as it seemed to mark the beginning of a counter-insurgency campaign in the northeast of the island just as it was ostensibly becoming a target for diplomatic efforts. By early November there were reports reaching Hobart of repeat attacks on farms, including attempts by the attackers to take firearms.[13] One correspondent claimed that 'guns appear to be the chief objects of their visits'.[14] Another settler wrote of a roving party catching up with these people, which potentially included Mungo-Jack, at Talbot's farm.[15] 'They commenced by spearing one of the party through the thigh,' the settler reported, 'but he fired at the moment and shot his assailant dead.' The wounded rover was sent to Campbell Town; apparently 'the spear was half through his thigh and remained fast in it'. Another report had the fellow differently wounded, but also reported another Aboriginal man being shot dead further afield while fleeing. Back on the farm, the man's corpse was left be. 'The dead Black was left as a decoy to his friends, who saw him fall, and as no doubt they will return for the body it is hoped they may be captured.'

Holding the Line

Meanwhile, the static line still occupied most of Arthur's attention. During the late morning of 27 October, according to one correspondent, 'a party of 6 men made their appearance on a rocky hill occupied by part of the Richmond force' and speared a sentry just as he was putting a log of wood on his fire.[16] As he turned and threw the log at his attacker, another spear struck him from a different angle. While he quickly raised the alarm, the attackers escaped into the area in front of the line. 'Several small parties were immediately formed and sent in pursuit,' while the wounded man was conveyed to hospital where the spears were removed.

About this time Emmett also had a close encounter. 'During the detention of the Line,' he recalled, 'one day, I heard dogs barking in front of my position, which I thought very unusual.' He took three men with him to investigate. As he 'started up a very pretty grassy valley', into the area in front of the line, he encountered evidence of the skirmishing:

> I saw almost immediately on the top of a hill a man who coo=ed [sic] that the blacks had run up the valley 12 in number and threw a spear at him, which actually struck his cap, knocking it off his head and pinning it to the ground. This man was one of Mr Walpoles, who had been sent down to the Line with a message. On proceeding a little further I came upon the Natives Camp, it seems that they had only just come evidently to watch an opportunity of escape. My appearance had started them off suddenly[,] evidenced, by my finding a fresh kangaroo on a small fire not skinned.

287

Emmett followed their tracks as best he could, finding a waddy and a puppy abandoned in their flight, before returning to the line. He thought he might have caught them if allowed to pursue them properly – perhaps a reflection of the way this event was later remembered, because he also mentioned an account of it recorded in Bonwick's 1870 history.[17] Emmett concluded his story of a close encounter by noting that 'Colonel Arthur & Judge Montagu visited me the next day, and inspected the trophies secured.'

Emmett then described the inaction of the daily line routine. He quipped that the task of gathering sufficient firewood for the night fires meant his party 'must have cleared ten acres of land for some ones benefit, for which we got no reward'. But soon enough his routine changed. The early skirmishing probes and repulsions along the line had proved encouraging. Arthur firmly believed the line was working. Moreover, the arrival of the reserve line under Donaldson meant that Arthur could soon advance with greater force, and Emmett was quick to volunteer. So too did Lawrence when he arrived with the reserves.

After marching to Bothwell, Lawrence and his fellow reserves were 'drawn up and ordered to march on the road to Richmond'. Apparently this proved a disorderly advance, and there was 'a great deal of squabbling among the men' over the speed they should walk. Because they were using the colonial roads, they now had access to various inns, and within a few days Lawrence was recording the result: 'Many of the people nearly drunk'. Soon, however, they were dining at Richmond, which Lawrence described as 'one of the prettiest and most english-like [sic] settlements'. But it was also a staging ground. Other reserve forces from Launceston and Norfolk Plains arrived, and all marshalled together to 'march in for the Governors camp in good order'. Lawrence was surprised by the good behaviour of the men, pleased when Arthur reviewed the volunteers, and soon took up his position on the line. Like Emmett, Lawrence also reported a close encounter on 3 November:

> In the course of the morning the cry of Look out came down the line, preceeded [sic] by several shots – We were all immediately on the alert. Capt Donaldson sent me with two soldiers to

ascertain the source of the firing ... It proved to be a Mr Glover and a constable, who had fallen in with a single native, at whom they fired several times without effect. He ran away and left his blanket. It is supposed he had been sent by the tribe to which he belonged to examine the strength of our part of the line.

The line was holding, but it was being probed for weak spots.

Skirmishing Out Front

Anticipating the arrival of Donaldson's reserves, Arthur had spent the final days of October planning to advance the line. He ordered a change in the maintenance of the static line, requesting that five-man patrols should 'continually during the day move along the front of their respective Corps at a distance of one mile from the Line'.[18] These were to 'make as much shew & noise as possible, & will leave a few fires at night to induce the Natives to believe that this advanced ground is also occupied'. By this Arthur hoped to give the impression that the line was impassable. The sentries were now posted between the 'double line of fires' instead of quietly out in front.

Arthur also changed the rationing arrangements to better reflect the circumstances. He inspected the lines personally, and commented approvingly of the cleared ground and various obstacles constructed along its length, but also pointed out that the line could be modified to better cover ground in some situations. He instructed the colonial surveyors to examine parts of the line and authorised partial advances if needed 'so as to make the most of every man in the Force'.

Douglas's daily reports reflect this focus on force maintenance.[19] He repeatedly claimed there was 'nothing extraordinary' to report to the Colonel Commanding in the first few days of November. He mainly dealt with a range of rationing matters – including noting the skirmishers who returned to the lines for rations and reports – and reported the situations of certain divisions or parties, including mentioning some deserters. After weeks of campaigning, some of the volunteers and conscripts were skulking away.

Various accounting documents survive from this period, in part because Arthur wanted to better understand the strength of the force at his disposal. From one of these reports of the size and composition of parties, which is undated but certainly made after the arrival of the reserves to the main line, it is possible to see that Donaldson's force comprised 307 men – including 80 soldiers. Moreover, it detailed that the party led by Lawrence consisted of 14 other men, needed seven pairs of shoes, had 47 rounds of ammunition, and wanted an additional 60 rounds.[20] This was just a small part of the needs of Donaldson's whole division, which required 899 rounds of ammunition and 180 shoes. But while this force did need material resupply, and was experiencing some issues with morale, it allowed Arthur to contemplate a final drive towards the neck.

With the arrival of the reserves Arthur was able to increase the numbers of skirmishing parties.[21] Arthur relieved some of the civil division leaders from their command, replaced them with soldiers, and put them on duties out front. This included Robertson, who Arthur delicately asked for his 'services as Leader of one of the scouring parties'. Arthur also made sure these parties had expert support, ordering 'Peter Scott to proceed to the Oatlands Division & attach himself to one of the scouring parties to whom he will act as Guide – Peter Scott will take his horse & deliver it over to Lt Pedder for his use'. This remarkable instruction reveals the way that Arthur had clearly ensured that some of the rangers had been given mounted duties during the main drive. But it also pointed to the ways in which Arthur was trying to put his most experienced men out front.

Arthur instructed Douglas to form '22 parties of seven men each', whose leaders he named. They were to be placed '50 paces in front of the Line', and Arthur even provided a diagram of where the parties were to be placed in relation to the main line. Among the chosen leaders were Walpole, Batman, Fortosa and Robertson. 'It is to be understood,' Arthur affirmed after stipulating the terms of composition and provision, 'that every man of these scouring parties is to be armed.'

Arthur gave a similar instruction to Wentworth, requesting him to form 15 similar parties for the line's right wing. Among the leaders was Emmett, who was posted near the centre of the whole line. Emmett had volunteered for the role. He was up for 'any thing to get away from the line', he recalled. Arthur's plan was that at noon on Monday 1 November, once Donaldson's forces had plugged the line, all of the scouring parties would 'advance towards the S.E. driving the Natives in the direction or capturing them'. On the fourth day he expected them to be at East Bay Neck, thereby sealing the peninsulas. The main line was kept in place, and Arthur warned the linesmen to be on their strictest guard because 'the Tribes will naturally redouble their attempts' at escape. Once Donaldson's force was in place Arthur wanted an immediate report on 'the quantity of Ammunition' carried by each party.[22] Arthur also ordered a further '2000 Rounds of Ball Cartridges' be sent from Hobart to the line.[23]

Donaldson's force was a day late, but at noon on 2 November the scouring commenced. Arthur was cautiously confident, writing that 'it ought to be successful; but these miserable Savages are not readily dislodged from the Tiers & Gullies where they secret themselves in a way that is quite extraordinary'.[24]

These operations were poorly recorded. 'That several of the Natives have already been killed', the *Colonial Times* claimed a few days into the movement, 'there is no doubt'.[25] But this was a mix of rumour and supposition, mainly intended to introduce the punchline that 'many, like our negligent Correspondent, G. A. WIDLIKINS, [were] most monstrously frightened'. Surviving documentation does not do a great deal to illuminate the movements, although it highlights the methodical nature of the intended advance. Among Assistant Surveyor Scott's papers is a sketch of the intended lines of daily movements, reportedly drawn by his colleague and superior, Surveyor General Frankland.[26] Emmett too highlighted the role of the survey department in planning the manoeuvres of these skirmishers. 'Mr Surveyor Sharland visited the parties,' he recalled, 'and instructed me in my course.'

Emmett also recalled that he 'had an interview with his Excellency and no doubt he spoke to all the Leaders of the advanced guard' as Emmett later styled his mission.

> He told me to proceed quietly, not to hurry, but to be very careful
> & watch for the Natives, not a shot was fired or word spoke and
> we proceeded in as extended a line as possible just in sight of
> each other.

But again the weather was against the colonists, as Emmett related:

> After starting about 24 hours it came on to blow rain a regular
> downpour for 48 hours, we were there on the top of very high
> land, and considered it useless to travel in such weather and
> from His Excellencys [sic] instructions not to hurry, we remained
> encamped, looked to our fires, arms &c. On the sixth morning
> we again started, when one of my men suddenly dropped
> from fatigue which caused a slight detention, until he revived
> somewhat. I was directed to examine on my journey down to the
> Neck, the numerous little projections of land in case the natives
> might have gone into any of them which greatly retarded the
> travelling of my party.

Eventually his party arrived at the neck without having spotted any Aboriginal people.

Others had closer encounters. George Lloyd, who had been one of those tasked with keeping the guidance bonfires burning during the drive, subsequently went ahead of the line during this skirmishing sweep. Lloyd did not form part of the skirmishing line as such. Like several other parties – including Kirby's – Lloyd's men were instead deployed on a variety of roving duties, some behind the line, others out front.[27] Lloyd narrated his experiences in a book detailing his time in the colonies, and from his own account 'was instructed to fit out eight of my best men as a roving party, and to scour the country between the advancing cordon and Tasman's Peninsula'.[28] With some flair and a bit of literary licence he described heading off 'into the wildest and most unfrequented country, famed and dreaded as the favourite haunt of the formidable Oyster Bay tribe of savages, known as Bream Creek' – the area of Walpole's raid.

Aware of his parallel with Walpole – whose encounter he mentioned – and a by-then established narrative of the campaign, Lloyd described a close encounter during this roving expedition when 'Mr. Tyro, my sagacious Newfoundland dog' alerted the party to nearby Aboriginal people. Carefully searching the area, Lloyd claimed that 'I caught sight of a sleek savage, partly enveloped in a new blanket'. But as the party advanced, one of his companions precipitously fired his gun, causing the man to flee. He outran his pursuers – including the dog – with almost implausible ease.

Concluding this recollection, Lloyd described the situation at East Bay Neck:

> Party after party arrived, all eagerly asking the question: 'Have the natives passed over the Neck?' Each inquiry, however, was met with a jeering negative; nor had a single black been seen – with the exception of the two captured by Mr. Walpole.[29]

He then went on to give an account of he and Walpole throwing spears for fun, whereby Walpole was injured in his knee.[30] Like Emmett's, Lloyd's remembrance of the event focused on parties reaching the neck without having captured anybody or even seeing them pass the commissariat ration station located in that vicinity.

Arthur visited East Bay Neck to see how these operations went.[31] Upon returning to Camp Sorell he set about addressing the security of some parts of the line. The poor weather, difficult duties, often inadequate rations and failing footwear were all affecting the vigilance and enthusiasm of the linesmen.

Ammunition was also running low, and some of the guns were in a poor state. 'Except the roving parties,' Jorgenson informed Arthur, 'the men in the Oatlands line have only about one ball cartridge each.'[32] The damp weather was also affecting the musketry. Jorgenson noted 'that few pieces would even so far strike a light as to kindle a fire, and few would go off'.[33] He went on to comment that 'the Sentries throughout the lines are not sufficiently vigilant'. He commented on one part being 'most unguarded' near the centre, and by suggesting the use of stone bases for fires on damp ground indicates that the linesmen may have been having trouble maintaining their fires during the wet nights. This was most worrying for Arthur, because as Jorgenson related, 'the Natives have made their appearance five miles up from here'. Jorgenson subsequently referred to 'firing in the lower part of the line' on Saturday 6 November because of 'a Knowledge the Natives were in front'.[34] He thought it was probably the tribe which he understood was 'pursued by Sergeant Kirby'. As Douglas reported to Arthur, 'Kirby's independent roving party' had been sent that day to investigate a reported sighting of 'six or seven' Aboriginal men.[35]

Jorgenson also explained that 'great numbers of Native Dogs have been seen and heard in front of the line'.[36] This was widely assumed to indicate the proximity of Aboriginal people, who were believed to be approaching the line rather than East Bay Neck. 'None could be caught,' Jorgenson explained, 'till Andrew Colbert and Black George went to them, and a fine bitch and its mother came to him, seeing he was a black man'. The captive dogs proved a source of some intelligence in a roundabout way:

> One of the Bitches had a string round her neck, and was so exhausted that she fell down before the fire in a state of excessive weakness, a clear indication that the Natives are driving away, and getting rid of their dogs, that they may not with their noise betray them should they succeed in getting through the line.

Furthering Jorgenson's impression that Aboriginal people were close, getting desperate, and attempting to break out, he mentioned how a few nights earlier 'the Natives passed along the Tier in front of Mr Pedders with fire sticks in their hands'.

Arthur got other reports that confirmed the skirmishing parties had failed to drive Aboriginal people over the East Bay Neck. On 8 November Arthur learned 'that a large Tribe of Natives were in the scrub w[hic]h extends from the Tiers before the Cherry Tree opening'.[37] He directed that 'the roving Parties w[hic]h have come in' should go and investigate, and instructed Donaldson and Wentworth to detach a further '50 or 60 Men & form them into parties to aid in the examination of this extensive scrub'. He also ordered Aubin to 'keep a particularly good look out' at the Three Thumbs Hills, where Aboriginal people would likely flee if flushed out of the scrub, and 'continue to harass them if they cannot be taken'. Arthur may have still hoped to capture Aboriginal people, but he was also fully prepared to engage them.

Arthur was also receiving fresh volunteers and conscripts, even while struggling with morale and provisions on the line. One person to arrive about this time was John Danvers, who Anstey had sent from Oatlands.[38] Knowing the ranger's experience, Jorgenson thought Arthur would wish Danvers 'be engaged in some special Service of more profit than being placed in the Line', and suggested one of the roving parties that currently lacked a guide. But Jorgenson also informed Arthur that 'the Oatlands bands were distressed for certain stores', and this was part of a broader phenomenon that seems to have motivated Arthur to make another push. Referring to the impatience of men 'to return to their Homes', Arthur recognised it was 'impossible to continue much longer to hold the present position'.[39] It was time for one last push.

Further Drives and Problems at the Rear

The advance was scheduled for Sunday 14 November, which Arthur hoped would provide sufficient time for the ground to be prepared. He wanted surveyors to map out the whole operation, trees marked in advance to help guide the parties, and bush cleared to create lines in predetermined daily positions. He even ordered a bugle for one of the divisions. The roving parties were placed under the command of Captain Moriarty and given dedicated lines of movements.[40] The main divisions would then similarly follow. It was close to the grand movement in microcosm, intending to methodically sweep Aboriginal people towards and then through the Neck.

On the day of the advance Douglas informed Arthur 'that uninterrupted tranquillity continues to prevail' along the line.[41] Reports continued to come in affirming that Aboriginal people were still before the line. One such report, sent to Douglas the day beforehand, referred to discoveries made by 'the party under the orders of Mr Lloyd' while returning to the main line from the Neck.[42] While it did not make it into his own book, Lloyd's party had 'traced the Natives in four different places moving in the direction of the three thumbs'. Apparently near one of the local farmhouses Lloyd's party 'found parts of Blankets, shirts, some waddies and three different Huts'.

As the line began moving the documentation slowed, but the operational plans survive, as do some of Douglas's daily briefings to Arthur. Two days in, Douglas again noted 'the same tranquillity' and 'there is nothing extraordinary to report'.[43] In a terse style he affirmed various divisions 'had completed the movement ... moving slowly ... agreeable to orders', with only a minor exception.

Arthur did not keep the new line in position for long. He planned another series of manoeuvres from Wednesday 17 November, with the divisions moving in a series of alternating lines, supported by roving parties, maintaining the advance.[44]

Unfortunately for Arthur, Eumarrah absconded during these movements, which was a cause of some concern. As one correspondent put it:

> Nu Marrah the black chief, who has been so long under tuition and on such friendly terms, was attached to Mr. Robertson's party in search of the blacks, has thought proper to decamp. This is bad; as the fellow knows the whole of our plan and operations. Mr. Massey has the young boy (taken the other day), with him for the same purpose.[45]

While the young captive was still in the field, the older of those taken by Walpole had been sent 'to Hobarton jail' at Arthur's insistence.[46] Surveyor General Frankland relayed this message to the relevant officer, noting that 'His Excellency entirely disapproves of the manner in which the elder Native, captured by Mr Walpole, has been suffered to walk about, unshackled, and <u>behind</u> the Constable who was supposed to be guarding him.'

By now there were numerous reports of Aboriginal people behind the line, but continued sightings in front of the advancing forces encouraged Arthur to continue the push. On Thursday 18 November, a farmer's son near Bream Creek claimed to have seen 'a black with his hair covered with red ochre, peeping at him from behind a tree, and … 6 or 7 more creeping among the bushes'.[47] Apparently Arthur was near enough to join a roving investigation:

> His Excellency, as soon as the intelligence reached him, proceeded to the spot with some parties, led by the black boy lately taken by Mr. Walpole, who on arriving near the spot speedily pointed out the tracts [sic], which he followed up like a dog on the scent. He led the party 3 miles in this manner towards Bream Creek, when night coming on obliged them to desist.[48]

Referring to this in an official report to London, which he wrote on Saturday 20 November, Arthur mentioned that these people 'were traced with great facility by one of the two blacks who had been recently captured'.[49] He did not mention that during this searching the parties reportedly found the body of an Aboriginal man who had been killed by having a pitchfork thrust into his chest on a prior confrontation at that farm. In fact, this official account of the campaign and the manoeuvres was surprisingly terse, written while 'in full hopes of success' while the forces were still moving forwards.

At the time of his hope-filled message to London, Arthur was ready for a final drive towards the Neck, aiming for the combined forces to converge there by Thursday 25 November.[50] Yet by this point the parties were in some disarray. Jorgenson wrote of how during this final stage one of the nearby units suddenly began moving on 21 November, 'and the Oatlands civil forces had to throw away their Tea etc – pack up – and hurry on in great confusion'.[51] As they marched forward the parties were drifting into each other or too far apart. By evening Jorgenson reported 'a vacancy of about 3 miles' between two groups, patchily resolved by his having 'lit 27 large fires … for the purpose of deception'. On the next day the story was similar. 'My little band of 15 now entered a thick, and sometimes, nearly impervious scrub', Jorgenson wrote, making them 'obliged to march one after the other'. They took turns at leading their group, 'clearing away the scrub before us'. As they camped by a creek that night, they were joined by a 'lost' group, and upon investigating a nearby noise discovered an injured man and two companions left to tend to him. Again they lit fires to plug a gap between the divisions.

As they advanced again on 23 November they found more men 'separated from the rest'. Jorgenson disposed of the growing force as best he could. That evening Jorgenson 'heard a shot fired', and upon investigating found a fire. Around it were '3 or 4 huts occupied by the 27th and 29th of Capt Macphearson's division, accompanied by Constables Benison and Lawrence'. They seemed out of place, as were other parties camped a few miles away. Even Jorgenson had trouble returning to his own camp once 'the moon went down'. Confusion continued the following day. 'We had received no specific instructions as to our movements,' he noted, 'except the vague order of steering SE two days, and South the other days.' They camped on a mountain that night, and resumed their march on Thursday. Jorgenson's account is telling of the final confusion and the dashing of Arthur's hopes:

> 25th Nov. We started by daybreak in the morning, moving on very slowly, so to be able to take up our position about 11 of the forenoon. In passing along we met several parties from various divisions all endeavouring to make the neck and it was only then I formed a vague conjecture that all the forces were to run to the Neck. We met one John Stacey who told us that the masses were ordered to break up, and proceed to Sorell, and believing what he said we made the rest of our way to the head-quarters of the Colonel Commanding.[52]

Other accounts similarly convey the disorganised state of the final stages of the campaign. Lawrence had joined the skirmishing operations in early November, met Emmett in the field and joined Batman for part of the operations, but got so confused about his position, dispirited and unwell, that he returned to Sorell on 17 November just as the final skirmishing drives began. He then simply stopped keeping his journal, only resuming it the next year.

But Lawrence was not the only one to leave a documentary gap. The later narratives of Emmett and Lloyd largely glossed the final stages of the operation, and even Arthur's written instructions and Douglas's daily reports ceased to be recorded as they had been weeks previously. The last memorandum in Arthur's campaign copybook recorded and ordered the dispersal of the military to Hobart, Sorell, Oatlands, New Norfolk, Bothwell, Hamilton, Waterloo Point, Spring Bay and Launceston.[53] A small detachment of one sergeant and 12 men were left 'to guard East Bay Neck until further notice'. Arthur returned to Hobart to see his infant son, born earlier that week. The rest of the Colonel Commanding's campaign copybook is blank. The largest military ground offensive ever conducted on Australian soil was over.

Demobilisation and Discretion

On the same day that the military were dispersed, Arthur issued a government notice explaining that the volunteers were released because further service 'would prove so detrimental to their Private Interests'.[54] He congratulated the volunteers, the conscripts, the military and the survey department for their good service, and affirmed that the movement mostly succeeded in driving the tribes as planned until 'their untimely dispersion by a party who too hastily attacked them before a sufficient force could arrive to capture them'. He was able to temper this with good news, noting 'that a body of natives have been captured without bloodshed on the northern coast'. This was a reference to Robinson, who with the aid of his companions, had some success capturing and removing some Aboriginal people to islands in Bass Strait.

Arthur also took the opportunity to briefly explain new measures. He referred to 'recent treacherous conduct of a party of natives, who had been received and treated with every species of kindness'. By this he meant Mungo-Jack and the women and men who had left Batman's farm. These people gave him proof, he claimed, 'that it would be in vain to expect any reformation in these savages while allowed to continue in their native habits'. Although exile had already been considered, this now became the official excuse for the policy. The current cohort of 'about 30' Aboriginal captives, along with any future captives, were going to be put 'upon an Island from where they cannot escape'.

But Arthur said little about the processes for making further captures. In referring to the dispersal of the forces from the field, the Colonial Secretary mentioned that this was 'with the exception of a small body whom the Lieutenant Governor has judged it expedient to detain for the protection of the settlements and the further pursuit of the Natives'. Moreover, while the late campaign had been performed with great publicity, future operations would not be publicised:

> The most active measures will be continued for vigorously pursuing the object in view, but as the Lieutenant Governor feels a strong persuasion that there are white men amongst the natives, His Excellency does not consider it prudent to detail any future operations in public notices.

Whether Arthur genuinely believed there were Europeans among the tribes was, like Mungo-Jack's supposed 'treachery', less relevant than the excuse it provided.

CHAPTER EIGHTEEN

From Open War to Black Operations

1830–31, Summer
Western Front and the Northeast

Audits and Operations

As the colonial forces dispersed, the book-keeping went on. Documentation from the campaign continued to be produced for months, accounting for men, muskets and munitions. Much of this material survives as lists or enumerations of men, assessing the force's strength in the final stages of the drive, or represents post-operational audits, concerned with issues like discrepancies in the stores and ledgers.

On 26 November 1830 a 'Nominal List of the Parties in Search of the Aborigines' was compiled.[1] It contains three groups of men, divided into four parties. The first group of 10 men was focused on the final stages of the campaign, and 'divided into two Parties under [William] Maginnis & [William] Grant in Search of the Stragglers who have been in Pursuit of the hostile Aborigines'. The disarray of the last drive left many small parties of men disoriented and potentially lost in the bush. The other two parties, headed by Thomas Guard and Ralph Dodge, were sent over the line into the peninsulas. 'These men under Thos Guard', one annotation recorded, 'are sent to ascertain if there be any of the Aborigines on Forrestiers Peninsula'. Dodge's team were sent further on to the Tasman Peninsula with similar instructions.

A few weeks later Guard reported to the police magistrate in Richmond, who in turn briefed the Colonial Secretary:

> by his [Guard's] Report to me it is very evident that no Natives have been in that Quarter for many Months; he states that he fell in with several of their Huts which did not appear to have been occupied for four of five months, as the Grass was grown very long and not the least trampled in the Vicinity, neither could any recent Tracks be observed in the Places which they have been accustomed to frequent, but what impresses on my mind the Certainty of their not having been there for several Months, is, the Saltwater Lagoon on the East side of the Peninsula being covered with young swans, from the Size of those nearly fledged to others not above ten Days or a Fortnight old, it being well Known that this Lagoon was their constant Resort from the Month of August till December for Eggs and young Swans.[2]

Guard's inspection confirmed that Aboriginal people had not been driven into the peninsula by the operation. But there was a clear subtext as well: the campaign may not have formally captured many people, but it certainly disrupted them – they had largely been effaced from this landscape.

Such reconnaissance was not just about assessing the efficacy of the General Movement, but was part of determining subsequent operations. Like the rangers in the midlands before him, Dodge recorded his journeying so that headquarters could build up a bigger picture. 'By a Diary which he Kept,' the Richmond police magistrate noted, 'it appears that the whole of the Land on Forrestier's Peninsula has been well scoured, that if any Natives had been there recently some Traces of them must have been observed.'

While Dodge had not yet returned, there was some news courtesy of 'one of the Party which was stationed at the lower Neck who ... had seen the Party under Ralph Dodge'. To that date in early December 'no Signs of the Natives had been observed in that Quarter'. While suggesting that Aboriginal people would not be caught on the peninsula as Arthur initially planned, this news also meant that by sealing the East Bay Neck with soldiers, Arthur had taken a large slab of territory. The newly established penal station at Port Arthur, located on a far point of the Tasman Peninsula in September, meant that the thin necks of land could now serve the twin purpose of excluding Aboriginal people and containing convict runaways.

The Western Front, Operations behind and beyond the Line

Other nominal lists reveal similar stories. One concerned a colonial victim of the campaign, Issac Hall, whose name appears on a list of 'Roving Parties Under Captain Moriarty'.[3] He is recorded at the bottom in a postscript section, beneath two volunteers registered as 'Sick at Sorrel'. Hall was described as 'Dead of the wounds in his Arm – This man came as a Volunteer from the Broad Marsh and was very attentive and an Active good man'. The burial register for Sorell and Richmond records that he was a farmer, aged 30, who lived at Old Black Brush.[4] He was buried on 17 November, in the final stages of the line. Other correspondence reveals that Hall 'came by his Death in consequence of receiving a Gunshot Wound'.[5] His death was likely an accident of the massed colonial firepower of the late campaign.

Another incident recorded in a 'Nominal Return of the Civil Force' under Wentworth's Western Division, dated 19 November, reveals one response to the reports of Aboriginal people in areas behind the line during the later stages of the General Movement.[6] A ticket-of-leaver named Fisher led six other men, and had 'gone Roving to Clyde'. The small note reveals that prior to the completion of the drive to the East Bay Neck, the successful if slightly controversial captor of Peletega was detached to go deal with renewed problems in the Bothwell district.

James Fisher's activities during this period, like most of the colony's military and paramilitary operations from this point onwards, are difficult to uncover. Arthur certainly kept his promise to keep colonial operations discreet, and surviving operational correspondence noticeably diminishes from late 1830 onwards, with the notable exception of what were called 'friendly missions'. Only hints of the campaigning in the Bothwell district really survive from this period. Certainly they continued into the new year because the Bothwell police magistrate complained that 'a difficulty exists in procuring supplies, for the commissariat store at this place, for men now employed on roving parties in this District'.[7] A few days later, the Colonial Secretary wrote to the police magistrate at Bothwell about a related matter:

> I beg to acknowledge the receipt of your letter of the 3rd instant forwarding the detail of a plan of James Fisher's ... 'for capturing the Aborigines alive' and in reply, I am directed to convey to you The Lieutenant Governor's approval of your immediately carrying it into effect.[8]

This seems to have been a scheme for using a hut filled with armed men as a decoy. A few weeks later another letter referred to 'an estimate of the expense which will attend the erection of the Hut proposed by James Fisher' to which 'Lieutenant Governor has signified his approval'.[9] Certainly it was a tactic that Arthur had long advocated, and hints at the networks of verbal communication now mostly invisible. Moreover, because Arthur wanted to ensure 'that the Hut in question is erected on Crown Land', it fitted into earlier patterns of such tactics already orchestrated with rovers. By targeting peripheral territory with few settlers it also produced fewer witnesses.

Fisher may also have been encouraged by the *Hobart Town Courier* advocating a similar scheme in early December 1830.[10] Discoursing on the question of 'what is now to be done with the blacks?', the paper advocated a range of options:

> Send numerous roving parties with skilful and expert leaders to guard and protect certain districts – to station as many outposts as possible ... let every one be well armed and constantly

prepared for them – round certain huts to erect such a sort of log fence or stockade ... to train dogs to give the alarm ... to shackle or chain those who are caught, and compel them to lead the parties to the haunts of their tribe.

Then, claiming no special knowledge of government intentions, the newspaper urged the use of strong parties in huts to ambush Aboriginal raiders. Despite its declarations of impartiality and ignorance, this newspaper had often reported views close to those of the government, and this seems likely to be another case of its getting inside information. The newspaper's editors may not have been aware that there were roving parties in the fields, but they did seem to know that these were proposals that the government was interested in receiving.

Yet while elements in the government were certainly directing forces to key situations, some of the other rovers left the General Movement with some confusion. John Sherwin Junior wrote to Arthur in early December that he had 'left the Lines on the 23rd Nov', but had not heard from Wentworth for some time.[11] It suggests that Sherwin too may have been detached from the operation with some expectation of further duties. As Sherwin explained, 'I thought it best to wait on your Excellency for your instructions, but as your Excellency at the present is so much engaged I will wait your answer at my father's.' He may have anticipated further roving duties. 'The object of my coming to Town has been for the express purpose of knowing what to do,' he explained. Precisely how Arthur ultimately responded is unclear, although annotations on the letter from Arthur and various government departments reveal that the terms of Sherwin's roving operations were rather fruitlessly investigated – in some minor ways the relative secrecy of paramilitary operations was coming back to frustrate the administration.

Not all news was hints and whispers. As Sherwin's query was followed up in Hobart, there had already been some success in the Bothwell district. On 19 December, Mr Howell – at whose property Fisher had captured Peletega a few months previously – learned that

Aboriginal people 'had gone into the Blue Hill' and so he 'went with a party of six men in pursuit of them'.[12]

> about one o'clock we came up with them eating dinner but [they] were informed of our approach by one of the tribe stationed on a distant hill. We were afterwards enabled to trace them by bits of fire they had here and there droped [sic] until about six o'clock in the afternoon when we came up with them on the banks of the Ouse and watched them walking on the side of the river about a mile down when they crossed the river and made up their fires for the night when it was sufficiently dark to approach them we got nearer to their camp when for the first time we discovered that they were on the opposite side of the river we then proceeded about a mile down the river and the six men crossed with great difficulty and came on them between three and four o'clock this morning and succeeded in capturing two of the natives a man and woman and took from the tribe two muskets and two fowling pieces ammunition several blankets knives and a quantity of spears

'The spears blankets &c have been destroyed', the Bothwell police magistrate explained to the Colonial Secretary, before drawing his attention to the confiscated weaponry and ammunition: 'It is an observation worthy of remark that these four stand of arms were loaded, and in perfect order, and that two of them had <u>native</u> flints in them.' It was evidence that Aboriginal people were using colonial weaponry and repairing them as well.

The Bothwell police magistrate also reported that a group of some hundred Aboriginal people 'attacked two of Mr Allardyce's men on the same day near the "Lagoon of Islands", one of whom was in a 'doubtful state at his master's residence on the Clyde'. This story was briefly repeated in some of the Hobart newspapers, showing a continued focus on Aboriginal aggressions while under-reporting the colonists' initiatives.[13] Only one of them mentioned the story about Howell, but it had morphed into a response to the attack at Allardyce's.

The Problems with Captives

The police magistrate of Bothwell took few chances with his new captives, arranging to send them to Hobart 'in charge of an escort of Soldiers, and a Constable'. They would be locked up at Hamilton and New Norfolk during the journey breaks, and no doubt chained to prevent escape.

This focus on ensuring captivity was sharpened when two of the Aboriginal men 'who have been living so long at Mr. [George Augustus] Robinson's house on the New Town road, absconded' on the morning of 26 November.[14] With increasing publicity about his expeditions, Robinson's house had become something of a local attraction, with one report claiming that 'Many of the inhabitants of New town were in the habit of stopping at the door and talking to them'. This part of the story was given as an illustration of these people's English-speaking capabilities – part of 'the mode of living of the white people'. But having divested 'themselves entirely of the cloathing [sic] given to them' the newspaper concluded that 'Nothing can tame them'.

Unfortunately for these two escapees from the Robinson residence, they happened to run into a pair of broom-makers armed with hatchets. These broom-makers 'exerted themselves considerably' and secured the men.[15] 'It was with difficulty indeed that one of them was found at all,' the *Hobart Town Courier* noted, 'for he was not discovered till after a search of upwards of an hour, when they came upon him almost by accident, coiled up, nearly imperceptible between two stones.' This image of a man lying between rocks in the bush near Hobart, sufficiently keen to leave the Robinson residence to attempt hiding from an armed search party, puts the lie to much of the discourse that later grew up about Robinson and the 'friendly missions'.

Another case from May and June a few months earlier tells a similar story of a young man's determination to leave Robinson's custody. This is revealed in a single letter from the police magistrate of New Norfolk to the chief police magistrate in Hobart:

> Sir, I beg to forward in charge of a Constable a black native boy, who came to Mr Thomson's house at Charlie's Hope on Friday

last. He appears to have ran away from Port Davey, or some roving party with whom he may have been sent as a guide. He evidently knows Mr Robinson, and says he got his clothes at Port Davey.[16]

That an absconder from Robinson's 'friendly mission' was captured and forwarded back to Hobart would be illustration enough that participation in such expeditions was not entirely voluntary, but the letter went further with a small postscript: 'Since writing the above the boy escaped, and was again taken near Mr Robt Bethune's farm on the 28th ultimo.'

Annotations on the same letter reveal relatively rare evidence of the custodial conundrum that Aboriginal captives could present the colony.[17] The chief police magistrate in Hobart noted that 'this is the Boy who escaped from the Native Establishment to which he has been returned, & strict order given for his safe keeping'. But clearly this was not necessarily considered sufficient for the Lieutenant Governor. 'If the Committee would wish to recommend it,' Arthur wrote, 'this Boy may be removed to Maria Island.' A final note reveals this was 'Referred to the Committee' the same day in June, but the neat record of committee meetings captures nothing of this or many other similar queries sent its way.

Through normal governmental processes, but particularly because it was a penal colony, there were whole documentary chains of custody produced by the administration of Van Diemen's Land. The arrival, assignment and punishment of convicts all produced documents for officialdom in the forms of registers, receipts and the like. While the major processes of arrival were kept in bulk because of their usefulness to centralised government agencies, with some very interesting exceptions, much of what was once a voluminous body of administrative minutiae from internal prisoner transfers has been lost. The same process similarly affects the records of Aboriginal captives, making it hard to assess any overall shift. But the peculiar wording of a letter from a division constable in Sorell to Hobart in early December 1830 hints again at the strong focus on custody in late 1830:

I am directed by the Police Magistrate to forward the Body of a Native youth recently captured by Mr Walpole to Hobart Town for the disposal of His Excellency the Lieut Governor.

Couched in terms familiar to the Common Law dictum of *habeas corpus*, this record was not about the disposal of a corpse, but rather custodial responsibility during prisoner transfer. As the colony absorbed more Aboriginal captives, who regularly escaped or absconded, Arthur wanted to focus on ensuring their better and more permanent detention. In January, he recalled the Aborigines Committee. Robinson was asked to attend their first meeting. He had a lot to relate.

Northeastern 'Friendly Missions'

Robinson had journeyed into northeastern Van Diemen's Land for the duration of Arthur's General Movement. His expedition was certainly a diplomatic overture that Arthur regarded as a prelude to a potential push into the northeast. While the Colonel Commanding was in the midlands in early October 1830 preparing his campaign, Robinson conferred with him at the residence of Roderic O'Connor, a prominent settler near Ross. Arthur wanted Robinson to have 'boats, presents for the natives, and whatever you may judge necessary to further the object of your expedition', which involved going into that area east of Launceston and north of Douglas's northern front.[18] This was outside of the General Movement, and Arthur reportedly wanted to give Robinson 'an opportunity of conciliating and bringing in these natives by gentle means'. Surveyor General Frankland understood that Arthur kept Batman from going 'to capture them', but told Robinson that Batman was supposed to have men 'in readiness to proceed by water from Spring Bay to Cape Portland whenever the advices from you make it appear desirable that he should come to your assistance'. As Frankland advised Robinson:

> Whatever humour you may find the native tribes in – it will be desirable that you should not lose sight of them – if you can

follow them, so that upon the arrival of parties, you may be able to bring them upon the tribes.

Robinson's expedition therefore had two key elements. It was a genuine attempt at diplomacy utilising Aboriginal intermediaries such as Kickerterpoller. But it also provided reconnaissance and intelligence for Arthur's wider military and paramilitary strategy.

Returning to Launceston after his meeting with Arthur, Robinson saw parties of volunteers departing for the front. He too readied a party and departed, albeit initially by boat and heading in a different direction. With Robinson's expedition was Alexander McKay, who had been part of the mission to Port Davey. Like Emmett, many years later McKay recounted his adventures and became an informant for local historians who recorded some of his testimony.[19] In addition to these snippets of oral history, a short account also survives in McKay's own handwriting, which describes elements of Robinson's mission to the northeast.[20] In this McKay refers to Arthur's instructions to Robinson 'to proceed to the East Coast and Capture what Natives he Could fall in with'. Also connected with this mission was a former sealer named James Parish, who was employed on boats supporting Robinson's expedition.

Ironically, despite heading off into territory nominally excluded from the military campaign, one of Robinson's earliest encounters during this mission was with an armed colonial roving party, guided by 'a person named Lucas'.[21] This was probably field policeman Lucas of the midlands roving parties, who was leading a party that 'had come from Mr Cox's near Launceston'. This was likely that roving group sent by Cox into the northeast that was later recalled at Arthur's insistence, and whose visit to Batman's farm documented the temporary return of the indigenous roving party headed by Aboriginal women. Robinson journaled that Lucas' party was 'astonished' at Robinson's own lack of firearms, although Robinson neglected to mention to either Lucas or in his own journal that the 'friendly mission' men had some pistols hidden away. There was a certain pacific mystique that Robinson seems to have liked to cultivate.

But Robinson's displays of pacifism were not just for other colonists, as he aimed to present himself and his mission as protecting Aboriginal people from violence throughout the colony. As he journeyed he often 'Conversed with the natives', as he put it, and in this expedition, shortly after the encounter with Lucas, Robinson collected information about the sealers who lived in the islands in Bass Strait. From his Aboriginal companions, particularly the women, Robinson learned that many of the sealers had taken women as concubines and servants, often treating them very badly. It became something of an obsession for Robinson to document this testimony in detail. One of the women, Bullrer, explained that the sealer 'Munro and others rushed them at their fires and took six, that she was a little girl and could just crawl'.[22] She went on to say that 'the white men tie the black women to trees and stretch out their arms ... and then they flog them very much, plenty blood, plenty cry'. She mimicked the gesture of being stretched out so that Robinson understood.

The testimony against the sealers sometimes got beyond generalisations into specific cases. Bullrer described a time when 'Jem Everitt, a red-haired man at Woody Island, shot a black woman'. Although frightened, she apparently asked him why he did it, and he 'said the rest of the men told him to shoot her because she would not get mutton birds'. When the expedition later reached Woody Island, Bullrer showed Robinson 'the grave where the woman had been buried who had been murdered by Jem', and gave more details of the incident.[23] 'She was up at the house and he stood in the bush and shot her through the breast,' Bullrer stated, explaining that it was 'because she did not clean the mutton birds to please him.' Even though Robinson readily tended to report hearsay and rumour into his journals, often very uncritically, the wealth of stories on this issue strongly suggest endemic domestic violence among sealers. 'Plenty children killed,' Bullrer said on another occasion, before going on to add that women would secretly 'kill them in their belly, beat their belly with their fist'.[24] She was trying to explain that this frontier was a bad place for children.

Such stories provided the main basis on which Robinson began to suspect the *Nimrod*'s report of hundreds of Aboriginal people in the direction he was heading was greatly overestimated. 'Their fear of the sealers is such the natives would approach the coast very cautiously, if at all,' Robinson wrote after asking some of the women about this supposed sighting.[25]

But the stories Robinson recorded were not all about predatory sealers. He also captured elements of intertribal relations. Although mentioned in only a few lines, Robinson's journal records confederated 'nations' joining together to fight their enemies. One man, Mutteele, told Robinson of 'a war expedition on the PYE.DARE.RER.ME nation of Tasmans Peninsula', where three groups combined to raid the territory. Mutteele also detailed other fights, which undermines simplistic notions of the Vandemonian War as only a two-sided conflict of 'whites' versus 'blacks':[26]

> The PYE.DARE.RER.ME see them coming and run in the bush, but they track out the PYE.DARE.RER.ME and kill them and take their women to Brune. When relating these exploits MUTTEELE appeared animated. He considered them as great achievements and honourable to his nation. Said at one time they attacked the PARE.DARE.RER.ME, who were fighting for oysters when they surrounded them. They had plenty of spears and killed several and took away some women. Said when he was a little boy he saw the MELL.ER.KER.DEE and the NEED. WON.NEE fight PAR.LEL.LER, a chief.

Similarly, Kickerterpoller told Robinson that his people, 'the PARE. DARE.RER.ME', with two allied groups, 'was engaged in war with the lakes or LUG.GER.MAIR.RER.NER nation and that this nation killed several of their women and took some away'. Kickerterpoller related the time his people hid from enemies attempting to attack their camp by night. They 'concealed themselves away from the fire', thereby surviving a volley of spears thrown at their camp, and 'in the morning they tracked them and fought with them and beat them off'. This second of Kickerterpoller's story was apparently caused by a broken 'treaty' between the groups about an exchange of beads and ochre.[27]

Through these sorts of conversations Robinson even learned that one Aboriginal group observed the *Nimrod* passing at sea when 'they had recently returned from fighting with the natives of the lakes'.²⁸ In that expedition they 'had killed three of that people and the rest fled'.

Much of this intertribal warfare Robinson recorded was clearly concurrent with the colony's war. The same group also told Robinson that while campaigning against their tribal enemies 'the soldiers had killed three of their people, and that they watched the soldiers asleep and killed two'.

'Friendly' Roving and Capture

The expedition established contact with this group on 1 November 1830 after tracking them by fire, smoke and footprints.²⁹ As was now standard practice, Kickerterpoller and a few of the other Aboriginal men began to 'take off their clothes' to make the first approach, but someone was spotted and an alarm raised. The group fled into the scrub, leaving their hut unattended. While Robinson went to inspect the hut, worried by barking dogs, Kickerterpoller and some other expedition members went 'to look for the natives'. They successfully established contact and in due course introduced a man to Robinson, who 'presented him with a few baubles'. Gradually other members of the group were introduced, and Robinson encouraged them all to join his own party:

> I had told them previously such a story of the soldiers killing the blacks that they would not stop on any account and all said they would accompany me. Having made them some tea I hurried them to set off, telling them the sooner we got away the better as the soldiers was [sic] coming.³⁰

As he made for the coast, happy to be 'accompanied by five fresh aborigines', he resisted all their requests to stop and look for the remainder of their group, thinking it was a stratagem for absconding.

Camping by a stream en route to the coast, Robinson learned more of the cultural significance of the moon, and witnessed various dances.³¹ 'One dance,' he noted, 'was a relation of a man who was with me named TAR.NE.BUN.NER, who had been chased by a man on horseback with a long whip, and of his out-running the horse.' When it was performed again a few weeks later Robinson added more detail, and even drew an illustration:

> Several men perform the part of horse: they stoop down and lean their hands upon the back of their companion and then walk round the fire singing; sometimes they run to imitate galloping. One man acts as driver and he has a bough for a whip, with horses in imitation of a dog – and performed his part exceeding well, shaking his head and appearing frightened, then stopping, then running &c.³²

This was clearly an important cultural development from within the colonial period, an illustration of cultural adaptation as well as a record of conflict. On another occasion when it was performed he admitted it was 'my favourite dance'.³³

While seemingly enjoying the spectacles, Robinson was also alert to the prospect of Aboriginal people attempting to leave the expedition.³⁴ He took various cautionary measures to ensure they remained. 'Ordered Stansfield to keep watch all night and not to sleep,' he noted, 'and I did the same and desired all the people to do so.' When he learned that the new group may have been planning to attack the expeditioners he ordered a servant 'to hide the spears in the bush.' In the morning Robinson 'hurried the people forward, being anxious to reach the boat', and took advantage of a serendipitous noise:

> Before setting off heard a sound at a distance, which the natives said was a musket: I did not imagine such a thing (I concluded it was a fallen tree or fragment of rock), but they saying it was soldiers I took occasion of the alarm and said the soldiers were coming ... Appeared myself alarmed, saying that I should be shot if I stopped and that I was anxious to get back before the soldiers had killed all the natives.³⁵

Yet the noise may have had further effect, because about midday two other Aboriginal people caught up and joined the party. Both of them 'seem dejected', Robinson noted.[36] Perhaps they realised elements of his scheme, perhaps there really were soldiers. Either way, some of the new arrivals were taken on hunting detours as the party advanced towards the sea. This was a deliberate strategy that ensured 'the people by this plan was kept apart', thereby discouraging a mass departure.

Much to his annoyance Robinson was forced to camp yet another night on the mainland, despite having reached the shore camp of his boatmen.[37] He instructed the boat crew, including McKay, 'to keep strict watch all night that the people did not get away'. The next day the weather was against a crossing to Swan Island, so Robinson 'gave them baubles and played the flute' to occupy them, as well as offering clothing to his new companions. 'Trousers is excellent things and confines their legs so they cannot run,' he smugly commented. For another night he had to camp on shore. 'Kept watch as usual', he noted, 'Greatly apprehensive the people would go away.'

When the weather was fine in the morning Robinson 'told them all to put on their trousers, as it would prevent them from running away', and convinced the group to get in the boat. 'I said come and they came, go and they went,' he later said, marvelling at his own success.[38] Soon they were deposited on the island. 'The natives were now at liberty to roam about,' Robinson explained, because there was now 'no necessity to watch them'.

Island Exiles

Robinson camped and conversed on the island while one of the boats was away. With its return Parish brought news of the war. 'Parish said Capt Donaldson had told his soldiers in his hearing not to spare man, woman or child,' Robinson noted, and 'not to parley with them', apparently because Aboriginal people had killed 'two of his soldiers'. On 9 November Robinson departed on one of the two boats to investigate some of the islands, visiting some of the sealers, and recording more conversations along the way. He also met some of the sealer's women, taking one woman from an old sealer with a parallel name: George Robinson.[39] In his journey he also transported some women between islands, and took yet more.[40] The integrated if reportedly dystopian straits community was being systematically segregated.

On 15 November Robinson returned to Swan Island to discover that more Aboriginal people had arrived. By targeting a smoke signal, a party that included Kickerterpoller and McKay succeeded in bringing more people to Swan Island.[41] McKay described the excursion succinctly:

> I went on the main land with some of the natives which went round the Island with us and found the natives near Mussell Row River where they were encamped and got them to the Boat landing them on Swan Island.[42]

McKay also mentioned that Robinson had gone to the islands during the sealing season when most of the sealers were away at work, facilitating his approaches to the women. For McKay's small trip the task was made much easier because Kickerterpoller was well acquainted with Luggenemenener, one of the women they met on the mainland. She was one of the women who recently returned to Batman's property as part of the indigenous roving party before departing again with Mungo-Jack.[43] Robinson inscribed a list of the new people, which included the following name and explication: 'TIL.LAR.BUN.NER (Jack's name; he was with Batman and is a native of the POOR.RER.MAIR.RE.NER nation)'. With so many Aboriginal people being called Jack, it is hard to be certain, and the tribal name was quite distinct from that recorded by Jorgenson, but it was possibly Mungo-Jack himself.

Luggenemenener brought news of the war to Swan Island. She explained to Robinson that she had taken the Aboriginal men she encountered 'to Mr Batman's, in consequence of there being so many soldiers in the bush and she was afraid they would shoot them. Her apprehensions, poor creature,' Robinson noted, 'was too well founded as they afterwards killed two of this number.' Luggenemenener also described her experience of being out while the General Movement was underway:

> she and the five young men had seen the soldiers, and had been inside the Line and had run away again, coming out in the morning. Described the soldiers as extending for a long way and that they kept firing off muskets. Said plenty of PAR.KUTE.TEN. NER horsemen, plenty of soldiers, plenty of big fires on the hills.[44]

But while lapping up this news of the war, Robinson was also concerned to get his own reports out from Swan Island, and dispatched letters with information for the Lieutenant Governor. The boat's departure seemed to precipitate a change in mood. 'The natives appeared dejected,' Robinson noted, learning that one of the women 'had circulated a story among the aborigines that the boat had gone to Launceston to bring soldiers to shoot them'. The terror with which Aboriginal people regarded the soldiery was one of Robinson's greatest tactical assets.

For the remainder of November Robinson stayed at Swan Island in what he referred to as 'this little black colony'.[45] In early December he again headed off 'to the mainland in quest of the aborigines … accompanied by six blacks, one white man and two dogs'.[46] He continued to learn and record stories, including the belief that the sickness which killed many of the people at the Bruny Island Establishment a few years previously was brought about by 'Boomer Jack that was shot by the soldiers, that his WRAYGEOWRAPPER came to his own country and killed all the people'.[47] But about a week into this expedition Robinson decided to return to Hobart. 'Conceived it would be advisable for me to proceed immediately to Hobart Town to confer with the Governor,' he noted, 'especially as he had expressed a wish at my conference with him at Ross to have my report to send to the Secretary of State.'[48] He also admitted to being short of supplies. Upon returning to Swan island he learned a little incorrectly 'that the Line had broken up at Pittwater and not a single native taken', but it was some time before he made the trip south.[49] 'There are now thirty-five natives collected together', Robinson reflected on Christmas Day 1830. 'I hope the prelude to many others.'

Humane Governance and Terror Justified

Only in January did Robinson make his journey to Hobart, walking south along the east coast of the Vandemonian mainland in company 'with one white man and five blacks', Kickerterpoller among them. As he entered the settled districts Robinson collected stories about local skirmishes, particularly those involving 'Meredith's people'.[50] On 11 January Robinson 'dined with Lieutenant Aubin' and 'stopped for the night' at Cotton's farm. 'The natives very unwell from cold', he noted, which was the only thing he described of the visit. Although not mentioning the 1829 attack on Cotton's farm, and the chases that followed, Robinson recorded various stories and locations of note as he progressed, including the graves of men 'killed by Mosquito and Black Jack' several years previously, presumably now sites of considerable local interest.[51]

But local memories of Aboriginal attacks were still raw. The day Robinson departed from his farm, Francis Cotton joined with other prominent settlers in the Great Swan Port district to publicly thank Arthur for 'his great exertions during the late operations against the Aborigines', particularly because they felt their district had to contend with 'the well known Hostile Tribe of Natives that infests it'.[52] While these settlers tacitly acknowledged 'friendly missions' – wishing the Lieutenant Governor would continue 'ameliorating the condition of these benighted people', and would 'bring them from their state of Pitiable Barbarism to enjoy some of the benefits of Civilized Life' – surviving drafts of their meeting reveal a strong focus on infestation, atrocities, outrages and murders. Their main concerns were their own fears and dangers 'while these people are at large'. In this meeting the Great Swan Port community was following other districts around the colony, holding meetings and subscribing letters during this summer of 1830–31, showing their support for the late military action and for continued vigilance.[53] Typical of petitions, the addresses also contained platitudinous conventions of the day, referring for instance to the Lieutenant Governor's 'humane intentions', 'paternal care' and his 'philanthropic purpose'.

Arthur thanked the settlers, responding to one that 'I receive with feelings of great satisfaction, and the assurance which is conveyed to me of your confidence in the measures of Government, for the purpose of subjugating the Aboriginal Natives, will, I trust, not be disappointed.' This was the political environment into which Robinson stepped as he journeyed through the settled districts. The war was not over; its direction had just become a state secret.

Eventually, on the evening of 17 January, Robinson 'Arrived in Hobart Town'.[54] The following day he was invited to 'wait upon the Governor' at 'a private interview' where Arthur's 'family were present, except Mrs Arthur'. The day after this social meeting, Robinson met with Arthur to discuss 'the civilisation of the aborigines', after which Robinson diarised Arthur's approbation of his services and promises of future reward.[55] On the next day, 20 January, Robinson's journal recorded that he 'Waited on the committee on the aborigines.'

The Aborigines Committee had nominally been 'Summoned ... after a long adjournment for the most Satisfactory and gratifying object; viz, of learning from Mr G A Robinson an account of his proceedings, since the period he Commenced his mission to the Black population of this Island under the auspices and Sanction of the Government'.[56] Robinson gave a short verbal summary of what he had learned from journeying south towards Port Davey, up the western coast, and along the north coast towards the northeast since his departure from Hobart a year earlier. He estimated there were only about 700 Aboriginal people across the island, and promised to produce a more detailed report for the committee. 'To Conciliate the Natives', he stated, was 'the main object' of his missions, and suggested 'the whole of the Native population can be brought in' and 'all removed to Some place of Security in three years'. Robinson said that he had explained his mission to Aboriginal people as 'to preserve them from injuries on the part of the Whites, and to place them in a Situation where they might be instructed in the modes and Customs of Civilized life'. No Aboriginal people were questioned by the committee.

This notion of Aboriginal protection underpinned the logic of Robinson's testimony and served to justify his mission, but Robinson was also conscious of the continuing warfare in the interior and its threat to settlers. Potentially echoing Fisher's operations being readied

319

in Bothwell and others like it, Robinson admitted that 'it would be prudent to afford protection to the remote Settlers and Stock-keepers. Stationary Parties is the only way to effect this' – past experience, Robinson suggested, 'proved that all the Roving Parties are of no use'.

Once again the roving parties were represented within the committee's minutes as a public foil for the lack of captives from the war-ravaged interior. But Robinson's testimony – like his assertion that 'after committing any Outrage they generally remove to a great distance immediately', and his opinion that Aboriginal people 'were very much intimidated by the operations which were carried on against them' – likely reflect a broader political reality. These two points seemed to justify the extension of martial law to the whole island and framed Arthur's campaign as a beneficial display of force. It is another useful reminder that the committee's public record was as much a political document as an administrative one, reflective of conversations at Government House as well as those with Aboriginal people in the bush. Robinson's thinking that 'even the better disposed look upon the Whites with terror', for instance, was potentially about more than stock-keeper misbehaviour and the predations of sealers on women. He had used stories of soldiers to scare people himself, after all, and within the broader political context it could also be taken to affirm that Arthur's original plan of terrorising the tribes into submission was becoming effective.

After Robinson left the meeting, the attendees focused on an appropriate island for 'an Establishment'. Opinions differed between Maria Island or somewhere in Bass Strait, and this discussion continued over subsequent days while Robinson prepared his report.[57] The idea of exiling all the tribes had become de-facto policy, summed up by the committee minutes on 27 January 1830:

> The object of the removal of the Natives from Van D Land is recommended for the purpose of protecting the Settlers and of Ameliorating the State and Condition of the Natives.[58]

A week later the committee recommended that Robinson 'remove the Natives from Swan Island, and after he has comfortably settled them in the Establishment he will renew his mission to the hostile Tribes'.[59] Robinson also reaffirmed for the committee that he was 'of opinion that placing Armed Men in the distant Stock Huts is a very judicious measure.'

Robinson's public support for such measures was made with fortunate timing, because a few days later the government received word about Fortosa, whose party had just made 'an excursion to George's River and the Country round the Bay of Fires'.[60] Fortosa had recently been scouring some of the same territory visited by Robinson over the past few months. Although 'having searched it without success', Fortosa was still in the field, and had switched from roving to waiting. 'The party is now stationed at a place called "Black Boy Plains" in the South Esk about the junction of the Breakaday River,' Simpson reported, 'in which neighbourhood the Natives were last seen, a few days previous to the party's arrival.' Robinson's mission may have attracted public attention, but other parties were quietly active in the field.

CHAPTER NINETEEN

The War after the War

1831, Summer and Autumn
The Midlands and the Western Front

The Oatlands Rangers after the Line

When Simpson updated Arthur about Fortosa's whereabouts in early February 1831, he offered to convey 'any communication' Arthur might have had for Fortosa.[1] The letter has no annotation, and the Colonial Secretary's letter copybook has no corresponding entry. If Arthur did send a message, he did not leave a clear paper trail. Typical of the whole conflict, outside of the Colonial Secretary's Office correspondence it was Jorgenson who produced the richest body of documentation of colonial manoeuvres in early 1831. While the operations of parties under Fortosa and Fisher remain mostly secret, thanks to Jorgenson the midlands roving parties can still be observed in detail a little longer.

Jorgenson was another of those men whose paramilitary operations continued as the line operations were breaking up in late November 1830. He appended a brief note to his journal of the final stages of the manoeuvre towards East Bay Neck, which reveals that 'At peep of day' on 28 November 1830, Jorgenson 'set off for the Brown Mountain' with four men.[2] Word had reached him the previous day at Sorell 'that the Natives had been seen at the White Marsh'. When he reached this area, he 'learned that a fine cow had been speared by the Natives' a few days previously. Heading in further pursuit to 'the White Kangaroo River', he 'learned that a boy had been chased by a Black' the day before the cow was speared. Nearby men formed a party and went in pursuit, and Jorgenson reportedly sent word to Arthur. He also wondered whether sticks placed in the ground that 'pointed towards the East' were a decoy. 'Some of the Blacks who have deserted from us, and who have been with us in the bush, may have told them that we take great notice of those sticks.'

Summarising the strategic situation in the midlands over the summer of 1830–31 in a report dated 1 March 1831, Jorgenson presented a period of relative quietude that seemed to reflect that wider conviction that the campaign had diminished the hostilities.[3] As Jorgenson claimed:

> The District, since the breaking up of the Line, has enjoyed a profound and uninterrupted tranquillity, free from all attacks on the part of the Aborigines, and even the Four Blacks who used to prowl about the Big Lagoon, Kangaroo River, and Jerusalem, have totally disappeared. The reports from Oyster Bay also state that the Aboriginal natives have not been seen in the Great and Little Swanport Divisions since the Line was dispersed, and as far as I can gather the same has been the case in the Carlton and Richmond districts.

Jorgenson nonetheless admitted that he had not received many 'regular reports ... for these last three months', and mentioned that those he had gotten from 'the various Leaders of the Oatlands Roving Bands present such a uniform sameness that nothing novel or interesting appear in any of them.' While reportedly incomplete, his disdain for poor record-keeping nonetheless highlights the continuation of roving patrols.

For some time after Arthur's campaign, Jorgenson explained, there was a 'general impression ... that the Blacks, from a variety of reasons, had come to a determination not to attack the settlements, but to remain in a state of quietude'. Yet this false peace did not hold, and reports of attacks started to come in, some of which Jorgenson detailed as 'proofs that the Aborigines still persevere in their hostile intentions and aggressions'. He also recorded a series of responses to false reports within the Oatlands district. One case concerned a supposed sighting of 'a Black' which turned out to be a settler 'who had lost his way, remained in the Bush all night, and was dressed in a black jacket, Waistcoat, and Trowsers [sic]'. Nonetheless, on the report reaching the authorities, 'Donald Mackenzie with his small band went instantly in pursuit'. Mackenzie had been with Jorgenson in the expedition towards the speared cow some months earlier.

Another report seemed similarly suspect, but still drew veteran rangers into a pursuit:

> Jillett's stock-keeper, who stated that he had been pursued across the two main roads as far as St Peter's Valley, and Peter Scott and Benjamin Allinson without a moment's delay formed a small volunteer party and proceeded in search. After scouring the Bush in every direction they could not discover a single track, neither in the Bush, nor in the sand on the Main-roads, and adding to this the improbability of chasing a man across two roads and in a place surrounded with stock huts and farms, within a couple of miles of a military station, and the general character of Jillett's stock-keeper, we could come to no other conclusion than that the whole was invention.

The third report derived from another witness subsequently thought to be unreliable, which partly seemed to have emanated from 'four distinct cooes ... heard at the Public house'. Yet it too had made a field policeman go in pursuit with company. They even encountered another party while chasing the source of these noises, demonstrating that the country swept by the General Movement was still being patrolled and regularly scoured.

Yet there were major changes afoot concerning the field police rangers. Jorgenson noted that many of the original rangers had now received their tickets of leave, and commented that some of their replacements were not suited to the service. He offered the example of James McCarthy who 'so far from being of any real service, requires watching'. McCarthy had previously been 'cruelly treated by the Blacks at the Big Lagoon, had his skull and jaw bone fractured by them, and otherwise wounded', Jorgenson reported, worrying that McCarthy's 'terror of the Blacks' would see him 'throw down his musket and make off' rather than fight. 'He certainly labours, at times,' Jorgenson claimed, 'under estrangement of mind, which manifests itself particularly in warm weather.' Between McCarthy's unsound mental state, another sick field policeman and the personnel changes, Jorgenson claimed there were 'only Nine effective men' in the Oatlands district.

At least three of the lead rangers had spent time in stationary huts attempting ambushes, which Jorgenson thought had proved an ineffective measure:

> Peter Scott on the Little Swan Port River, Benjamin Allinson in the Vicinity of the Big Lagoon, and Richard Tyrrell in Davy's bottom all erected huts at the places named, and these remained with their parties for upwards of one month each, exercising the most especial care, caution, and patience, but to no purpose; huts within a mile or two of them were robbed by the Blacks with impunity and there is not an instance that they have approached any hut of any description where a roving party was concealed.

He concluded that Aboriginal people were 'perfectly aware when they may attack a hut with safety, and when not'. Because of this, combined with various military withdrawals from old stations in the area, Jorgenson shifted these three parties back to mobile duties to 'rove incessantly round the District'. He directed them 'to confine their exertions merely for the protection of the settlers, particularly on the out-runs, and leave capture entirely out of the question, unless they should actually fall upon the traces of the Blacks'. Anstey annotated this report, explaining that this was Jorgenson's order rather than his own, possibly aware it may have met with Arthur's displeasure. Jorgenson explained that his scheme was to maintain an impression that the country was swarming with armed parties, and he credited this plan with keeping the district safe. Anstey annotated this too with a sarcastic comment about 'three small Parties' keeping the tribes at bay as being 'Prodigious!'

Nonetheless, the parties did report some useful information, describing a series of stationary smoke plumes in the distance that suggested Aboriginal people could have been staying away from the settled districts. 'It might very well happen that some of the Aboriginal tribes might be pacifically disposed, and others not,' Jorgenson commented, adding a little hopefully that the concept of the line of demarcation had been explained to Mungo-Jack, who might have conveyed the concept to the tribes after his escape. Anstey agreed that this was plausible. Jorgenson proposed a multi-week expedition into the highlands and towards the west, but in the margin Arthur made only a non-committal comment about its probable uselessness.

Autumn Hostilities in the Interior

A few days before Jorgenson finished his report of the past few months, an Aboriginal group was spotted near 'the upper Macquarie' descending from Tooms Lake.[4] George Scott, one of the settlers in the area, wrote to Anstey to alert him:

> My splitters in coming from the tier yesterday saw ten of them. They did not seem to observe the splitters, but walked slowly on. John Telford's party, your shepherd Wilson, and all my men started after them. They came home about 12 o'Clock today, but without success.[5]

Telford was one of the field police rangers roving the district, clearly in place to respond to sightings. Fortunately, Scott's letter of 27 February helps illuminate more of the rangers' actions during this relatively undocumented period. Scott informed Anstey that a nearby hut 'was robbed':

> Telford went there this afternoon, and discovered the prints of their feet in several places not far from the hut. He is gone

to your hut tonight to search round the tiers tomorrow, round Stocker's and Bell's bottom.

The result of these searches is unclear. But Scott's letter, which survives in excerpt within another letter by Jorgenson, reveals that the arrival of this Aboriginal group in the midlands elicited a coordinated colonial response.

On 3 March Telford received orders to 'proceed without delay to the Eastward with his party ... keep a sharp look out, put everyone on his guard, and if necessary, again muster a party, for the purpose of capture'. As Telford was preparing to leave, 'intelligence came in from the Police Magistrate at Campbell Town of an attack'. Two men were wounded, one badly, and this Aboriginal group was thought to be 'likely to fall down on the Oatlands district'. Because of this, Telford was also instructed 'to direct Robert Hyatt to remove his party to the Big Lagoon, and to cruise between there, the Little Lovely Banks, and the Quoin at the back of the Green Ponds.' Jorgenson also described roving directions given to two other parties. Once again the district was being scoured.

But the field police were not the only agents at play. Forwarding Jorgenson's letter to Hobart because it contained 'an authentic Report of the re-appearance of the Aborigines', Anstey commented that 'Captain Anley, 17th Regt, not having yet received any Orders from the Colonel Commanding touching the Blacks, I have not reported it to Capt Anley'.[6] While on the surface it would appear to suggest that dealing with Aboriginal people was now primarily a police initiative, on closer examination it proves to be the opposite. Anley had only arrived in Van Diemen's Land from England in late January.[7] He was part of a cohort of the 17th Regiment, including two sergeants and 27 privates, nominally sent as part of the guard for a shipload of male convicts, but now on duty in the interior. Anstey was intimating to Arthur that the new officer needed to be told, through military channels, how things were done in Van Diemen's Land.

As it happened, the same day that Anstey was writing this slightly coded comment, out at the Eastern Marshes Anley's men were already engaged in the war. As it was tersely reported by Jorgenson, 'the military chased the natives and actually came within twenty yards of them, when they got into a scrub, and disappeared as if by magic.'[8] News of this chase reached Oatlands on Wednesday 9 March, one of numerous reports reaching Jorgenson, Anstey and Anley of trouble throughout the district. Some of these were just sightings of Aboriginal people in the distance, others close encounters. Of the latter sort, there was the case of a ticket-of-leaver who 'had fell in with the Blacks, but did not dare to fire at them, for fear of being rushed', and an incident where 'three of the hostile aborigines seized George Campbell's dog'. Fear clearly gripped the district. When two men 'went into the tiers for sawed stuff, they heard cooing, and dogs barking in the scrub'. Anstey claimed that 'no blood has yet been shed', although he was meaning colonial blood, adding that he was 'in hourly expectation of news of murders'.

But the authorities were not just going to wait for the tribes to strike first. As Jorgenson detailed, the military response to these varied reports was swift:

> On Wednesday (9th) Captain Anley sent out from Oatlands three parties of six soldiers each in pursuit, under the direction of Field police Constables ... The first party by the Big Lagoon, Malcolm Logan's marshes, and Johnson's Quoin as far as Constitution Hill. The second party along the Jordan through Abysinia, and the hunting ground, and the third across Harrison's tier, through Michael Howe's marsh, as far as Osborne's marsh. Another party of military stationed in the Eastern marshes received orders on the same day to go in pursuit.

The field police parties continued their roving operations too:

> Robert Hyatt's roving band scoured about the Table Land, and Davis's bottom. Moaby and Caines at the back of Michael Howe's marsh and John Telford with his party about Mac Gill's marsh, Hobbe's Bluff, and at Mr Adey's, Little Swan port river.

There was general agreement, Jorgenson claimed, 'that the district is on all sides invaded'. But so far it was safe, Jorgenson asserted, because of 'the vigilance of the military, the roving bands, and the volunteers (joining the latter)'.

Then, just as the war again seemed to be spilling into another confused round of raids and strikes, Jorgenson's correspondence stops. This was the last letter filed in the section of the CSO1/1/320 (7578) volume that compiled Jorgenson's reports. But Jorgenson's final lines are telling. Before posting this letter on 15 March 1831 Jorgenson had time to add a postscript, which conveys neatly the sense of a conflict now being conducted with stealth and discretion, albeit through the description of a missed opportunity:

> Since writing the above news is arrived that on Saturday last Henry Pratt, Parker, and Foley, all on horseback, passed a Tribe of Blacks in Black Johnny's marsh Salt pan plains within twenty yards, without seeing them. Cassidy's Shepherd was at some distance behind when the Blacks squatted down, and saw them, but the horsemen were too far off, and rode so swiftly, that they could not hear him. Traces of the Aborigines are now seen everywhere.[9]

With that last image of horsemen prowling an increasingly agitated district, the war in the midlands shifts. And with it, the official wartime documentation ceases.

Disbanding the Rangers and Changing the Code

The documentary quietude reflected in the surviving records may have come from a higher directive. On 25 March the Colonial Secretary informed Anstey 'that the Executive Council having particularly advised the recommendation of the Aboriginal Committee that the roving parties should be discontinued'.[10] Anstey was again thanked for his service, and the midlands roving parties were again supposed to be disbanded. The Colonial Secretary mentioned that the useful members of these teams 'may be attached to the Field Police in those Districts, that are most exposed to the incursion of the Savages'. The letter was coded 10,852/64 – the 64th communication in the 10,852 file. It was a relatively new coding, one of several being used to address issues connected with Aboriginal people and their detention.

This archival shift partly reflects the probable convenience of a replacement numerator – the volume of correspondence filed as 7578 was heading towards a thousand communiques, after all – but it also highlights that the Colonial Secretary's Office was now fully on top of its archiving. The winding down of code 7578 still had some way to go, but it was rapidly diminishing in proportion to increasing use of alternate file numbers. Like the roving parties themselves, the 7578 code gave way in part because of political circumstances.

In late February 1831 the Executive Council discussed the removal of Aboriginal people from mainland Van Diemen's Land to an island in Bass Strait, and almost as an afterthought 'advised the Lieutenant-Governor to discontinue the roving parties, as the measure appeared to have a bad effect upon the Natives'.[11] Instead, the council advocated Arthur should 'station small parties of military in the remote stock-huts in the interior'. It was part of that quiet shift back to a full military frontier, defensively arranged, much as had been the case when Arthur partitioned the colony in 1828. While most of the recorded discourse centred on issues of protective captivity and prospects for 'negotiation', it was geared towards the tribes in the west of the island who were not yet embroiled in full conflict with the colony. It was another case of diplomacy before force.

This ostensibly protective and conciliatory focus continued in the following month, further highlighting the sense that diplomacy preceded active colonisation, rather than soothed its results. On 14 March the Executive Council again met to discuss this issue, with Arthur concluding that negotiation in the warring interior was unlikely to succeed. But he did think it was 'most proper that an embassy should be again sent to the tribes inhabiting the Western Country, and that blankets and food should be given them'.[12] While this was underway, stationary military posts would be deployed to protect the settled districts and if possible capture Aboriginal people. Moreover, 'all the Natives at Swan Island, and in possession of the government either at Hobart or at Launceston, or indeed in any other part of the Island, should be removed to some eligible Island in the Straits'. Robinson was now given proper authority to collect Aboriginal women living on the islands of Bass Strait. On the surface, as far as the documentation of executive deliberations was concerned, there seemed to be a shift away from paramilitary operations and offensive military ones. The new approach seemed to be mobile conciliation and static defence.

But to some extent this was just for show. Likely aware of the potential for international repercussions from military operations in Van Diemen's Land, Arthur was concerned to ensure the case of military necessity was proven, even if it meant collecting information after the fact. In early 1831 Arthur followed up his request for information from police magistrates per Government Order 12 of 1830 regarding 'all such outrages as may have taken place ... within the last five years ... not only of all persons who may have been murdered or wounded by the Aborigines, but also of all houses which have been attacked or plundered by them'.[13] Clearly, he was not satisfied with the responses. On 14 January 1831, for instance, the assistant police magistrate at Brighton was told that 'you will forthwith revise your Report, as it does not comprize but a very small part of the information which was required by the Government Order'.[14] A few days later the police magistrate of New Norfolk was informed that 'The Lieut: Governor is satisfied with the Report as far as it goes, it nevertheless appears to His Excellency that many cases of outrage must have been omitted ... you will have the goodness further to investigate the subject and report thereon.'[15] Similarly, the police magistrate of Campbell Town was told that Arthur had 'perused the report of the atrocities committed by the Aborigines in your District', but that 'it does not fully comprize the information required by the Government Order'.[16] It was a peculiarity of the moment that even while government documentation seemed to be recording much discussion about conciliation, the Lieutenant Governor was actively generating evidence of past violence, focusing on the acts of Aboriginal people against colonists.

All the while the war continued. On 10 March 1831, only a few days before declaring that a conciliatory mission to the far western tribes was 'proper', Arthur ordered troops into the hills west of Hobart.

Colonial Celebrity and the New Norfolk Campaign

Arriving in Hobart on 27 February by the *Merope* from China was celebrity travel writer and half-pay lieutenant James Holman.[17] He was famously blind, yet also a keen observer of events in his popular works.[18] Through many old military friends stationed around the world, or simply well-wishers, he often received warm treatment. On 2 March, the day after taking a hotel room in Hobart, Holman was taken on a guided tour by 'a lady this morning to visit the Female Factory, about two miles from Hobart Town'.[19] He recorded a sudden decline in the weather on Saturday 5 March, when the thermometer dropped 25 degrees Fahrenheit and the day became 'exceedingly bleak and cold'. A few days later, on Tuesday 8 March, Holman 'had the honor of dining to-day with His Excellency, the Lieutenant-Governor, who entertained a mixed party of official persons, visitors to the Island, and settlers'.

On 9 March, while the Oatlands authorities were busy dealing with reports of Aboriginal people in the interior, Holman visited a settler's house at 'Risden Farm', the site of the original settlement, which Holman commented was 'A corruption of Restdown, its original name, so called from its having been the first place in which a tent was pitched on taking possession of the colony'. This piece of local storytelling prompted more, as he went on to relate 'the first act of hostility, between the natives and a party of soldiers' which, he thought, became the source of 'a deep-rooted hatred for the strangers'. By the time of Holman's visit this was the usual version of the story told in polite circles, a sort of Vandemonian Garden of Eden with its own original sin, followed by 'cruelties' inflicted 'by the bush-rangers, and convict-servants in charge of sheep and cattle'. Holman then went on to relate that 'there is but one British resident, who is enabled to hold communion with the natives', namely 'Mr Robinson', capturing another polite myth. Unsurprisingly, reliant on local informants and information, Holman had effectively recorded the version of the Vandemonian War advocated by the Aborigines Committee: a distant sin and a reconciliatory conclusion.

But the very next day Holman recorded proof that the normal narrative was wrong, and that a war was continuing:

> Thursday, March 10. Colonel Logan left Hobart Town to-day, with a detachment of the 63rd regiment, to scour the country about New Norfolk, twenty-two miles distant from the capital, as some depredations had been committed lately, either by the bush-rangers, or the aborigines. I dined with my friend Major Fairtclough [sic], at the 63rd mess, where there was but a small party, as many of the officers had accompanied the Colonel.[20]

On Friday, Holman mentioned that Mount Wellington 'is covered with snow' and that he dined 'with Mr. Burnett, the Colonial Secretary', where he 'had the pleasure of meeting my old friends, Major Douglas of the 63rd, and Mr. Hamilton, R.N.'. If they informed him of the exact nature of the military operations in New Norfolk, then he did not record it. He said nothing of the General Movement in which Douglas played such a prominent role. There were some things gentlemen did not talk about, at least in very public books.

Aboriginal people were observed in the district of New Norfolk on Wednesday 9 March, the same day that word reached Oatlands of their arrival in that district, and the police magistrate wrote to Hobart at 5:00 pm. Upon receiving this letter the next day, the Colonial Secretary 'lost not a moment in submitting it to The Lieut. Governor', who was unimpressed that the news had not been reported sooner.[21] Arthur thought that this intelligence 'should have been more expeditiously transmitted, so that measures, might have been adopted by day light this morning'. Nonetheless, his response was clear:

> a Detachment of Eighty Soldiers, will march this afternoon for the Black Snake, and from thence, divided into parties, they will strike into the Tiers, and move along their summit towards

New Norfolk – In the mean time the Troops at New Norfolk will, on your application to the Officer commanding, be formed into parties, and follow the course, which the Natives may be supposed to have taken – This arrangement, however you may perhaps have already adopted – I am to desire if any further information has reached you, that you will acquaint Lieut Colonel Logan, who proceeds with the Troops to the Black Snake, and will advance with them in the direction of New Norfolk.[22]

Arthur even instructed 'six active prisoners' should be ordered 'to carry the luggage of the officers'.[23] Their departure from Hobart was only quietly noted.[24] The *Colonial Times* made the most of the story, suggesting there were exaggerated reports behind the 'soldiers marching, drums beating' and 'other demonstrations of alarm' as the 80 troops departed.[25]

Presumably the soldiers did their duty but the action was not reported in the press in any detail. Over the subsequent editions of the Hobart newspapers, the New Town Races attracted much more attention than the military operations in the New Norfolk district, or any other district for that matter. These scouring operations had likely concluded or diminished within a month when Holman 'dined to-day with Colonel Logan, and the officers of the 63rd regiment' on 14 April.[26] Some of his dinner companions were old friends from England, but if they told him anything of the recent excursion to New Norfolk, the conversation remained private.

Holman may, however, have started to form an opinion that all was not quite what the Hobart authorities and Aborigines Committee liked to suggest. Shortly after Logan departed Hobart for his campaign in the New Norfolk district, Holman took a tour of the interior settled districts, travelling from Hobart to Launceston and back. He commented in passing on military stations being at Oatlands, Ross and Campbell Town, although he was generally focused on the settlers and the progress of settlement. But in the Oatlands district he commented that there were 'few settlers', ascribing this to 'the best land having been principally granted to the magistrate ... a great favourite with the Governor', clearly picking up Anstey's significant role in ruling the midlands.²⁷ Holman also noted the origins of certain place names that interested him, one of which captured the sense of a landscape of conflict:

> a hillock rises abruptly, with a flat summit, which received the name of Don's Battery, in consequence of a man, nicknamed Don Morris, having defended himself on it for twenty-four hours against a number of the aborigines.²⁸

In this way Holman conveyed that phenomenon of a colony starting to tell stories about its own past.

But Holman was also faced with evidence of the colony's often unspoken present. In Launceston on 29 March Holman visited the town gaol.

> I found here also a native boy, who had been employed as a guide to some soldiers in pursuit of his black brethren, and who, having naturally endeavoured to escape, was placed here for security, and not for punishment, as appeared from his being well taken care of, and allowed to go about the jail, and amuse himself as he thought proper. He was a heavy, stupid boy, apparently little better than an idiot: he slept the greater part of his time, seeming indeed to care for little else but eating and sleeping. This description may be applied, with truth, to the majority of the aborigines, who appear to be a treacherous, bloodthirsty, and barbarous race; though the severity with which they are treated, and the provocation they have received, are, I fear, much greater than the authorities are either aware of, or willing to acknowledge.²⁹

While condescending in his description of the boy, and quick to generalise from limited personal observation, Holman was clearly starting to recognise that there were disjunctions between the official pronouncements and the attitude of many settlers. He also captured the sense of an ongoing threat, describing one track as 'dangerous, from the chance of being waylaid, and killed, by the aborigines', and offering his readers the story of Aboriginal people attacking a woman 'with a child in her arms'.[30] This 'barbarous murder was perpetrated by them, about this time', he reported, meaning to let his readers know that the conflict continued at the time of his passing through. With similar purpose, when Holman stopped at the Lawrence farm on his way south, he noted that 'Mr. Lawrence's son is one of the best botanists in the island', referring to the former line party leader.[31] This proved an introduction for another comment about the dangerous bush. 'In the course of his rambles through the woods,' Holman added of Lawrence, 'he has had two or three narrow escapes from being speared by the natives.'[32]

Like the good colonial enthusiast and public observer that he was, Holman had hinted at the war without really detailing it. Before departing Hobart for Sydney he 'met with the celebrated painter, Mr. Glover, who had just arrived in the colony.'[33] John Glover's paintings of the Vandemonian landscape became significant visual evidence of the progress of settlement and the precolonial wild. He often painted farmed landscapes devoid of Aboriginal people, or bush scenes of Aboriginal people inhabiting country from which they had often already been removed.

On his departure, Holman wrote at length about 'the system of granting land', convict discipline, and the most desirable British emigrants for 'the welfare of the settlement'.[34] His allusions to conflict, like the under-reporting of Logan's New Norfolk operations, reflected a new focus on putting the war behind the colony – even if it was not yet completely over.

But the end was certainly approaching. Shortly before Holman's arrival, the government had announced Robinson's mission 'to the Tribes resident on the Western Coast amongst whom it is desirable to distribute some presents'.[35] Through this government order Arthur also announced that he wanted 'to engage the services of a few respectable persons to aid in similar conciliatory measures':

Two or three other Missions will be made in cooperation with
Mr. Robinson for the purpose of conferring with the hostile
Tribes to the Eastward, and those usually frequenting the country
on the banks of the Tamar, the Mersey, the Clyde, the Shannon,
and the Lakes.

Concurrent with Holman's visit, and the deployment of a large detachment to the New Norfolk district, the Colonial Secretary received letters from several prospective conciliatory volunteers. Among the correspondents were experienced party leaders like Batman and Walpole.[36] There were also lesser-known applicants, like a servant of 'Mr E Lawrence of Launceston' who knew a little of the languages of Aboriginal people he had encountered 'about Table Cape & Rocky Cape' in the northwest.[37]

Like the application process for the Bruny Island Establishment a few years previously, this government order elicited evidence of a variety of colonial figures, some seemingly qualified, others not. But filed among the same batch is another letter, which captures the machinations of nineteenth-century patronage at work. Charles Arthur, secretary to the Aborigines Committee, wrote to the Colonial Secretary about clothing for 'Tyrrell, whose services, in the undertaking in which Mr. Robinson is engaged, the Lieut Governor has notified his approval of accepting'.[38] The former roving party leader and ranger was joining the 'friendly missions'.

CHAPTER TWENTY

Allies, Enemies and Ambiguities

1831, Autumn and Winter Northern Fronts

Fisher and Fortosa: Special Forces on Secretive Duties

The 'friendly missions' were never the total of colonial government policy. After announcing Robinson's mission and calling for further volunteers, Arthur asserted that force would continue to be used:

> Whilst these measures are in progress, the utmost possible disposable force, will continue to be employed for the protection of the Settlers resident at the most distant and exposed situations, and to afford countenance and protection to the friendly Missions.[1]

The records disbanding the roving parties reveal some of the ongoing colonial paramilitary operations of early 1831. Dutifully responding to Arthur's instructions, Anstey wound down the midlands roving parties, recommending many rovers for tickets of leave and forwarding their petitions to Hobart, while suggesting others be appointed to the field police of New Norfolk or other general police duties.[2] The Colonial

Secretary followed up with other districts, revealing that at least 28 convicts ceased roving the districts of Norfolk Plains, Richmond, Campbell Town, Bothwell and Oatlands.[3] The several parties affected included those led by Sherwin and Batman. But this disarmament was not universal. In a query to the assistant police magistrate of Bothwell about clothing for three men 'not known in this office as being employed upon the service of which James Fisher is engaged', the Colonial Secretary wanted to know 'whether they have been selected from the Roving Parties, whom, with this exception, The Lieutenant Governor considers to have been entirely useless, and, unless you see any good reason to the contrary, the sooner they are discontinued the better'.[4]

While the quip about their usefulness perhaps captures part of Arthur's frustration with these cohorts, the record itself points to Fisher's continued deployment. In fact, while his secretive operations are scarcely documented within the colonial archive, Fisher's mission clearly absorbed some of the slack of other rovers' duties. In early April the Colonial Secretary clarified that three convict servants attached to Fisher were 'to be victualled from His Majesty's Stores in the same manner as the roving parties'.[5] Yet he also added that they did not require special clothing because 'they are chiefly to be employed in watching within doors'. They were hiding in ambush in huts.

All three of Fisher's convicts had been transported for life, one for 'Shooting with intent to Murder'.[6] Nonetheless, despite this history – or perhaps because of it – the government was keen to ensure that they were adequately armed for their mission. Following up the return of 'Arms and Ammunition' as the final phase of disbanding the old convict roving parties a week later, the Colonial Secretary informed the Bothwell police magistrate to ensure this was done quickly, 'except as regards the party remaining out with "Fisher"'.[7] Another week after that, Bothwell was still attracting attention for 'very superior Arms having been issued to Dorans, and also to some other parties', that were still outstanding in that district.[8] With that last burst of correspondence about guns, the documentary trail of Fisher's party ends.

Traces of Fortosa's expedition similarly reveal his continued deployment in the field over the first half of 1831, largely through the administration of his party. In March Arthur approved the removal of a member of Fortosa's party to the Campbell Town field police when a position opened, because he was 'unequal to the fatigue of the enterprise'.[9] Presumably following on with the topic of Fortosa's mission, the Colonial Secretary mentioned that 'with regard to the men recently employed under Mr Batman, it is probable that he will require some of them to accompany him on the mission he is now engaged upon, in conjunction with Mr George Robinson'.

Little else appears regarding Fortosa until May, when Simpson reported 'that "James Brown" one of Nicholas Fortosa's party has been sent … into the Colonial Hospital at Launceston in consequence of a severe Gun Shot wound in the right Hand'.[10] Simpson added that 'Fortosa is anxious to have another man or two; his party being now four less than was at first proposed.' In response, Arthur had 'very little hope that Nicholas Fortosa will succeed in the undertaking against the hostile Aborigines'.[11] Apparently Fortosa's health was suffering, so Arthur left Simpson to decide whether the mission should continue or not.

But Simpson had good news as well. 'Fortosa has within this week', Simpson commented in May, 'at last found recent traces of a Tribe of Blacks up the South Esk and is now in pursuit'. But after several weeks there were no captures. Fortosa spent the remainder of May and a few weeks of June 'searching the Tiers round Ben Lomond for the Native Tribes; but without success'.[12] 'His party is so much reduced,' Simpson stated, 'that he has requested me to supply him with Three or four Men in addition to enable him to post himself and party on the Coast between "The Bay of Fires["] and "George's River".' Like Jorgenson before him, Fortosa struggled to maintain his force's strength, but also like Danvers and Batman, his prowling drew him further north.

Simpson vacillated over Fortosa's request, ordering him 'to scour the South Esk Tiers until I am favoured with His Excellency's wishes'. Knowing that Fortosa's contract only had about three months to run, Simpson was uncertain whether Arthur would approve the additional men. He appended 'a list of the men now effective' for Arthur's attention, which included only five names, including Fortosa's. There were two others that Simpson mentioned, explaining that 'Brown is in hospital having accidentally discharged his gun through his hand and Field is employed on <u>Special Service with Mr W T Massey</u>; which circumstance I believe His Excellency is informed'. He was likely referring to a member of the Massey family of Ben Lomond, whose servants had been attacked in March. Aboriginal people had speared them, acquired their guns, and taken 'a black girl who had been brought up from her infancy among the white People'.[13] In the wake of this raid 'a party of 8 men ... were despatched in pursuit' from Massey's farm, joined by Massey himself when he returned from town a few days later. While 'fruitless', it seems to have prompted one of the Masseys to take more active measures within the district, much as Batman and others had on previous occasions. Just as Fortosa's own mission is mentioned only in snippets, generally because of the convict servants assigned by the government, so too were there other missions known to Arthur with even fainter documentary trails.

Arthur was 'not inclined, to offer either a Conditional Pardon, or a Ticket of Leave to any of the men who may be now placed there for the remainder of Fortosa's engagement'.[14] It suggested Fortosa's party was going to be wound down. But Simpson was allowed to 'recommend two or three who have otherwise claims of Indulgence', which Arthur would approve as additions to Fortosa's force, and sure enough in July Arthur confirmed two convicts appointed to 'the party under Nicholas Fortosa in pursuit of the Aborigines'.[15] With that, the mission continued, but its documentary trail fades.

Fresh Recruits and McKay's 'Friendly Mission'

The last additions to Fortosa's party, approved on 6 July, corresponded with a communication of the same date from the Colonial Secretary to Simpson regarding 'the capture of a man, woman, and child of the Aborigines'.[16] These three had been caught a few days earlier on 2 July when they 'were observed approaching Mr. Headlam's house, on the Macquarie River'.[17] The Headlams, like the Masseys and other settlers, were taking charge of the protection of their farms and districts. As the *Launceston Advertiser* described the event:

The alarm being given, Master Charles Headlam and two assigned servants armed themselves and went in pursuit of them. They soon came up with them; and on approaching within gun-shot, Master Headlam (a youth of about 14 years of age) presented his gun at the black man, who immediately held up his hands and afterwards his feet, thereby intimating that he had no spears, or other weapons. The 2 servants then came up and the blacks were secured.

Their dogs were also taken captive. While the three Aboriginal captives were fed, 'a strong detachment went out' looking for more of their tribe, but none were reportedly found. The captives were sent to Campbell Town in the custody of a constable. When they arrived, Simpson reported they 'shall remain in the Gaol', but he also wanted them moved quickly because of 'the very confined accommodation'.[18] But rather than being sent to Hobart or Launceston, they remained in Campbell Town Gaol.

An unnamed correspondent subsequently relayed the story of this capture to Hobart, also describing his observations of the captives for readers of the *Hobart Town Courier*:

I saw them in Campbelltown gaol last Saturday [9 July], & a very harmless & pacific trio they appear. I felt particularly interested in the woman ('Dembrona' is her name) for her manners are pleasing, her buoyancy of spirits is great, and her features and gait are very superior to the miserable, untutored Blacks of this island whom you meet with. She and the boy 'Medroolmilla' eat mutton, but the man 'Meelaletta' cannot be induced to touch it. Opossum, (or 'Pothum' as he pronounces the word) is his favourite; they do not belong to Umarrah's tribe, but they say that it frequently comes to 'Wacoondina,' the lofty mountain on the west of the Isis, and that it is *it* which perpetrates robberies and murders. 'O Umarrah – no good – speared white man.' They are all three passionately fond of smoking.[19]

On learning of these captives Arthur 'approved of Tea Sugar and Tobacco forming part of their rations'.[20] Arthur wanted 'these poor people to be treated with every possible kindness' but Simpson was also told that 'if you can ascertain from them where any of their companions can be found … you will use every effort to discover them.'[21] The kind treatment was not just an expression of philanthropy. They were being interrogated for information.

Eumarrah's continued evasion was a political embarrassment for Arthur, one of several he faced in the early part of 1831. The cost of the late campaign was lambasted in sections of the press as a waste of money.[22] Moreover, the site of the new Aboriginal Establishment at Gun Carriage Island in Bass Strait was reportedly unsuitable, leaving the inhabitants 'very sickly', meaning that an alternative had to be found.[23] To deal with some of this Arthur again recalled the Aborigines Committee, which now became much more permanent, meeting almost every month into early 1833 as it oversaw aspects of the 'friendly missions' and the Aboriginal Establishment. Through their minuted meetings, however, more information about the captives in Campbell Town survives. In early August Bedford showed the committee 'a letter from a man named McKay, stating that he had some Conversation with three Natives at Campbeltown [sic] who had been Captured'.[24]

> [They] appeared to be very unhappy on account of their Country Men having Searched all over the Country without being able to find them, and when informed by McKay that they were living with the White People at Swan Island they were much delighted and expressed a Wish that their Tribes Should be informed of it. McKay also ascertained that Eumariah [sic] is now with a Tribe to the Westward of Launceston, and has offered his Services to proceed with one of the Captured Natives to Endeavor to Conciliate him and his Tribe.

At the next meeting, McKay attended in person and 'Offered his Services to proceed with the Native Woman, with the view of Conciliating

Eumariah [sic] and his Tribe.'[25] The committee recommended his services be accepted, but restricted to the west so as to avoid interference 'with Mr Robinson's proceedings', and suggested McKay be given a salary of 'a pound a week for 3 Months'.

The most successful strategies for capture had generally involved the use of Aboriginal auxiliaries, so there was little new in this approach. Eumarrah's original capture was facilitated by Kickerterpoller, for instance, who was now helping the colony capture more people for the new Aboriginal Establishment. Even before McKay offered to use these new captives, Batman had made a similar offer, but Arthur decided 'not to send out Mr Batman's party at present [30 July] on any fresh pursuit, while the Natives continue quiet, and commit no new aggressions'.[26] Arthur potentially thought Batman was too well known, and his methods possibly a little indelicate for the present political circumstance. Instead, Arthur authorised McKay taking the captives 'for the purpose of effecting a friendly intercourse with their Tribe, and if possible of communicating with "Eumarrah"'.[27]

McKay returned to Campbell Town, got 'the Native woman and Boy', and went 'in search of the Tribe to the northwest' in mid-August.[28] 'I was obliged to take them to Mr Batman's', he wrote in his brief journal, 'as she would not concent [sic] to leave him any other place'.[29] But after McKay's little 'friendly mission' departed, Batman proposed raising another indigenous roving party using 'Seven Sydney Natives who have recently arrived from New South Wales', in concert with 'the Native now Confined in Campbell Town Gaol, and the Boy he has at his own house'.[30] Subsequently attending the Aborigines Committee to further explain his plan, Batman was reportedly 'Confident' that the young Aboriginal man 'would not attempt to leave the party, and he thinks his presence would induce the Native Black to remain with them'. Moreover, two of the New South Welshmen had previously served with Batman, and had learned a bit of local language. Batman proposed attaching James Gunn, one of his servants, to the mission. The committee was enthusiastic, and on 1 September reported they 'urge the <u>immediate</u> employment of the Services of these people'.

In the meantime, McKay and the Aboriginal woman known to him as 'Sall' reached Launceston, and headed west. The pair 'Crossd at the cataract river', and the next day 'walkd ... over scrubby and stony hills' before reaching 'a small plain where we slept the night'.[31] The same rough territory caused problems the following day. McKay reported 'very bad walking all this day the womans [sic] feet much cut with the stones'. But there was some progress, as they 'came to a place where the natives often stops [sic] at between two hills'. There they 'found the remains of a Kangaroo several spears which they left and three muskets hid under a tree which was laid on the ground'. But these muskets were 'all of them over rusted and not in a state of use'.

Another day of 'very bad walking' followed. The next morning they 'came to a very thick myrtle forest which we travelld in all this day keeping the natives path'. Regular Aboriginal pathways were often obvious in certain portions of the landscape, and much of coastal Van Diemen's Land had distinct trails. In the most settled districts, however, many of these Aboriginal paths had already been turned into colonial roads. On the sixth day since leaving Launceston, the pair left the forest, and 'came to a plain abounding with Kangaroo and emu'. They also 'found two natives [sic] huts where they had been about three days ago'. They camped the night, and in the morning Sall found Aboriginal tracks. The pair followed them through 'Country very Scrubby and wet'.

The next morning they found 'more natives huts' beside a creek. Footprints on either side suggested there had been some 'ten or twelve' people. Abandoned at the camp were 'pieces of Kangaroo quite fresh', which suggested these people had been there very recently. There was also 'part of a jacket', which further indicated that this group had contact with settlers, or at least their property. But this was unsurprising. The next day the Aboriginal tracks intersected with 'cattle tracks'. In the evening the pair 'heard some one cutting wood'. It proved to be three servants 'splitting timber at the North side of Pipers Lagoons'. They were now re-entering the most northern of the contiguous interior settled areas, and were only several miles from the military station at Westbury. The splitters, McKay noted, 'told me that the natives had been here two days ago and made an attempt to rob the hut'. That attempted raid was on 31 August. After only a few days in the bush McKay had returned to the war, now most active in the northwest midlands and beyond.

Domestic Warfare and Colonial Fidelity

The attempted robbery on the woodcutters' hut was just one of several raids throughout the Norfolk Plains district at that time. A week earlier, on 22 August, one of the most infamous attacks in the colony took place at Stocker's hut:

> There was no person in the hut when they first appeared but a Woman named Dalrymple Briggs with her two female children, observing some little noise outside she sent the elder child to see what was the matter, and hearing her shriek went out herself with a musquet; on reaching the door she found the poor child had been speared[;] the spear enter'd close up in the inner part of the thigh, and had been driv[en] so far thro' as to create a momentary difficulty in securing the child from its catching against either door post[;] having effected this object, she barricaded the door and windows, and availed herself of every opportunity to fire at them but as they kept very close either to the chimney, or the stumps around the hut and she had nothing but duck shot with little effect, tho' she imagines she did hit one of them: Their plan was evidently to pull down the chimney and thus effect an entrance, but they were intimidated by her resolution, finding this fail, they went off and returned again in about an hour; this interval had been employed by them in procuring materials for, and forming faggots; which, on their return, they kept lighting and throwing on the roof (to windward) with a view to burn her out; she however shook them off as fast as they threw them on, and maintained her position with admirable composure, till the return of Thomas Johnson the stockkeeper pointed out to them the necessity of a retreat.[32]

Afterwards Dalrymple described the assault to Captain William Moriarty, a local Justice of the Peace, who penned a lengthy account for the authorities. 'She reports that there were eight men at the hut, and that she saw a small mob going across the plain besides'.

The day following Dalrymple's fight, another hut was attacked in the district. On 23 August Aboriginal people 'speared James Cubitt at the run of Mr Gibson'. Moriarty added that 'this is the ninth time this unfortunate man has been speared, and he would certainly have been murdered in this instance but for the promptitude, and good conduct of Peter McGuire, 14 years, Bengal Merchant'.

Moriarty's response was swift. Learning that these people's tracks 'directed towards the locations higher up, on the first information I dispatched the detachment stationed here, for the purpose of putting the settlers in that quarter on their guard'. He reported this, along with the statement about the attack on Stocker's hut, in a letter to the Colonial Secretary. Upon receipt, it was coded 7578/1000, and the Colonial Secretary drew it to Arthur's attention. 'I do hope Your Excellency will cause the <u>Heroine</u> Dalrymple Briggs to be rewarded in some way or other', he wrote, suggesting that the letter could be published 'with some remarks on the conduct of this intrepid <u>Female</u>, as an example to the Colonists in general'. It was a politically savvy suggestion. It would neatly respond to earlier tragedies and colonial agitation about unattended women and children requiring military protection – such as the slaying of Alicia Gough – while also continuing to advance Arthur's longstanding argument that settlers needed to take care to arm and protect themselves.

Arthur agreed with the Colonial Secretary's suggestion. 'Certainly this woman should be rewarded,' Arthur noted, 'but first, I should wish to examine some more particular information respecting her – who is she – from where did she come &c &c'. As it was, Dalrymple Briggs was among the most famous children in the colony, and was described in books published in London, Hamburg and Paris.[33] Reportedly the first child born in Van Diemen's Land to an Aboriginal woman and a European father, a sailor named Briggs, she was apparently named for the first British settlement in the north of the island: Port Dalrymple.

Before she was old enough to fight off Aboriginal assailants in defence of her own children, a description of Dalrymple's childhood physique had been published and translated multiple times over. The 'remarkably handsome' child with 'light copper' complexion and 'rosy cheeks' was a noted curiosity. Yet in records of colonial Van Diemen's Land, her mixed birth had little real consequence – she was simply considered a member of the colony – despite being known as the daughter of an Aboriginal woman. In fact, because Arthur approved the publication of Moriarty's letter in Government Notice 196 – 'in order to show how these wretched people may be intimidated' – she was actually presented as a model of colonial womanhood.[34]

Murder, Culpability and the Politics of Conciliation

The public and political praise of Dalrymple Briggs' fortitude in fighting off her attackers was still being worked out as McKay entered Norfolk Plains, certainly now on high alert. The Colonial Secretary had drawn Moriarty's letter to Arthur's attention on the same day McKay learned of the attempted robbery of the splitters. Yet soon after this, McKay and Sall 'lost the Natives tracks'. Taking Sall's advice 'that the natives go to one part of the country for a particular sort of stuff to paint with', the pair 'set off for this place'. McKay and Sall soon found 'several huts where they had been lately', and made their way to 'a place like a quarry where they dig out their stuff'. There were, McKay noted, 'heaps of Kangaroo bones and by the appearance of the place they come here often'. But they were too late. McKay recorded that 'the woman says umarah and his tribe has gone to the East'. They camped there the night, and headed to Moriarty's place the next morning. There McKay likely learned of the recent attacks, including the spearing of Dalrymple Briggs's daughter, and possibly learned of the mysterious disappearance of Captain Thomas and Mr Parker. McKay and Sall then headed further west to the Mersey River, and followed this river until they 'came on the natives tracks where they had crossd'. But Sall was unwilling to pursue this tribe, 'telling me the[y] would kill us both', McKay recorded.[35] Almost as if to match this prescience, the next day McKay 'came to Captain Thom[as's] and went in search of his body'.

It took time for the full circumstances of Thomas's disappearance to come to light, but by 10 September the news that he had 'been murdered by the natives' was being reported in Hobart.[36] The news was shocking for several reasons. Thomas was an 'accomplished cavalry officer' who served in the 9th Dragoons in South America, and was related 'to Sir Henry Parnell, the new Secretary at war'. He was a warrior from a warrior's family, and none expected him to meet this end. But, as the *Launceston Advertiser* lamented when news of Thomas's fate was 'still impenetrable', his death came about through his own good intentions:

> It seems that in endeavouring to carry into effect the conciliatory measures which the Government have in view towards the Aborigines, Captain THOMAS, and Mr. PARKER, his overseer, went in pursuit of a tribe which appeared in the vicinity of Port Sorell, very insufficiently armed. Having some civilized blacks in company, they came up with the savages, some of whom were secured by the black pursuers, and taken by them to Port Sorell. Captain THOMAS and Mr. PARKER were thus separated from their party and have not since been heard of.[37]

Because of the circumstances and the profile of the victims, the case attracted widespread attention.

A key witness of the disappearance was Thomas Carter, an assigned servant to Thomas, who was part of a boat crew.[38] On 31 August he and three other men were camped at Port Sorell. 'I was standing by the tent, eating some damper,' Carter later deposed, 'when I saw two natives coming along the Bank; immediately they saw me they held up their hands and sung out "Breadlie, Breadlie"'. Carter cut some bread for them, and then offered them some tea.

Shortly after, Thomas 'came riding down to the boat', followed by Parker. With two Aboriginal people eating and drinking in the servants' tent, Thomas seems to have seen an opportunity. He asked whether others were nearby, and the men held up their extended hands, saying 'Good many more'. Thomas asked them 'if they would shew them where the others were', and soon he and they 'went into the bush together'. Parker, suspicious of the plan, followed with a gun under his arm. Carter reported that a few hours later the two Aboriginal men returned in company with another Aboriginal man and two Aboriginal women. Two more Aboriginal people followed behind, although the last to arrive left again before night. These six accompanied Carter and the other men back to the farm, and were soon in captivity in George Town. Neither Thomas nor Parker were heard from again.

McKay arrived in time to be part of an early search. But, after failing to find the bodies, Moriarty ordered McKay and Sall to George Town to interrogate the captives and gain help. They returned with one of the women, who soon led them to the bodies. McKay described them as being 'in a shocking state being speared all over'. The coronial inquest described the bodies struck from various angles multiple times.[39] There were at least 'ten spear wounds' in the body of Parker, slumped against a tree, and 12 in the thigh, side, and back of Thomas, laying in 'a great deal of blood' among tall grass. They had also been beaten. Being some time before their discovery, the bodies were in a state of putrefaction. The constable deposed that 'part of the neck of Mr Thomas had been eaten by crows or cats, and I saw a number of worms on the face and in the eyes'.

Once the bodies were examined and retrieved they were taken to Launceston for the inquest. So too were the captives at George Town, who were placed in the Launceston 'watch-house', and then removed to Launceston Gaol. When McKay, Sall, and the other woman arrived, McKay gave evidence to the inquest. He affirmed that these people had admitted to killing Thomas and Parker, before giving details of the event as relayed to him by the captives:

> one of the white men had a double-barrelled gun, and that *Wow-wee* seized the gun by the lock and gave him a twist round, and at the same time another native struck him with a waddy; he fell, and the smallest white man ran away; part of

the natives followed him, and the rest killed the white man who was knocked down; the natives who followed the man who fled speared him as he ran and killed him; she told me that while this transaction was going on the women attempted to stop it, but the men would kill them[.][40]

Seemingly confirming their unwilling association, witnesses reported the women crying when the bodies were found. The woman Nongoneepitta was then questioned, with McKay interpreting. She confirmed one of the men had 'a double-barrelled gun ("loweena – shoot twice") ... under his arm', and then tried to explain which of the prisoners was involved in perpetrating the killings. The coroner concluded that 'the verdict must depend upon the feelings of the jury, as to a belief in the story of the black woman' pertaining to two of the men in custody. Despite Nongoneepitta's initial statements, the jury soon found that Thomas and Parker were 'treacherously murdered' by these people, 'assisted by the residue of the tribe known by the name of the Big River tribe ... whilst endeavouring to carry into effect the conciliatory measures recommended by the Government.'

While the jury verdict was in some ways a typically bellicose rejection of conciliatory overtures, it did prompt further public discussion of the whole phenomenon of conflict between the colony and Aboriginal people, and treatment of captives. One correspondent to the *Launceston Advertiser* asked 'Are these unhappy creatures the subjects of our king, in a state of rebellion? or are they an injured people, whom we have invaded and with whom we are at war?'[41] An editorial in the Hobart *Tasmanian* took a different view, asserting 'the Government to have been unfairly treated in every matter connected with this most important subject':

> The only two remedies then which remain are a vigorous offensive prosecution of the war, even to extermination, *bellum internecinum*, or measures wholly DEFENSIVE, and His Excellency seems to have decided upon most judiciously – determined *resistance* but undeviating *conciliation*![42]

Essentially, the twin phenomena of continued conflict and increasing numbers of captives meant that some in the colony questioned the legality of exile. But the very public tragedy of Thomas and Parker also seemed to reflect poorly on the expediency of negotiation, and highlighted the very political reality behind the application of the rigours of English criminal law. The slayers of Thomas were found responsible by coronial inquest, were already in custody, yet were not charged with murder. To some it seemed a just measure of humanity towards what was generally perceived as a childlike people; to others in a colony populated by convicted felons it seemed like a double standard.

Despite the press attention they attracted, the group associated with the deaths of Thomas and Parker were not the only captives taken about this time. In fact, the Aborigines Committee were mainly focused on supporting Robinson's mission, in part because of the strong patronage he received from Bedford, but also because about the same time that Thomas was killed Robinson reported 'that Six Men and one woman of the Tribe which has so long committed atrocities on the East Bank of the Tamar have been conciliated and joined his party, and that amongst the number is "Eumarrah"'.[43]

Tribal Enmities and Colonial Service

Since meeting the Aborigines Committee at the start of the year, Robinson's 'friendly missions' had passed through two broad stages, roughly corresponding with the seasons. During autumn he mostly focused on the new Aboriginal Establishment and women in the Bass Strait Islands. He continued visiting islands and recording the atrocities of sealers as he sought to remove women to the establishment. During a journey to Preservation Island in early May he was 'accompanied by one male aborigine named Jack, who', as Robinson put it, 'formerly belonged to Mr Batman'.[44] A month later Robinson recorded 'the death of three aborigines', including 'Jack', presumably the same person.[45] Robinson recorded few specifics, but it seems likely that Mungo-Jack, the former roving party guide, died of an undisclosed illness on one of the islands in Bass Strait early in the winter of 1831. Many of his countrymen suffered similar fates in the years to come.

Another former ranger was now also helping Robinson's mission, again cooperating with Aboriginal people to make captures. Richard Tyrrell joined the friendly missions in April, and quickly made himself useful. 'Tyrrell said Brumby had a black boy at Norfolk Plains,' Robinson noted within days of his arrival, so Robinson 'Sent Tyrrell to Norfolk Plains for Mr Brumby's farm for the purpose of obtaining a domesticated aborigine residing there.'[46] Two days later 'Tyrrell returned with the aborigine,' who was reportedly 'in a shamefully ragged state, not having sufficient to conceal his nakedness.'[47] Highlighting the way that the 'friendly missions' involved the centralisation of many already-captive Aboriginal people, Robinson also noted that 'Major Abbott ordered the black in the penitentiary to be rendered up to me; also the one with the military'.[48] It was never as if Robinson personally rounded up all the people he soon held captive.

Tyrrell, like others attached to the Robinson mission, was often employed in these sorts of side-capture operations, generally only sparsely recorded among the documentation produced by and centred on Robinson. In Robinson's journals, for instance, Tyrrell often serves as a vehicle for introducing some gossip or alleged slight that Robinson wished to record.[49] Tyrrell's movements between islands, towns and campsites are mostly just passing mentions.[50] In early June, for instance, Tyrrell 'and the two native women', as Robinson put it, were sent to join another 'friendly' roving expedition being conducted by Daniel Clucas. Like McKay, although more closely allied with Robinson's own mission, Clucas was engaged in his own expeditions of conciliatory capture.

Tyrrell's June departure marked the shift to Robinson's second operational phase, back to actively seeking Aboriginal people in northeastern Van Diemen's Land in person. Two days earlier Robinson moved his party away from the islands. 'I ordered the two boats to be manned,' Robinson noted, 'when myself and the whole of the white and black people, with the exception of R Surridge who was left in charge of the stores, crossed over to the main'.[51] Robert Surrage was yet another of the key support staff, often engaged in his own conciliatory captures.

Among the Aboriginal members of Robinson's own party were Kickerterpoller and Wooraddy. These two continued to regale Robinson with stories of past exploits as they traversed the territory seeking signs of other tribes. In July, for example, Robinson recorded that the land northeast of Ben Lomond 'was formerly occupied by the PY.EM. MAIR.RE.NER.PAIR.RE.NER nation, who were a fierce people'.

> The last chief of the nation was CUMMENER, the husband of the woman of that name at my house. They are now extinct. The country had formerly been burnt, and many trees were notched where the native women had ascended in quest of opossums. Tom [Kickerterpoller] related some exploits of his nation in their wars with these people.[52]

Later in the month, Wooraddy 'entertained us with a relation of the exploits of his nation and neighbouring nations or allies', telling more stories of fights including 'the manner of fighting, the blows given, where inflicted and how'.[53] Yet in contrast the expedition also faced the reality of a depopulated landscape. 'My sable companions frequently asked me what had become of the natives, as they had not discovered any traces of them', Robinson recorded.[54] 'They supposed that they had been shot by the soldiers.'

But eventually they did find traces of some Aboriginal people, largely through the direction of the 'chief' Mannalargenna, who left the Establishment in August to join this roving expedition.[55] Describing 'my plans to the chief', Robinson reportedly 'explained to him the benevolent views of the government towards himself and people'.[56] Apparently he 'cordially acquiesced'. But the whole conversation was clearly taking place in translation:

> I informed him in the presence of KICKERTERPOLLER that I was commissioned by the Governor to inform them that, if the natives would desist from their wonted outrages upon the whites,

they would be allowed to remain in their respective districts and would have flour, tea and sugar, clothes &c given them; that a good white man would dwell with them who would take care of them and would not allow any bad white man to shoot them, and he would go with them about the bush like myself and they then could hunt. He was much delighted.

Robinson believed that it was this potentially duplicitous conversation that convinced Mannalargenna to find Eumarrah's people, but Mannalargenna's motives were likely more complex than Robinson realised. A few days later Mannarlargenna 'related some of the exploits' of his own past battles, mentioning that 'he had fought with UMARRAH and that UMARRAH was frightened of him and begged for mercy.'[57] They were old enemies.

Mannarlargenna found tracks of Eumarrah's people while on a hunting excursion.[58] It was the same day that Tyrrell returned to the party, but Tyrrell was despatched on another side mission before the final encounter occurred.[59] Robinson reported that Kickerterpoller was frightened, and repeatedly held back from the pursuit, but he insisted that Kickerterpoller go out with Mannalargenna and three women to make initial contact. While these five went in pursuit, Robinson came upon a campsite, with the largest bark hut he had yet seen made by Aboriginal people.[60] Fires were still burning out front. And then, with what Robinson saw as providential significance, he found 'some pieces of the leaves of the Common Prayer Book, covered with red ochre.' He was particularly struck by the significance of some of the printed verses, including Psalm 33:13-14: 'The Lord looked down from heaven and beheld all the children of men'.

But the advance party were out for days, and Robinson began to worry. 'The general opinion of those aborigines with me', he wrote, 'is that Black Tom [Kickerterpoller] is speared by the native tribe and that they have taken away the women'.[61]

Kickerterpoller occupied an unusual position in the expedition. He was part of the leadership team, the main translator and had personally met with the Lieutenant Governor prior to joining Robinson. He was often caught between tradition and cultural transition. When creation stories had been told one night several weeks earlier, for instance, he 'said he would not believe it, he only believed the white people's story'.[62] In response 'TRUGERNANNA was angry with him and said: "Where did you come from? White woman?", denigrating his apparent conversion. When Mannalargenna was angry with the government pandering to the sealers over their occupation of the islands and treatment of Aboriginal women – saying 'No, no, no, they be bad men and by and by me tell the Governor' – it was Kickerterpoller who mollified him by asserting that 'Yes, when we have done we will let the Governor know all about it.'[63] He was a representative of government and Aboriginal people, needed by both, and often reviled by both.

Robinson expressed some of this mixed attitude when Kickerterpoller and the others returned. 'I was much disappointed to see my party return alone,' Robinson wrote, although admitting he 'was glad they had returned inviolate'.[64] Soon enough they tried again, and met with success. Spotting smoke in the distance, a plan was formed. Robinson and the main party camped by a lagoon, while Kickerterpoller and the others went out again. On 29 August Robinson was 'busy writing' when he was informed 'that there was plenty smoke coming this way that the natives were making as a signal of their approach'.[65] Out in the bush Kickerterpoller, Mannalargenna, and the three women had made contact with Eumarrah, and were guiding him in. As they approached the camp someone cooeed, so Robinson made sure an Aboriginal person answered. Soon there was talking, as Robinson described:

> I saw them leaving the copse and coming on towards me. They were all loaded and walking in single file. They had fourteen dogs. I saw six men and one woman. It gladdened my heart: it was a blessed sight. They were headed by the chief MANNALARGENNA and Tom and the woman Jock, who had a brother among them. Tom informed me UMARRAH was with them, and how I rejoiced to hear that this man was in being. He shortly approached me and gave me a hearty shake of the hand.[66]

The newcomers spent part of the evening dancing with the others, although Mannalargenna disarmed them and kept watch during the night as they lay by their fires.

'The natives complain of the outrages which have been committed upon them and their progenitors,' Robinson noted, 'and in bitter terms complain of their women having been stole from them.' Proving the point, the very next day 'a party of armed sealers' approached the camp, 'and behaved in a very abusive manner', Robinson reported.[67] 'The murderer Everitt demanded an aboriginal female named Jock who was with her brother, one of the strangers,' and 'placed himself on a hill with his gun in front of the people' when he did not get what he wanted. This was the area where the Vandemonian War – between the colony and various tribes – blurred into the violence of clannish frontier relationships. The incursion fretted the party, and Robinson reported the Aboriginal people were soon 'at variance and quarelling', with Mannalargenna and Kickerterpoller asserting that Eumarrah's Stoney Creek tribe 'were a savage lot and would kill white and black together'.

Mannalargenna carried a spear for the next few days and nights, wary of the newcomers, but the whole party managed to stay together with no actual fighting.[68] On 1 September they reached the main expedition encampment at the Forester River, where Tyrrell was stationed. A delicate routine of hunting and conversing was established while Robinson waited for a boat. Tyrrell, like the others, was sent running errands and messages, including to and from George Town. Over subsequent days Robinson learned of public adulation of his success, as well as the death of Thomas.[69] The day after receiving this news Robinson succeeded in getting the new people on a boat and deposited them at Waterhouse Island.[70] The process of exile was now underway. As Robinson described it:

> The chief MANNALARGENNA and other natives were much pleased at the strangers being placed on the island, and indeed it was the most humane as being the only way to save their lives. Here they can remain and when by a proper discipline

their ferocious dispositions are subdued, they can be brought on the main, should it be proper to do so, and placed under the protection of a missionary.[71]

Robinson then headed to George Town. On the way he met Tyrrell leading pack horses, and learned that Thomas's body had been found. Tyrrell went to erect Robinson's tent. On 16 September Robinson reached George Town, where he heard that McKay was still at Port Sorell.[72]

Consultations and Plans

Soon both Robinson and McKay were in Launceston. There Robinson learned the verdict of the coronial inquest into Thomas's death, and met with the Aboriginal captives in the gaol.[73] 'Both men and women were allowed to commix with the felons,' Robinson was distressed to see, advocating to the gaoler for 'their being separately confined'. But this was not his only challenge for the day. 'Whilst here McKay had the effrontery to come into the gaol,' he noted. The two had fallen out earlier in the year, so much so that the government even got involved, weighing up differences in the respective descriptions of events in which both had participated.[74] Their separate employment was part of the attempted resolution. Robinson was unimpressed when he was 'informed that McKay had been engaged by the government':

> to go in quest of the natives and had an order from the Governor to get a native woman from Campbelltown, who was with him. ... This man McKay subsequently took another black woman from the gaol, and has gone away with her, this before my face and whilst I was here in Launceston.

Robinson appears to have increasingly seen the control of Aboriginal people as his sole prerogative. But he had another meeting that day in Launceston with 'Mr Batman', which reveals he was well aware he was not the sole operator concerned with making captures. Robinson

ALLIES, ENEMIES AND AMBIGUITIES

and Batman discussed 'employing the Sydney natives'. A few days previously two of them 'named Crook and Stewart' had joined Robinson's party, but Batman also had others ready for deployment.[75] Batman explained that 'he did not intend going himself in quest of the natives, but recommended Mr Cottrell.' This was Anthony Cottrell, a close neighbour of Batman, who had been with Batman in some of his earliest expeditions against Aboriginal people in the Ben Lomond area a few years previously, as well as serving during Arthur's campaign.[76]

The next morning 'Tyrrell proceeded at 6am on his way to Waterhouse Point in order to bring up the natives'. Robinson meanwhile 'Took breakfast with H Arthur esq, the Collector of Customs', who 'had received a letter from his brother Charles Arthur'. Robinson learned that the Lieutenant Governor wished to meet him and some of the Aboriginal people in the midlands.

After a few more days in Launceston, Robinson was ready to go to Campbell Town. His journal succinctly records the process, but also something of his attitude: 'Pleasant weather. Preparing to set off. Visited the gaol. Took my blacks.'[77] He often wrote of being their saviour, but in terms that suggested he was their owner.

But Arthur was delayed, so Robinson waited to meet him in Launceston. Arthur arrived on 5 October, with Robinson reporting his own prominent, almost medieval role in the pageantry of a Lieutenant Governor's arrival:

> The guns announced his approach. Went on horseback and met him at the entrance of the town. In the afternoon had a conference with the Governor and the whole of the natives waited on him.[78]

The content of the discussion remains unclear, but likely followed those Arthur had previously had with Kickerterpoller and Eumarrah about protective exile. In the evening Robinson and Arthur met again. The next morning Arthur reviewed some of the troops before leaving town.[79]

A week later Robinson and Cottrell met in Campbell Town to plan the next stages of the conciliatory capture expeditions. Robinson headed east, as did Cottrell via a different route. Arthur meanwhile approved changes to the administration of the 'friendly missions'. Campbell Town was made 'the central situation for the conciliatory mission to the Aborigines'.[80] McKay was ordered to 'forthwith return with the two native women to the Establishment at Campbell Town', workmen from the roads department were seconded to building duties on the site, and Arthur specifically approved the construction of a hut for Mannalargenna. But Arthur's strategy relied on more than diplomacy and allies. Over the following days he stationed mounted troopers at Campbell Town and Oatlands to facilitate the rapid sharing of 'information connected with the natives'.[81] And when word was received of fresh hostilities in the 'White Marsh', Arthur announced he would try to arrange for 'a few more Soldiers to be sent to Richmond District'.[82] Just as peace seemed possible, another campaign season was starting.

CHAPTER TWENTY-ONE

Ending the Vandemonian War

1831, Spring–Summer
East and West

Terminus 7578

Anthony Cottrell's correspondence provides the last comprehensive batch of letters filed as 7578 roving party war reports. They capture the movements of Cottrell's roving party in considerable detail, like many other rovers before him, giving one last cohesive look at the Vandemonian War in its final stages. On 29 October 1831 Cottrell reported directly to the Colonial Secretary on his recent movements, illustrating the government's close surveillance of his operations:

> I beg leave to acquaint you, for the information of His Excellency, the Lieut Governor, that on the 13th inst, I received instructions from Mr Robinson, and on the 14th proceeded with the Sydney blacks across the tiers towards St Paul's plains. On the 15th, 16th, 17th, and 18th, travelling through the tiers towards the East Coast, and on the 19th made the Coast about twelve miles north of the Schoutens, without having seen any traces of the Aborigines.[1]

Even such tersely recorded movements allow Cottrell's expedition to be seen in connection with other expeditions, all of them part of a larger and coordinated whole. Further south, for instance, Robinson's party was also heading east into the hills of the eastern midlands. Eumarrah told Robinson a story of being attacked at a certain spot, and as Robinson put it, one of his servants 'behaved in a rude manner towards me'. The Aboriginal expedition members hunted, more servants were rude, and on 20 October Robinson found 'a native hut and the skull of a female aborigine'. Reportedly the Aboriginal people were 'alarmed when I laid hold of it'.[2] The country was being scoured so thoroughly that even the dead could not rest.

Cottrell spent 20 October 'looking for tracks', and then headed further north:

> on the 21st, according to instructions received from Mr Robinson proceeded towards St Patricks head beating to and from the coast. On the 24th reached Dr Andersons farm, and learnt that the Blacks had been seen in the neighbourhood of Georges river. On the 25th, proceeded towards the head of Georges river, and on the 27th fell in with the tracks of the natives and followed them til dark. On the 28th continued on the tracks round the South East end of Benlomond when owing to the heavy rain fallen during the day lost all traces.

With that, his party returned to Batman's farm hoping for 'further instructions'.

To the west, yet to receive his orders to return to Campbell Town, McKay was having more luck. George Robson, superintendent of the Van Diemen's Land Company, reported McKay's success to Charles Arthur:

> On Friday October the 21st about midnight McKay, the two female trackers and my own two Men, perceived the native fire and Hut, in a ravine of dense forest and remote from the settlement.[3]

McKay's party rushed the camp, 'and the struggle between the two parties was a desperate one'. Six people and two dogs were caught. But then one of the men got loose and ran, so one of the servants chased him down, 'caught him after another struggle, and brought him back'. To remedy such attempts, Robson reported, 'McKay proposed that my men should suffer themselves to be lashed hand to hand to the captured natives'. Now inhibited, McKay's own party fought a running battle through the night to escape 'an infuriated, and savage tribe, clamorous for the rescue of their captured friends'.

McKay's party was 'pursued during the night'. Two of the captives were in fact rescued, but McKay kept going, and reportedly 'considered it better to let them have two, than run the risk of losing the whole.' He reached the company settlement with two men, a woman and a boy. Reporting this to Hobart, Robson mentioned that McKay was 'with other men again in pursuit of the committers of fresh attacks', before recommending his two servants for reward. An annotation by Arthur asking for their police characters shows he considered this, and tickets of leave were soon granted to these servants, Thomas Ward and William Wells.[4] Arthur was publicly supporting conciliation, but privately still rewarding more blunt forms of capture. Meanwhile, in the public press McKay was praised for 'being persevering, intrepid, and humane'.[5]

The Schoutens Operation

That October Arthur also discreetly launched another military campaign. While Robinson, Batman and Cottrell were strategising at Campbell Town on 13 October, the *Colonial Times* reported that Aboriginal people 'attacked and plundered the premises of constable A. Reid' in the Great Swan Port district.[6] Reid and his men had been ploughing a field when their weapons, hidden nearby while they worked, were stolen by an Aboriginal group. The frightened and disarmed men fled to a neighbour, chief district constable Amos, who promptly formed a pursuit party. It was the trigger for the last major campaign in the core settled districts.

Word shot through the district as Reid's men informed Captain Watson, who visited Mr Lyne. That much is clear. The remainder of the story is less so, as over subsequent months several different printed accounts of the incident surfaced, slightly at odds in some details, but essentially the same in broad outline.[7] The first of these was by a 'Subscriber' of the *Colonial Times* that was written 17–19 October. John Lyne told his version of events on 15 November, and Thomas Watson Junior – one of the men robbed of their guns – wrote his account on 16 December. Another letter detailing the events survives, which was penned for Arthur by the settler George Meredith on 21 October, was quite similar to Subscriber's, and also later became public.[8]

Basically, news of the Aboriginal arrivals reached Lyne's hut in the evening of the raid at Reid's. Further afield were more men who needed to be warned. These were stationed in a remote hut occupied by Amos Junior with two soldiers, although another account claimed they were Lyne's stock-keepers. Either way, these outlying men remained unaware of the return of danger to their district. As John Lyne wrote:

> I set off with one soldier, but upon second thought, I could not see any good to be done in going, for if the men were hurt in the bush, it was not possible for me to find them, as they roved near forty miles distant after their stock.

Precisely when Lyne set off was a matter for dispute, with multiple reports affirming unnecessary delays, which left the men at Amos Junior's undefended.

Following the Aboriginal trail, the initial pursuit party from Amos's found the distant hut 'plundered of every thing'. These pursuers then headed back to Lyne's hut, possibly prompting Lyne's own brief excursion. All agree that some soldiers got a guide and went off themselves. Apparently, this group 'happily found the men safe'. In short, there was local confusion and a haphazard response among the settlers, but there were also soldiers stationed throughout the district responding to developments. On Saturday 15 October, a report of recent events was sent to Francis Aubin at Waterloo Point.

Meanwhile, the prominent settler George Meredith was organising a plan. Having learned of the Aboriginal arrivals and thinking that they would make for the Schoutens, he requested a military party be sent to the peninsula. He had a whaling station there, and likely was hoping for some protection for his men and business, 'but no party was sent'. Aubin apparently wanted to wait for some of the soldiers to return to base before sending another party out. Nonetheless, Meredith's son Charles 'went over immediately, and established a signal with the persons there, in case of the arrival of the natives'. They needed a signal so they could spring a trap.

On Wednesday 19 October the whalers gave the signal. This information was sent to Waterloo Point for Aubin's attention, but he had gone to Richmond, leaving a sergeant in charge. Some correspondents scoffed at Aubin's absence, and also at reports that the government boat was under repair and under-crewed. Nonetheless, the military responded, and Subscriber had time to append the details to his letter to the *Colonial Times*:

> the Sergeant in command, ordered a small party to be in readiness, and they were sent off without loss of time, in the best way, the boat and remaining crew admitted. The natives are now at the place where they might *all* have been captured in *Capt. Hibbert's* time, had the Government proclamations been such as to have justified that officer in acting as he was inclined to do; and the whole district would *now* rise as one man, and act cheerfully under *proper* authority and guidance.[9]

The next day two more parties went to the Schoutens. One was sent by Amos, another led by Charles Meredith. The Meredith party prepared to take up positions on the neck near the whaling station, trying again to seal the Aboriginal people in the peninsula.

Friday brought evidence that the trap was sprung. Rushing home to tell his father, Charles Meredith had news from the whaling station 'that the natives were in the vicinity', but also mentioned that the troops had already returned to base at Waterloo Point. A 14-man party of civilians comprised the only force holding the position. Meredith immediately wrote to Amos for aid:

> [T]he 'NATIVES' are now between my Fishery and the Passage ... the party which went over yesterday will keep guard at the neck, at the head of Fishery bay to-night, waiting for assistance to be sent over to-morrow; and it is highly proper, that either yourself, or some other *constable* should accompany the additional party, and I am sorry to find the constable and few military we saw go over on Wednesday, returned again to Waterloo Point yesterday; and the duty of keeping the Aborigines in their present long-wished-for situation, appears to devolve wholly upon the settlers and their servants. Under such circumstances, I intend to send off an express to the Government; and until some military or civil force arrives, I am ready to furnish boats and provisions, with every man I can spare from the needful protection of my different establishments, but we have no arms for them.

He also wrote 'To the person in command at Waterloo Point', remonstrating about the untimely withdrawal of military forces from the Schoutens. Meredith then composed a lengthy account of the situation for the Lieutenant Governor. He sent the letter to Hobart and circulated the news throughout the district, asking the settlers to help hold the new line until the government could respond.

By Monday 24 October there were reportedly 'between seventy and eighty persons' forming a line across the peninsula. This soon rose to 'ninety-eight' by one count. The force included at least a corporal and a 'few military', as well as a 'prisoner constable', likely from the field police, giving some impression of civil authority.

Dr George Fordyce Story, the government storekeeper at Waterloo Point, consulted with Meredith to ensure the force was adequately provisioned.[10] Once again colonial forces were maintaining a static perimeter against Aboriginal movements. The line of men 'was not quite 1700 yards' across mostly flat ground, one participant noted, which was clear of scrub. He added that 'there were about forty huts, with two men stationed in each, the remainder being placed along the beaches, to prevent a possibility of their swimming round'. Following the precedent from a year ago, 'good fires were kept in advance of the line'.

In the peninsula were an indeterminate number of Aboriginal people. Meredith reported to Arthur that 'only two have been *seen*, and not more than twelve or fourteen footsteps have been counted'. A firsthand report said much the same, adding 'one child' to some 16 pairs of adult footprints noticed on the beaches. There were still high hopes that the scheme would work.

News of these developments on the east coast reached Arthur in Hobart the following evening, Tuesday 25 October.[11] Arthur's response was swift. As he directed the police magistrate at Richmond:

> use every possible exertion with the utmost promptitude to aid the Assist Police Magistrate, at Waterloo Point, with the Civil and Military force of your district; as the situation where the natives are reported to be, is supposed to afford great facilities for their capture.

At Waterloo Point, 'in conjunction with the Officer commanding at Spring Bay', Aubin was similarly ordered into action. Just as the 'friendly missions' were supposedly heading towards the east coast, the Colonel Commanding had ordered three military stations to deploy to the Schoutens.

But Arthur's reaction came too late. The same night he learned of the new line, it reportedly failed. According to Meredith, 'the Aborigines succeeded in passing through the line of posts ... on the night of the 25th instant, near the centre of the line where the military were stationed'. He added that a volunteer party had gone in pursuit. Subsequent commentators implied that military pursuits also continued in the area over following weeks.[12]

Like so much of the Vandemonian War, the broader outcome of this short-lived Schoutens campaign fell into documentary oblivion. The newspapers falsely reported that Aboriginal people had 'been secured on the Schouten island' after their escape. Accounts of the escapees 'making a sudden rush through the line' were published later still.[13] Some witnesses supposedly characterised this charge as 'equal to that of a mob of wild cattle'.[14] Certainly the Aboriginal people on the Schoutens appear to have been alert to the danger. A few days after escaping this trap 'sixteen adults and one child ... were seen passing from the direction of Swan Port in great haste, towards the Break-o'day-Plains'. With a major military deployment behind them, they were now heading towards the area being patrolled by Cottrell.

Interceptions

News reached Cottrell on 31 October, relayed to him via Simpson at Campbell Town, 'that a tribe of the hostile aborigines had a few days previously escaped from the settlers on the Schoutens'.[15] Cottrell immediately made for the coast, hoping 'to intercept them'. It was 13 November before he 'received information that sixteen Blacks had been seen near Dr Brock's farm on St Paul's plains'. Heading that way, the next day he 'found tracks of the Natives, apparently making for B'lomond'. He kept on these tracks for four days but 'lost them between the South Esk and Benlomond' on 18 November. 'On the 19th went to the station at Mr Batman's,' he explained, 'the party being in a wretched state from want of shoes and clothing'.

At Batman's he received further help, an Aboriginal woman named 'Timbrunah', who joined him when he headed off in later November. Cottrell was aiming to try his luck in the territory northeast of Ben Lomond. He again found traces of Aboriginal people:

> In the course of this route I fell in with natives' huts, and fires, and continued on their tracks in active pursuit until the 4th inst when a smoke which I had made on an eminence to the East of Benlomond was recognised and answered by the Blacks. On the following day I succeeded in coming up and establishing a friendly intercourse with the natives consisting of two men and one woman[.] One of the former is the man that escaped from

> Campbell Town Gaol. Having adopted every precaution to
> prevent their escape I was happy to find that no resistance was
> offered on their part and that I was enabled to lodge them here
> [at Batman's farm] without having recourse to force or violence.

Once again, the use of Aboriginal auxiliaries seems to have assisted effecting a colonial capture. Although Timbrunah's role was not described at length, she was attached to Cottrell's party shortly before he began using smoke signals, which suggests she assisted in such decoying operations. Similarly complicating his brief synopsis of peaceful surrender, Cottrell mentioned that 'I possessed myself of their offensive weapons consisting of a Musket, with ammunition, & shot belt, and a bundle of spears.' Surrender did not just mean detention, it meant disarmament.

Yet these new captives seem to have opted to assist Cottrell make further captures. He notified the authorities that he planned to go towards 'the North Esk in consequence of information ... that a man had been speared in that quarter'. 'I shall be accompanied on this occasion by the three Natives I have recently captured,' he said, 'as they are very anxious to bring in the remainder of their tribe consisting of six men & one woman, some of whom are their relations'. When he read Cottrell's report, Arthur's response was to note that 'I am very apprehensive that Mr Cotterel [sic] may lose the natives he has already taken, and I trust he will take the greatest precautions, to prevent their escape.'

Further north, another roving conciliatory capture party also had success. Robert Surridge, one of the servants attached to the Aboriginal Establishment like Tyrrell, had led a party with Aboriginal auxiliaries helping him make contact on the coast directly north of Ben Lomond.

> [The party came upon] a tribe of Natives near Waterhouse Point
> after fourteen days pursuit tracing them all the time by their
> smokes, & by means of the native women who accompanied
> them succeeded in bringing about a conference on sunday last

[18 November], & on the following day placed them all, ten in number – 8 men & 2 women – by persuasion & force, in security on the Island.[16]

This party was similarly disarmed of their spears. Arthur thought this was 'very satisfactory!'.

Other accounts of this incident reveal yet more tactics. One of the servants went out with the two women to make initial contact.[17] When Aboriginal people surrounded and threatened these three, one of the women 'screamed out … recognising her own husband'. Once again, interpersonal and familial relationships had facilitated contact. While colonial commentators rarely recognised it, such kinship relations appear to have been among the most significant factors aiding the conciliatory capture missions. Either way, with hostilities averted, the women attached to Surridge's party gave the new group 'Bread Blankets & many fine things if they would come down to the Boat'.

Waiting with the boat was Charles Scott, another of the men attached to the Establishment, who penned an account of what followed:

> they came back the next morning bringing a party of natives with them[.] we told them we was a Sealing Boat and if they would go in the boat we would get them plenty of eggs[.] five of the men agreed to go with us and the others agreeing to remain till they came back[.] we immediately made for waterhouse Island where we landed them and returned to the others but they would not be enticed in the boat so we slept on the main all night keeping a man on the look out till day light when we asked the natives to help us to launch our boat and we would bring the natives back[.] they consented and as soon as we got the boat in the water we rushd [sic] upon them and after a struggle of some minutes we overpowerd them and secured them in the boat and landed them on waterhouse Island[.][18]

Afterwards, they returned to the site of the capture and found 17 spears.

Cottrell meanwhile had continued prowling around Ben Lomond and the upper rivers in that area, targeting the occasional signs of smoke, and sometimes following Aboriginal tracks.[19] Eventually, after spotting a campfire in early January 1832, he had another success:

> I then sent forward three of the Sydney Natives and one female aborigine of this Island to communicate and explain the intention of Government towards them. Some time after the party returned bringing with them one aboriginal female who readily agreed to join the party & return with us. I returned to the station [Batman's farm] the same evening. This woman calls herself 'Toolamworrah', and had been formerly in Launceston jail and had been taken from there by Mr Robinson from whom she states she ran away some short time since, Eumarrah and Black Tom having beaten her, she says she came over to this side to join a small tribe that she knows to be to the Eastward.

Toolamworrah now joined Cottrell, helping him find some Aboriginal huts, more tracks, and although he made no more immediate captures, he did get close enough to hear some of them hunting.

Within a few weeks Cottrell expressed an interest in going 'to the westward ... having been informed that there are a considerable number of Hostile Aborigines in the neighbourhood of Port Sorell & along the next coast towards Circular Head'.[20] It reflected something of a strategic shift. By the end of 1831 the old settled districts were increasingly clear of Aboriginal people. Certainly the opportunities for capture parties were diminishing in the midlands and east coast districts. Even the Schoutens campaign, ill-documented as it was, suggested that tribal groups were small and scared.

Moreover, the documented encounters highlight the ways that tribal social structures were observably distorted. Capture parties tended to bring in groups that were disproportionately male, and with very few children, which both pointed to the collapse of anything approaching demographic normality. Moreover, new captives and auxiliaries facilitated further captures, making the process of 'conciliation' relatively organic, growing from those early pursuit and roving parties of the late 1820s into the ostensibly conciliatory capture parties of the early 1830s. But as the opportunities for capture diminished in the settled districts of the east, contracted rovers looked to the west where the colony was expanding through the business interests of the Van Diemen's Land Company.[21]

McKay helped lead this drive to the west in early 1832. With him was an Aboriginal woman and a party that included the recently rewarded Thomas Ward and William Wells, as well as another man named Richard Dagnell, one of Robinson's former servants.[22] McKay reportedly left Launceston on 1 December 1831 for the Hampshire Hills, which he only reached near the end of the month because of 'the rivers being overflowed'. Roving into early January 1832, they eventually 'saw a native smoke', which gave them a target to approach. On 3 January they 'halted at the edge of a plain to have breakfast'. Hearing 'the natives Hunting' in the area, they quickly extinguished their fire, and McKay and the woman cautiously approached, followed by the remainder of the party, and all hid in the bush. McKay and the woman then advanced alone. McKay 'made the woman to take off her cloathes' as part of their approach. Although the Aboriginal people 'ran off a little way', they were stayed from full flight because 'the woman went forward and addressed them in the Native language'. Promising kindly treatment and bread, two were enticed to come over and sit, and gradually more joined until there were eight sharing tea, tobacco and food with McKay's group. The rest of McKay's party also joined them, although making sure to keep 'the arms out of sight'.

Meanwhile, McKay reported, 'our woman learnt by the native language that their intention was to rush us'. McKay reached for his pistol, but in a reverse of his own plan was seized instead. An old man grabbed McKay, other men grabbed his fellows, and a 'great scuffle' ensued. Meanwhile, more Aboriginal people armed with 'spears and waddies' were seen approaching.

Scrambling with each other, McKay and his combatant 'fell into the fire'. The captor released his grip, McKay got his pistol, and pointed it at those approaching, slowing their advance. He then quickly turned to help his own companions, clubbing one of the men 'with the butt of the pistol which laid him senseless on the ground'. Then he got a musket. The woman had retrieved it from its hiding place and ran with it to McKay. At this, the assailants ran away. Packing their goods, and securing the unconscious Aboriginal man, the party beat a retreat to the settlement at Emu Bay. 'I hope that we will be successful in capturing a few more natives before my return to Launceston', he wrote towards the end of his report to the Secretary of the Aborigines Committee. But unbeknown to McKay or Cottrell, the Vandemonian War had already ended.

Surrender

On 4 January 1832 Captain Wentworth, the police magistrate of Bothwell, reported to Arthur 'the surrender of <u>the whole</u> of the Big River and Oyster Bay tribes to Mr Robinson'.[23] The Colonial Secretary coded Wentworth's letter 7578/1056, and Arthur insisted that 'Every precaution sho[ul]d be taken to prevent their escape!' Reportedly 26 people had surrendered, comprising '16 men 9 women and one child'. After patrolling the eastern midlands about the time of the Schoutens campaign, Robinson and his party had gradually headed west into the highlands and lakes districts. On 31 December 1831, he made contact with the combined relic of these two tribes in the usual fashion, with several of the Aboriginal members of the 'friendly mission' going out first 'as an embassy to the hostile natives'.[24] Once contacted, these tribes then approached the remainder of the expedition, Robinson shook some hands, and they all conversed. Robinson 'promised them a conference with the Lieut Govr and that the Governor will be sure to redress all their grievances'.

The capture of this group was a tremendous political coup, and served to help the colony believe that the war had been concluded through negotiation. When Robinson 'made his triumphant entry' into Hobart on Saturday 7 January 1832, as the *Hobart Town Courier* reported, it was with a party of 40 Aboriginal people.[25] One of the men was singled out for mention, because he had 'lost his arm ... in the rat trap that happened to be set in the flour cask in Mr. Adey's stock-keeper's hut' a few years previously. But for the most part the description was pure propaganda:

> They walked very leisurely along the road, followed by a large pack of dogs, and were received by the inhabitants on their entry into town with the most lively curiosity and delight. Soon after their arrival they walked up to the Government house, and were introduced to His Excellency and the interview that took place was truly interesting. They are delighted at the idea of proceeding to Great Island, where they will enjoy peace and plenty uninterrupted. ... After, in the greatest good humour and with an evident desire to make themselves agreeable, going through various feats of their wonderful dexterity, they proceeded on board the Swan river packet.

'The removal of these blacks will be of essential benefit both to themselves and the colony', the *Hobart Town Courier* argued, before turning to the problems caused by 'dogs which these poor people have nursed and bred up' and 'ravages committed by the opossums in like manner ... equally ruinous to the hopes of the farmer'. Elsewhere on the page the newspaper casually reported that 'Aborigines were very troublesome at Bathurst, carrying off whole flocks of sheep.' There were other fights in other colonies, but no more in Van Diemen's Land.

Of course the contest for Van Diemen's Land did not stop, and the harrying, capturing and removing of Aboriginal people continued. Robinson, Cottrell and others pursued the remaining tribes of Van Diemen's Land across the west coast. For instance, more than a year later, in February 1833, Cottrell informed the Colonial Secretary about an encounter on the west coast near Macquarie Harbour:

> again fell in with traces of the natives and on the following day came up with them and succeeded in inducing eight (having five women two men and boy) to join us. The remainder of the tribe would not allow us to come up with them but evinced a hostile

feeling shaking their spears at our people when they advanced towards them.[26]

Nonetheless, despite the relative isolation of this region and the obvious unwillingness of these people to be taken, more roving conciliatory capture expeditions followed in the remote west.[27]

Some of the veterans of the Vandemonian War were there, too. The former volunteer party leader Henry James Emmett – who also claimed to have witnessed the Big River and Oyster Bay tribes 'regaled on the lawn at Government House' by 'the band of the 63 reg' – moved to Circular Head at the far northwest of the island, and subsequently remembered conflict in that region. 'Since I have resided at Circular Head poor Neil McDonald was speared by the natives at the Surry Hills,' he later wrote, before listing several hut raids. He also recounted the time 'at Woolnorth when the men gave chase and caught one young woman who was taken to Launceston', and the final well-known capture in the colony: 'the remainder of the natives were decoyed by some halfcasts [sic] beyond Woolnorth and Captured ... for which the party who caught them received £100.'

These seven Aboriginal people were captured in 1842 – over a decade after the war-ending surrender – through the agency of some sealers' wives. They were temporarily lodged in Launceston Gaol before being exiled.[28] Old William Coventry, another veteran volunteer of the General Movement, also remembered this capture into his later years.[29] But these recollections, like this supposed last capture, in some respects reflect the blurring of the colonial frontier into the historiographical one. Only a couple of years after this capture, in 1844, the *Launceston Examiner* was discoursing on the 'formation of a yeomanry corps', and in doing so referred to the military exertions of the past, asserting that 'the black war will not soon be forgotten by those who shouldered the musket and kept watch during the campaign'.[30] It is an eerily familiar concept about sacrificial effort and never forgetting.

Afterword

The surviving Aboriginal people of Van Diemen's Land mostly died in exile and the Vandemonian War disappeared from public memory with them. In its place, coincident with a rising fascination with 'race', grew a scientific obsession with their physiognomy and culture. The Aboriginal Vandemonians were studied into absurdity with unwittingly circular chains of evidence that corrupted the intellectual integrity of the whole process. By the end of the nineteenth century scientists believed that these people could not make fire on their own, did not eat fish, and that their women had suckled puppies.

Commentators believed that the conflict was mostly about wild convict stockmen, that the roving parties were a short-lived experiment, that military manoeuvres had little effect, and that 'conciliation' won the day. Kickerterpoller and Mungo-Jack largely faded from memory, their significance deliberately underplayed and then quickly and genuinely forgotten. The Vandemonian War was too ambiguous for the binary politics of race and culture. It did not meet narrative conventions of clear goodies and baddies, winners and losers, whites and blacks. A different story replaced the truth.

In the meantime, Robinson's fame continued to grow, Arthur earned international acclaim as a great humanitarian, and Batman was feted as a treaty-maker and the founder of Melbourne. These great men of the age passed into the canon of Australian history, reputations largely intact. Danvers, Tyrrell, Scott and hundreds of others like them passed into oblivion, marrying, settling and conveniently disappearing. So too did an indeterminate number of non-exiled Aboriginal people, living as members of the colony by the war's end. It was never about race, until later it was, retrospectively warping the whole story with yet more bad history and even worse science. Some families kept stories, some even made up stories, but most just got on with life until the documentary darkness gradually covered their own roles or structural complicities. For as long as the war was remembered it was mostly unwritten. Like the First World War, it took the passing of a generation to make it an appropriate subject for entertaining and populist history.

By then the intensely militaristic past had been trumped by stories of largely peaceful civil settlement. Thousands of tourists flock to Tasmania without realising that many convicts fought for the prospect of freedom from bondage. Visitors use roads built to carry armies, cross the site of the line on their way to Port Arthur, and photograph gaols that held Aboriginal prisoners of war as well as colonial captives. In part this is because the red-coated soldiers left to fight other wars, guard other colonies, and eventually never returned. Their absence from the landscape left room for the frontier wars to become gradually de-militarised in favour of a narrative focused on sporadic frontier skirmishes. The embarrassingly named 'History Wars' of recent times, at least pertaining to Van Diemen's Land, turned not so much on the evidence or actuality of history as on different versions of the same lie.

Such contestation is not new. Stories of the 'Black War' in Van Diemen's Land proliferated for the better part of two centuries. Such tales grew and changed with the telling, but the characters, scenes and plot lines largely derived from the early 1830s when the colonial government and newspapermen articulated them. Falsehoods became facts and coincidences became causal.

In trying to make sense of the past, even chronological sequences became fluid, and were sometimes made subject to narrative necessity. All genuinely became oral tradition as people heard and read falsehoods and told them to their children who passed the half-truths on as history and tradition. The past was soon populated with heroes and villains, making a folkloric tableau, a sort of Tasmanian *Iliad*. It was clumsily and simplistically drawn from old propaganda and wartime obfuscations, and effectively mashed with elements of *Genesis* and

AFTERWORD

Exodus to attempt to speak in the familiar languages of original sin and salvation. Risdon became a serpent, Robinson a messiah.

Even in text this master narrative influenced each subsequent telling down the ages, gradually strangling history with mythology. Out of this mix, lived history coalesced into narrative history, national history and then nationalist history. As it did, it grew but became a diminished truth. Whole campaigns fell into void and silent amnesia. Rewards for captures and records of killings dropped out of biographies. Despite avid antiquarianism and persistent historical nit-picking, the real story was lost, buried by habits of mind. Van Diemen's Land became Tasmania, and Tasmanian history had no room for the Vandemonian War.

Precisely how this all came to be is most easily discerned through brief reference to a select group of writers. First among these is Jorgenson, who hoped to write a history of the Vandemonian War even before it terminated. Writing to Charles Arthur on 30 November 1830, as Arthur's campaign waned, Jorgenson asked Charles:

> would you be so good as to solicit your honoured uncle to permit me to have a sight of all the various reports I have from time to time addressed to Mr Anstey concerning the Aborigines, and the movements of the Roving parties against them. ... I intend to write a work on the Subject of the Aborigines, and the history of the late warlike movements against them.[1]

Perhaps recognising that his own period of service was nearing its end, Jorgenson admitted there might be some financial profit in such a work. The war had been lucrative for many people, who afterwards all had to turn to other things.

Understanding his proposed book's potential military import, Jorgenson hoped 'to dedicate it to the King of Prussia'. With its coordinated formations and sweeping drives, Jorgenson seems to have thought that studying the Vandemonian War could be useful for future armies and empire-builders. Sometime after his retirement from the roving parties, Jorgenson did write an account of Aboriginal cultural practices and narrated a short history of the conflict, but it was far from this early proposal. A draft manuscript survives in the State Library of New South Wales.²

Curiously, Jorgenson glossed over the roving parties, and much of the war to which he was privy, but repeatedly stressed that he had examined manuscripts in the colonial archive, some of the same ones used for this book. It was quite a bizarre document, more revealing of Jorgenson's persistent jealousies than reliably illuminating the past, perhaps reflecting the way that the profits from victory tended to benefit higher classes of men than this ex-convict and his fellow rangers. It is tempting to see his references to these government-held documents as a coded pointer to the truth he was overlooking, but that could be giving him too much credit. No longer of great utility to his government, Jorgenson was now severely limited by class and a lack of patronage, and was not well placed to challenge the already-strong master narratives. 'The reports written by Mr Jorgen Jorgenson are very voluminous, and embrace every object' he made sure to state, adding a prefix to his name that the original reports lacked. He was never Mr Jorgenson to his masters, only Jorgenson. An ex-convict could not challenge what the Lieutenant Governor had authorised as truth.

Although unpublished under his own name in his lifetime, parts of Jorgenson's manuscript were used in James Bonwick's *The Last of the Tasmanians; or, The Black War of Van Diemen's Land* of 1870. Bonwick constructed his history from some government records and populated it with colourful and often fanciful anecdotes. One of Jorgenson's unattributed contributions was an absurd version of Dalrymple Briggs's defence of her children at Stocker's hut.³ Similar stories had similarly stupid trails of transmission into the historical and literary canon – even surviving into present times. When Louisa Ann Meredith wrote of her husband's experiences of the war, she entirely omitted the Schoutens campaign, despite his prominent role and it being his father's idea.⁴ Some of the Cottons insisted they kept Aboriginal people safely and secretly on their property into the years of exile, possibly misunderstanding family traditions that hearkened back to their very real collection of Aboriginal skulls, which was well known to the scientific community.⁵ The war served later colonial audiences

AFTERWORD

as a sort of gothic whimsy, offering terrible tales from yore, and it has often continued to do so.

This old story of the Aboriginal peoples of Van Diemen's Land has also frequently served as a morality tale. As Bonwick wrote to his friends when he first conceived of his work in the 1850s:

> it is the desire of my heart to write a full & particular account of that melancholy period, the Black War; it is not mere curiosity nor thought of money making, badly as I want cash. Mr West, in his history, has not detailed the events of that sad story. The race is passing away & no proper memorial of their struggles exists.[6]

For Bonwick, this story was intended to elicit 'the sympathy of philanthropists', popularising notions of racial extinction and historical tragedy, thereby contributing to contemporary debates about the nature and behaviour of empire. 'Have we not often been, in our civilizing processes,' Bonwick asked in the condensed reprint of his book, 'more savage than the Savages?'[7] The Vandemonian War thereby became a cautionary lesson for the empire drawn from its own genocidal past.[8]

But the people who helped inform that story were often tainted as participants, either in the war or in its misremembering. The timeless and savage Aboriginal tribes, violent and criminal stockmen, humane administrators, and absent soldiers of the old 'Black War' narrative were products of this later moment of gentile reflection. This unfortunate and unofficial war of previous memory, this accidental genocide, was a classed construction, a shared fantasy, the direct result of wartime propaganda and mutual interest.

Until now, the real Vandemonian War was hidden by the strength of this antiquated 'Black War' tradition obsessed with race and reputation, and made resilient through repetition. But there is great irony here as well. Certainly, the colonial government constructed a public narrative of what happened and why, massaged at times to suit circumstances, which persisted beyond its immediate context and political purpose. But the orders to troops, the cataloguing of arms and ammunitions, the mission reports of movements, captures and killings derive from the documentary by-products of that same misrepresented history. They capture history as it happened. The Vandemonian War was written as it was fought.

It would be easy to fall into the old habit of the 'Black War' narrative and turn a complex war into an ethno-cultural morality tale or resistance fable. A final platitude about fallen warriors, the shared experiences of war, the survival and renewal of culture and identity, or any other cliché could help conform this work to narrative convention and round it to a fitting end. But the Vandemonian War has a grimmer message more pertinent for the present – this age of half-truths, cultural and ethnic partisanship and the intellectual vacuum left by that great postmodern conceit that all truth is relative. Unearthed after nearly two centuries of established history, the Vandemonian War allows us to see that a society can be led to do almost anything – and then come to believe it did not do it at all.

Endnotes

Some Notes on the Notes

To keep hundreds of references from becoming thousands, and to keep them useful without becoming burdensome, I have adopted a few referencing conventions.

Unless otherwise specified, all archival citations refer to the Tasmanian Archive and Heritage Office housed within the State Library of Tasmania. This mostly concerns series of volumes from the Colonial Secretary's Office (CSO), the Governor's Office (GO), and convict (CON) and police (POL) records. Individual documents (e.g. letters and reports) are cited at first use per their full pagination within relevant volumes. Subsequent quotations are identifiable by context and preceding reference(s).

Government pronouncements such as proclamations, government orders, and government notices are identified by their date of issue, and any original numerator where such was used. These can most easily be identified by searching colonial newspapers for their reproduction.

A range of other government material (including selective garrison orders) were compiled and printed for the British House of Commons in 1831. This provides a convenient means of citing otherwise disparate or missing material. Officially titled *Return to an Address of the Honourable The House of Commons, dated 19th July 1831; – for, Copies of all Correspondence between Lieutenant-Governor Arthur and His Majesty's Secretary of State for the Colonies, on the Subject of the Military Operations lately carried on against the Aboriginal Inhabitants of Van Diemen's Land*, documents from this compilation will be cited per the abbreviation 'Commons Return'.

Note that the much-used CSO1/1/320 (7578) volume has a pagination error, meaning that most of the 300s are duplicated. References are given per the uncorrected manuscript page numbers to avoid further confusion, but are easily identifiable by context and discoverable by the volume's own organising sections.

Preface
1. On the resonance of the Vandemonian genocide within British history, see Tom Lawson's *The Last Man: A British Genocide in Tasmania* (London: I. B. Taurus, 2014). See also the sizeable appendix 'Towards Genocide' in James Boyce's *Van Diemen's Land* (Melbourne: Black Inc., 2008). *The Vandemonian War* builds significantly on these lines of enquiry with more evidence.
2. For a recent survey of the field, see Murray Johnson and Ian McFarlane's *Van Diemen's Land: An Aboriginal History* (Sydney: University of New South Wales Press, 2015). On experiential aspects of the conflict, see Nicholas Clements's *The Black War: Fear, Sex and Resistance in Tasmania* (St Lucia: University of Queensland Press, 2014). On military involvement see John F. McMahon, 'The British Army: Its Role in Counter-Insurgency in the Black War in Van Diemen's Land', *Tasmanian Historical Studies* 5, 1996, pp. 56–63; and John Connor, 'The Tasmanian Frontier and Military History', *Tasmanian Historical Studies* 9, 2004, pp. 89–99. Other works of note include: Clive Turnbull, *Black War: The Extermination of the Tasmanian Aborigines* (Melbourne: F. W. Cheshire, 1943); Lyndall Ryan, *The Aboriginal Tasmanians* (St Lucia: University of Queensland Press, 1981), updated as *Tasmanian Aborigines: A History Since 1803* (Crows Nest: Allen and Unwin, 2012); and Henry Reynolds's body of work, especially *Fate of a Free People* (Ringwood: Penguin, 1995), and *An Indelible Stain? The Question of Genocide in Australia's History* (Ringwood: Penguin, 2001).

Chapter One – Conquest and Division
1. See my *1787: The Lost Chapters of Australia's Beginnings* (Melbourne: Hardie Grant, 2016).
2. An excellent impression of the varied encounters can be found in James Kelly's account of circumnavigating Van Diemen's Land in 1815–16: University of Tasmania Library Special and Rare Collections, RS 99 (1).
3. *Hobart Town Gazette*, 5 November 1824, p. 2.

ENDNOTES

4 *Hobart Town Gazette*, 5 November 1824, p. 2.
5 Mary Nicholls (ed.), *The Diary of the Reverend Robert Knopwood 1803–1838* (Sandy Bay: Tasmanian Historical Research Association, 1977), pp. 182, 217, 232, 293–94.
6 Grant Finlay, 'Always Crackne in Heaven', PhD Thesis, University of Tasmania, 2015, Appendix A, pp. 345–49. Note that some known Aboriginal offspring were baptised without specifically being labelled as 'Aboriginal' or similar, meaning these are at best indicative minimum figures.
7 Zoe Lawson, 'George Vandiemen: A Tasmanian Aborigine in Lancashire, England, (1822–27)', *Journal of the Royal Australian Historical Society*, 99(2), 2013, pp. 153–69.
8 *Hobart Town Courier*, 3 May 1828, p. 4.
9 GO54/1/3, p. 292.
10 GO54/1/3, p. 310.
11 Proclamation, 15 April 1828. See Commons Return, pp. 22–24.
12 Historical Records of Australia (HRA), Series 3, Volume 4, pp. 134–54.
13 HRA 3(4), p. 149.
14 HRA 3(4), pp. 155–56.
15 HRA 3(4), pp. 162–63.
16 HRA 3(4), pp. 307–08.
17 Stefan Petrow, 'Policing in a Penal Colony: Governor Arthur's Police System in Van Diemen's Land, 1826–1836', *Law and History Review* 18(2), 2000, pp. 351–95.
18 Government Order, 19 February 1827.
19 *Hobart Town Gazette*, 7 July 1827, p. 2.
20 *Hobart Town Courier*, 24 November 1827, p. 2.
21 CSO41/1/1, pp. 2–5.
22 CSO41/1/1, pp. 6–10.
23 GO54/1/3, p. 257.
24 GO54/1/3, p. 253.
25 Government Notice, 29 November 1826. See Commons Return, pp. 20–21.
26 *Colonial Times and Tasmanian Advertiser*, 13 July 1827, p. 2.
27 CSO41/1/1, pp. 13, 119–20.
28 CSO41/1/1, pp. 119–20.
29 Government Notice, 29 November 1827. See Commons Return, p. 21.
30 Commons Return, pp. 21–22.
31 State Library of New South Wales, A 773 (Safe 1/360), 10 April 1816.
32 HRA 1(9), p. 54.
33 Kristyn Harman, *Aboriginal Convicts: Australian, Khoisan, and Māori Exiles* (Sydney: University of New South Wales Press, 2012).
34 See Harman, *Aboriginal Convicts*, and Naomi Parry, '"Hanging no good for blackfellow": Looking into the Life of Musquito', in I. Macfarlane and M. Hannah (eds), *Transgressions: Critical Australian Indigenous Histories* (Acton: ANU E Press, 2007), pp. 153–76.
35 EC4/1/1, pp. 236–37.
36 EC4/1/1, p. 303.

37 Nicholas Dean Brodie, "'He Had Been a Faithful Servant': Henry Melville's Lost Manuscripts, Black Tom, and Aboriginal Negotiations in Van Diemen's Land", *Journal of Australian Colonial History* 17, 2015, pp. 45–64.
38 CSO1/1/321, pp. 295–96.
39 GO54/1/3, pp. 234–35.
40 *Hobart Town Courier*, 22 March 1828, p. 3.
41 *Hobart Town Courier*, 12 April 1828, p. 3.
42 *Hobart Town Courier*, 19 April 1828, p. 3.
43 *Hobart Town Courier*, 22 March 1828, p. 3; *Hobart Town Courier*, 3 May 1828, p. 3.

Chapter Two – Scouring the Country
1 *Hobart Town Courier*, 12 April 1828, p. 3.
2 *Hobart Town Courier*, 7 June 1828, p. 2.
3 CSO41/1/1, p. 152.
4 CSO41/1/1, pp. 154–55.
5 CSO41/1/1, p. 156.
6 Brigade Major to Captain Walpole, 30 September 1828, Commons Return, pp. 25–26.
7 *Hobart Town Courier*, 18 October 1828, pp. 1–2.
8 CSO1/1/316, pp. 166–72.
9 CSO1/1/329, p. 284.
10 Danvers' convict history is contained in CON31/1/9, no. 330, p. 111; CON32/1/1, no. D330; CON13/1/3.
11 CSO1/1/320, p. 6.
12 Proclamation, 1 November 1828, Commons Return, pp. 27–28.
13 Circular to the Magistrates, 1 November 1828, Commons Return, p. 28.
14 Brigade Major to Officers on Detachment, 3 November 1828, Commons Return, pp. 29–30.
15 CSO1/1/320, p. 7.
16 CSO1/1/320, pp. 8–10.
17 CSO41/1/1, p. 176.
18 CSO1/1/320, pp. 12–14.
19 CSO41/1/1, pp. 183–84.
20 CON31/1/18, no. 464, p. 155.
21 *Hobart Town Courier*, 6 September 1828, p. 2.
22 *Hobart Town Courier*, 15 November 1828, p. 2.
23 CSO1/1/320, p. 18.
24 CSO1/1/320, pp. 320–23.
25 *Hobart Town Courier*, 13 December 1828, p. 2.
26 CSO1/1/320, pp. 531–32.
27 CSO1/1/320, pp. 353–54.

Chapter Three – Clearing the Settled Districts
1 Commons Return, p. 9 [sic proferred].
2 Commons Return, p. 14.
3 CSO1/1/320, pp. 324–33.

4   CSO41/1/1, p. 204.
5   CSO1/1/320, p. 357.
6   CSO1/1/320, p. 361.
7   CSO1/1/320, p. 362.
8   CSO1/1/320, p. 360.
9   *Hobart Town Courier*, 20 December 1828, p. 2.
10   CSO1/1/320, p. 359.
11   *Hobart Town Courier*, 20 December 1828, p. 2.
12   CSO1/1/320, pp. 19–21.
13   CSO41/1/1, p. 191.
14   CSO41/1/1, p. 203.
15   CSO1/1/320, pp. 26–28.
16   CSO1/1/320, pp. 30–32.
17   GO54/1/1, pp. 167–68.
18   GO54/1/4, p. 117.
19   GO54/1/4, p. 132.
20   GO54/1/4, p. 129.
21   GO54/1/4, p. 155.
22   CD7/1/1.
23   CD7/1/1, pp. 136, 299–300, 309, 539, 701, 719.
24   CD7/1/1, pp. 30, 165.
25   CD7/1/1, pp. 22, 98.
26   CD7/1/1, pp. 211, 424.
27   *Hobart Town Courier*, 24 January 1829, p. 2; *Hobart Town Courier*, 31 January 1829, p. 2.
28   GO54/1/4, p. 27.
29   GO54/1/4, p. 130.
30   *Hobart Town Courier*, 17 January 1829, pp. 1–2.
31   *Colonial Times*, 30 January 1829, p. 3.
32   *Launceston Advertiser*, 9 February 1829, p. 3.
33   *Hobart Town Courier*, 24 January 1829, p. 2.
34   *Colonial Times*, 23 January 1829, p. 2.
35   Garrison Orders, 12 December 1828, Commons Return, p. 31.
36   *Colonial Times*, 30 January 1829, p. 3.
37   CSO41/1/1, p. 265.
38   CSO1/1/320, pp. 364–65.
39   *Hobart Town Courier*, 17 January 1829, p. 1.

Chapter Four – Mercenaries and Aboriginal Guides
1   GO54/1/4, p. 172.
2   CSO1/1/331, pp. 168–78.
3   CSO1/1/331, pp. 169–70.
4   *Hobart Town Courier*, 22 November 1828, p. 2.
5   GO54/1/4, pp. 120–21.
6   CSO1/1/331, pp. 158–60.
7   CSO1/1/331, p. 159.
8   CSO1/1/329, p. 269.

9   CSO41/1/1, pp. 250–51.
10 CSO41/1/1, pp. 185–86.
11 CSO41/1/1, p. 187.
12 CON31/1/1, no. 113, p. 29; CON31/1/27, no. 8, p. 3.
13 CSO41/1/1, p. 211.
14 CSO1/1/329, p. 278.
15 CSO1/1/331, p. 63.
16 CSO41/1/1, p. 207.
17 CSO1/1/331, pp. 79–92, 114–44. The latter document includes a copy of William Grant's journal in pp. 123–31.
18 CSO1/1/331, pp. 186–88.
19 CSO1/1/331, p. 172.
20 CSO1/1/331, pp. 172–73.
21 CSO1/1/331, pp. 119–23.
22 CSO1/1/331, pp. 123–31.
23 CON31/1/15, no. 261, p. 87; CON13/1/2, p. 245.
24 CON31/1/15, no. 455, p. 152.
25 CON31/1/15, no. 518, p. 173.
26 CON31/1/27, no. 332, p. 111; CON14/1/1, no. 332, p. 2.
27 CSO1/1/331, p. 126.
28 CSO1/1/331, p. 127.
29 CSO1/1/320, p. 39.
30 CSO41/1/1, p. 223.
31 CSO41/1/1, pp. 231–34.
32 CSO1/1/331, p. 79.
33 CSO41/1/1, pp. 246–47.
34 CSO1/1/331, p. 79.
35 CSO41/1/1, pp. 216–17.
36 CSO1/1/331, p. 81.

Chapter Five – The Oatlands Roving Parties
1   CSO41/1/1, pp. 274–75. A copy also survives in POL576/1/1, bundle 5761.
2   CSO41/1/1, p. 281.
3   CSO41/1/1, pp. 277–78.
4   CSO41/1/1, p. 274.
5   Commons Return, p. 31; *Colonial Times*, 13 March 1829, p. 4.
6   GO54/1/4, pp. 244, 248.
7   GO54/1/4, p. 262.
8   Robinson's journals are published in *Friendly Mission: The Tasmanian Journals and Papers of George Augustus Robinson, 1829–1834*, edited by N. J. B. Plomley, 2nd edition (Launceston: QVMAG and Quintus, 2008), p. 57.
9   GO54/1/5, pp. 149–51.
10 CSO41/1/1, p. 269.
11 GO54/1/4, pp. 327–29.
12 CSO41/1/1, pp. 272–73.
13 CSO1/1/320, pp. 40–41.

14 CSO41/1/1, p. 280.
15 As above, but see also CSO41/1/1, p. 284.
16 CSO1/1/320, p. 42.
17 CSO1/1/320, p. 45; see in connection CSO41/1/1, pp. 293–95.
18 CSO41/1/1, pp. 281–83.
19 CSO1/1/321, pp. 57–60.
20 For a full biography see Sarah Bakewell's *The English Dane: From King of Iceland to Tasmanian Convict* (London: Vintage, 2006).
21 CON31/1/23, no. 298, p. 100.
22 *Hobart Town Gazette*, 6 May 1826, p. 2.
23 CSO41/1/1, p. 18.
24 CSO41/1/1, p. 64; Government Notice 105, 25 May 1828; *Hobart Town Courier*, 24 May 1828, p. 2.
25 CSO41/1/1, pp. 146–47, 157.
26 CSO1/1/320, pp. 275–78.
27 CSO41/1/1, pp. 304–05.
28 CSO1/1/320, pp. 295–96.
29 CSO1/1/320, pp. 279–94.
30 CSO1/1/320, pp. 280–81.
31 CSO1/1/320, p. 294.

Chapter Six – Offensive Defence in Reality and Record
1 *Launceston Advertiser*, 6 July 1829, p. 3.
2 CSO1/1/320, pp. 297–16.
3 CSO41/1/1, p. 298.
4 CSO41/1/1, p. 300.
5 CSO1/1/331, pp. 36–42.
6 CSO1/1/320, pp. 317–24.
7 CSO1/1/320, pp. 325–30.
8 CSO1/1/331, pp. 27–50.
9 CSO1/1/331, p. 50.
10 CSO1/1/331, pp. 27–31.
11 CSO1/1/331, p. 83.
12 CSO1/1/320, pp. 366–67.
13 CSO1/1/320, pp. 378–81.
14 GO54/1/5, pp. 19–20.
15 GO54/1/5, pp. 8–9; CSO41/1/1, p. 299.
16 GO54/1/5, pp. 25–27; CSO41/1/1, pp. 303–04.
17 CSO1/1/321, pp. 87–89.
18 CSO1/1/321, pp. 87–89.
19 CSO41/1/1, p. 307.
20 CSO1/1/321, pp. 57–59.
21 CSO1/1/321, p. 89.
22 *Hobart Town Courier*, 30 May 1829, p. 2.
23 *Hobart Town Courier*, 25 July 1829, p. 2.
24 *Colonial Times*, 28 August 1829, p. 3.
25 *Launceston Advertiser*, 24 August 1829, p. 3.

26 For more on these men, see Kristyn Harman, 'Send in the Sydney Natives! Deploying Mainlanders against Tasmanian Aborigines', *Tasmanian Historical Studies* 14, 2009, pp. 5–24.
27 CSO1/1/320, pp. 142–44.
28 *Hobart Town Courier*, 12 September 1829, p. 2.
29 CSO1/1/320, p. 143.
30 CSO41/1/1, p. 311; emphasis added.
31 CSO41/1/1, p. 311.
32 GO54/1/5, p. 51.
33 *Launceston Advertiser*, 7 September 1829, p. 2.
34 *Hobart Town Courier*, 12 September 1829, p. 2.
35 *Colonial Times*, 18 September 1829, p. 3.
36 CSO41/1/1, pp. 316–20.

Chapter Seven – The Methods and Landscape of Settlement
1 CSO1/1/320, pp. 146–48.
2 CSO1/1/320, pp. 155–58.
3 CSO41/1/1, p. 326.
4 CSO41/1/1, p. 327.
5 *Hobart Town Courier*, 3 October 1829, p. 2.
6 GO54/1/5, p. 35.
7 GO54/1/4, p. 243.
8 CSO1/1/330, pp. 40–48.
9 CSO1/1/320, pp. 389–90.
10 CSO1/1/320, pp. 382–83.
11 CSO1/1/320, pp. 334–37.
12 CSO41/1/1, pp. 327, 333–34, 343.
13 CSO41/1/1, p. 338.
14 CSO41/1/1, pp. 333, 350–51.
15 CSO1/1/330, pp. 47–50.
16 CSO41/1/1, p. 339.
17 CSO41/1/1, pp. 324–25.
18 CSO41/1/1, p. 343.
19 CSO41/1/1, p. 315.
20 *Hobart Town Courier*, 21 November 1829, p. 2.
21 CSO41/1/1, p. 343.
22 *Colonial Times*, 13 November 1829, p. 3.
23 CSO41/1/1, pp. 352–53.
24 HRA 3 (5), pp. 361–62, 612.
25 HRA 3 (5), pp. 651–53.
26 HRA 3 (6), pp. 116–18.
27 HRA 3 (6), pp. 150–51.
28 HRA 3 (6), pp. 376–77.
29 GO54/1/4, pp. 168–69.
30 *Hobart Town Courier*, 19 December 1829, p. 3.
31 GO54/1/4, p. 333; GO54/1/4, pp. 31, 73.
32 GO54/1/5, p. 136.

ENDNOTES

33 *Hobart Town Courier*, 17 October 1829, p. 2.
34 *Colonial Times*, 16 October 1829, p. 3; *Hobart Town Courier*, 24 October 1829, p. 2.
35 *Hobart Town Courier*, 23 January 1830, p. 3; CON31/1/1, no. 1180, p. 306.
36 CSO1/1/320, pp. 395–96.
37 CSO1/1/320, pp. 338–41.
38 *Hobart Town Courier*, 17 October 1829, p. 2.
39 *Hobart Town Courier*, 17 October 1829, p. 2.
40 *Colonial Times*, 6 November 1829, p. 3; *Colonial Times*, 13 November 1829, p. 3.
41 CSO1/1/320, pp. 385–87.
42 CSO1/1/331, pp. 71–74.
43 CSO41/1/1, p. 349.
44 *Hobart Town Courier*, 21 November 1829, p. 3; GO54/1/5, pp. 209–10: indicates that Vicary's replacement assumed duties in Oatlands on 20 November 1829.
45 *Hobart Town Courier*, 28 November 1829, p. 2.
46 CSO41/1/1, p. 353.
47 *Hobart Town Courier*, 13 December 1828, p. 2.
48 *Hobart Town Courier*, 7 March 1829, p. 2.
49 *Hobart Town Courier*, 12 December 1829, p. 2.
50 CSO41/1/1, pp. 236–37.
51 *Hobart Town Courier*, 14 November 1829, p. 2.
52 *Hobart Town Courier*, 14 November 1829, p. 2.
53 CSO1/1/320, p. 52; CSO41/1/1, pp. 353–54.
54 CSO1/1/320, pp. 337–48.
55 CSO1/1/320, p. 335.
56 CSO41/1/1, p. 343.
57 CSO1/1/320, pp. 349–50.
58 CSO1/1/320, p. 351.

Chapter Eight – Aboriginal Auxiliaries

1 CSO41/1/1, p. 357; CSO1/1/320, pp. 57–58.
2 CSO1/1/320, p. 55.
3 CSO1/1/320, pp. 50–51.
4 CSO41/1/1, p. 356.
5 CSO1/1/331, pp. 6–8.
6 CSO1/1/331, pp. 2–5.
7 CSO41/1/1, p. 355.
8 CSO41/1/1, p. 359.
9 *Hobart Town Courier*, 20 June 1829, p. 2.
10 *Hobart Town Courier*, 1 March 1828, p. 4.
11 *Hobart Town Courier*, 7 March 1829, p. 3.
12 *Hobart Town Courier*, 4 April 1829, p. 2.
13 *Friendly Mission*, p. 66.
14 *Hobart Town Courier*, 18 July 1829, p. 2.
15 *Hobart Town Courier*, 4 April 1829, p. 2.

16 CSO41/1/1, pp. 149–51.
17 CSO41/1/1, p. 150.
18 *Hobart Town Courier*, 7 November 1829, p. 2.
19 CSO41/1/1, pp. 82, 96–97, 129, 141.
20 CSO41/1/1, pp. 124–25.
21 CSO41/1/1, pp. 162–63.
22 *Hobart Town Courier*, 28 February 1829, p. 2.
23 *Hobart Town Courier*, 7 March 1829, p. 4.
24 *Hobart Town Courier*, 16 August 1829, p. 1; *Hobart Town Courier*, 18 July 1829, p. 3.
25 CSO1/1/323, pp. 79–81.
26 *Hobart Town Courier*, 23 January 1830, p. 4.
27 CSO1/1/332, p. 1.
28 *Hobart Town Courier*, 21 March 1829, p. 2.
29 *Colonial Times*, 12 February 1830, p. 4.
30 *Friendly Mission*, p. 143.
31 *Friendly Mission*, p. 143.
32 CSO1/1/331, pp. 199–200.
33 CSO1/1/320, pp. 409–10.
34 CSO1/1/320, pp. 405–08.
35 CON31/1/42, no. 247, p. 83.
36 CON31/1/1, p. 217, no. 866.
37 CSO1/1/323, pp. 117–52.
38 LSD17/1/1, p. 23.
39 *Colonial Times*, 5 March 1830, p. 2; *Colonial Times*, 14 January 1831, p. 2.
40 See Tyrrell's fascinating retraction in CSO1/1/320, pp. 425–28.
41 CSO1/1/320, pp. 61–62.
42 CSO1/1/320, p. 403.
43 CSO1/1/320, p. 340.
44 CSO1/1/320, pp. 335–36.
45 CSO1/1/320, pp. 337–40.
46 CSO41/1/1, p. 361.
47 CSO1/1/320, pp. 341–42.
48 CSO1/1/320, pp. 167–70.
49 CSO41/1/1, p. 368.

Chapter Nine – Pushing Further while Debating Peace
1 CSO1/1/320, pp. 411–13.
2 CSO1/1/320, pp. 351–55.
3 CSO1/1/320, pp. 355–68.
4 *Hobart Town Courier*, 13 February 1830, p. 2.
5 CSO41/1/1, p. 365.
6 CSO41/1/1, p. 369.
7 *Hobart Town Courier*, 20 February 1830, p. 2: Government Order 1, 19 February 1830.
8 *Colonial Times*, 19 February 1830, p. 3. It was also published in the *Hobart Town Courier*, 20 February 1830, p. 2.

9 *Colonial Times*, 19 February 1830, p. 3.
10 CBE1/1/1, pp. 3–6.
11 The testimony is recorded in two different volumes. One is the committee's formal minutes, kept in clean copy: CBE1/1/1, pp. 3–6. The other is a rougher copy, with slightly different (but not mutually exclusive) commentary: CSO1/1/332, pp. 71–72.
12 CBE1/1/1, pp. 6–7; CSO1/1/332, pp. 72–74.
13 CBE1/1/1, pp. 7–8; CSO1/1/332, pp. 74–75.
14 CBE1/1/1, pp. 8–9.
15 GO54/1/5, pp. 236–38; Government Order 2, 25 February 1830. See Commons Return, p. 35 and *Hobart Town Courier*, 27 February 1830, p. 2.
16 Un-numbered notices immediately below the Government Order in *Hobart Town Courier*, 27 February 1830, p. 2.
17 GO54/1/5, p. 234.
18 GO54/1/5, p. 234; CSO41/1/1, p. 371.
19 GO54/1/5, p. 235; Government Notice 47, 26 February 1830, *Hobart Town Courier*, 27 February 1830, p. 2. It became law on 12 March: 11 Geo. IV, No. 2.

Chapter Ten – Roving Still
1 CBE1/1/1, pp. 10–14.
2 CBE1/1/1, pp. 49–80. See also Commons Return, pp. 35–46.
3 GO54/1/5, pp. 235–36.
4 GO54/1/5, pp. 235–36.
5 GO54/1/5, p. 241.
6 CSO41/1/1, p. 372.
7 CSO41/1/1, pp. 373–75.
8 CSO1/1/320, pp. 369–70.
9 *Hobart Town Courier*, 27 March 1830, p. 3.
10 *Hobart Town Courier*, 13 March 1830, p. 2.
11 *Colonial Times*, 19 March 1830, p. 3.
12 *Hobart Town Courier*, 13 March 1830, p. 3.
13 *Colonial Times*, 19 March 1830, p. 3.
14 *Hobart Town Courier*, 27 March 1830, p. 2: Commissariat Office, 25 March 1830.
15 CSO1/1/320, pp. 373–76.
16 *Friendly Mission*, pp. 167–68.
17 *Friendly Mission*, pp. 168–69.
18 CSO41/1/1, p. 375.
19 CSO1/1/320, p. 68.
20 *Launceston Advertiser*, 29 March 1830, p. 3.
21 *Colonial Times*, 2 April 1830, p. 3.
22 GO54/1/5, pp. 252–53.
23 *Hobart Town Courier*, 3 April 1830, p. 2.
24 GO54/1/5, pp. 252–53.
25 CSO41/1/1, p. 378.
26 CBE1/1/1, pp. 49–80.

27 CBE1/1/1, pp. 76–77.
28 CBE1/1/1, p. 76.
29 *Launceston Advertiser*, 5 April 1830, p. 2.
30 CSO/1/320, pp. 178–81.
31 GO54/1/5, p. 311.
32 CSO1/1/320, pp. 182–83.
33 CSO1/1/320, pp. 184–86.
34 CSO1/1/320, pp. 187–89.
35 *Hobart Town Courier*, 10 April 1830, p. 2; Government Notice 71, 7 April 1830.
36 CSO1/1/320, pp. 192–94.
37 CSO1/1/320, pp. 342–52.
38 CSO1/1/320, pp. 70–71.
39 CSO41/1/1, pp. 393–94.
40 CSO1/1/320, pp. 190–91.
41 CSO1/1/320, pp. 86–89.
42 *Hobart Town Courier*, 19 June 1830, p. 2; *Launceston Advertiser*, 21 June 1830, p. 3.
43 *Hobart Town Courier*, 19 June 1830, p. 2.
44 *Hobart Town Courier*, 5 June 1830, p. 3.
45 *Hobart Town Courier*, 17 April 1830, p. 2; Government Notice 73, 15 April 1830.
46 CSO41/1/1, p. 382.
47 CSO41/1/1, p. 387.

Chapter Eleven – Beyond the Limits of Law and Documentation
1 CSO1/1/320, pp. 379–81.
2 *Colonial Times*, 12 March 1830, p. 3.
3 *Colonial Times*, 12 March 1830, p. 3.
4 *Colonial Times*, 26 March 1830, p. 3; *Hobart Town Courier*, 27 March 1830, pp. 3–4.
5 *Colonial Times*, 12 March 1830, p. 3.
6 CSO1/1/320, pp. 377–78.
7 CSO1/1/320, pp. 379–81.
8 CSO41/1/1, pp. 382–83.
9 CSO1/1/320, pp. 379–82.
10 CSO1/1/228, pp. 211–14.
11 CSO1/1/228, pp. 211–14.
12 CSO1/1/320, pp. 425–28.
13 *Launceston Advertiser*, 22 March 1830, p. 2.
14 CSO1/1/320, pp. 415–18.
15 CSO1/1/320, p. 419. This mission was also reported in some detail in a letter to the *Hobart Town Courier*, 29 May 1830, p. 2.
16 *Colonial Times*, 11 June 1830, p. 3.
17 *Colonial Times*, 30 April 1830, p. 2.
18 *Hobart Town Courier*, 8 May 1830, p. 2; Government Notice 95, 5 May 1830; CSO41/1/1, p. 390; GO54/1/5, p. 268.

ENDNOTES

19 *Colonial Times*, 28 May 1830, p. 4.
20 *Hobart Town Courier*, 27 March 1830, p. 2.
21 GO54/1/5, p. 302.
22 CSO41/1/1, pp. 394–96.
23 CSO41/1/1, pp. 395–96.
24 CSO41/1/1, p. 418.
25 CSO41/1/1, p. 397.
26 CSO1/1/320, pp. 453–54.
27 *Launceston Advertiser*, 22 March 1830, p. 2.
28 *Hobart Town Courier*, 29 May 1830, p. 2.
29 *Hobart Town Courier*, 29 May 1830, p. 2.
30 CSO1/1/320, pp. 453–54.
31 CSO41/1/1, pp. 399–400.
32 CBE1/1/1, pp. 43–47.
33 CSO1/1/320, pp. 72–73.
34 CSO1/1/320, p. 197.
35 CSO1/1/320, p. 454; CSO41/1/1, p. 408.
36 GO51/1/5, pp. 310–11.
37 CSO1/1/320, pp. 453–54.
38 *Hobart Town Courier*, 29 May 1830, p. 2.
39 CSO1/1/320, pp. 74–76.
40 CSO41/1/1, p. 403.
41 CSO1/1/320, pp. 77–78.

Chapter Twelve – Keeping up the Pretence and the Pressure
1   CSO1/1/320, pp. 80–81.
2   CSO1/1/320, pp. 82–85.
3   *Colonial Times*, 18 June 1830, p. 3; *Hobart Town Courier*, 19 June 1830, p. 2.
4   RDG36/1/1, no. 1370, p. 11.
5   CSO41/1/1, p. 413.
6   *Colonial Times*, 25 June 1830, p. 3.
7   *Colonial Times*, 25 June 1830, p. 3.
8   GO54/1/5, pp. 316–17.
9   *Hobart Town Courier*, 19 June 1830, p. 2; Government Notice 118, 16 June 1830.
10 CSO1/1/320, pp. 383–84.
11 CSO41/1/1, p. 423.
12 CSO1/1/320, p. 93.
13 CSO1/1/320, pp. 91–92.
14 *Colonial Times*, 16 July 1830, p. 3.
15 *Colonial Times*, 16 July 1830, p. 3.
16 CSO1/1/320, p. 427.
17 CSO1/1/320, pp. 348–49.
18 *Colonial Times*, 30 July 1830, p. 2.
19 *Colonial Times*, 23 July 1830, p. 3.
20 *Colonial Times*, 16 July 1830, p. 3.
21 *Colonial Times*, 26 February 1830, p. 3.

22 CSO41/1/1, pp. 428–29.
23 CSO1/1/320, pp. 98–101.
24 CON31/1/42, no. 58, p. 53.
25 CSO41/1/1, p. 435.
26 CSO1/1/320, pp. 429–30.
27 CSO1/1/320, pp. 95–96.
28 *Hobart Town Courier*, 31 July 1830, p. 3; Government Notice 146, 30 July 1830; GO54/1/6, pp. 31–32.
29 CSO1/1/320, pp. 431–32.
30 *Colonial Times*, 13 August 1830, p. 3.

Chapter Thirteen – Captivity, Qualms and Escalation
1 CSO1/1/320, pp. 102–05.
2 *Hobart Town Courier*, 14 August 1830, p. 2.
3 *Hobart Town Courier*, 14 August 1830, p. 2.
4 *Colonial Times*, 20 August 1830, p. 3.
5 CSO41/1/1, pp. 439–41.
6 *Launceston Advertiser*, 26 July 1830, p. 2.
7 *Hobart Town Courier*, 4 September 1830, p. 2.
8 *Hobart Town Courier*, 14 August 1830, p. 3.
9 *Colonial Times*, 27 August 1830, p. 2.
10 *Colonial Times*, 19 February 1830, p. 3.
11 CSO41/1/1, pp. 439–41.
12 *Colonial Times*, 10 September 1830, p. 1; Government Notice 175, 9 September 1830.
13 *Colonial Times*, 10 September 1830, p. 1; Government Notice 177, 9 September 1830.
14 *Hobart Town Courier*, 21 August 1830, p. 2; Government Notice 159, 11 August 1830.
15 CSO41/1/1, pp. 439–41.
16 CON31/1/13, no. 123, p. 42.
17 CON21/1/1, no. F123.
18 *Hobart Town Gazette*, 29 September 1827, p. 9.
19 State Library of New South Wales, DLADD 83.
20 *Hobart Town Courier*, 28 August 1830, p. 2; Government Notice 161, 20 August 1830.
21 *Colonial Times*, 3 September 1830, p. 3.
22 *Colonial Times*, 27 August 1830, p. 3.
23 *Hobart Town Courier*, 28 August 1830, p. 2.
24 CBE1/1/1, p. 81.
25 *Colonial Times*, 20 August 1830, p. 1; Government Notice 160, 19 August 1830.
26 Government Notice 166, 27 August 1830.
27 Commons Return, pp. 62–64.
28 Government Order 9, 9 September 1830. See Commons Return, pp. 64–66.
29 CSO41/1/1, p. 434.
30 CSO41/1/1, p. 437.

31 CSO41/1/1, pp. 439–41.
32 *Colonial Times*, 20 August 1830, p. 2.
33 CSO41/1/1, pp. 445–46.
34 CSO41/1/1, p. 449.
35 *Launceston Advertiser*, 16 August 1830, p. 2; *Friendly Mission*, p. 225.
36 CSO1/1/320, pp. 106–07.

Chapter Fourteen – Agitation and Armament

1 CSO41/1/1, p. 450.
2 CSO41/1/1, pp. 449–50.
3 CSO1/1/321, pp. 141–42.
4 CSO1/1/321, pp. 138–40.
5 CSO1/1/321, pp. 154–57.
6 CSO1/1/321, pp. 163–64.
7 CSO1/1/321, pp. 165–68.
8 CSO41/1/1, pp. 451–52.
9 CSO1/1/321, pp. 172–74.
10 CON31/1/13, no. 9, p. 4; CON23/1/1, no. F9; CON13/1/1, p. 3.
11 Probably the case of William Morgan, sentenced to death for sheep stealing: *Sydney Gazette*, 25 September 1819, p. 3.
12 Phillip J. Hilton, '"Branded D on the Left Side": A Study of Former Soldiers and Marines Transported to Van Diemen's Land: 1804–1854', PhD Thesis, University of Tasmania, 2010, pp. 114, 425.
13 CSO1/1/321, pp. 192–93.
14 CSO1/1/321, pp. 194–96; CON31/1/9, no. 275, p. 92; Hilton, 'Branded D on the Left Side', p. 422.
15 CSO1/1/321, pp. 205–08; GO54/1/6, pp. 32–34.
16 CSO41/1/1, pp. 451–52.
17 CSO41/1/1, pp. 451–52.
18 *Hobart Town Courier*, 11 September 1830, p. 3.
19 University of Tasmania Library Special and Rare Collections, RS48, 30 August 1830.
20 CSO1/1/320, pp. 385–91.
21 Government Order 11, 22 September 1830. See Commons Return, pp. 66–70.
22 *Colonial Times*, 17 September 1830, p. 1.
23 CSO41/1/1, p. 452.
24 *Launceston Advertiser*, 27 September 1830, p. 3.
25 *Colonial Times*, 24 September 1830, pp. 3–4; *Hobart Town Courier*, 25 September 1830, p. 2.
26 CSO41/1/1, p. 453.
27 CSO41/1/1, p. 457.
28 CSO1/1/329, pp. 85–88.
29 CSO41/1/1, p. 458; CSO1/1/329, pp. 16–19.
30 CSO41/1/1, p. 459.
31 CSO41/1/1, p. 458; CSO1/1/329, pp. 16–19.
32 CSO41/1/1, p. 457.
33 CSO1/1/329, pp. 75–76.

34 CSO41/1/1, p. 461.
35 CSO1/1/329, pp. 69–72, 136–37.
36 CSO1/1/329, p. 63.
37 CSO1/1/329, p. 67.
38 CSO1/1/329, pp. 3–5.
39 CSO1/1/329, pp. 14, 81.
40 CSO1/1/329, pp. 12, 79, 99.
41 CSO1/1/329, pp. 89–90.
42 *Hobart Town Courier*, 2 October 1830, p. 2.
43 CSO1/1/329, pp. 105–07.
44 CSO1/1/329, pp. 101–02.
45 CSO1/1/329, pp. 69–72.
46 *Launceston Advertiser*, 4 October 1830, p. 1.

Chapter Fifteen – Propaganda and the Preliminary Manoeuvres
1 CSO1/1/324.
2 National Library of Australia, MS 3311. See also Nicholas Dean Brodie, 'It Is "a Matter of History and Mentioned in Several Authoritative Writings": Reminiscing "The Line" in Tasmania's "Black War", c. 1830 – 1916', *Tasmanian Historical Studies* 20, 2015, pp. 41–63.
3 CSO41/1/1, p. 456.
4 Proclamation, 1 October 1830. See Commons Return, p. 71.
5 A phenomenon I became aware of undertaking doctoral research: Nicholas Dean Brodie, 'Beggary, Vagabondage, and Poor Relief: English Statutes in the Urban Context, 1495–1572', PhD Thesis, University of Tasmania, 2010.
6 *Colonial Times*, 1 October 1830, p. 3.
7 *Hobart Town Courier*, 2 October 1830, p. 2.
8 *Hobart Town Courier*, 2 October 1830, p. 4.
9 *Colonial Times*, 8 October 1830, pp. 2–3.
10 Government Order 11, 22 September 1830.
11 CSO1/1/324, pp. 17–19.
12 CSO1/1/324, pp. 19–22.
13 State Library of New South Wales, A 1055/2; the manuscript is unpaginated.
14 *Hobart Town Courier*, 4 September 1830, p. 1.
15 CSO41/1/1, p. 456.
16 State Library of New South Wales, A 1055/2.
17 CSO1/1/324, pp. 373–74.
18 CSO1/1/324, pp. 375–77.
19 CSO1/1/324, pp. 19–22.
20 CSO1/1/324, pp. 127–28.
21 Copies of Robert Lawrence's diaries survive in the Queen Victoria Museum and Art Gallery in Launceston, Plomley Collection CHS 53 33/2. I have used a transcript of this material very kindly supplied by Dr Eleanor Cave. For more on this source see Eleanor Cave, '"Journal during the Expedition against the Blacks": Robert Lawrence's Experience on the Black Line', *Journal of Australian Studies* 37(1), 2013, pp. 34–47.
22 *Launceston Advertiser*, 27 September 1830, p. 2.

23 *Launceston Advertiser*, 27 September 1830, p. 2.
24 *Launceston Advertiser*, 4 October 1830, p. 2.
25 CSO41/1/1, p. 456.
26 *Launceston Advertiser*, 27 September 1830, p. 2.
27 *Launceston Advertiser*, 4 October 1830, p. 2.
28 *Launceston Advertiser*, 27 September 1830, p. 2.
29 Government Notice 183, 16 September 1830; *Hobart Town Courier*, 18 September 1830, p. 2.
30 Government Notice 182, 15 September 1830; Government Notice 184, 16 September 1830; *Hobart Town Courier*, 18 September 1830, p. 2.
31 Government Notice 186, 17 September 1830; The rewards were printed as 'a thousand acres' each in the *Hobart Town Courier*, 18 September 1830, p. 2, but corrected a week later in the *Hobart Town Courier*, 25 September 1830, p. 3.
32 CSO41/1/1, pp. 461–62; Government Notice 193, 2 October 1830; Government Order 12, 7 October 1830, p. 2.

Chapter Sixteen – Necessity Has No Law
1 CSO1/1/324, pp. 24–25.
2 *Colonial Times*, 15 October 1830, p. 3.
3 *Colonial Times*, 15 October 1830, p. 3.
4 *Colonial Times*, 22 October 1830, p. 3.
5 *Colonial Times*, 29 October 1830, p. 3.
6 *Colonial Times*, 22 October 1830, p. 3.
7 James Bonwick, *The Last of the Tasmanians; or, The Black War of Van Diemen's Land* (London: Sampson Low, 1870).
8 CSO1/1/324, pp. 26–29.
9 CSO1/1/324, p. 30.
10 CSO1/1/324, pp. 123–25.
11 CSO1/1/324, pp. 31–32.
12 University of Tasmania Library Special and Rare Collections, RS131(1), pp. 1–2.
13 *Colonial Times*, 15 October 1830, p. 4.
14 CSO1/1/324, pp. 37–38.
15 Government Notice 203, 18 October 1830; *Hobart Town Courier*, 18 October 1830, p. 1.
16 Government Notice 203, 18 October 1830; *Hobart Town Courier*, 18 October 1830, p. 1.
17 CSO1/1/324, pp. 40–41.
18 William Henry Breton, *Excursions in New South Wales, Western Australia, and Van Diemen's Land* (London, 1833), pp. 402–03.
19 CSO1/1/329, pp. 166–67.
20 Lawrence's Journal, 8 October 1830.
21 *Hobart Town Courier*, 30 October 1830, p. 2.
22 CSO1/1/324, pp. 133–34.
23 State Library of New South Wales, A 1055/2. See the letter from Douglas, 'Sent Near Hobb's Bluff', 18 October 1830.

24　*Colonial Times*, 29 October 1830, p. 3.
25　*Hobart Town Courier*, 23 October 1830, p. 2.
26　*Hobart Town Courier*, 30 October 1830, p. 2.
27　CSO1/1/324, pp. 43–45.
28　CSO1/1/324, pp. 46–48.
29　CSO1/1/324, pp. 47–48. This record appears misdated 30 October instead of 20 October. Another copy of this memorandum survives in Scott's collection, dated 20 October.
30　CSO1/1/324, pp. 48–49.
31　CSO1/1/324, pp. 50–51.
32　CSO1/1/324, pp. 135–36.
33　CSO1/1/324, pp. 52–53.
34　CSO1/1/324, pp. 54–57.
35　CSO1/1/324, pp. 139–40. See other reports of this incident in the *Hobart Town Courier*, 30 October 1830, p. 2.
36　CSO1/1/324, pp. 141–42.
37　CSO1/1/324, p. 58.
38　CSO1/1/324, p. 57.

Chapter Seventeen – Harass Them if They Cannot Be Taken
1　CSO1/1/324, pp. 409–12.
2　*Hobart Town Courier*, 6 November 1830, p. 2.
3　University of Tasmania Library Special and Rare Collections RS131(1), p. 2.
4　CSO1/1/328, p. 16.
5　There was also a 'Black Christie' serving under Field Policeman Nicholas Carr: CSO1/1/328, p. 34. While admittedly not necessarily an Aboriginal man, it nonetheless contradicts simplistic notions that the Vandemonian War was a race or colour war.
6　CSO1/1/329, pp. 159–60.
7　CSO1/1/324, pp. 33–36.
8　CSO1/1/324, pp. 397–402.
9　CSO1/1/324, pp. 407–08.
10　*Hobart Town Courier*, 23 October 1830, p. 2.
11　*Hobart Town Courier*, 16 October 1830, p. 2.
12　*Hobart Town Courier*, 6 November 1830, p. 2; *Hobart Town Courier*, 13 November 1830, p. 2.
13　*Tasmanian*, 5 November 1830, p. 3.
14　*Hobart Town Courier*, 13 November 1830, p. 2.
15　*Tasmanian*, 5 November 1830, p. 3.
16　*Hobart Town Courier*, 30 October 1830, p. 2.
17　Bonwick, *Last of the Tasmanians*, p. 163.
18　CSO1/1/232, pp. 59–66.
19　CSO1/1/324, pp. 143–56.
20　CSO1/1/324, pp. 327–28.
21　CSO1/1/324, pp. 66–70.
22　CSO1/1/324, pp. 71–77.
23　CSO1/1/324, p. 80; CSO1/1/329, p. 134.

24 CSO1/1/324, p. 79.
25 *Colonial Times*, 5 November 1830, p. 3.
26 State Library of New South Wales, A 1055/2; *Tasmanian*, 5 November 1830, p. 3.
27 CSO1/1/324, p. 69.
28 George Thomas Lloyd, *Thirty-Three Years in Tasmania and Victoria; Being the Actual Experience of the Author, Interspersed with Historic Jottings, Narratives, and Counsel to Emigrants* (London, 1862), p. 225. The chapter dealing with the subject was titled 'Colonists v. Natives'.
29 Lloyd, *Thirty-Three Years in Tasmania and Victoria*, p. 231.
30 Lloyd, *Thirty-Three Years in Tasmania and Victoria*, pp. 231–32.
31 CSO1/1/324, pp. 73–85.
32 CSO1/1/324, pp. 433–37.
33 CSO1/1/324, pp. 439–40.
34 CSO1/1/324, pp. 441–42.
35 CSO1/1/324, p. 181.
36 CSO1/1/324, pp. 443–45.
37 CSO1/1/324, p. 85.
38 CSO1/1/324, pp. 443–45.
39 CSO1/1/324, pp. 88–89.
40 CSO1/1/324, pp. 90–94.
41 CSO1/1/324, p. 221.
42 CSO1/1/324, pp. 223–24.
43 CSO1/1/324, pp. 229–30.
44 CSO1/1/324, pp. 96–98.
45 *Tasmanian*, 19 November 1830, p. 6.
46 CSO1/1/324, p. 95.
47 *Hobart Town Courier*, 20 November 1830, p. 2.
48 *Hobart Town Courier*, 20 November 1830, p. 2.
49 Commons Return, p. 74 [the original is misprinted as 47].
50 CSO1/1/324, pp. 99–103.
51 CSO1/1/320, pp. 396–98.
52 CSO1/1/320, p. 398.
53 CSO1/1/324, pp. 106–07.
54 Government Order 13, 26 November 1830.

Chapter Eighteen – From Open War to Black Operations
1 CSO1/1/324, p. 325.
2 CSO1/1/320, pp. 112–13.
3 CSO1/1/324, p. 343.
4 RGD341/1/, no. 2342.
5 CSO1/1/324, pp. 471–73.
6 CSO1/1/324, pp. 360–61.
7 CSO1/1/320, pp. 120–21.
8 CSO41/1/1, p. 482.
9 CSO41/1/1, p. 491.
10 *Hobart Town Courier*, 11 December 1830, p. 2.

11 CSO1/1/324, pp. 487–88.
12 CSO1/1/320, pp. 115–19.
13 *Tasmanian*, 24 December 1830, p. 1; *Hobart Town Courier*, 25 December 1830, p. 3.
14 *Hobart Town Courier*, 27 November 1830, p. 2.
15 *Hobart Town Courier*, 4 December 1830, p. 2.
16 CSO1/1/320, pp. 125–26.
17 CSO1/1/320, p. 126.
18 *Friendly Mission*, note 6, pp. 466–67.
19 See James Erskine Calder, *Some Account of the Wars, Extirpation, Habits, etc. of the Native Tribes of Tasmania* (Hobart, 1876).
20 State Library of New South Wales, A 597, pp. 73–76.
21 *Friendly Mission*, p. 282.
22 *Friendly Mission*, p. 284.
23 *Friendly Mission*, p. 304.
24 *Friendly Mission*, p. 291.
25 *Friendly Mission*, p. 291.
26 *Friendly Mission*, p. 292.
27 *Friendly Mission*, p. 292.
28 *Friendly Mission*, p. 297.
29 *Friendly Mission*, pp. 295–96.
30 *Friendly Mission*, p. 296.
31 *Friendly Mission*, p. 297.
32 *Friendly Mission*, p. 312.
33 *Friendly Mission*, p. 316.
34 *Friendly Mission*, pp. 297–98.
35 *Friendly Mission*, p. 298.
36 *Friendly Mission*, pp. 298–99.
37 *Friendly Mission*, p. 300.
38 *Friendly Mission*, p. 301.
39 *Friendly Mission*, pp. 302–04.
40 *Friendly Mission*, pp. 305–06.
41 *Friendly Mission*, p. 309.
42 State Library of New South Wales, A 597, pp. 73–76 (1–4).
43 *Friendly Mission*, pp. 309–11.
44 *Friendly Mission*, p. 311.
45 *Friendly Mission*, p. 319.
46 *Friendly Mission*, p. 319.
47 *Friendly Mission*, p. 319.
48 *Friendly Mission*, p. 322.
49 *Friendly Mission*, pp. 323–24.
50 *Friendly Mission*, p. 344.
51 *Friendly Mission*, p. 347.
52 University of Tasmania Library Special and Rare Collections, Cotton Family Papers, C7/58(1), p. 1.
53 For example: *Hobart Town Courier*, 25 December 1830, p. 3 (New Norfolk); *Launceston Advertiser*, 3 January 1831, p. 7 (Launceston);

Colonial Times, 7 January 1831, p. 4 (Richmond); *Colonial Times*, 7 January 1831, p. 1 (Campbell Town); *Hobart Town Courier*, 15 January 1831, p. 2 (Richmond); *Hobart Town Courier*, 22 January 1831, p. 2 (Norfolk Plains); *Hobart Town Courier*, 26 February 1831, p. 4 (Hobart).
54 *Friendly Mission*, p. 349.
55 *Friendly Mission*, pp. 349–50.
56 CBE1/1/1, pp. 84–86.
57 CBE1/1/1, pp. 87–95.
58 CBE1/1/1, pp. 92–93.
59 CBE1/1/1, pp. 94–95.
60 CSO1/1/320, pp. 122–24.

Chapter Nineteen – The War after the War
1   CSO1/1/320, pp. 122–24.
2   CSO1/1/320, p. 398.
3   CSO1/1/320, pp. 399–309 [Sic]. As noted earlier, there is a pagination error in the volume commencing during this report. After page 405 the sequence runs from 306.
4   CSO1/1/320, pp. 310–13.
5   CSO1/1/320, p. 312.
6   CSO1/1/320, p. 310.
7   *Colonial Times*, 1 February 1831, p. 2.
8   CSO1/1/320, pp. 315–17.
9   CSO1/1/320, p. 317.
10 CSO41/1/2, p. 8.
11 Commons Return, p. 82.
12 Commons Return, pp. 83–84.
13 Government Order 12, 7 October 1830.
14 CSO41/1/1, p. 487.
15 CSO41/1/1, pp. 489–90.
16 CSO41/1/1, p. 499.
17 *Colonial Times*, 1 March 1831, p. 2.
18 *Hobart Town Courier*, 5 March 1831, p. 2.
19 James Holman, *Travels in China, New Zealand, New South Wales, Van Diemen's Land, Cape Horn, Etc. Etc.*, Second Edition (London, 1840), pp. 394–442.
20 Holman, *Travels*, p. 406.
21 CSO41/1/1, unpaginated, 10 March 1831 (10,854/21).
22 CSO41/1/1, unpaginated, 10 March 1831 (10,854/21); CSO1/1/495, p. 64.
23 CSO1/1/495, p. 66.
24 *Hobart Town Courier*, 12 March 1831, p. 2.
25 *Colonial Times*, 22 March 1831, pp. 2–3.
26 Holman, *Travels*, p. 436.
27 Holman, *Travels*, pp. 412–13.
28 Holman, *Travels*, p. 414.
29 Holman, *Travels*, pp. 422–23.
30 Holman, *Travels*, p. 425.

31 Holman *Travels*, p. 432.
32 Lawrence's diary reveals he had visited Holman earlier while in Hobart.
33 Holman, *Travels*, p. 437.
34 Holman, *Travels*, pp. 437–41.
35 Government Notice 39, 25 February 1831.
36 CSO1/1/495, pp. 26–27, 61–62.
37 CSO1/1/495, pp. 14–15.
38 CSO1/1/495, pp. 39–40.

Chapter Twenty – Allies, Enemies and Ambiguities
1 Government Order 39, 25 February 1831.
2 CSO1/1/495, pp. 81–86.
3 CSO41/1/2, pp. 13–15.
4 CSO41/1/1, unpaginated, 9 March 1831 (10,852/59).
5 CSO41/1/2, pp. 9–10.
6 CON31/1/6, no. 436, p. 146.
7 CSO41/1/2, p. 15.
8 CSO41/1/2, pp. 2, 20, 22.
9 CSO41/1/2, pp. 1–2.
10 CSO1/1/495, pp. 112–13.
11 CSO1/1/495, p. 113; CSO41/1/2, p. 30.
12 CSO1/1/495, pp. 136–38.
13 *Launceston Advertiser*, 14 March 1831, p. 85.
14 CSO41/1/2, pp. 40–41.
15 CSO41/1/1, unpaginated, 6 July 1831 (10,854/54); CSO41/1/2, p. 49.
16 CSO41/1/2, pp. 45–46.
17 *Launceston Advertiser*, 11 July 1831, p. 213.
18 CSO1/1/320, pp. 127–28.
19 *Hobart Town Courier*, 16 July 1831, p. 3.
20 CSO41/1/2, pp. 55–56.
21 CSO41/1/2, pp. 45–46.
22 *Colonial Times*, 14 January 1831, p. 2.
23 CBE1/1/1, pp. 97–107.
24 CBE1/1/1, p. 105b.
25 CBE1/1/1, p. 106.
26 CSO41/1/2, p. 54.
27 CSO41/1/2, pp. 55–56.
28 CSO1/1/495, p. 155.
29 CSO1/1/320, pp. 449–52.
30 CBE1/1/1, pp. 109–11.
31 CSO1/1/320, pp. 449–52.
32 CSO1/1/316, pp. 941–44.
33 For more details, see Nicholas Dean Brodie, 'From "Miss Dalrymple" to "Daring Dolly": A Life of Two Historiographical Episodes', *Aboriginal History* 38, 2014, pp. 89–107.
34 Government Notice 196, 22 September 1831.
35 CSO1/1/320, pp. 447–48.

36 *Tasmanian*, 10 September 1831, p. 6.
37 *Launceston Advertiser*, 12 September 1831, p. 287.
38 *Launceston Advertiser*, 19 September 1831, pp. 291–92.
39 *Launceston Advertiser*, 19 September 1831, pp. 291–92.
40 *Launceston Advertiser*, 19 September 1831, pp. 291–92.
41 *Launceston Advertiser*, 26 September 1831, p. 299.
42 *Tasmanian*, 1 October 1831, p. 309.
43 CBE1/1/1, pp. 111–12.
44 *Friendly Mission*, p. 382.
45 *Friendly Mission*, p. 392.
46 *Friendly Mission*, pp. 375–76.
47 *Friendly Mission*, p. 377.
48 *Friendly Mission*, p. 377.
49 *Friendly Mission*, pp. 387, 389–90.
50 *Friendly Mission*, pp. 378, 388–89.
51 *Friendly Mission*, p. 391.
52 *Friendly Mission*, p. 404.
53 *Friendly Mission*, p. 411.
54 *Friendly Mission*, p. 412.
55 *Friendly Mission*, pp. 426–27.
56 *Friendly Mission*, p. 427.
57 *Friendly Mission*, p. 429.
58 *Friendly Mission*, p. 440.
59 *Friendly Mission*, pp. 441–42.
60 *Friendly Mission*, pp. 442–43.
61 *Friendly Mission*, p. 444.
62 *Friendly Mission*, p. 411.
63 *Friendly Mission*, p. 432.
64 *Friendly Mission*, p. 445.
65 *Friendly Mission*, p. 447.
66 *Friendly Mission*, p. 447.
67 *Friendly Mission*, p. 448.
68 *Friendly Mission*, pp. 449–50.
69 *Friendly Mission*, pp. 451–55.
70 *Friendly Mission*, pp. 456–57.
71 *Friendly Mission*, p. 457.
72 *Friendly Mission*, p. 495.
73 *Friendly Mission*, p. 461.
74 CSO1/1/320, pp. 441–45.
75 *Friendly Mission*, pp. 459, 461.
76 For instance: *Hobart Town Courier*, 12 April 1828, p. 3.
77 *Friendly Mission*, pp. 462–63.
78 *Friendly Mission*, p. 517.
79 *Launceston Advertiser*, 12 October 1831, p. 318.
80 CSO41/1/2, pp. 73–74.
81 CSO41/1/2, pp. 82–83.
82 CSO41/1/2, p. 84.

Chapter Twenty-one – Ending the Vandemonian War
1   CSO1/1/320, pp. 199–201.
2   *Friendly Mission*, pp. 520–21.
3   CSO1/1/320, pp. 456–59.
4   Government Notice 235, 30 November 1831.
5   *Launceston Advertiser*, 23 November 1831, p. 365.
6   *Colonial Times*, 26 October 1831, pp. 2, 4.
7   *Colonial Times*, 26 October 1831, pp. 2, 4; *Colonial Times*, 23 November 1831, p. 3; *Colonial Times*, 28 December 1831, p. 3.
8   *The Colonist and Van Diemen's Land Commercial and Agricultural Advertiser*, 28 December 1832, pp. 2–3.
9   *Colonial Times*, 26 October 1831, p. 4.
10 For more on Story's involvement in supplying military and paramilitary operations, see Nicholas Dean Brodie, 'Quaker Dreaming: The "Lost" Cotton Archive and the Aborigines of Van Diemen's Land', *Journal of Religious History* 30(3), 2016, pp. 303–25.
11 CSO41/1/2, pp. 85–87.
12 *Hobart Town Courier*, 26 November 1831, p. 2
13 *Hobart Town Courier*, 29 October 1831, p. 2; *Launceston Advertiser*, 2 November 1831, p. 341; *Hobart Town Courier*, 5 November 1831, p. 2.
14 *Colonial Times*, 28 December 1831, p. 3.
15 CSO1/1/320, pp. 201–09.
16 CSO1/1/320, pp. 134–35.
17 CSO1/1/320, pp. 483–86.
18 CSO1/1/320, pp. 136–37.
19 CSO1/1/320, pp. 214–17.
20 CSO1/1/320, p. 218.
21 For more about the situation in the northwest and concerning the Van Diemen's Land Company, see Ian McFarlane, *Beyond Awakening: The Aboriginal Tribes of North West Tasmania, A History* (Launceston: Fullers, 2008).
22 CSO1/1/320, pp. 460–63.
23 CSO1/1/320, pp. 138–40.
24 *Friendly Mission*, pp. 601–04.
25 *Hobart Town Courier*, 14 January 1832, p. 2.
26 CSO1/1/320, pp. 255–60.
27 See Nicholas Dean Brodie, '"The Last Man Left to Tell the Tale": Challenging the Conciliation Master Narrative in Van Diemen's Land', *Australian Historical Studies* 48(1), 2017, pp. 87–103.
28 *Launceston Advertiser*, 14 December 1842, p. 4.
29 University of Tasmania Library Special and Rare Collections, RS131(1), pp. 2–3.
30 *Launceston Examiner*, 20 January 1844, p. 3.

Afterword
1   CSO1/1/320, pp. 392–95.
2   State Library of New South Wales, A 614, titled 'Aborigines of Van Diemen's

Land, 1830–1840'. See N. J. B. Plomley (ed.), *Jorgen Jorgenson and the Aborigines of Van Diemen's Land* (Hobart: Blubber Head Press, 1991) for a transcript.
3   Nicholas Dean Brodie, 'From "Miss Dalrymple" to "Daring Dolly": A Life of Two Historiographical Episodes', *Aboriginal History* 38, 2014, pp. 89–107.
4   Mrs Charles [Louisa Anne] Meredith, *My Home in Tasmania, During a Residence of Nine Years* (London: John Murray, 1852), pp. 188–218.
5   Nicholas Dean Brodie, 'Quaker Dreaming: The "Lost" Cotton Archive and the Aborigines of Van Diemen's Land', *Journal of Religious History* 30(3), 2016, pp. 303–25.
6   University of Tasmania Library Special and Rare Collections, W7/24(1), J. Bonwick to G. W. Walker, 22 March 1856.
7   James Bonwick, *The Lost Tasmanian Race* (London: Sampson Low, Marston, Searle, and Rivington, 1884), preface.
8   As noted above, see Tom Lawson's *The Last Man: A British Genocide in Tasmania* (London: I. B. Taurus, 2014) for an excellent discussion of this.

Acknowledgements

Historians are trained to see everything as source material and look for underlying patterns. Like Colonel Arthur's government notices, even book acknowledgements reveal as much about professional networks, patronage and aspirations as they ever do about personal support. But while I habitually view them as the great propaganda pieces of the genre, I trust the undermentioned people will not see the following that way, or will at least be amused if they do.

Kristyn Harman was there from the beginning, when this was a much smaller project, and gave helpful commentary on questions of style and substance throughout. I am grateful to her, and my family and friends, for constant support and motivation, and I apologise for those moments of absence when my mind strays to another century.

For hearing me talk through questions of law, politics and history over repeated coffees during the long research and writing months, I want to especially thank Michael Tate and Anthony Ray. For designing another brilliant cover, perfectly capturing the essence of the story, I applaud Nada Backovic's talent. With this image in mind, my copyeditor Dale Campisi helped me trim and polish the narrative and I thank him for helping me continue to become a better writer in the process.

Hardie Grant Books provided magnificent support, and I am humbled that they continue to do so for such an atypically young historian. Thanks to Pam and Sandy for seeing the topic's potential, and to everyone who has helped me see it through. This includes (but is not limited to) Roxy, Kasi, Olivia, Jodie, Jane and of course my

ACKNOWLEDGEMENTS

publicist Kirstie. It is constantly wonderful to work with professionals who are so dedicated to combining research credibility with popular accessibility.

Archivally, the staff of the State Library of Tasmania tolerated my repeated visits to the Tasmanian Archive and Heritage Office with good humour. Anthony Black deserves special mention for smoothing my access to the manuscripts and their secrets, and for going beyond the call of duty at the end with his own camera. So too, Ian Morrison proved a good source of tips and conversation. At the University of Tasmania Library Special and Rare Collections, Heather Excell helped immensely with sourcing and supplying manuscript evidence that gave me the confidence and proof to call a broken spade a broken spade. I also owe a huge thanks to Tania Colwell for helping me with Emmett's reminiscence manuscript and to Eleanor Cave for furnishing me with a copy of her transcript of Lawrence's journal, both of which helped greatly in the later chapters. Similarly, David Flegg at the State Library of Victoria kindly stepped in on multiple occasions to help with parts of old Vandemonian newspapers torn from the digitised copies. And thanks to Pru Francis at the Archdiocese of Hobart Archives and Heritage Collection for giving me flexibility to manage writing and working.

In addition to these individuals and repositories, three more institutions proved crucial to the completion of this project. The National Library of Australia's Trove is still the best research tool in the world, and kept getting better even while I wrote. I had the good fortune to access manuscripts directly at the State Library of New South Wales, but I have also benefited greatly from their ongoing program of digitisation. And the *Australian Dictionary of Biography*, available online courtesy of the Australian National University's National Centre of Biography, provided essential information about many of the senior figures in this work.

Finally, a series of historians helped inspire my entry into this epoch of Vandemonian history. Murray Johnson, Ian McFarlane, Kristyn Harman (again), James Boyce, Nicholas Clements and Tom Lawson have all given me things to muse upon over the past few years in one way or another. My mentor in medieval history at the Australian National University, John Tillotson, was also particularly influential during this project, at least in a broadly professional sense. John fostered my scepticism about established historical narratives and encouraged me to use primary sources ever more critically and comprehensively. I am sure he will recognise in this colonial history the methodologies of a fellow medievalist.

Index

Aboriginal attacks 25, 87, 97, 114, 240, 286–7, 323, 363
  Ben Lomond (Mar 1831) 341
  Big Lagoon (Jan 1830) 134
  Blue Hill (Feb 1830) 143
  Boomer Creek (1830) 250
  Bothwell (1830) 149–50, 195
  Campbell Town (1828–31) 24, 327
  Clyde River (1829–30) 109
  Clyde River (Feb 1829–30) 150–1
  Coal River (1830) 275
  Great Swan Port (Winter 1828) 88
  Hone's hut (Mar 1830) 178
  Lagoon of Islands (1830) 306
  New Norfolk (Oct 1829) 116–17
  Oatlands (1828) 25–6
  Ouse River (Oct 1829) 113
  Oyster Bay 251, 285
  Pittwater (1830) 276
  Southern Midlands (May 1830) 181
  Stocker's hut (Aug 1831) 346–7
Aboriginal captives 55–6
  after the General Movement 307–9, 353
  capture and treatment 72–3, 125, 210–12
  escapes 207–9
  Maria Island 308
  Swan Island (Dec 1830) 315–17
Aboriginal people
  as auxiliaries with colonial forces 165–8, 282–3
  to be shot if not captured 249
  concerns about extermination 127
  deaths at St Paul's River (Jan 1829) 51
  deaths in custody 99, 105
  deaths in exile 125, 377
  early treatment 6–8
  effects of the War 132–3, 206–7
  extermination 51, 151, 218–20, 237–238
  impact of settlers 6
  Oatlands district (Mar 1831) 328
  taken by sealers 311–12
  tribal animosities 6, 61
  tribal confederation 146
Aborigines Committee 128, 343
  Aboriginal culture & customs 131–2
  assessment of the War (Autumn 1830) 156–8, 164
  bounty system 152
  on conciliation 149, 219
  on contradictions in War Policy 218–19
  on exile for all Aboriginal people 125, 320
  formation 125
  reports of attacks (early 1830) 151
  Robinson's report (Jan 1831) 309, 320–1
  submissions on capture or extermination 151–2
  support for Robinson's missions 352
Allardyce, Mr 306
Allen, John 20

Allinson, Benjamin
  East Coast (Autumn 1830) 196
  the Quoin district (Winter 1830) 201
  St Peter's Valley (early 1831) 324–5
Anley, (Capt.) 327–8
Anstey, George Alexander 207, 327
  bounty for captives 204–5
  militia joins Major Douglas (Oct 1830) 258
  Oatlands district (Winter 1830) 204–5
Anstey, Thomas (Oatlands police magistrate) 14, 93, 108, 165, 168
  activities (late 1828) 30–1
  deployment of constables 28
  Lake Fergus operation (early 1830) 139–41
  Martial Law boundary 137, 139
  missions to the south and east 37–9
  the need for force (May 1830) 170
  Oatlands (Autumn 1830) 176
  Oatlands (Dec 1828) 35–6
  plan for 'capture of aborigines' 30–1
  reorganisation of the Field Police 74–7
  roving parties (1830) 174
  roving parties (late 1828) 42–5
  roving parties (late 1829) 119
  supports Jorgenson's tactics (1829) 117–18, 120
Apsley 41
Arthur, Charles (Aborigines Committee secretary) 152
Arthur, Colonel George (Lieutenant Governor 1824–1836) 1, 7
  Aboriginal threat (early 1830) 153
  action beyond Martial Law boundary (1830) 136–7
  after the War 377
  allows arrest without warrant 154
  arms requisitions 12–13, 271
  bounties for Aboriginal people captured 152–3, 222
  bounties for Aboriginal people killed 229
  Bruny Island Establishment 9
  centralised command of the Great Movement 266

  on 'civilising' Aboriginal people 106
  as Colonel Commanding 18–19
  commander of the war effort 174
  commends Danvers (1829) 108
  conciliation as a strategy 144
  conciliation fails 219–20
  contradictions in War Policy 218–19
  decentralises the roving parties 163–5
  deploys military in Bothwell (late 1829) 115–16
  diplomacy using tribal reunions 162
  discussions with Batman (April 1830) 165
  discussions with Robinson (Oct 1831) 359
  district tour (Autumn 1830) 163–4
  dual military & civil roles 185
  East Coast Campaign (1829) 88–9, 92, 95–8, 100–3
  enthusiasm for ambush tactics 199–200
  exile of Aboriginal people 300
  exonerates Batman after deaths in custody 105
  the extirpation of the entire colony 284
  general mobilisation (Oct 1830) 220–2
  on Gilbert Robertson 109
  hunting dogs as weapons 203
  inspection tour north 45–6
  investigates mistreatment of captives 188–9
  Launceston (April 1830) 165
  martial law (Oct 1830) 249
  mercenaries 202–3
  in the Midlands (Oct 1830) 256
  militaristic pretensions 262
  military power 184
  militia groups 110, 153–4
  orders troops west of Hobart (Mar 1831) 332–4
  oversight of the War 46, 56
  para–military forces 71
  Port Davey mission 124
  reasserts the use of force (early 1831) 338
  rewards for colonists 215

INDEX

secretive missions (late 1830) 300, 303–4
settler protection (1827) 17
soldier–settlers 110
terror as a weapon 37, 50–1
Tyrrell's report (1830) 133
war propaganda 261
Arthur, Thomas 56
Ashton, George (district constable) 194
Aubin, Francis (town adjutant) 178, 184, 258, 280, 318, 364
  the General Movement 233
  Three Thumbs district (Nov 1830) 295
Auxiliary Bible Society 126, 127

Bagshaw, George 193–4
Barry, Andrew 224
Bathurst, Earl (Secretary of State for War and the Colonies) 12, 13
Batman, John 23, 77, 78, 140, 162, 178, 309, 340, 344
  Aboriginal captives (Oct 1830) 284–5, 286
  Aboriginal deaths in custody 99, 105
  Aboriginal deaths near Ben Lomond 187–8
  after the War 377
  Ben Lomond area (May 1830) 170
  conciliatory mission to the east (1831) 336
  East Coast (1829–30) 88, 92, 96–105, 136–7
  exonerated for deaths in custody 105
  final report (Aug 1830) 222
  the General Movement 232
  history of expeditions 97
  independent action in Ben Lomond 164–6
  land grant 214
  in Launceston (Spring 1831) 358–9
  at the Line (Nov 1830) 278, 290, 298
  north–east (Autumn 1830) 191
  a political liability 170
  report of attacks (Sept 1830) 251
  use of Aboriginal auxiliaries 118, 165–6

Bedford, Rev. William (Colonial Chaplain) 9, 352
  Aborigines Committee 125
  at the Bruny Island Establishment 126
  promotes conciliation 149
Ben Lomond 97–8
Ben Lomond tribe 146
Benison, Thomas (Constable) 40–1, 298
Bethune, Robert 308
Betts, Lieut. 198
Bevan (bushranger) 185
Big River 41
Big River tribe 6, 276
  surrenders (Jan 1832) 373–4
  united with Oyster Bay tribe 283
'Black Christie' (Aboriginal auxiliary) 398n5
'Black George' (Aboriginal auxiliary) 294
'Black Jack' (Aboriginal auxiliary) 94–5
the Black Line (*see* General Movement)
Black Marsh 43
'black rangers' 173–4
'Black Tom' (*see* Kickerterpoller)
'Black War' 378
Blue Hill 142
Bonwick, James 266, 380, 381
'Boomer' (Aboriginal auxiliary) 47–9
Boswood, John 75
Bothwell
  military action (late 1828) 44–5
  military station 29
bounty system 186–7, 189–90, 204, 215–16, 222
  includes Aboriginal people killed 229
Boxall, James 242
Boxall, Margaret 242
Briggs, Dalrymple 346–8
British colonial strategies 11
Brodie, John Sinclair 151, 159
Brompton, Rev. 156
Brown, James (Convict) 112
Brown (tribal member) 269
Browne, Francis (convict) 131–2

413

'Bruné Island Jack' 47–9
Bruny Island 6, 19
Bruny Island Establishment 8–9, 47, 55,
    106, 122, 124, 317
  Aboriginal detention 71–2, 74
  conditions of detention 125
  fatalities and illness 129
  G A Robinson as overseer 73–4
  paternalism 127
Bullrer 311
Burnett, John (Colonial Secretary) 24,
    184 (see also Colonial Secretary)
bushranging 111

Caines, Mr. (Field police) 328
Cains, Francis 226
Campbell, George 328
Campbell Town 30, 105
Carr, Nicholas (Field Police) 398n5
Carter, Thomas 349
Cascades Female Factory 243
Champ, Lieut. 255
Chinese labour 211–12
Circular Head 371
civilians authorised to shoot 17
Clark, Capt. William (Justice of the
    Peace) 113, 140
  ambush plans 110
  attack (Feb 1830) 142–4
  local militia 108–10
Clark's Hut 113
Clyde River 12, 158–9
Coal River Valley 138
Colbert, Andrew 294
Collins, Mr 273
Colonial Secretary 2–4, 24, 184
  East Coast campaign (1829) 88,
    92–3, 100–2
  on the Roving Parties (late 1829) 120
  on Tyrrell's report (1830) 131
Colonial Secretary's Office archive 2–4
Colonial Times 252–3
  coverage of the War 49–50
  on the General Movement 262–3
  inaccurate reportage 149–50
  reports on attacks (Winter 1830)
    195–6, 198
  reports on conflict (1829) 102

colonial warfare 19
Command Structures and Designation
    7578 24
convicts
  conscripts 221
  potential uprising 111
  rewards 121
Cotton, Francis 88–90, 318
Cottrell, Anthony
  Ben Lomond district 1831 359
  Ben Lomond district (Jan 1832)
    3710
  East Van Diemen's Land (Oct 1831)
    361–2
  Macquarie Harbour (Feb 1833)
    374–5
  North–East (Nov 1831) 368
Coventry, William
  recollects The General Movement
    267–8
  use of Aboriginal auxiliaries 283
Cox, James 136, 283–4
Croly, Lieut.
  and the General Movement 233
Cubitt, James 347
Cummener 354
Curtin, Lieut. Joseph (Police
    Magistrate) 14, 29

Dalrymple, Capt. (Police Magistrate)
    39, 42
Daniels, Mary 195–6
Daniels, Richard 195
Danvers, John 31, 166, 177
  Ben Lomond (April 1830) 168–72
  Big River area (Autumn 1830)
    158–60
  Bothwell district (late 1829) 112, 114
  engaged as a para–military 27
  Lake Fergus operation (early 1830)
    141–2, 149
  at the Line (Nov 1830) 295
  Midlands (early 1830) 134
  Oatlands district (1830) 135, 257
  'particular service' (1830) 226
  pursuit of convicts 112
  the Quoin (Autumn 1830) 196,
    200–1

INDEX

roving early (1831) 340
south and east 37–9
St Patrick's Head mission 41–2
Tooms Lake 32–4
Western Tiers (1829) 108
working with John Batman (May 1830) 167, 169, 170–1
D'Arcy, Capt. John (Police Magistrate) 14, 55
Darke, William 224
Davey, Thomas (Lieutenant Governor 1813–1817) 8
Dembrona (Aboriginal captive) 342
Dodge, Ralph 301–3
Donaldson, Capt. 242, 258, 273
Coles Bay (Nov 1830) 294–5
the General Movement 234, 267
orders the killing of Aboriginal people 315
Doran, John 202, 233
Douglas, Major Sholto (JP) 184, 185, 266–7, 333
command of military districts 220
the General Movement 232, 277
at the Line 278
northern district (Oct 1830) 256, 267, 274
northern volunteers 242
Dray (Part Davey tribe) 130
Dromedary Hill 138

Eagle, John 242
Eagle, Mary Ann 242
East Bay Neck 291–3
Emmett, Henry James 375
Blue Hills (Oct 1830) 263–6
Bothwell district (Oct 1830) 253–5
the General Movement 246–8, 265–7
at the Line (Oct–Nov 1830) 287–8, 290–2, 298
Espie, George 134, 148, 151
ethnic cleansing 51, 151, 218–20, 237–8
Eumarrah 54, 61, 72, 342–3, 355, 356, 362
aboriginal auxiliary 285–6
absconds 296

captured 352
Port Davey Mission 129
Eumarrah's tribe 283
Everitt, Jem 311, 357
Executive Council
on Aboriginal exile 330–1
disbanding the roving parties 330
Extreme Western Bluff 119

Field Police
armaments 46–7
deployment 15–17
expansion (1829) 74–7
formation 14–15
militarisation 30, 81
para-militaries 15–17
Fisher, Constable
background 214
operations (early 1831) 322
Shannon River (Winter 1830) 210
Fisher, James
Bothwell district (Dec 1830) 303–4
roving (early 1831) 339–41
Flexmore, Francis (district constable) 194
Ford, Francis (bushranger) 172, 173–4
Fortosa, Nicholas 227–8
Bay of Fires (Jan 1831) 321
the General Movement 277
at the Line (Nov 1830) 290
operations (1831) 322, 339–41
Special Force 228–9
Frankland, George (Surveyor-General) 128, 131–2, 291
Franks, Edward 193–4
Fry, Lieut. 116

Geary, Anne 25–6
Gee, William 186
Gellibrand, Joseph 236
General Movement
Aboriginal people to be shot if not captured 249–50
advancing the Line (Nov 1830) 262–71, 277–8, 289, 295–9
arms and weaponry 241–2, 271
cordon breached 268
counter-insurgency 286–7

415

debated in Hobart (Sept 1830) 235–9
demobilisation 299–300
failure to achieve objectives 293, 302
fortifying the Line 278–9
Hobart on a war footing 231–44, 237, 267
Hobart volunteers relieved 279
inherent contradictions 235
legalities 249–50
the Line breached 296
military involvement 267
preparations 231–44
provisioning the Line (Nov 1830) 289
public enthusiasm 235–9
record of action 245–6, 256–7, 259, 298–9
Reserve Line 271–4
skirmishing parties 276–8, 290
volunteers 267
volunteers from Hobart 234, 267
George Town 12
Gibbons, Lieut. 115
Giles, George 67
Glover, John 336
Gordon, James (Richmond police magistrate) 117
Gough family of Oatlands 25–6, 347
Government Notices
   193 261
   196 (mid 1831) 348
   160 of 20 Aug 1830 218
   161 of 20 Aug 1830 215, 218
   146 of 30 July 1830 205
   193 of Oct 1830 261
   182 of 15 Sept 1830 260
   183 of 16 Sept 1830 260
   186 of 17 Sept 1830 260–1
Government Orders
   7 Oct 1830 261
   12 of 1830 331
Gracie, Ralph 66
Grant, William 62, 65, 76, 93–5, 107, 122, 301
   application for pardon 121
   Arthur's review of the Jan 1828 mission 68–70

Bothwell (late 1829) 114
Robertson mission (1829) 64–8
Great Island Aboriginal Establishment 374
Great Swan Port 17, 20, 31
   attacks (Oct 1831) 363
Guard, Thomas 301–2
Gun Carriage Island Aboriginal establishment 343
Gunn, Harry 66

Hall, Isaac
   death at the Line (Nov 1830) 303
Hamilton, William (Police Magistrate) 14, 333
Hamilton garrison (late 1829) 115
Headlam, Charles 341–2
Henderson, Dr 171
Hewitt, James 226
Hibbert, Capt. George (Police Magistrate) 14, 17, 18, 20
'History Wars' 378
Hobart 5, 12
   on a war footing 231–44
Hobart Town Courier 8, 22–3, 24, 112, 143
   on Aboriginal attacks (Winter 1830) 195–6
   on Aboriginal captives (mid 1831) 342
   on captives 105
   coverage of the War 49–50, 101–2
   on the Great Movement 273, 275–6
   on Tooms Lake mission 34
   on Walpole's skirmish (Oct 1830) 281–2
   on the War (Winter 1830) 217
Hobbs, Mr 181
Hobbs Lagoon 183
Hodgson, Edward Wilson 225
Holman, James 332–6
Holmes, William 34, 207
   East Coast (1829) 91
   late 1828 mission 41–2
   missions to the south and east (late 1828) 37–9
Hone, Joseph (Hobart JP) 177
Hopkins, James 31

INDEX

Bothwell district (late 1829) 118
East Coast (Autumn 1830) 196
Oatlands mission (late 1828) 35–6
Oyster Bay (Winter 1830) 199
Horne, Thomas 236
Howell, Humphrey 142, 159
  Blue Hills mission (Dec 1830) 305–6
  property attacked 149–50
  reward for services 213–14
Hubbard, Elizabeth 242
Hubbard, Thomas 242
Humarra 171
Huon River 123
Hyatt, Robert
  Quoin district (Feb 1831) 327
  Table Land district (early 1831) 328
Hyett, Mr 118

inter-tribal wars 207

Jack (Aboriginal auxiliary) 59–64, 131, 135–6, 139, 180–3
Jackson, Corporal 160
James, George (Constable) 80
  Oatlands (May 1830) 181–3
  Oyster Bay (Winter 1830) 199
Jemmie 54
Jericho 12
Johnson, Thomas 346
Jones, Henry 43
Jones, James 43
Jones, Michael 43
Jones, (overseer) 189
Jones, William 186
Jordan River 43, 138
Jorgenson, Jorgen 77–87, 164, 178
  after the War 379–80
  Bothwell district (late 1829) 112, 114
  Bothwell district (Sept 1830) 230
  Brown Mountain district (Nov 1830) 322–3
  Clyde River area (Autumn 1830) 158
  conditional pardon 197
  conflict with Robertson 93
  East Coast (1829) 88–93, 95–103
  Highlands mission (mid-1829) 81–5
  joins the Field Police 78
  joins the mobilisation (1830) 230–1
  justifies roving parties 161
  Lake Fergus operation (early 1830) 139–49
  letter to the press 199
  at the Line (Nov 1830) 293–4, 297–8
  martial law boundary (Jan 1830) 139
  midlands observations (1830–31) 323, 329
  Oatlands (Autumn 1830) 130–1, 176
  Oatlands (Oct 1830) 257–8
  optimism about the War (late 1829) 117
  plans new expedition to the west 326
  record of the War 78, 329, 379–80
  report on Aboriginal activity (Jan 1830) 134–5
  strategies for capture 92
  use of Aboriginal auxiliaries 117–18

Kickerterpoller ('Black Tom') (Aboriginal auxiliary) 92
  discussions with Arthur 20, 356
  Eumarrah's capture 344
  fades from history 377
  in Hobart (Jan 1831) 318
  with McKay (1830) 316
  Port Davey Mission 129
  with Robertson (1828) 53–4, 58, 60–1, 64
  with Robinson (1829) 129
  with Robinson (1830) 310, 312, 313
  with Robinson (1831) 318, 354–7
  Swan Island (Nov 1830) 316
  treatment of captives 109
Kingston 97
Kirby, (Sergeant)
  at the Line (Nov 1830) 294
Kirkwood, Major Tobias (Field Police Commandant) 15
Knopwood, Rev. Robert 8

Laing Smith, Malcolm (Police Magistrate) 14

417

Lake Fergus 139–49
Lake Sorell 43
Lane, Lieut. (Police Magistrate) 51, 184
   East Coast (1829) 88–92, 95
Langworth, Constable 32
Lascelles, Thomas (Police Magistrate) 14, 56, 69
Launceston 5, 12
Launceston Advertiser
   on Aboriginal captives (mid 1831) 342
   on Aboriginal trackers 98
   on the General Movement 244
   murders of Thomas and Parker 351
   support for war effort 259–60
   War reportage 87, 101, 217
Lawrence, Robert 259
   Bothwell district (Oct 1830) 274
   at the Line (Nov 1830) 288–9, 298
   Norfolk Plains (Oct 1830) 263
   Reserve Line (Oct 1830) 271–4
   Richmond district (Oct 1830) 288
Lee, Robert 56–7, 80
Leith, Mr 273
Lieutenant Governor (*see* Arthur, Colonel George (Lieutenant Governor 1824–1836))
Lieutenant Governor's Office records 3–4
Lightfoot, John 66
Limaganny tribe 146
Little, William 75, 80
Little Swan Port 38, 88, 91
Lloyd, George 296
   at the Line (Nov 1830) 292–3
Lockyer, Ensign 31, 35–6
Logan, (Lieut. Colonel) 334
Lucas, George (Field Policeman) 107
Luggenemenener 316–17
LUG.GER.MAIR.RER.NER nation 312
Lyne, John 364

Macguire, Patrick 80
MacKenzie, Donald 324
MacPherson, Captain 298
Macquarie Harbour 12, 123
Maginnis, William 301

Mahon, Capt 258
Malony, Private 48
man-traps 183
Mannalargenna 354–7
Maria Island 38, 308
martial law
   boundary 42, 63, 136–7, 139
   declared (Nov 1828) 28–9
   no investigation of Aboriginal deaths 41
Massey, W T 341
Maynes, Arthur 188
McCarthy, James 324–5
McDonald, Neil 375
McGill's Marsh 182
McGuire, Patrick 75
McGuire, Peter 347
McKay, Alexander 358
   Norfolk Plains (mid 1831) 348
   North-West (early 1832) 372–3
   Swan Island (Nov 1830) 316
   west of Launceston (late 1831) 343–5, 362–3
McLeod, Mr 226
Medroomilla (Aboriginal captive) 342
Meelaletta (Aboriginal captive) 342
MELL.ER.KER.DEE nation 312
Meredith, George 38, 62, 318, 364
   requests military at the Schoutens (Oct 1831) 365
Meredith, Luisa Ann 380
military
   deployments 15–17, 115–16
   and the Field Police 30, 81
   garrisons 16, 25, 111
   given police powers 30
   strategy (late 1829) 117
militias 12, 44, 110, 177
Moaby, (Field police) 328
Monaghan, Private 40
Moriarty, Capt. William 295, 300, 347
Mungo (*see* Mungo-Jack)
Mungo-Jack 191–2, 299, 326, 377
   in Bothwell 142
   with Danvers (1829) 159–60, 168–9
   departs (Oct 1830) 286–7
   dies 352–3
   ill 171–3

with Jorgenson (1829) 118–19, 135–6
Lake Fergus operation (early 1830) 145–9
negotiator 161
Murray, Lieut. 233
Musquito 19
Mutteele 312

'Native Hut Valley' 31
New Norfolk 12
  attacks (late 1829) 116–17
  military station 29
Nicholls, Mr 198
Nongoneepitta (Aboriginal captive) 351

Oatlands 18, 30
  receives captives 105
  volunteer levy (Oct 1830) 257
O'Connor, Roderic 188, 309
Oliver, John 226
Oyster Bay 17, 30, 41
Oyster Bay tribe 6, 61, 91, 276
  surrenders (Jan 1832) 373–4
  united with Big River tribe 283

paramilitary forces 108
  after the General Movement (early 1831) 338
  combined action with regulars 117
  deployment 15–17
  operations prior to 1928 23
  rewards 71
PARE.DARE.RER.ME nation 312
Parker, Mr 348–52
PAR.KUTE.TEN.NER horsemen 317
PAR.LEL.LER (Aboriginal chief) 312
PAR.LER.DY (Aboriginal spirit) 124
Parnell, Sir Henry 349
Parramore, William 227
Partition Proclamation (1828) 10–11, 21
Peak of Teneriffe 119
Peletega
  bounty paid for capture 215
  capture and treatment 210–12
Pennington, Mr 181, 183
'Pigeon' (Aboriginal auxiliary) 98, 104

poison baits 151
Police Magistrates 14–15
POOR.RER.MAIR.RE.NER nation 316
Port Dalrymple tribe 55, 61
Port Davey 123
Port Davey mission (early 1830) 128–30
  Aboriginal auxiliaries 122, 124
  George Robinson leading 122
  paternalism 127
Port Davey tribe 129–30, 162
Price, Private 40
Prosser's Plains 30
PYE.DARE.RER.ME tribe 312
PY.EM.MAIR.RE.NER.PAIR.RE.NER nation 354

Rangers 112
RARGEERWROPPER (Aboriginal spirit) 129
Reid, Const. A 363
'Reminiscences of the Black War by Leader' by Henry Emmett 246
Reynolds, John 24, 75, 80, 118
Richmond Gaol 57
  Aboriginal incarceration 69, 72, 109
Risdon Cove conflict (1804) 5
Robert (Aboriginal auxiliary) 129
Robertson, Gilbert (Richmond Chief District Constable) 53–4, 178, 197–8, 266, 277
  Aborigines Committee inquiry (Mar 1830) 157
  Arthur's review of the Jan 1828 mission 68–70
  Bothwell district (late 1829) 114
  Coal River (1829) 109
  conflict with Jorgenson 93
  crosses the line of martial law 63
  East Coast (1829) 91–7, 103
  at the Line (Nov 1830) 290
  Little Swan Port River (Oct 1830) 275
  missions of 1829 57–64, 68
  tensions with Anstey 120–1
  use of Aboriginal auxiliaries 118

419

Robinson, George Augustus
  Aboriginal Establishment in Bass Strait 352
  after the War 377, 379
  Big River and Oyster Bay tribes surrender (Jan 1832) 373–4
  Bruny Island Establishment 9
  Georgetown district (Oct 1830) 285
  in Hobart (Jan 1831) 318
  holding captives 307
  meeting with Arthur (Oct 1831) 359
  new mission to the West (1831) 336
  North-East 'Friendly Missions' 309–17
  north-east Van Diemen's Land (mid 1831) 352–8
  Port Davey mission (early 1830) 122, 128–30, 161–2, 211
  records predations by sealers 311–12
  report to the Aborigines Committee (Jan 1831) 320–1
  roving in early 1831 340
  Swan Island (Dec 1830) 315–17
  visits sealers (Nov 1830) 315–16
  and William Bedford 126
Robinson, George (son of George Augustus) 283
Robinson, Sam (convict servant) 121–2, 138–9, 204–6
Rogers, Mr 90
Ross 12
Ross Bridge 17
Rosvere, Mr 189–90
roving parties 30–2, 76
  applications to join 223–4
  attached to Field Police (Mar 1831) 329, 338–41
  expansion in 1829 74–7
  lack of success (late 1829) 119
  Oatlands (early 1831) 323
  Oatlands (mid-1829) 71–86
  remote west (1833) 374–5

Savage, Thomas 269
the Schoutens 92
  military action (Oct 1831) 363–8
Scott, (Assistant Surveyor) 291
Scott, Charles 370

Scott, George 326
Scott, Peter
  ambush tactics (early 1831) 325
  appointed to the Field police 174
  Bothwell district late 1829 114, 118
  Coal River (May 1830) 181
  east of Bothwell (Autumn 1830) 160
  Eastern region (Autumn 1830) 196
  Lake Fergus operation (early 1830) 142
  Oatlands (Autumn 1830) 176
  Oatlands (Winter 1830) 199
  Prosser Plains (Oct 1830) 275
  roving St Peter's Valley (early 1831) 324
  skirmishing at the Line (Nov 1830) 290
  'special service' (1830) 227
Scott, Thomas (Assistant Surveyor) 256
  'Papers - Connected with the Campaign after the Natives' 256
sealers in Bass strait 311–12, 357
7578 records 4, 24, 197, 198, 200, 245, 247, 329, 330, 361, 373, 384
Shannon River conflict 44
Sharland, (Surveyor) 291
Sherwin, John (Junior) 157, 159, 164, 305
  Clyde River area (early 1830) 157
  the General Movement 233
  River Ouse (Winter 1830) 203–4
Sherwin, Mr (Senior)
  property attacked 149–51
  supports capture or extermination 151–2
  on the use of poison 151
Simpson, James (Police Magistrate) 14, 24, 25, 97, 169–70
  directs north-east operation (Autumn 1830) 190–2
Smith, Malcolm Laing (Police Magistrate) 14, 180
  at Norfolk Plains 30
soldier-settlers 110–11
Sorell, William (Lieutenant Governor 1817–1824) 12
Spangle, James 186
Splint, Private 40

INDEX

Spotswood, John (Capt.) 111
St Paul's Plains 18, 30
Standing, Thomas 70
Steele, Mr 172
Stephen, Alfred 180, 236
Stirling, Charles (convict servant) 162
Stoney Creek tribe 61
Surrage, Robert 353–4
Surridge, Robert 369–70
Swan Island exile 315–17
Swan Port tribe 61

TAR.NE.BUN.NER (Aboriginal man) 314
Tasmanian Archives & Records Office 2
Tasmanian (newspaper) 351
Tattersall, John (Constable) 42
Telford, John (Field Police) 326–7, 328
terror as a weapon 19, 37
'The Last of the Tasmanians; or, The Black War of Van Diemen's Land' by James Bonwick (pub. 1870) 266, 380–1
Thomas, (Capt.) 348–52
Thompson, Henry 172
Thompson, James 252
Thomson, Henry 226, 307
Thorp, Charles 189–90
TIL.LAR.BUN.NER ('Jack's' name) 316
Timbrunah (Aboriginal auxiliary) 368–9
Tooms Lake 32–4
  deaths of Aboriginal people 41
trackers 97–8
Triffitts, Mr 113
TRUGERNANNA 356
Truighilly, Liangla 66–8
Turnbull, Adam 236, 251
Turton, Major 17
Tyrrell, Richard 207
  ambush tactics (early 1831) 325
  conciliatory missions (1831) 336
  death of Aboriginal person 133–4
  highlands lakes (Jan 1830) 131–4
  joins GA Robinson (Winter 1831) 353

Lake Fergus operation (early 1830) 142, 147
  missing (Autumn 1830) 158, 177–80
  Norfolk Plains (Autumn 1830) 180–1
  Oatlands district (Jan 1830) 135
  Ouse River district (1829–30) 112, 114, 118, 135
  pursuit of convicts 112
  taking skulls 132

Umarrah (*see* Eumarrah)

Van Diemen's Land
  bounty system 187
  history 1, 5–6, 10–11
Van Diemen's Land Company 7, 16, 45, 106, 130, 177, 372
  employs Jorgenson 78
Van Diemen's Land Philosophical Society 127–8
Vandemonian War
  Aboriginal auxiliaries 344
  Aboriginal captives 55–6
  Aboriginal people to be shot if not captured 249–50
  Aborigines Committee inquiry (Mar 1830) 157
  after the General Movement 322–9
  after the War (1842) 373–5
  ambush tactics 199
  arming the General Movement 241–2, 271
  Arthur reasserts the use of force (early 1831) 338
  Big River and Oyster Bay tribes surrender (Jan 1832) 373–5
  the Black Line 231–2
  bounty system 186, 204, 215–16, 229
  British war veterans 39
  convict conscripts 221
  ethnic cleansing 51, 218–20, 237–8
  'friendly missions' 1831 336–7
  general mobilisation (Oct 1830) 220–2, 223

General Movement preparations 231–44
the General Movement's failure 301–3
hunting dogs 203
increased politicisation (1830) 158–9
man-traps 183
mercenaries 202–3
military deployment to Richmond (Oct 1831) 360
military responses (early 1831) 328, 330
press coverage 49–50
propaganda use 205–6
reward system 215
Roving Parties 163–4
roving parties (early 1831) 321
Schoutens military action (Oct 1831) 365–8
secretive missions (late 1830) 301–3
terror as a weapon 19, 37, 50–1
tradition and history 377–82
use of captives 189–90
voices against extermination 251–2
war records 2–4, 178, 204–7, 298–9
winds down 373–5
Veteran Company 111
Vicary, Capt. (Bothwell police magistrate) 116, 142, 144, 162
Arthur's proclamation on conciliation 149
the General Movement 233
use of mercenaries 202–3

Wacoondina 342
Walpole, Capt. 25
conciliatory mission (1831) 336
at the Line (Nov 1830) 287, 290
Walpole, Edward Atkyns 277
skirmishing party (Oct 1830) 279–83, 285, 287
Waterhouse Island 370
aboriginal captives 357–8
Watson, Capt. 364
Watson, Thomas Junior 364
Wedge, John Helder 224
Wentworth, Capt. 254
Blue Hills (Oct 1830) 265
Coles Bay district (Nov 1830) 294–5
the General Movement 232, 277
Jordan River (Oct 1830) 268–9
at the Line (Nov 1830) 290
western front (Oct 1830) 267
Westbury garrison 16, 17
Western River garrison 16
Widlikens, George Augustus 263, 273, 275, 291
Williams, Constable 113
Williams, Lieut. (Bothwell police magistrate) 43–4, 80–1, 83, 109–10, 112, 114–16
at Bothwell 29
Wilson, William (Constable) 131
Wood, Capt. 195–6, 198, 216
Wood, Private 40
Woorrady (Port Davey tribe) 130, 354
WRAYGEOWRAPPER (spirit) 317

Young, Constable 44–5
Yumârra (*see* Eumarrah)